SMALL WONDER

WALTER HENRY NELSON

Small Wonder

The amazing story of the Volkswagen

HUTCHINSON OF LONDON

HUTCHINSON & CO (*Publishers*) LTD
178–202 Great Portland Street, London W1

London Melbourne Sydney
Auckland Johannesburg Cape Town
and agencies throughout the world

First published 1967
Revised edition 1970

Printed in Great Britain by litho on antique wove paper
by Anchor Press, and bound by Wm. Brendon,
both of Tiptree, Essex

To
Art Railton

Contents

factories—and eventually takes his company from the ruins to its present position: the fourth largest motor-car manufacturer in the world, the largest industrial enterprise in West Germany, and the tenth largest industry in Europe. Nordhoff, the man, evaluated—what sort of man does a 'miracle' require?

Illustrations

Preface

This history of the Volkswagen, the company that builds it, and the persons who made its success possible, was independently written, without financial support from VW. It is a free-lance view and, if it is admittedly an enthusiastic one, then it is so because I do not believe that a fair observer could render a judgement other than enthusiastic about the VW or its company. This is a story of staggering achievements in the face, often, of overwhelming odds and, always, of enormous challenges. Thus, it is a story which provides its own 'lesson', not only for leaders in industry, but also for individual men and women who may believe that the era of opportunity lies somewhere in the lost past.

This present edition of *Small Wonder* is only superficially comparable with the one that initially appeared in the United States. I have completely revised the book, not only bringing it up to date, but making it far more comprehensive in scope. Not only have sections been added on the Volkswagen in the United Kingdom, Australia, and South Africa, making it of greater interest to readers within that area and throughout the Commonwealth, but at least one-third of the remaining text has been newly added. The 'romantic' early years of VW in the United States, given only brief attention in the first US edition, have here been given the space they deserve; an overall view of Volkswagen exports throughout the world has been added; the story of how a group of British officers administered the VW company and saved the VW motor-car has been greatly expanded; the contribution of many important individuals within the organisation has been gone into more fully. In general, the 'human' anecdotal material has been given greater scope.

Had this book been written by someone who is a purer 'car-buff' than I am, it might have included more technical data; had it been written by someone more industry-oriented, it might have supplied more information about the Volkswagen company as a business enterprise. I took another approach: to me, the story of the Volkswagen is not primarily a technical nor even an industrial story, but a human one. I wrote about the things which interested me: a man's long dream and his hard work to realise that dream, the nightmare of seeing that dream shattered, and the near-miraculous fulfilment of it after World War II. I wrote for those who are more interested in men than in machines, for those more keen on cars than assembly-lines, and for all those who have been amused, bemused, or puzzled by this strange little motor car which so many people the world over have taken to heart.

WALTER HENRY NELSON

London, 1970

I

The Years of Preparation

IN MARCH 1948 Henry Ford II seated himself at a conference table
in Cologne, Germany, to help decide the fate of the Volkswagen.
With him on the 'Ford side' of the negotiating table were Ernest
Breech, chairman of the board of Ford Motor Company, and the
heads of Ford's German and British companies. Across the table sat
Colonel C. R. Radclyffe, representing British Military Government, and Heinz Nordhoff, a German engineer, who had recently
been appointed head of the Volkswagen factory.

Nordhoff attended the meeting with mixed feelings. He knew
that the British had been trying to give the Volkswagen factory
away ever since World War II. Now Henry Ford was being offered
the plant, gratis. 'Perhaps,' Nordhoff thought, 'it would be for the
best. Perhaps the only hope for this company is to be taken under
the wing of a powerful American manufacturer.' He had been with
Volkswagen only two months and was not yet really confident of
the company's future. Production was insignificant and the factory
was in ruins.

'It was plain,' Nordhoff says, 'that Sir Patrick Hennessy, head of
British Ford at Dagenham, did not want to see Volkswagen come
into the Ford family. Perhaps Sir Patrick felt that if we were combined with Taunus [German Ford], it would make Ford's German
subsidiaries too strong.'

Finally, Colonel Radclyffe ended the discussion and asked Henry
Ford to decide if he wanted to take over the Volkswagen plant.
Ford turned to Ernest Breech and asked for his opinion. He
received a famous answer.

'Mr. Ford,' Breech said, 'I don't think what we are being offered
here is worth a damn!'

The factory nobody wanted was turned over to the Germans.

Nordhoff began trying to sell Volkswagens. He had his problems. In 1949 he arrived in New York City to look for American customers for his product. By this time, he had developed a fondness for his beetle-like car and hoped that others, perhaps even American car dealers, would share his feelings. He was disappointed; no one took him seriously. His car, according to all the American experts and to the British, who had preceded them, was just what Ernie Breech said, not worth a damn.

Not only was the car strange-looking, but its history was suspicious. Nordhoff could hardly expect to sell 'a Nazi creation' to Americans four years after the war. The Volkswagen was out of date politically, and its design was out of tune with public tastes. In those days, the beetle didn't even have a petrol gauge; today, it's lost its clutch pedal, having gained an automatic transmission. It's come a long way. Today more than twelve million Volkswagens have been sold in about 130 countries, as painful a fact for the marketing men of Detroit to face as it is to those British motor industry men who predicted no future for the VW. More than two and a half million Americans have already bought this car, several hundred thousand more Americans buy it each year, and Heinz Nordhoff's company today is the world's fourth largest producer of motor-cars, following General Motors, Ford and Chrysler. It is West Germany's biggest corporation, and it stands among the top corporations in Europe today.

How this was achieved, how a bombed-out plant in which cars could be produced only if it didn't rain could grow into a colossus which builds—and sells—a Volkswagen every eight seconds, is only part of the story.

Nobody had wanted the Volkswagen—except people. Hitler gave the car its impetus, then throttled it with his war. Three hundred thousand Germans fell for his propaganda and started saving for the car, but the Führer was to disappoint them here as elsewhere. He never produced a single Volkswagen for the public, despite his boasts of outproducing Henry Ford.

After the war, what was left of Hitler's preposterously ambitious plant was offered to all comers. The car it now produced in tiny quantities was one no 'expert' took seriously. Finally the British had no choice. They had to find someone to run it and give its workers something to do. They turned to Heinz Nordhoff, who took the job only because he was broke and hungry. He also disliked the Volkswagen at first, but came to love it later.

In 1950, Nordhoff showed the factory's production line to a small, chunky old man in a rumpled suit. Ferdinand Porsche, who recently had been freed after two years in a French prison, had come to see the plant which owed its existence to him.

'Yes, Herr Nordhoff,' said Porsche, 'that's how I always imagined it!' He was finally seeing the fulfilment of a dream which had obsessed him throughout his life. Since the end of World War I, when he was a young car designer full of visions which no one would share, he had planned a Volkswagen, a people's car. At a time when cars were thought to be only 'for the rich and for the very rich', he had dared design for the man on foot or on a bicycle. His idea was rejected year after year. He left one company after another, usually because he was not allowed to pursue his vision. Had it not been for the fact that he built at the same time some of the fastest, biggest, most luxurious, and finest cars in the world, he might have been discredited.

Then Hitler wanted just such a small car, and for his own reasons. He provided Porsche with the means to build his people's car and Porsche perfected the beetle. Today, more than thirty years later, his car still bears the advanced design he gave it then.

There was talk of this car proving that National Socialism could do what free enterprise could never do. Under Hitler, the Nazi propagandists said, every German would have his own Volkswagen within ten years. Instead, he had defeat and desolation.

Yet ideas do not easily die and the idea behind the Volkswagen was an honest one. How it originated and was finally made to prevail is the story of many men, but primarily three: Ferdinand Porsche, who had the dream; Adolf Hitler, who sought to exploit it, and Heinz Nordhoff, who turned Porsche's vision into reality.

The first of these, Ferdinand Porsche, was to spend much of his strength, genius, and almost all his years on his dream, and crowning achievement; the story of his first sixty years of life is the story of how the Volkswagen story got started in the first place. A brief glance at this man and his years of preparation sets the scene for the beetle.

Ferdinand Porsche was born on September 3, 1875, in Maffersdorf rechts der Neisse, a town lying in the backwoods of the sprawling Austro-Hungarian Empire. Electric power, new in the world, was unknown there until Willy Ginskey installed it to light his carpet factory, and it was there that fifteen-year-old tinsmith's

apprentice Ferdinand Porsche, arriving to fix the drains, encountered it first. His interest was caught; Porsche learned fast and two
years later had wired his father's home for electricity, installing
incandescent lights, electric chimes, and even an intercom.

There were rapid changes in other fields as well, even though the
change was hardly noticeable to the average man. The petrol
internal combustion engine had been developed; the Lanchester
brothers were already producing motor cars in Britain; in 1890
Gottlieb Daimler formed the Daimler Motor Company to manufacture his first car, the Phoenix; in 1896, Daimler cars went into production in Britain, at Coventry; Karl Benz had formed Benz & Cie;
Panhard & Levassor started producing in 1891, and Louis Renault,
Armand Peugeot, August Horch and Wilhelm Maybach entered the
infant industry as well. In America, others started in business during
those early decades: Charles E. and J. Frank Duryea, Elwood G.
Haynes, Henry Ford and Ransom Eli Olds. By 1900, Sunbeam, Riley,
Humber and Wolseley cars were being produced in Britain as well.

Ferdinand Porsche did not, of course, know of these events. Yet
he was excited by the smell of the burgeoning technology, and after
a while persuaded his father to send him to the trade school at
Reichenberg, to test his talent. There he attended only the Werk-
meisterschule, to be trained as a factory foreman. After he had
finished (leaving with the lowest grades in his class), his brother
Oskar took over the family tinsmiths' trade and Ferdinand left for
Vienna.

He left Maffersdorf on April 18, 1894, with an introduction to
Bela Egger, owner of the United Electrical Company at Fernkorn-
gasse No. 16, who put Ferdinand to work sweeping the floor and
greasing machinery. Within four years Porsche had been put in
charge of the experimental shop. Here he could learn and experiment, absorb technical knowledge, and devote himself to his passion, electricity. After work, he illegally attended the technical
university, sneaking into the lecture galleries. He found time to court
another Egger employee, Aloisia Kaes, and soon had both won the
girl and produced his first industrial design. Porsche designs ultimately would total more than 380 and include the Volkswagen.

The electromobile was the rage now, however. A number of
inventors had tried their best to make such a car efficient. In the
1880's a succession of cumbersome models appeared. Such battery-
driven cars may seem strange to us today, as we roar along behind
(or in front of) our internal combusion engines, but these motors

had and still have much to recommend them. For one thing, they were noiseless and free of fumes. To Porsche, the electromobile's shortcomings seemed the big challenge in Vienna. At twenty-four, he tried to eliminate them.

He designed an electromotor to power the inside of a wheel's rim, placing the power squarely where it was needed. As Porsche told the story, this first of his designs was stolen from him at the Egger offices. Although his fiancée, Aloisia, was outraged and urged Ferdinand to press the matter, he refused to do so. 'Don't bother yourself about it,' he told her. 'I've already got something better.'

He produced it for Ludwig Lohner, owner of a court carriage factory, in Vienna-Florisdorf, who hired him as his designer in 1898. Lohner, who intended to produce motor-cars, was interested in this design, which placed the electric motor right inside the hubs, eliminating belts or chain drives completely. Utilising this principle, Porsche built the Porsche-Lohner Chaise, capable of travelling fifty miles without recharging. A car which only an Imperial and Royal Court Carriagemaker like Lohner would produce, it looked like a cross between a victoria and a surrey, and was a beautiful sight to Lohner and his young designer. They decided the village lad from Maffersdorf would take it to the great 1900 Exposition at Paris and enter it for whatever interest it might generate. This was quite a move for a former tinsmith's apprentice. At twenty-five, he was about to compete with engineers, scientists and technicians from all over the world.

No grander fair had ever been organised than the 1900 Universal Exposition. It was attended by 51 million visitors and was described by a contemporary as seeming 'as fairy-like as a stage-setting . . . creating in the heart of Paris a veritable city of dreams and illusions'.

In the midst of all this, Porsche explained his car without a trans- mission system, powered by hubcap motors, and exhibited it in a nine-mile-per-hour run to Versailles and back. When the awards were announced, Porsche won a grand prize. It made him famous. Motoring had captured the imagination of most men by this time. In Britain, by 1904, there were almost 8500 privately-owned passenger cars on the roads, along with more than 5000 'hackneys' and 4000 vans and trucks.

In Vienna, the delighted Lohner studied the future and Porsche developed a new principle. Combining a petrol engine with an electric motor, he produced what he called a 'Mixt' car. Its petrol engine powered the generators, feeding the electric motors in the wheels. They nicknamed the car 'Aunt Eulalia' and in it Porsche drove home to Maffersdorf to show off his technical ability, as well as his fiancée, whom he married on October 17, 1903.

This automobile did more than astound the rustics of Maffersdorf; it became the hit of the *haut monde*. Baron Nathan Rothschild of Vienna bought one in 1905 and Archduke Franz Ferdinand drove in one during the Austrian manœuvres of 1902, chauffeured by reservist Porsche.[1] In the same year, a Prussian general used it at the German Imperial War Games. Bureaucrats as well as aristocrats bought it and municipal authorities used it for fire-prevention vehicles and omnibuses. Now Porsche turned to plans for further cars.

Yet Ludwig Lohner was hesitant to spend more money on further advanced designs. He already had spent a million crowns on Porsche's development costs and wanted to concentrate on selling the popular 'Mixt' car. It was at this time that Porsche received a tempting offer to join Austro-Daimler. His name was already famous in 1905. Austria had awarded him its coveted Poetting Prize that year, marking him at the age of thirty as having made the greatest contribution to the nation's car industry. It was the highest honour that Porsche could receive in his field at the time. Yet he had few ambitions for himself and little desire for the perquisites of corporate position. He was too busy with his workers in the shop. 'Fundamentally', to quote Charles Lam Markmann and Mark Sherwin in *The Book of Sports Cars*, Porsche 'was an engine man. Those who observed him say they could see his eyes grow brighter as he listened to the purr or the roar of one of his creations, making mental notes of what had to be adjusted, changed, or redesigned. Some have called him a martinet in his pursuit of perfection, but a listing of his accomplishments is enough to dispel any criticism of his method or manner.'

In 1906, this gifted, brusque and as-yet-unpolished man took over as technical director and board member of staid Austro-Daimler, the independent Austrian offshoot of Daimler in Germany. (British Daimler, holder of the Royal Warrant for many years, began as a

1. On November 8, 1902, Franz Ferdinand wrote an archducal note to Porsche styled in the elaborate language of the court:

'His Imperial and Royal Highness, the gracious Archduke Franz Ferdinand, deigns to transmit to your honourable person a memento of this year's manœuvres in West Hungary. The performance of your automobile, as well as your sure and exact guidance of it, have satisfied His Imperial and Royal Highness in every particular.'

(*'Seine Kaiserliche und Königliche Hoheit, der durchlauchtigste Herr Erzherzog Franz Ferdinand geruhen Euer Wohlgeboren beiliegend eine Erinnerung an die heurigen Manöver in West-Ungarn übersenden zu lassen. Die Leistung Ihres Automobils sowie Ihre sichere und exakte Führung desselben aben Seine Kaiserliche und Königliche Hoheit in jeder Beziehung befriedigt.'*)

Daimler patent licensee and soon came to be totally independent also of 'Cannstatt-Daimler', as the German company in Bad Cannstatt came to be called.) Porsche was to stay at Austro-Daimler until 1923, resigning eventually in an ugly argument about finances. By the time he quit, he had risen to Generaldirektor, or chief executive, a position equivalent to managing director. In the meantime, he did what he liked best: he produced great cars.

The staple workhorse of Austro-Daimler was the Maja, a car named after a daughter of Emil Jellinek, a financier and consular official who helped finance the Daimler Company in Germany. Another of Jellinek's daughters provided the name for German Daimler's prize car, the Mercedes.[1]

The Maja, in which Porsche first used the purely internal combustion engine, found a market in Austria; it had a four-cylinder engine, and an early Porsche redesign of this model generated 32 hp and included a four-speed transmission.

In order to sell the company cars by demonstrating them, Porsche entered them in races. The first major event in which he took part— and he would enter a host of races in the future—was the Prinz Heinrich race of 1909. This event, to which the car-enthusiast son of the German Kaiser lent his name, was less a race than a week-long endurance run throughout much of Central Europe. All three Austro-Daimler cars, one driven by Porsche himself, won top honours.

After the race ended, the rules for the 1910 runs were announced. Porsche, it is said, ducked out of Prince Heinrich's banquet and into an anteroom that night, leaving his wife with the dignitaries, so as to mull over his chances of winning next year, whilst munching a hard roll.

For the 1910 event, he wanted to design a truly notable motorcar; the one he entered was just that. The 80-hp Prinz-Heinrich-Wagen, achieving 90 mph, startled the other drivers and onlookers at the race. It was quickly nicknamed the *Tulpenform* (tulip shape).

It hardly looked like a blossom, but it certainly was streamlined in contrast to the boxes then sputtering down the road. Instead of a conventional square grille, it sported a moderately curved one. Its body sloped back in an unbroken line and even door handles had been eliminated. Austro-Daimler cars won twelve of the seventeen tests, three won the first three prizes in a field of over 170, and Porsche,

1. Markmann and Sherwin point out that 'it is a nice irony of history that Adolf Hitler's favourite car was named for the grand-daughter of a Hungarian rabbi'.

who had driven the lead car himself, was commended by Franz Joseph. Austro-Daimler knew that now Porsche would want more money to carry the design forward.

But the designer was called to aid his country; the year was 1911 and Europe had begun to arm.[1] Porsche had already designed airplane engines for Austro-Daimler. Although they generated more than 300 hp, they were lighter in weight than those in existence before. They helped Porsche perfect powerful yet lightweight engines for cars, and weight as well as power was becoming a prime Porsche obsession. Now, building airplanes and dirigibles, he intended to test them himself.

'Already before 1914, at Austro-Daimler, we had started to build the first aeroplane engines and also small motors for dirigibles,' he recalled years later to his son Ferry. 'And since I test all my children, I willy-nilly had to make at least one ascent in one of these balloons. It was rather stormy and, in order not to run into a church spire, we were forced to jettison some ballast. A little too much of it! As a result, the balloon rapidly gained height, and the pressure could not be controlled by the safety valve. I was watching the manometer intently and saw that the pressure was continuing to increase. I could calculate exactly when it would reach the point at which the fabric of the balloon would burst. We had no parachutes—we hadn't even heard of them. . . . The pressure gauge had long passed the red line; but the ascent stopped just as the pressure had reached its limit. We were able to land.

'Back on firm ground, I said to the balloon crew: "I have a nice salami sausage which my wife packed for me; that's just what we need after all this excitement." However, how great was our disappointment, when I unpacked the parcel and found that my wife had made a mistake; there was no sausage, but instead a new corset.'

In 1913, the Austro-Hungarian military developed a heavy 305-mm mortar which fired a shell weighing more than 700 pounds and Porsche designed a 100-hp vehicle to draw this monster, utilising an adaptation of the 'Mixt' car principle. After the war began, Porsche motorised an even bigger 42-cm mortar, similar to Germany's 420-mm Big Bertha. Its barrel alone weighed 26 tons and its shell another 2000 pounds. Porsche powered its tractor-like cab with a petrol

1. During this period, one of Porsche's test-drivers and mechanics was Josip Broz, later Tito, president of Yugoslavia. 'In 1912,' he is quoted in Dedijer's *Tito* as saying, 'I got a job in the Daimler factory in Wiener-Neustadt . . . The work here interested me more than in any other actory. I even became a test driver, running the big powerful cars with their heavy brasswork, rubber-bulb horns, and outside hand brakes, to put them through their paces.'

engine. This was hooked to a generator feeding hubcap motors in the eight trailer wheels. Thus, cab and trailer were both motorised.

In 1917 Porsche received an honorary doctorate in engineering from Vienna Technical University. Herr Doktor Porsche, General-direktor of Austro-Daimler, had achieved academic acceptance and the proud title never left his calling cards.

Porsche's motorised trailer found other uses. As many as ten huge troop-carrying trailers were strung behind the petrol-powered cab, each separately made mobile by means of hubcap electro-motors. The entire effect was that of an undulating caterpillar, moving troop trains along the French, Italian, and Russian fronts.

The troops, however, only moved faster towards defeat. The war's end brought economic ruin and an end to the Empire. Porsche now worked in a minor republic called Austria. Maffersdorf, in the meantime, had become part of Czechoslovakia, and Porsche found himself to be a citizen of that country.

If the age of the Volkswagen were more accurately reckoned from conception, rather than from date of delivery, then today's Volks-wagen would date back to the beginning of the 1920's. It was at Austro-Daimler, shortly after the end of World War I, that Ferdi-nand Porsche first thought of his small car for everyman, his 'people's car'.

In Porsche's mind, the 1920's and the social changes in Europe meant an opportunity for Austro-Daimler. They could now produce a small car for everyman, much as Henry Ford was doing with such spectacular success in the United States. Yet, despite Ford's exam-ple, Porsche's idea was a radical one not only for Austro-Daimler, but for the entire car industry. Even in the United States and despite the impact of Ford sales, cars remained mostly for the well-to-do, and many were luxury models imported from Europe. In Britain, Rolls-Royce, founded in 1904, entered a decade of producing luxury limousines tailored to the whims of wealthy clients (who stopped in-dulging themselves as much after the 1929 crash) by a host of great English coach-builders.

Porsche, in Austria, shared Ford's vision of a cheap car for the millions, but was scorned for it. Almost to a man, the leaders of European car companies discounted the general public and certainly the worker as a potential customer. The worker in Germany and Austria bicycled to his job if he did not take a bus or a trolley. When he had saved some money, he bought a motor-cycle perhaps, but never a car. The board of directors of Austro-Daimler reasoned that many Austrians would continue to want big, showy automobiles, a point which Porsche did not dispute. Porsche merely saw that market as too limited and regarded as narrow those who could not share his vision. This time, however, he agreed to devote himself to designing large and expensive motor-cars.

And so, in 1921, the company offered a select public a large six-cylinder, 60-hp touring car displacing 4·5 litres and called it the AD for Austro-Daimler Motors. It was followed by a somewhat bewildering succession of varying models, eventually with a lower displacement, desirable in Europe because car taxes were rated in accordance with engine size, and also because of the high cost of petrol.

Then, suddenly, the direction changed. An investor, film company president Count Sascha Kolowrat, wanted a small, one-litre displacement, lightweight, but high-powered racing car. Porsche built it and, of course, called it the Sascha. These were quickly entered in several European races, including the demanding Targa Florio event in Sicily, where they won both first and second places on April 2, 1922.

Porsche had proved his point: a high-performance car could be small and lightweight. After rebuilding the original Sascha, Porsche boosted displacement to two litres, transforming the tiny car into a powerhouse capable of 106 mph. The board of directors threw up their hands. They had reluctantly gone along with racing small cars but now refused further funds. Transforming Saschas into small, efficient cars for the public did not interest them. They wanted to sell aristocratic cars to rich people—'even though they may be Social Democrats'.

The largest shareholder in Austro-Daimler was a bank headed by Camillo Castiglioni. Austro-Daimler's foreign income was exchanged for Austrian schillings, the foreign currencies being retained by the bank. The schilling, however, was deteriorating so rapidly in value that the entire foreign profits could be wiped out in an afternoon. At a board meeting, Porsche demanded that the hard currencies, rather than their equivalents in schillings, be credited to his company. Castiglioni refused. As Ferdinand Porsche's son Ferry today puts it, 'They were, after all, primarily interested in making money for the bank.' Then Castiglioni insisted Austro-Daimler economise by dismissing two thousand workers. Porsche exploded, shouted an obscenity at the board, and stormed out. In his outrage, Ferry says, he picked up a gold table lighter and hurled it on to the table in front of the directors.

Although Castiglioni has often been depicted as a villain, the fact is that Porsche and he were and remained friends, addressing each other with the familiar '*du*'. When the explosive board meeting ended Porsche's career at Austro-Daimler, German Daimler called for him. Porsche's son and daughter remember that Castiglioni later visited them at German Daimler and that, after World War II, Castiglioni did what he could to get Porsche out of the French prison in which he languished in 1947. The truth was that the legitimate interests of the bank and of the company it controlled came into conflict. The bank won.

From the top spot at Austro-Daimler, Porsche moved to the position of technical director and member of the board of the Daimler Motor Company in Stuttgart, Germany. (The German and Austrian Daimler companies were independent though related.) There was here a tradition of aloofness which Porsche soon shattered, to the consternation of the rather stodgy management. The front office was remote from the shop and executives kept themselves distant from those who worked in the factory. *Der Spiegel* refers to German Daimler as 'arch-conservative' and as being organised like 'a monastic order'. Here Porsche's swearing and blunt talk often seemed out of place. The reception accorded Porsche in the shop itself was of course different. It was enthusiastic, if a little apprehensive, for Porsche had a habit of lavishing praise on bright designers while denouncing as 'manure' the work of those of limited ability.

He inspired considerable loyalty among those whose talents approached his own, just as he provoked the enmity of lesser men. From Austria, Porsche brought Otto Koehler, who served Porsche as his personal technical aide in Stuttgart, Alfred Neubauer, a top-flight mechanic and racing driver, and others. He felt at home with them and they, in turn, lavished devotion on their chief. Markmann and Sherwin call Porsche a man who 'worked hard and faithfully at his drawing board, in the machine shop or even the pits to make certain that his machines performed as promised. He was a prim little man with an amiable moustache and a sharp twinkle that could become a bolt of electricity when he chose. His attire was almost a trademark. He would wear a loose-fitting tweed suit with giant patch pockets and a cloth cap pulled down to his ears. At races, a pair of binoculars would dangle from his neck and a pair of goggles would be perched on top of his cap. His demeanour was one of intense dignity and concentration. . . .'

A story is told of an important car being inspected ceremoniously by a group of white-smocked front-office designers who endlessly discussed what might be wrong without once checking for themselves. Porsche climbed into overalls, crawled under the car, found the trouble, answered his colleagues' queries with a snarling 'Look for yourselves', and stalked off. This was the nature of the man. He was not easy to work with. Volatile, irrepressible, deficient in the technical theory taught at school, he designed with pure fingertip feel and sure instinct, often going directly against accepted principles of design because he knew his ideas were right. His understanding of engines was uncanny; their very sound often told him what was the matter with them or what new feature needed to be incorporated into them.

The star of the German Daimler salon was the Mercedes (known as the Mercedes-Benz only after 1926), but the 1923 Indianapolis 500-mile event, the first race the company entered after Porsche joined it, proved existing Mercedes cars were too heavy.

Porsche improved the Mercedes supercharger and engine and later designed a 100- and 140-hp, six-cylinder model better suited to competitive events. He entered this in the 1924 Targa Florio race in Sicily, averaging 41 miles an hour. Considering the terrain, the speed was remarkable, and it won for Porsche a warm endorsement from the previously reserved management as well as a new doctorate, from Stuttgart's technical university. (This was most welcome, for Porsche had found out that the Germans considered Viennese honorary doctorates meaningless.)

At German Daimler, Porsche produced a number of great Mercedes cars. Six-cylinder, six-litre engines generating 140 horsepower brought the company 21 racing victories in 27 starts from 1925 to 1927. Several of these are classics of an era renowned for power, elegance, and fine coachwork; their gleaming outside exhaust pipes, together with their superchargers, became almost synonymous with the Mercedes name, for German Daimler was first in offering superchargers on its regular passenger line.[1]

1. Specifications of five notable Mercedes models by Porsche:

K (1927)   Horsepower: 110 (at 3000 rpm), supercharged to 160; Engine displacement: 6·2 litres (378 cu. in.); Bore: 3·70 in.; Stroke: 5·91 in.

S (1927)   Weight: 3600 lbs.; Wheelbase: 134 in.; Cylinders: 6; Horsepower: 120 (supercharged, 180); Engine displacement: 6·8 litres (414·8 cu in.); Compression ratio: 5 to 1. Also, dual ignition and carburettors; optional 2·5, 2·76, and 3·09 axle ratios.

SS (1928)   Weight: 3630 lbs.; Wheelbase: 134 in.; Engine displacement: 7022 cc (428 cu. in.); Cylinders: 6; Horsepower: 170 at 3200 rpm (supercharged, 225); Compression ratio: 5 to 1; Bore: 3·94 in.; Stroke: 5·91 in.; magnesium block.

SSK (1928)   Modified SS on 116-in. wheelbase, generating 170 hp (supercharged, 225).

SSKL (1931)   Modified SSK. Weight 3960 lbs.; Horsepower (supercharged): 300. Actually produced after Porsche's departure, but retained most of his design features. 'K' stands for *Kurz* (short wheelbase); 'L' for *Leicht* (light); 'S' for *Sport*; 'SS' for *Super-Sport*.

Again, Porsche pressed for his ideal of the small car for everyman. And again he was turned down by the management. The design, he was told, would be too costly and the car would not be profitable. Porsche was asked to take note of the times. Germany was floundering in a depression which had wiped out all purchasing power and made the Reichsmark nearly worthless. The very man whom Porsche proposed to motorise was, in point of fact, mainly worried about whether there would be enough to eat. Germany in 1926 had one car for every 211 persons (compared with one for every 5·7 persons in the United States that year). Yet the wealthy did more than survive; many prospered, and they remained the heart of the motor-car market. In Britain (in 1925) 579,901 motor-cars and 571,552 motor-cycles were registered, a sizeable increase from 1920, when there were only 186,801 private cars as against 287,739 motor-cycles on British roads. Porsche noted the trend and felt ever more strongly that the private motor-car should become a vehicle for popular use in Germany as well.

Porsche now planned to build a modified version of the company's medium-sized Stuttgart and Mannheim models. These had solid axles, four-wheel brakes, three-speed transmissions, semi-elliptical springs, and box-type bodies. To adapt them to the demands of a truly small vehicle, Porsche developed a 1·3 litre four-cylinder engine producing 38 horsepower. Three prototypes were built, but the plans were abandoned. The question of building a small car created frictions. So did the company's 1926 merger with Benz & Cie., which created Daimler-Benz A.G. The Benz 'outsiders' had better bank connections and the board was weighted in their favour. The merger doubled the managerial personnel and cost the new company a great deal. The board decided to get rid of a large number of former Daimler people, Porsche included.

The overt cause was the 38-hp Stuttgart car, which, the board claimed, failed to start in cold weather. Fifteen Stuttgarts were parked overnight in the company lot during cold weather. On the next morning Porsche was challenged to start even one of them. Fuming, Porsche went from car to car in the early morning hours and, unfortunately, not one started immediately. A bitter argument with General-direktor Wilhelm Kissel ensued, and the designer flew into a rage, tore off his hat, trampled it in the snow, and marched out of the plant, never to return.

The cars apparently started during another test three weeks later at —20° centigrade, the anger abated, and the management suggested that Porsche tour the United States, studying car design and production, and return to serve the company as a consultant. Porsche, however, declined. He felt, his son remembers, that they were trying to shunt him aside politely. An offer came from Vienna's Steyr Works, which had switched from production of arms to cars at the war's end, and Porsche accepted. On January 1, 1929, he became technical director, chief engineer, and a member of the board.

He returned to Austria at the age of fifty-three something of a hero, which may have surprised him, considering the stormy way he left the country five years earlier. Austria, however, was eager to industrialise and regarded Porsche as the man to help. Steyr did seem the right place; its prosperous past endowed it with vast holdings, including a rolling mill, a foundry, and a forge. Steyr could build a car without recourse to outside suppliers. Here, Porsche produced two which were noteworthy. The first was a modification of the 'Stuttgart'; the second was the 'Austria', a big five-passenger limousine. Technically a great achievement and ranking with some of the great classics of the time, it was the centre of attention at the 1929 Paris Auto Show, and Porsche knew he had a winner.

A few days later, however, he picked up a newspaper in Paris to find he had no job. Steyr's finances had collapsed, and, ironically, the company fell into the hands of the very financiers who controlled Austro-Daimler. When Porsche got home, he found he was unwelcome and that his 'Austria' was doomed. The new bankers refused to let Steyr produce a big luxury car, since Austro-Daimler already did so. The decision outraged Porsche and eighteen months after joining Steyr, he quit. This time he stopped trying to fit himself into the car industry. Fed up, he left the country.

Where should he go? He was fifty-five, had no taste for corporate positions and yet no wish to retire. The solution seemed to lie in a career as an independent consultant, in which his responsibility for a car might end after he designed it.

On January 1, 1931, Porsche opened up shop in Stuttgart. He chose this city because it was a centre of the German car industry, with many parts plants and machine shops. His shingle—which seemed to invite all comers—read, 'Doctor, Engineer (*honoris causa*) Ferdinand Porsche G.m.b.H., Construction Bureau for the Manufacture of Motors, Motor Vehicles, Aircraft, and Ships.'[1]

1. *Dr. Ing. h.c. F. Porsche G.m.b.H., Konstruktionsbüro für Motoren-, Fahrzeug-, Luftfahrzeug-und Wasserfahrzeugbau.*

As it turned out, Porsche's venture into business for himself proved crucial to the future of the Volkswagen. From this time on, his designs for the car moved forward, if somewhat spasmodically. Events were moving rapidly to push the designer into a 'socialistic partnership' with Adolf Hitler, who could provide or extort the funds needed. In the meantime, Porsche produced two 'Volkswagens' for two car manufacturers, neither of whom would benefit from them.

First to hire the Porsche Bureau at 24 Kronenstrasse in 1931 was the Wanderer Auto Company, for whom Porsche delivered the designs and prototypes of a medium-priced, six-cylinder car and a larger, eight-cylinder car. Again on contract to Wanderer in 1932 Porsche developed a new type of suspension system which eventually proved to be a radical feature of the Volkswagen. Porsche felt that leaf and coil springs were unsatisfactory. Both types were too heavy, cumbersome, and unadaptable to a small, lightweight, yet high-performance car. Porsche's solution was the torsion-bar suspension system. After its initial weaknesses had been worked out, it proved a major invention. Until 1950, when his patent ran out, Porsche licensed its use in many other cars, including the Volkswagen. After 1950, it became public property. As a recent Volkswagen advertisement put it, however, the number of sedans having *both* this system *and* four-wheeled independent suspension 'can be counted on one finger'. Both features were part of the *original* design by Porsche.[1]

Two proposals were presented to the designer in 1932. One was an offer to build a small car; the second came from the USSR, inviting Porsche to become a top Soviet industrial designer. A Soviet delegation had come to Porsche's Stuttgart office, listened attentively, said little and taken careful note of everything being done. It was not long afterward that Porsche received an invitation to the USSR.

He left on July 20, 1932, and after three weeks in a Moscow bed, nursing a foot he had hurt alighting from his train, he toured much of the country. His hosts were eager to impress him with their technological growth and hospitality. Once, when Porsche complained of the vodka which was endlessly served to him and expressed

1. The principle behind Volkswagen's torsion-bar suspension system was that a bar was held on one end and twisted from the other, where the wheel moved up and down. Such a bar, made of laminated strips of steel, will twist as it absorbs a shock. The harder the bump, the more the twist and the greater the resistance to further twisting, a principle which may be tested by twisting an ordinary piece of rubber garden hose. These laminated strips, bound together and clamped at the centre to prevent them from rotating when twisted, are attached to 'trailing arms' fastened on to the VW's front wheels. The rear suspension is similar, but two torsion bars, one for each wheel, are used. The outer ends of each bar are splined so that they can be adjusted to maintain correct rear suspension geometry. Each bar is a single piece of steel, pre-stressed for use on either the left or right side.

a wish for some beer, a case of Pilsner awaited him at the next stop. Negotiations began. Porsche was offered a luxurious Crimean villa for his family and entire staff, as well as a blank cheque. He would never again have to concern himself with personal or developmental expenses. The Russians were even interested in small car designs and had shown Porsche some preliminary plans of their own. When Porsche returned home, he confessed he was tempted—and impressed. 'Well, one isn't supposed to say it, but what I saw was wonderful!' he said to Ghislaine Kaes, his nephew and by then his secretary. Still, he declined the offer. It required him to break all ties with his homeland. Porsche felt too old to make the change.

He returned instead to his offices in the Ulrich Building on Stuttgart's Kronenstrasse. His hand-picked staff consisted of many who had followed him from company to company: Karl Rabe, his chief designer; Karl Fröhlich (gearboxes); Josef Kales (engines); Josef Zahradnik (axles, springing and steering) and Erwin Komenda (bodies). Among them was Ferry Porsche, the designer's twenty-one-year-old son, who was beginning his own brilliant career as a car designer under his father's tutelage and who today heads the Porsche company in Stuttgart. The business manager was Adolf Rosenberger, a businessman whose hobby was racing, and who owned 15 per cent of the firm. (Porsche owned 70 per cent and Dr. Anton Piëch, his son-in-law, 15 per cent.) Rosenberger, however, was Jewish and had to flee the country after 1933, moving to Paris, where he was secretly appointed the Bureau's sales manager abroad, representing the firm until World War II, and selling Porsche designs to foreign companies. At the outbreak of war, he made his way to the United States.

Fritz Neumeyer of Nuremberg's Zündapp Works, one of Germany's biggest motor-cycle manufacturers, was now convinced the time was right for a small car, a *Kleinauto*. Before he visited the Porsche Bureau in November 1931, the designer had already become involved in perfecting similar designs on his own.

Such a vehicle was badly needed. All existing models were, for one reason or another, unsatisfactory. Porsche wanted to build a car which would rank as a major technical achievement. 'By a "people's car",' as he explained on another occasion, 'I do not understand a small car which . . . carries on the tradition of previous products in this field and continues to copy them exactly.' He referred to the fact that most small cars were merely scaled-down big cars. Porsche considered them uneconomic and unsafe. 'By a "people's car" I understand only a completely practical vehicle which can compete with every other practical vehicle on equal terms. In my opinion, a fundamentally new approach is needed to turn "normal vehicles" existing hitherto into "people's cars".'

The small car he wanted to build would have to be designed from the chassis up. It would have to be an unconventional car, built in accordance with its own demands, if it were to be the ideal small car Porsche wanted. He called it Project No. 12 and was now willing to gamble his own money on it.

He could afford little. While the Wanderer contracts had set him up in business, there was not much of it. His staff was extraordinarily devoted to the choleric little designer and many had accepted lower salaries than they could have earned elsewhere, just to work with the Master; still, there was one occasion when Porsche was driven to the extremity of borrowing on his life insurance to meet the payroll. Project 12, however, had been the hub around which his thoughts had turned so long that he launched it anyway. The fact that Neumeyer would be interested was unknown to him as he assembled his staff in September of 1931, to tell them of his plans.

He never had a drawing board of his own and so, on this as on other occasions, he simply gathered his men around any convenient board and then began to talk and sketch. Usually, he did so with lightning speed and the meetings were short; this time, he spoke and sketched from early afternoon into the evening. The room was littered with his drawings by the time he had finished.

These sketches were certainly radical and illustrated an odd-looking car. The hood dropped forward in a graceless curve to the front fender; the windscreen stood upright and robbed the car of any slipstream look; the sharply sloping roof line seemed to allow little or no headroom for rear-seat passengers, and the rear window would apparently afford a view only of the sky. No question about it: the designer who had built some of the most elegant automobiles known to date was planning a weird one. It hardly looked like a car. It resembled a bug—a beetle.

As the afternoon wore on, Porsche covered one detail of the construction after another. His assistants saw that he had thought out everything, in broad strokes, to be sure, but masterful ones. It was now to be their task to provide the detailed drawings, offering Porsche several solutions to each problem, until the 'ideal small car' would have every nut, bolt, and cotter pin assigned. There was to be an air-cooled 26-hp engine mounted just aft of the rear axle, for this position would allow the cheaper, lower-horsepower motor to deliver torque more directly to the rear wheels, without wasting precious power to turn a driveshaft from the front of the car. Engine weight placed over the rear wheels would also improve traction and offset the effect of the car's light weight. He planned at first a design wherein three cylinders were arranged in a radial pattern around the crankshaft, and the gearbox and differential were to be worked into a single unit just ahead of the engine. He wanted air cooling because it would also cut weight and cost by eliminating the water jacket which surrounds the cylinders of liquid-cooled engines. An air-cooled car also would need no antifreeze in winter and could cross deserts or labour endlessly up mountain roads without over-heating.

Porsche insisted his car was to have a four-wheel independent suspension system utilising the torsion bars he had just invented (but which had not yet been perfected). Any car, no matter what its size, benefits by having each of its four wheels suspended independently, but in a small car this is even more desirable. Short-wheelbase cars bang and bounce on bumps; the impacts are even worse if both rear wheels are sprung together, as they are on most cars, for then the shock travels the full width of the rear axle.

The Project 12 car was to be lightweight, so as to make its low-horsepower engine sufficient. Porsche, remembering his Austro-Daimler aircraft experience, cut weight sharply by eliminating the heavy steel or timbered frames of the day and using instead a prin-ciple of aircraft design. He mounted all his car's components on a large sheet-steel floor plan made stiff by shaping ripples and ridges into the metal and by forming a tunnel along the front-to-rear centreline.[1] When the upper portion of the body was bolted to the floor plan, the effect was the same as the 'unit body' (or monoque construction) used in building aircraft; it provides the strength and stiffness of a steel pipe without involving a heavy frame.

Porsche gave his designers ninety days to finish the job. In the meantime, he sent out feelers to the car industry, hoping to find a sponsor. No one seemed interested. Just as Porsche called a halt to the project, which had consumed all the money he could allocate, Neumeyer heard of his designs. He thought he would have a look at them, for he badly needed a new product; he had already decided a small car would enable his motor-cycle customers to 'trade up'. Neumeyer had even gone so far as to give the car its name, before

---

1. The principle is the same one that stiffens a sheet of paper if one folds it several times.

he even had a design. He decided to call it the Zündapp Volksauto, or people's car.

The word Volksauto had already been used a great deal in the Germany of the 1920's, and indeed, a car called the Bergmann Volksauto had even appeared on the market in 1904. The impetus given the Volksauto idea in the 1920's can above all be credited to *Motorkritik* and its editor, Ganz. Neumeyer thus was planning to give his car a name much in vogue at the time.

When he saw the designs at the Porsche Bureau, he had only one reservation. He used air-cooled engines in his motor-cycles and felt they were too noisy for an automobile. He wanted his Volksauto to have a water-cooled five-cylinder radial engine, so as to eliminate the siren scream which an air blower, mounted in an auto chassis, makes in forcing cooling air over the cylinders. The water jacket, he further pointed out, would also help dampen much engine noise. Although Porsche never received such drastic suggestions gracefully, he acquiesced without a murmur in this case. He needed a patron badly and Dr. Neumeyer was the only one he could find. Neumeyer's factory was to make the engine and gearboxes for three prototypes; the bodies were to be built at the Reutter coachworks in Stuttgart, under Porsche's supervision. The final Volksauto was to have an all-steel body, but the prototypes were made of aluminium stretched over a wooden frame. At the end of April 1932, the completed bodies were shipped to Nuremberg to be mated with the rest of the car, and Zündapp drivers began their tests.

Disasters happened daily. The cars had hardly sputtered the first six miles down the road when the engine oil began to boil. The great heat actually welded the pistons to the cylinder walls of two of the test cars and they screeched to a halt. Back at the factory, the cooling system was redesigned. While mechanics struggled to make these modifications, Porsche saw that the radial engine, its five cylinders splaying out around the clock, would always prove a nightmare for mechanics.

Once the cars were back on the road, the teeth on the gears began snapping off; once more everything halted for repairs. Finally, the Volksautos were ready for high-speed long-distance tests—or at least Porsche thought they were. As the drivers raced them along the highways there was a sharp crack, like a rifle shot. Slivers of steel flew out from one of the cars; it sagged helplessly over one of its front wheels. Porsche's torsion bar had shattered under the strain. From then on the rifle reports sounded one after another as torsion bars gave out on all the cars. This problem was so basic that it could be set right only by tedious experimentation in metallurgical laboratories. These would have to produce just the right temper in the steel to make the bars more supple. Neumeyer's enthusiasm, not to speak of his funds, began to dwindle. He was also beginning to realise how costly the heavy stamping presses needed to shape the steel body parts would be. He decided to cut short his gamble on the Volksauto. Porsche was paid 85,000 marks and was allowed to keep one of the prototypes. (A company car in constant use, it was destroyed twelve years later in a 1944 air raid.) Disappointed, Porsche at this juncture received his welcomed invitation from the Soviets. By the time he returned, he had broken free of his depression.

Before the year ended, another 'Volksauto' customer had presented himself at number 24 Kronenstrasse. He was Fritz von Falkenhayn, head of Germany's NSU Works in Neckarsulm, also interested in a small car. Porsche had the designs ready in his Bureau drawer. What emerged in 1933 was a car even more similar to the Volkswagen of today, although it was bulkier and contained a 1·5 litre engine (at NSU's request).

Again, the strange cars were built at Stuttgart. This time, engines were constructed at NSU's Neckarsulm factory, under Ferry Porsche's supervision. Three prototypes of this direct forerunner of the Volkswagen were rolled out of the plant, gassed up, tested, and performed successfully.[1]

Porsche had applied his Zündapp experience to modify the car for NSU. The body was now a bit more shapely, the headlights were recessed into the fenders and, most important, Porsche had talked Von Falkenhayn into trying an air-cooled engine. This time, however, it had four cylinders lying on their sides, opposing each other two by two; very much as in Porsche's 1912 airplane engine, which had proved most durable, there was a large blower to direct the cooling air over the cylinders.

'Sounds like a worn-out stonecrusher,' the good-natured Von Falkenhayn told Porsche after his ride in the noisy car. But he liked its performance: it whipped along at a top speed of 72 mph without

1. The three prototypes vanished until December 1950 when one of them unexpectedly reappeared in Stuttgart, driven by a crippled German war veteran who was a former NSU engineer. This ancient forerunner of the VW was parked in front of the Porsche Bureau headquarters and ogled 'with curiosity and awe like a prehistoric fossil'. Driven almost daily before the outbreak of World War II, it survived the war and the immediate postwar years in the deserted Friedrichsruh Castle of the Hohenlohes near Öhringen. There the NSU veteran found it in 1948 and bought it for next to nothing. He installed new headlights and a new battery and tested the engine. It worked as though it were brand new.

ever threatening to overheat. The same old trouble with the 'exploding' torsion bars remained, however. Deciding nevertheless that the car had real possibilities, the NSU chief arranged for its manufacture while Porsche pushed ahead with new enthusiasm to exterminate the bugs in the beetle.

Events, however, were moving fast now—and in many directions. While Von Falkenhayn and Ferdinand Porsche were poring over paper plans for their car, other forces were forming. As unlikely as it seemed, all were to play their part in Porsche's life and, even more so, in the life of the car that would outlive him. They involved many men: a new Chancellor who was a car-buff, a Munich car salesman who became a courtier, and a lot of smart industrialists who proved in the end not to have been so smart after all.

2

Hitler and the Changed Atmosphere

I T WAS on January 30, 1933, that Adolf Hitler returned triumphant to his Nazi Party cronies in Berlin's Kaiserhof Hotel. As they recalled it, he greeted them with eyes full of tears. He had just been named Chancellor of Germany by President Paul von Hindenburg. It was shortly after noon and Adolf Hitler's sun, too, stood at the zenith.

Before three weeks had passed, he summoned Germany's top industrialists, including the heads of Krupp, I. G. Farben, and United Steel Works, to the offices of Hermann Goering, who was now President of the Reichstag. An election was scheduled for March 5, and Hitler wanted to fleece the 'fat cats' for contributions to the Nazi fund. He assured them that the sacrifices 'surely would be much easier for industry to bear if it realised that the election of March fifth will surely be the last one for the next ten years, probably even for the next hundred years'.

As was his custom, he proceeded to cozen his listeners by appealing to their prejudices. In the presidential offices of the very Reichstag building which would be set afire within seven days, Hitler held out the promise of a chastened labour force, accompanied by a policy of governmental support for a reactionary form of capitalism.

'Private enterprise,' he told them, 'cannot be maintained in the age of democracy. It is conceivable only if the people have a sound idea of authority.' Then, in a philosophical aside, he ventured: 'All the worldly goods we possess we owe to the struggle of the chosen . . . all benefits of culture must be introduced more or less with an iron fist.'

His vision of a rapacious, state-protected *laissez-faire* economy was designed to please the industrialists. Krupp reportedly jumped up at the end of the meeting to express the 'gratitude' of those present for his clear statement of Nazi policy towards industry. The short speech earned Hitler three million marks.

It is not surprising that industrialists hoped for a 'clear picture' of intent from the new Chancellor. The economy was chaotic: more than six million workers were out of jobs and fifteen million Germans were on relief. Tight wage- and price-control measures had succeeded mainly in stifling initiative. No group of industrialists had less of this particular commodity at the time than the car manufacturers, whose sales had plummeted and some of whom were considering clósing down their plants.

True, they had heard some good news from Chancellor Hitler at the Motor Show in Berlin. An annual event staged in the second week of February, this exhibition in 1933 was to have been a modest one, as befitted the shrinking wallets of the industrialists who were to pay for it. Yet all plans for simplicity had been forcibly cast aside a few days after Hitler came to power, for a Nazi Party official let the show managers know that the exhibition was to be the new Chancellor's first public forum. He would address the show and the Party was to see to it that the surroundings matched the dignity of the office. The man who received the telephone call from Party headquarters was Director Allmers of the German Automobile Industry Association (the RDA, for Reichsverband der deutschen Automobilindustrie), and he was not happy about it. He was even less happy next day, when uniformed Party officers took over the exhibition hall to make sure the decorations were lavish. The conservative industry leaders who were to pay the expenses dug deep, and grumbled.

They grumbled less when they heard Hitler's speech at the Grand Opening. Dressed in black jacket and striped pants and flanked by the two other Nazis in his eleven-man cabinet (Interior Minister Wilhelm Frick and Hermann Goering, then minister without portfolio), and accompanied also by propaganda chief Goebbels, Hitler made what seemed to the industrialists an utterly amazing speech. They may not have realised it then, but it was the speech of a confirmed car buff.

A nation, the Führer said, is no longer judged by other nations by its miles of railroad track, but by its miles of paved highways. He promised to build a vast network. Nothing, he went on to say, gives a nation greater prestige in the age of the motor-car than leadership in motor racing; he called upon the German car companies to win the victories. Speaking with moderation for once, he analysed the economy of Germany, and he did so much as the manufacturers would have done. They found his statements and his critique startling, for no other government leader they knew of had ever shown so great an understanding of the car industry or of motorisation as a whole. They were more than startled when they heard his promises; they were elated. Hitler promised to reduce the confiscatory car taxes, ease the stringent traffic laws, and make it easier to obtain drivers' licences. Clearly, the new regime planned to encourage car ownership and to help them sell cars.

For a brief while after the show was over, Hitler's speech continued to intoxicate the car manufacturers, but they later grew cynical and marked the promises down as pie-in-the-sky political propaganda for the March 5 elections. As for a request Hitler had made during his speech—that they develop a cheap, small car for the masses—most of them never expected to hear of that again. It sounded like another demagogic 'promise' at election time.

The manufacturers were wrong on all counts. Hitler meant what he said. He built the highways, cut the taxes, eased ownership and traffic laws, encouraged motoring holidays—and pressed for his small car. As a matter of fact, he had had that idea even before he became Chancellor. A year earlier, in 1932, he spoke about a small car with Jakob Werlin, a Munich Mercedes-Benz salesman, and had asked him to suggest to Daimler-Benz that they build one. The directors of the company turned the idea down flatly. Hitler was not Chancellor yet and a suggestion by Werlin in 1932 didn't carry the weight it later would.

Werlin had sold Adolf Hitler his first Mercedes, a 60-hp limousine, which the Nazi leader bought in 1923 out of Party funds, despite the impoverished state of Nazi finances at the time. He never learned to drive, but loved the sensation of being raced at top speed through Germany, and he became the first German politician to use a car extensively for political campaigns. So intrigued was he with cars, and especially with the powerful, large Mercedes limousines which Jakob Werlin sold, that Werlin from that time on became Hitler's crony and personal adviser on all motoring matters. Daimler-Benz, spotting an inside track once Hitler had become Chancellor, made Werlin a member of its board of directors then, hoping for advantages.

There are those who argue that Hitler most probably was captivated by the idea of a cheap car for the masses while he was imprisoned in Landsberg Fortress in November 1923. Sentenced to five years, Hitler served only nine months and used the time to write *Mein Kampf*—and to read a biography of Henry Ford. The fact that the elder Ford was a notorious anti-Semite, as well as a production genius, prompted Hitler to call him the 'greatest American' of all time; the story of Ford's motor-car achievements, in any case, also impressed him, and it may have been while reading this biography that the Nazi leader became interested in the subject.

Whatever the reason, Hitler's passion for cars was real and his sense that the issue could be exploited propagandistically was realistic. Once in power after January 1933, he set about to act. The idea of a car for the masses, coming from a Chancellor, was novel— and audacious. It had appeal.

The long night of the inflation and Great Depression had cheated the German worker out of even dreaming of owning a family car, yet it was well known that, in America as early as 1929, one out of every six Americans owned his own car, and the United States, with 23,122,000 cars, had reached the stage where an entire population could simultaneously be moved about by car. In Germany, however, few hoped for something comparable. It all seemed a mad fantasy.

Years later, Heinz Nordhoff discussed European small-car development and set the scene.

'During the early twenties,' he said, 'a wave of American cars swept over the countries of Europe which were still dazed by the aftermath of the First World War. . . . They were big, powerful, quiet, and they made all European cars of similar size obsolete overnight. These magnificent machines came as a shock to our engineers and manufacturers. . . .'

This invasion, Nordhoff noted, ended soon, for few Europeans could afford to buy or operate such American cars. Inadequate roads, expensive fuel, and meagre repair facilities plagued Europe. Nevertheless, these cars proved, Nordhoff says, 'the hopelessness of hybridising a comparable strain in Europe. . . . The European engineer was forced to take a different approach.' This, Nordhoff says, was 'a new trend of thought, the revelation of a secret love, long cultivated, often in secret, among European designers, for a small car'.

In Britain, during the 1920's, Austin, Morris, and Singer had begun production and the development of the Austin 7 (as well as Fiat's Topolino in Italy) did much to inspire those elsewhere in Europe who urged the development of small cars. Indeed, both Herbert Austin and William R. Morris were planning 'motors for the millions', along Ford's lines. Nordhoff watched these develop-

ments in the 1920's and 1930's from his vantage point at Adam
Opel, which also was working on small cars. But those which existed
on the Continent, he says, were *ersatz* cars for those who could not
afford the real thing. Most were meant only for two passengers and,
says Nordhoff, 'while their size was reduced, their faults were
doubled'.

Young designers throughout Austria, Czechoslovakia, and
Germany, joined later by French and Italian designers, revolted.
As they questioned all the old ideas and conceptions, debates became
heated. In meetings and in the engineering press, they argued about
front and rear engines, front and rear drives, water and air cooling
systems, and the questions of weight and air resistance. The Continental car manufacturers resisted this debate. Their great investments, shaky finances and innate conservatism compelled them to
discourage innovations. And so, new designs came from the drawing
boards of independent and consulting engineers, like Ferdinand
Porsche.

'The severe depression after the crash of 1929,' says Nordhoff,
'aggravated the reluctance among the struggling automobile companies. At the same time, it increased the unrest among the young
and enthusiastic designers. It was during this period of turmoil,
uncertainty, and fear, that Hitler came to power. Demagogue that
he was, he was quick to realise the propaganda value of favouring
the public demand for the automobile.'

The congenial atmosphere created by Nazism for his car and for
car production in general was not lost on Porsche. It was at this very
time that he was working on the final paper designs for NSU. Then,
in May 1933, Baron Klaus D. von Oertzen, a board member of the
new Auto-Union company, asked Porsche to accompany him to see
the new Chancellor. Von Oertzen needed Porsche to help convince
the Führer that Auto-Union ought to obtain a financial subsidy
equal to the one Hitler gave Daimler-Benz to finance a German
Grand Prix racing car.

When Adolf Hitler entered the room, he strode up to the designer
with an enthusiastic 'We've met before, Dr. Porsche!' Although
Porsche had no idea when this might have occurred, the encounter
had indeed taken place in 1924. At the time, Porsche was already
famous, and Hitler was a regional politician of questionable importance. The men had met at the Solitude Race near Stuttgart, where
Hitler had been introduced to Porsche by Daimler's press chief, Dr.

Völter. Porsche's son Ferry recalls the event, but says his father never did remember it, and cites this fact as an example of how little interest Ferdinand Porsche had in politics or politicians. After the auspicious beginning, however, the mood at the meeting changed. Hitler, who loved the big Mercedes cars, had become an admirer of Daimler-Benz and saw no reason why Germany needed two factory racing teams in order to win all the prizes. Daimler-Benz would do nicely. He was frank in telling Baron von Oertzen and Porsche that Auto-Union (formed in 1932 through a merger of Wanderer, Horch, Audi and DKW) was a company 'no one had heard of', with no record in racing even remotely comparable to that of Daimler-Benz. 'What an outrageous request you make, gentlemen!' he concluded.

Now Porsche took the floor and argued for twenty-five minutes without letting Hitler interrupt him once. At first surprised, the Chancellor gradually became more and more impressed, for Porsche was pouring out a hypnotic mixture of technical language and layman's jargon, just the sort of talk that would captivate a car buff. He argued that no single German manufacturer could compete alone against all the foreign factory teams and that, furthermore, what was important was not the company, but the car. He, Porsche, had the car, and he proceeded to explain it to the Führer.

He told of the racer he was then planning for Auto-Union, with a sixteen-cylinder engine shaped in a V with eight cylinders on each side, the engine mounted just ahead of the driving wheels in the rear. It would have Porsche's new torsion-bar and trailing-arm suspension, now being perfected. The racer would have better traction because of the engine weight over the rear wheels and the suspension would make it superior in holding the road. Hitler may have understood little of the technical side, but Porsche's confidence affected him. He did a complete turnabout and promised Auto-Union the same million mark subsidy granted to Daimler-Benz.

Porsche's racing car did everything he said it would. It was first put on the racing circuits in 1934, at a time when Grand Prix cars had been limited to a weight of 1653 pounds as a safety precaution, the argument being that so lightweight a car could not achieve dangerously high speeds. Yet Porsche's Auto-Union racer with its 16-cylinder engine, although weighing less than the VW 'beetle' does today, developed between 550 and 600 horsepower and went blazing down the tracks at 250 mph. (In comparison, an Alfa-Romeo of the same period, though 110 pounds heavier, developed only 220 hp and could go no faster than 156 mph.) Porsche had indeed given

Auto-Union (and Hitler's Third Reich) a running start in the racing business.

He was far ahead of the rest of the world with his rear-engine racer design. In 1963 a group of European Grand Prix drivers invaded the Indianapolis 500 race, and all were driving rear-engined cars made by different companies. A Scot, Jimmy Clark, amazed American car-racing experts by driving to an easy second; some observers believed that he was kept from first place only by a poor ruling on the part of the judges. Writing for *Life* just before the race began, Britain's great racing driver Stirling Moss had this to say about rear engines:

The battle [at the Indianapolis Speedway] will be easy to follow. All your regular Indy drivers will be in front-engine cars—all of them except one or two powered by old reliable Offenhauser engines. All our Grand Prix boys will be in cars with engines in the rear. In Europe the front-engine racing car is regarded as hopelessly out of fashion. We have learned that engines in the rear give better traction, eliminate the driveshaft beside the driver and cut down on frontal area, which means less wind resistance. I can tell you, too, that it's usually cooler for the driver with the engine in the rear—even inside the car I used to drive, the temperature got up to 160 degrees. It's a bloody sauna bath.

What Moss said may seem obvious today, but Porsche recognised it well before most others did. So much was he convinced of the merits of the rear-engine cars he was working on in 1933 that he prepared a lengthy memorandum to the German Government's Transport Ministry, spelling out the specifications of just the small car for the masses which Hitler had called for in February, at the 1933 Motor Show. He sent it off on January 17, 1934, just before the 1934 Berlin Motor Show.

While he was still planning it, two different events had occurred. The time was late 1933. Porsche was told that NSU had decided to abandon preparations to build motor-cars. For one thing, the investment required would be too high and, for another, it had an agreement with Fiat in Italy never to build a four-wheeled vehicle under the NSU name. As Von Falkenhayn himself explained a few years ago, it was hard at the time to obtain credits for the investment required (he estimated it would be between 15 and 20 million marks); further, bicycle and motor-cycle sales were picking up so satisfactorily that he could hardly meet the demand and decided to concentrate on doing so. Yet Porsche was nevertheless to construct three prototypes of the NSU cars he was designing, for that was part of their contractual agreement.

The news from NSU came as a severe blow to Porsche and his staff. It seemed to them that their small car would never be built. Just then, and entirely coincidentally, Jakob Werlin showed up at the Porsche Bureau headquarters. He had come down from Berlin that very day and had some time to kill before his first important appointment. Not having seen Ferdinand Porsche for five years, since the designer had left Daimler-Benz, Werlin thought he would find out what Porsche was planning.

Porsche greeted him with reserve, for he thought Werlin might be trying to find out as much as he could about the Auto-Union racer then being designed, which would be competing against racers of the company the Mercedes dealer represented. And so, rather than talk too much about his rear-engined racing car, Porsche told Werlin about his rear-engined small car for the average driver. Chafing at the news of Von Falkenhayn's withdrawal, he spoke passionately. Knowing the interest Hitler had in an inexpensive small car, Jakob Werlin listened more and more attentively. This talk of Porsche's, he well knew, would interest the Chancellor, and Werlin, more and more the courtier, no doubt also realised that the Führer would be grateful to the man who brought him news of it.

By the time Hitler addressed the 1934 Berlin Motor Show in January, it was clear that he did know already that Ferdinand Porsche was working on a car more or less of the kind he himself wanted. Some of this he must have gained from his May 1933 meeting with Porsche and Von Oertzen, some he learned from Werlin after the latter's autumn 1933 visit to Stuttgart, and some he may have gathered from Porsche's memorandum to the Transport Ministry.

Firmly in power by 1934, Hitler appeared in his Nazi Party uniform, instead of conservative dress, and his far less temperate speech underlined the tougher posture. 'So long as the motor-car remains only a means of transportation for especially privileged circles,' he said, 'it is with bitter feelings that we see millions of honest, hard-working, and capable fellow-men whose opportunities in life are already limited, cut off from the use of a vehicle which would be a special source of yet-unknown happiness to them, particularly on Sundays and holidays. One must have the courage to grasp this problem in a decided and comprehensive manner. What will not be possible in one year will, perhaps, prove to be a commonplace fact ten years hence.'

This message had an impact on the car industry. Hitler in 1934 was

already Der Führer, and '*Der Führer wünscht*'—'the leader wishes'—
already had assumed the nature of a command.

'To placate this dangerous man, the car manufacturers decided to
give at least lip-service to his fantastic scheme,' said Heinz Nordhoff.
The extent of even their lip-service was minimal and their foot-
dragging, which was monumental, would cause them plenty of verbal
abuse—and more—at the hands of Hitler. They would learn in no
uncertain terms that it was not the age of democracy which made
free enterprise impossible, but the *Führer-prinzip*—the 'leadership
principle'—on which the German state was now organised.

In May 1934 Porsche was summoned from his offices in Stuttgart
to Berlin. His document urging the construction of a *Kleinauto* had
come to Hitler's personal attention. He wanted to meet the designer
again and spell out some of his own requirements. Accompanied by
Werlin, Hitler met Porsche at the Kaiserhof Hotel.

The two men saw eye-to-eye for several reasons. Both came from
small towns in the old Austro-Hungarian Empire and, in a very real
way, spoke each other's language; both were always to feel more
comfortable among backwoods Austrians than among the polished
members of Germany's industrial society. Both mistrusted the
wealthy industrialists: Porsche because they had always frustrated
his plans, Hitler for less clear-cut reasons rooted in his arsenal of
hatreds. They were linked on that day in the Kaiserhof Hotel by a
common boyhood, by a sense of jousting against the giants of
capitalism, and by their love of cars. They got along well. The
politically disinterested Porsche saw the new Chancellor simply as
someone in a position of power who shared his enthusiasm about
motor-cars and his vision of the small car. For the first time, the
possibility of a Volkswagen dawned for the general run of the
people. Porsche was delighted with the events as they were unfolding
themselves.

He outlined his ideas for a small car. In its essentials, he proposed
a 26-hp (at 3500 rpm) car weighing 1430 pounds, with four-wheel
independent suspension, capable of achieving 100 kilometres (62·2
miles) per hour, and with a one-litre (61 cu. in.) engine displacement.

Hitler liked what he heard, then added a few more of his own
ideas. Such a car, he insisted, should use up no more than seven litres
of petrol per 100 kilometres (approximately 40 miles per gallon, and
one litre less than Porsche proposed); must be a four-seater to
accommodate the family; should be air-cooled to protect the car in

cold weather (because private garages were few); and should maintain, not just reach, 100 kilometres per hour.

A few more details were ironed out before the two men parted
company. Porsche asked to be paid for all expenses and a royalty per
car built. Then came the matter of price; Porsche had calculated this
carefully and suggested 1550 marks, a sum which, he believed, would
just cover the costs.

Shortly, word was passed on to the car manufacturers' trade
association, the RDA, that the Führer had decided to move ahead,
as he had warned, with the development of a *Kleinauto*. It was to be
placed under the wing of the RDA. The RDA contract with Porsche
was 'to further the motorisation of the German people on the basis
of co-operative action and by enlisting the best talents of German car
manufacture'.

There was nothing for the RDA to do but co-operate. Adolf Hitler
had made up his mind, and the industry had learned that the dictator-
ship which was 'to keep the workers in line' was keeping them in line
as well. Wilhelm Vorwig, then head of the RDA's technical department (and today director of its postwar successor organisation), says,
'We knew we had to do something, because this was not a government to fool around with.'

Nordhoff, discussing these events later, said: 'It soon became
apparent that the jealousy between the automobile companies was
far too deep-rooted to make a concerted effort possible . . . Porsche
was chosen . . . How and where such a car would be manufactured
after a satisfactory design had been achieved, remained completely
open, and there might have been a hidden hope that the whole very
unwelcome plan would go on the rocks when this decision had to be
faced.' A suggestion by the RDA that this 'people's car' be a three-
wheeled vehicle was rejected out of hand by Hitler, for he had
already seen Porsche's plans for a four-wheeler. Vorwig says the
three-wheeled car was proposed because it was unheard of in
Germany that 'the common man would be driving a car and we were
thinking more of a sort of covered-up motor-cycle'. Yet, once the
contract was drawn up, Vorwig claims, the RDA 'honestly intended
to build a car'. None of its members, he says, 'were keen on it', but
they were willing to give it a try.

The contract between the RDA and the designer contained two
clauses which shocked Porsche: he was not given a full year, as he
had requested, but only ten months, and worst of all, his price of
1550 marks had been shaved to 900. The new price was a serious blow

threatening the whole design concept and Porsche at first considered it 'idiotic'.

The price had been arrived at for several reasons. For one thing, it was good politics. The average German's savings in 1934 fell below 1000 marks; thus the 900-mark price had great appeal. For another, the Opel entry into the small-car field, the P–4 then being developed, was to sell for around 1550 marks—and out of this had to come a 20 or 25 per cent dealer commission. Because even the early Volkswagen plans counted on no dealers who would require commissions, it was felt that the car could be realistically priced below 1000 marks Ferdinand Porsche's son Ferry says that his father let himself be convinced by this argument; he thought at least 'it might be possible'.

The contract negotiations had begun in May (with Heinz Nordhoff representing the Opel company); the signatures were affixed on June 22, 1934. Liaison man between the Porsche Bureau in Stuttgart and the RDA was to be Wilhelm Vorwig. As for money, Porsche was to submit monthly statements and time-sheets, covering staff hours, overhead, and a salary for himself. These, says Vorwig, 'always were very correct'. They began by running about 20,000 marks a month, later climbed slowly to 50,000 as more staff was required, then levelled off at about 40,000. Porsche, returning home to Stuttgart in June 1934, was to build three prototype automobiles. But no one volunteered to help him.[1]

Despite the conditions, Porsche and his team began work in earnest. 'They meant business, not lip-service,' Heinz Nordhoff remarked later. 'This outstanding man was engineer and designer not by profession, but at heart. Short-tempered and energetic . . . he was not regarded as being successful in the normal sense of the word, but he was a fanatic and an unusually gifted engineer. He had his own very clear ideas about a small car, and he gripped with all ten fingers this opportunity to materialise his dreams. He had the rare gift of surrounding himself with a team of devoted followers who loved him and were dedicated to his ideas. Among them there was a unity and a determination to accomplish the outstanding and an unbounded willingness to follow their leader and idol.'

---

1. According to author Herbert Quint, one manufacturer said to Porsche, after the RDA contract had been signed, 'Right, Herr Porsche? You'll design what they demand and then, when the budget is exhausted, you'll tell them it won't work.' He quotes another as claiming Volkswagens weren't necessary: 'One should build omnibuses; the worker can ride those into the countryside, if he absolutely must go. But not everybody needs a car!' According to Ferry Porsche, this latter remark was made by the head of BMW (Bayerische Motoren-Werke).

Idol and idolaters started building their small cars. Since they did not have a factory or a machine shop at their disposal they built the cars in the garage of Porsche's home on Stuttgart's Killesberg. They brought to the garage a couple of lathes, a drill press, a milling machine, a grinder, and some other equipment, made room for a dozen workers, and proceeded to hand-tool the cars. Ten months later, when the contract came due, they were still trying.

Another motor show was held in Berlin. Even with the prototypes uncompleted, Hitler sounded optimistic in 1935.

'I am happy,' he said, 'that due to the abilities of the superb designer Porsche and his staff, we have succeeded in completing preliminary designs for a German people's car, so that the first models will finally be tested by the middle of this year. It *must* be possible to make the German people a gift of a motor vehicle which will not cost them more than they have heretofore been accustomed to paying for a medium-priced motor-cycle and whose petrol consumption will be low!'

Much of this was stalling for time, and Hitler knew it. He was well aware of how slowly the little garage in Stuttgart was forced to operate and knew the car could not reach the test stage by mid-1935.

Nevertheless Hitler took great pride in his designer. In 1934 he had learned to his apparent dismay that Ferdinand Porsche was a Czech citizen and had taken immediate steps to 'Germanise' him. On December 17, 1934, Ferdinand Porsche received a letter from the man in charge of sports activities under the Nazis, Reichssportführer von Tschammer und Osten, which stated: 'The Führer wishes that the greatest German automobile designer become a German citizen. I urge you to use this letter as the basis for your application for naturalisation.' The matter of citizenship meant little to Porsche. Ghislaine Kaes remembers the morning when he showed the designer the letter. Porsche cast his eyes over it and handed it back with the remark: 'Well, I guess we can't do anything about it. Take care of the matter today.'

In 1936 Hitler continued to sound optimistic at the Berlin Motor Show. To make certain that his message regarding a small car was not lost on those most important to its fulfilment, the Ministry for Propaganda and People's Enlightenment broadcast the Führer's address into every motor-vehicle and car-accessories plant in Germany. Hitler's February 15 speech held out 'no doubt' that the day was dawning on which three to four million Germans would be driving their own cars.[1]

Hitler said the purchase price and upkeep costs of the car must be 'brought into conformity with the owner's income'. He sought to dispose of the argument (no doubt raised by the car manufacturers) that a small car would elbow big ones off the market. The opposite was true, he said, for 'it has been conclusively demonstrated that the low-priced car had not only popularised the motoring habit, but had gradually stimulated the demand for more expensive makes'.

'I have no doubt,' he concluded in his address to the still-ambulatory worker, 'that the costs of this car will be brought into a tolerable relationship with the income of the broadest masses of our German people, as we have seen this done so brilliantly in America.'

The problem in Germany, however, was not one of lowering a car's costs artificially, by fiat as it were, in order to meet the generally low wages of 1936, but of raising personal income to a level where a car might be a reasonable investment. Even at the low 900-mark price, Hitler's *Kleinauto* would cost the German worker more than three times as much in man-hours as one of the low-priced three Detroit cars cost an American worker of that day.

To many at the time, the entire scheme seemed crazy, just an idea being insisted upon by the Chancellor who already was declared absolute ruler over all phases of German life. Little except the design being produced in Stuttgart made sense.

And while the ideas were Porsche's, the designs also owed much to Karl Rabe, who made them work. This brilliant engineer, a first-rate motor-car designer in his own right, with several cars to his personal credit, had served with Porsche ever since 1913, when he met him first at Austro-Daimler. Rabe stayed at Austro-Daimler during Porsche's stormy sessions with German Daimler and with Steyr, but when Porsche set himself up in business as a consultant, Karl Rabe could not resist his call. He rejoined Porsche in 1931; today, more than thirty-five years later, and more than half a century after first meeting Porsche, Rabe continues serving the Porsche company as a consultant near Stuttgart. Until a few years ago, he continued on in his

1. The U.S.A. in 1936 contained 24 times as many cars as did Germany, despite the fact that its population was only twice as large; 70 per cent of the world's 40,287,000 motor vehicles were in the US. (Actual figures: USA—24,219,000 passenger cars; Germany—1,061,000). In relation to population, there was one car per 4·5 Americans, versus one per 49 Germans. (Other nations in 1936: Italy—103 persons per car; Belgium—41; Denmark—27; Great Britain—21; France—19; Canada—9; and New Zealand—7.) The number of all types of motor vehicles in Britain had risen from about 2,274,000 in 1930 to 3,150,000 in 1939; of these, the number of motor-cars were, respectively, 1,056,214 and 2,034,400, the remainder being motor-cycles.

capacity as Chefkonstrukteur (chief designer) for Ferry Porsche as he had for Ferry's father before. Says Vorwig, 'Rabe is actually the man responsible for the finished design. Porsche had the grand idea and the concepts, but it was Rabe who designed a mechanism that worked. Porsche could not have performed without Karl Rabe.' No doubt this is true, for those who deal with grand concepts usually need others to deal with details. Rabe was a far more technically-skilled designer than Ferdinand Porsche ever was; he just lacked Porsche's genius.

From 1934 to 1938, says Heinz Nordhoff, Porsche and this team fought against great odds. 'Without question,' he says, 'Porsche led a fight against the entire German car industry . . . a secret, underground fight of course and one which ended to his and the Volkswagen's benefit only because Hitler stood behind the entire plan.' Even Nordhoff was involved, as the Opel man on the RDA. Vorwig remembers him saying at an RDA meeting which discussed Porsche's initial engine design, 'This is an airplane engine. We can't produce that at this price.' 'He was completely disdainful,' says Vorwig. 'He never dreamed he'd one day be the man who'd build the car.'

Porsche now decided to visit the United States to see at first hand how cars were mass-produced. No comparable facilities existed in Europe and Porsche was, as always, interested only in using the most advanced methods. On September 19, 1936, he told his secretary, Ghislaine Kaes, to prepare to accompany him, and on October 1 they left for Paris by train. Kaes would be indispensable, not only as Porsche's travelling companion and secretary, but also as an interpreter, for English was his native tongue. He was a British subject, born in London, where his father, Otto Kaes, had represented Ferdinand Porsche as far back as the end of World War I, when Porsche was with Austro-Daimler. Otto Kaes was the brother of Ferdinand Porsche's wife Aloisia and his son Ghislaine was, therefore, the designer's nephew by marriage.

The two men boarded the North German Lloyd liner *Bremen* at Cherbourg on October 3 (after spending a day at the Paris Motor Show) and arrived in New York City on the eighth. There they checked into the Hotel Commodore and gaped at the city like tourists. Kaes's notebooks began to fill with the specifications of Radio City Music Hall, the Empire State Building, and New York highways. Everything interested the designer—and everything was noted down for future reference. On October 12, they drove to Roosevelt Raceway at Westbury, Long Island, where they saw Tazio

Nuvolari win the Vanderbilt Cup. Racing drivers and team managers recognised the famed designer instantly and deplored the fact that no Porsche racer was running at Roosevelt that year. Porsche studied the track carefully and, no doubt, began formulating his plans for the 1937 event. In that year, a Porsche-designed car would sweep the field at Westbury.

From New York, they took a train to Detroit on October 13, where they remained until October 22, touring the Ford Motor Company's River Rouge plant, the Lincoln factory, Packard, General Motors, Fisher Body, and other plants. Then they took a train to Chicago and on October 27 visited Bendix Aviation Corporation in South Bend, Indiana, as well as Notre Dame University. From there they travelled to Cincinnati, Ohio, and on October 29 returned to Detroit. Porsche had hoped to buy a new model Ford, but the car he wanted was not ready yet and instead he bought a six-cylinder Packard for $1000. With it, he drove to Niagara Falls, to Albany, and back to New York City. On November 4, after observing the US elections, he and Kaes boarded the *Queen Mary* for Europe, and sorted out their impressions. While aboard the liner, Porsche's fame permitted him the freedom of the ship and he spent endless hours questioning the ship's officers about the ship's technical specifications. Kaes, who acted as interpreter, took countless notes, for both men were enthralled by the huge liner.

A few months later, on January 29, 1937, Ghislaine Kaes spoke in Germany about his tour of the United States. He gave largely a technical lecture, detailing facts and figures of every factory they visited. He did, however, include some observations of American life, particularly of facets which had impressed the designer and his aide. In making the transcript of this lecture available, Kaes explained to me: 'Sentences in it appear which were not written by me. When I finished drafting it, I had to present it to a German censor who added a few sentences to please himself and those he served. Mainly, these disparaged the French. Well, I don't have to tell you about the "thousand-year-*Reich*" we have somehow survived . . .'

One of their first New York impressions was of the 'courtly' American behaviour. Kaes said they obediently drove for hours, one behind the other, without impatience or attempting to force their way ahead. The courtesy American men showed towards women was also a surprise. In Detroit, Porsche and some top executives were kept waiting (Porsche very impatiently) while a receptionist finished speaking to her friends. The prosperity of American workers impressed them and they noted down exact pay scales, working conditions, holiday schedules, and the means by which workers bought homes, motor-cars, and appliances on hire purchase plans. Time and again, they compared conditions with those then prevailing in European industry. 'One's heart leaps with joy to see how spotlessly clean American factories are,' Kaes reported. At Bendix Aviation and 'in all the factories we visited', he said, they were impressed by the 'relaxed and polite manner in which even high executives address the lowliest workers'. (At Bendix, however, they noted a sign which read, 'No one here has to belong to a union to keep his job!') In general, they found the trip exhilarating, if sometimes puzzling. At the Cincinnati Milling Machine Company, for example, where they ate in the workers' cafeteria and carried their trays about by themselves, Kaes wrote, 'I had to laugh heartily at the sight of Herr Dr. Porsche managing his own plates. Well, other lands, other customs!'

From Cherbourg, where the *Queen Mary* docked, they travelled to Great Britain, to see a British motor-car factory. On November 10, they toured Austin Motors in Longbridge, near Birmingham, where they were greeted by Lord Austin. After a day there, they left, singularly unimpressed. 'Compared with the manufacturing facilities of US factories, Austin is a poor, old, small plant,' Kaes noted in his lecture. On November 14, they returned to Stuttgart, Porsche by train, and Kaes by Packard.

The official RDA road-test of three prototype *Volksautos* (as the German and US press were calling them) had already begun, on October 12, 1936. Two had earlier been tested by the Porsche Bureau, in Alpine conditions, one for 500, the other for 3000 miles. The third was not ready until the last minute and joined the RDA test on October 13, a day late. In point of fact, all three were almost eighteen months late, for the June 1934 RDA contract demanded Porsche deliver his car by April 1935, evidence again that the car manufacturers hoped to kill the project with impossible conditions. Hitler had, however, insisted they extend the contract to give Porsche more time. (Whereupon Wilhelm von Opel reportedly told the designer: 'You'll give up in a year or so. You'll have earned enough money by then and that should satisfy you.')

If Opel said that, it shows he did not understand Porsche. Money interested Porsche very little; all he ever was interested in was seeing his ideas actualised. As a matter of fact, it may have been his personality as much as anything that caused delays. Vorwig, watching everything as RDA's 'project manager', grew increasingly concerned as month after month went by. 'Porsche kept rushing in while they were building his cars,' Vorwig says. 'He'd always have another change to make in the design, more or less like a woman building a house. There was just no arguing with him. If one's objections ran counter to his ideas, he'd just pooh-pooh them.' Just as it had been at Austro-Daimler, where Porsche turned out a bewildering series of changed designs, so it was in Stuttgart in 1935 and 1936. The cars were at first to be powered by a variation of Porsche's 1912 Austro-Daimler airplane engine; it was this idea that prompted an exasperated protest from Opel's Heinz Nordhoff at the time. Later, Porsche installed a two-cylinder, two-cycle, water-cooled engine into one of the three prototypes being built; this was an improvement over the principle used in the Puch motor-cycle engine, but it proved unfit for long distances. Then he tried an air-cooled, four-cycle, two-cylinder engine, but this turned out to have too little power in the low ranges. Ultimately, he settled on an air-cooled flat-four engine similar to the one designed for NSU, and it was this that was installed in all three test cars. The bodies of two of these cars were of wood and thin metal; only one had an all-steel body.

The test conditions were gruelling, for both cars and drivers. Each car was to cover a total of 30,000 miles, the drivers logging 200 miles of rough or hilly country roads each morning and another 300 miles along the Stuttgart–Bad Nauheim Autobahn each afternoon. Although there was to be no night driving, the cars were to be kept running six days a week. At night, they were to be kept outside, under canvas, so as to subject them to cold starts in the mornings.

'Because the production had been improvised and specifications were not always adhered to,' Vorwig later stated, 'errors had to be expected from the start.' As it did not have the necessary equipment, the Porsche Bureau was unable to test all the materials going into the prototypes for reliability; Porsche's men had, in Vorwig's words, virtually 'knitted' the car together, and didn't have enough spare parts. All this of course was the result of the lack of co-operation of the car companies; no doubt they hoped that their man Vorwig would test the cars to death.

Vorwig, however, says he was professionally interested in checking the cars out, not in burying them. He may have expected errors to crop up, but their number began to amaze even him over the months.

'Once we started testing,' he says, 'I found out just how much could go wrong with a car.' On car No. 1, the headlights turned out to be too weak, the gearshift broke, the front wheels began to wobble after 5000 miles, the valves needed to be reground at 10,000 miles, the brakes gave out at 13,000 and again at 16,000, and a rear shock absorber broke at 27,000.

The other two cars had even more problems; one which plagued all three was broken crankshafts. 'The sound a crankshaft makes as it breaks,' says Vorwig, 'is enough to turn you pale.' After a while, they were breaking with monotonous regularity and soon the entire reserve stock had been used up. Daimler-Benz produced a new supply in two days' time. But these, like the original shafts, were cast, and the breaks did not stop until forged crankshafts were used. (Although some manufacturers even today employ cast crankshafts, VW has never gone back to them after that experience.)

A Bureau service vehicle followed the cars around—and towed them in as they became disabled. Back in Stuttgart, a workshop was set up to repair the cars throughout the nights. Bad luck plagued the test drivers even when the cars were performing well. One car ran into a lorry, another into a motor-cyclist, and once a car hit a large deer at full speed going down the Autobahn. The collision knocked out a headlight and demolished the front-end bodywork. 'In this case,' Vorwig remembers, 'the results weren't entirely negative. The crew of the vehicle tossed the stag into the rear seat, its four legs sticking out a window, and raced back home at full speed, to get it there before it began to stink. We had a feast of venison and the accident further proved that a rear-engine vehicle can drive away from a collision.'

Vorwig and his drivers maintained their optimism, and of course Ferdinand Porsche maintained his confidence. As Vorwig noted later, only developmental mishaps were occurring, not basic ones. Nevertheless, these—and the fact that they were short of drivers— were causing delays. To counter this, tests were now being run on Sundays and at night as well, and even Vorwig took to the road. 'We were pushing hard to get through before Christmas,' he explains. 'None of us wanted to be driving cars on Christmas Eve.' They just barely made it. On December 23, each of the three cars had covered 30,000 miles. The drivers, exhausted, went home for the holidays; Vorwig prepared his report. If the manufacturers whose narrow interests he was supposed to have solely served thought he would now issue a death sentence, they were disappointed. They were not alone, for if Hitler expected the wildly enthusiastic judgment which a more sycophantic official might have given him, knowing his wishes, then he too must have been disappointed. Vorwig's report, in the light of the Führer's interests, seemed impertinently chilly in its dispassionate tone. He stuck to the facts and offered few value judgments. The furthest he went was to say that a continued development of the design could be recommended and that most of the shortcomings might be overcome without great difficulty. Vorwig himself today regards his report as positive and says it did not place undue emphasis on the difficulties. 'I liked the vehicle,' he says. 'I thought it was a good and unique design. I felt the concept was good and hoped the difficulties could be surmounted.' He did not, however, let this note of enthusiasm creep into his report. Its ruthlessly factual tone continues to be interpreted by many, including the Porsche family, as an expression of the RDA's negative attitude; there are those who believe that Vorwig's post-war claim that his had been a positive attitude towards the design reflects the beetle's post-war successes rather than mirroring the expression of his own views while he served the RDA. Referring to it in 1949, Vorwig admitted, 'It is clear that a privately owned industry had no interest whatever in a Volkswagen with which it would actually be in competition.' Yet his report, filed in January 1937, did urge further testing on a larger scale. This time thirty *Volksautos* should be used, these to be manufactured under better conditions, in the factories of RDA member companies.

Necessary or not, the further tests now being recommended would further delay the project. Hitler, never known for patience, began losing his temper. It was now four years since he first broached the subject of a 'people's car' at the 1933 Motor Show. He felt, and with justification, that a good deal of foot-dragging was going on. He read the riot act to the manufacturers on Sunday, February 28, 1937. The occasion was his opening speech at the Berlin Motor Show that year. The previous day, the government had announced a price reduction on motor-car spare parts and 'the production of a small car to be called a *Volksauto*, a people's car'. Hitler hailed this latter announcement, and then in loud and angry tones shouted:

'It is my irrevocable decision to make the German motor-car industry, one of our greatest industries, independent of the insecurity of international importations and place it on a solid and sure basis. *And let there be no doubt: so-called private business is either capable of solving this problem or it is not capable of continuing as private business. The National Socialist State will under no circumstances capitulate before either the convenience, the limitations, or the ill-will of individual Germans.*' (Italics are mine.)

These were the words of a ruler who would brook no opposition. Germany had already been converted into a Roman state with the panoply of the Imperium. When Hitler drove to the 1937 Motor Show, he was paced to the exhibition hall from the Chancellery by Germany's top racing drivers and driven through streets lined by 12,000 motorised storm troopers, black helmets gleaming over their brown shirts. Once in the hall, he was angered by an exhibit of Opel's own small-car entry and in his speech also warned the German car industry that only one model of *Kleinauto* would be permitted.

Heinz Nordhoff stood beside the ageing Herr Geheimrat von Opel as Adolf Hitler passed the Opel exhibit. Opel showed the Führer his new small car, with its sign, 'Opel's latest achievement, P-4, the motor-car of the little man: 1450 marks.' With paternal pride, he said to Hitler, 'And that, my Führer, is *our* Volkswagen!' Whereupon Hitler whirled around, his face red, and marched off without a word in reply. To demonstrate that he would not brook any last-ditch attempts by private companies to enter the small-car field on a competitive basis, Hitler made it difficult for the company to obtain materials necessary for the car. Later, when Opel offered to shave the P-4's price by 200 marks, the company was told unofficially that such price cuts would not be permitted, because no German car would be allowed to approach the price set for the Volkswagen.

In the spring, progress remained questionable. The New York *Times*' Associated Press report from Berlin on April 23 read:

HITLER'S CAR REMAINS A MYSTERY

Chancellor Adolph Hitler's cheap people's car, which he promised Germans for three years and with which the Führer dreams of conquering the European Market, will remain a myth for at least two years.

Three models of the mysterious 'Volkswagen' were secretly put on test runs before Hitler proudly exclaimed on opening the 1935 Berlin Auto Show: 'We will solve the problem of the cheap car. Production of this newly-designed car, which will be as inexpensive as a middle-priced motorcycle, will be started this year.'

But Hitler's midget car failed to make the grade and will have to continue trials 'at least until 1938', it was learned from the Federation of the German Automobile Industry.

Finally, inaugurating the 1937 Auto Exhibition, Hitler banged his fist on the speaker's table as he burst out: 'Either automobile makers produce the cheap car or they go out of business. I will not tolerate the plea, "It can't be done!" '

In the spring, the Nazi brass discussed the overwhelming question of how actually to produce the car. The manufacturers schemed in every way possible to frustrate these plans. They suggested that each company might supply a portion of the parts for the car, or that each manufacturer could produce a set number of Volkswagens alongside regular production. Both suggestions, Nordhoff believes, were stalling tactics. Finally, says Ferry Porsche, the manufacturers told Hitler that they could produce a Volkswagen themselves if the government would subsidise them to the extent of 200 marks per car. Hitler figured that this would come to 200 million marks for the one million cars a year he wanted to produce, and decided that it would be money down the drain. He would have nothing to show for it. The 200 million marks could instead be used to build a factory. It was in this way, Ferry Porsche believes, that the decision was reached that the State itself would produce the Volkswagen in its own plant.

'The car manufacturers were foolish,' says Dr. Volkmar Köhler, the archivist of today's Volkswagen company. 'Had they been smarter, they might have produced a cheap "people's car" for Hitler just as the radio manufacturers produced a "people's radio" (*Volksempfänger*) when he asked for it. It might have been enough to satisfy Hitler. Instead, because they thought they could out-stall and out-fox Hitler, they ended up having the Volkswagen as competition.'

3

The Nazis Lay Their Plans

FOR the first time in his life, Ferdinand Porsche was not beset by money worries. For the first time, too, he was free of the dictates of car manufacturers. The State, with its unlimited power and apparently endless funds, had decided it would build the small car of which Porsche had dreamt for years.

In late May 1937, the Nazi brass formed a new firm, the Volkswagen Development Company (Gesellschaft zur Vorbereitung des Volkswagens[1]), capitalised with 480,000 marks. (On July 1, 1939, the company's capital was increased to 150 million marks.) Its management consisted of Ferdinand Porsche, Hitler's confidant Jakob Werlin, and Dr. Bodo Lafferentz, aide to German Labour Front chief Robert Ley, whose organisation was to supply the necessary funds. Now the sizeable capital of the German Labour Front was at Porsche's disposal and he could move forward energetically. Concern over budgets—which he so despised—plagued Porsche no longer; Ley's organisation, by extension, had at its disposal the funds of the Nazi Party and, by further extension, those of the German Government.

The decision was made to go ahead with the RDA plan and test thirty more prototypes; later, another thirty prototypes were built for propaganda and sales promotional purposes. Porsche set up a large factory-like shop in Zuffenhausen, an industrial suburb of Stuttgart. The first thirty prototypes took shape there and at the Daimler-Benz plant in Stuttgart-Untertürkheim, the very one in which Porsche had worked years earlier. These and the second series of thirty cars which followed them all had 60·7-cubic-inch engine displacements, a fraction smaller than the 61 originally envisaged.

All sorts of facilities became available. A command from Berlin was all that was needed for the Porsche-*Gezuvor* group to borrow

1. Promptly nicknamed *Gezuvor* ('After you!') for its initial syllables.

the large-scale motor pool, garages, and service facilities of the German Army's Kornwestheim barracks near Stuttgart, and it was there that test headquarters were established. The RDA had now been shunted completely out of the picture. 'I was not even called upon for advice when the tests started,' says Vorwig, 'even though I knew more about the car than many others.' As for personnel, Werlin came up with two hundred SS men who were experienced drivers drawn from all over Germany. The tests were continuous and demanding. As soon as a driver brought his car back to the Kornwestheim barracks, it was inspected, re-fuelled, and taken out again. When the tests were over, the Volkswagen prototypes had been driven *more than 1,242,000 miles!* Ferry Porsche says, 'This was the first time in Europe that as many as thirty test cars had been used by a manufacturer.' The cost of production-plus-testing of the prototypes alone rose astronomically to an estimated thirty million marks, resulting in a car which, as events have proved, was far ahead of its time. What was being perfected was a uniquely efficient, serviceable, yet low-cost vehicle. Not one feature of Ferdinand Porsche's *Kleinauto* of the mid-1930s was for show; each served a distinct purpose. The now familiar sloping bonnet of the car's beetle shape, for example, was designed to minimise the power needed in high-speed driving, for a car with a blunt bonnet requires far more power to push air forward at high speeds than does the VW.

By the early summer of 1937 Hitler actually had his Volkswagen, at least in prototype, as he had promised the Germans for years. Now what he said earlier in the year at the 1937 Motor Show really had come true: all that remained was to go into production. But that was to pose its own problems.

Porsche, still impressed by his last pilgrimage to the mass-production mecca of America, Detroit, was determined that his cars would be produced along American lines. Yet there were not enough German engineers and production men familiar with these methods. The solution suddenly seemed clear: drain such brains from America!

And so another trip to Detroit took place and a meeting was planned with Henry Ford, whom the German government decorated in 1938 with the Grand Cross of the German Eagle for his pioneer work in 'giving cars to the masses'. On his previous visit, Porsche had arrived with just his secretary; this time, he had an entourage and a new rank.[1] With him went Bodo Lafferentz; Jakob Werlin;

1. Hitler had designated Porsche Reich Car Designer (Reichs-Autokonstrukteur), a laureate-like title which apparently only amused the designer.

Ghislaine Kaes; Ferry, his son; Dr. Anton Piëch, his son-in-law; and Otto Dyckhoff, a production and design expert.

Arriving in New York City aboard the *Bremen*, they immediately went to Roosevelt Raceway in Long Island to prepare for the Vanderbilt Cup Race in which one of Ferdinand Porsche's Auto-Union cars was entered. From there, they went to Detroit, where they met Henry Ford. Porsche regarded this meeting as the high point of his visit. He idolised Ford as a genius who had materialised Porsche's own personal dream in another country. They conversed through interpreters and Porsche poured out all his plans for the Volkswagen. Did they worry the elder Ford? Not in the least. 'If anyone can build a car better or cheaper than I can, that serves me right,' he said.

Ferry Porsche, in his mid-twenties, was present at this meeting and Henry Ford asked him to talk about the car of the future, not necessarily the Volkswagen, but the 'ideal' European car of the next decade. 'Let *him* tell me,' Ford said. 'The young are the ones who will build that car.'

Ferry spoke of independent suspension, streamlining, low petrol consumption—actually enumerating the VW's specifications. Would Ford care to visit Germany, asked Ferdinand Porsche? Would he like to see what they were building? That would be impossible, said Henry Ford, because there would be a war in the near future.

Porsche was astounded. He and his colleagues looked at each other with the naïveté of those who read only the technical press. 'No!' said Porsche. 'We cannot believe that! We live in an era of economic improvement, in which many problems exist which take time to solve. Why should there be a war?' Ford murmured that he hoped they were right, but he had his doubts. Then he excused himself. Four hundred orphans were waiting to see him.

After the meeting with Henry Ford, they revisited New York City for the July 5, 1937, race, returning directly afterwards to Detroit to recruit German-Americans for the projected factory. They bought a Ford V-8 and drove through Canada to Niagara Falls, to Albany, New York City, and Philadelphia. En route, they stopped at various manufacturers to buy machinery for the factory in Germany. From the US, Porsche also shot back a telegram ordering a further change in the design of his car. All the *Volksautos* so far had doors which opened from the front (as had many other German cars); Porsche ordered these changed, to open from the rear. In the US, he had learned that this was the trend now, and also safer.

The recruiting of US-trained personnel continued through 1938, carried on by German consuls in various cities. Altogether, about twenty signed up. Most of them were German nationals working in the United States; a few were American citizens of German descent. All of the latter returned home from Germany after World War II started in 1939.

'My wife received a telephone call one day in spring 1937, asking me to see a Dr. Porsche in the Book-Cadillac Hotel,' says Joseph Werner, then a special machine designer at Ford's River Rouge plant. 'I assume he got my name through the German consul. My wife warned me to be careful—that she didn't know what they were after. I went anyway and met Porsche, Dyckhoff, and Lafferentz. They told me they were going to build a Volkswagen and needed American-trained designers and production men. I remember asking them if they had any idea how much just the machines for such a project would cost. They answered that they had plenty of money. Then they mentioned that they were also going to build their own factory. When I heard that, I knew it was one of those dreams of Hitler's, but I never thought he'd actually carry it out.' Werner, who had been away from his home in Germany for ten years, finally agreed to go, 'because my parents were still there and I'd always intended to come back. Still, I didn't think it was very sound for them to try to start a company when they didn't even have a factory.' They offered him a salary of 1250 marks a month ('about what I'd been earning at Ford,' he said) and agreed to pay all moving expenses, including the cost of transporting his car and furniture to Germany. He and several others who had been recruited from Ford and General Motors—all of them designers—sailed together and started working for Porsche in Stuttgart on September 1, 1937. Werner has remained with the company ever since and is today head of Volkswagen's huge factory in Hanover.

Another of today's Volkswagen's executives who was recruited in the USA at the time is Otto Hoehne, now production chief of the Volkswagenwerk and a member of its Vorstand, or management board. He had lived in Chicago from 1926 to 1939 and was thirty-three years old when he first read an offer of a job with Porsche in a US German-language newspaper. Hoehne had spent some years on the assembly line at International Harvester and moved from there to the National Tea Company, where he was in charge of night truck maintenance, working twelve hours a night, six days a week. This was an unpleasant and dirty job and Hoehne disliked being away from home each night (he even had to work the night of Christmas Eve). He submitted a résumé to the German consul in Chicago and was hired. They offered him free transportation, a flat, and at least one mark per hour. 'What attracted me,' he says, 'was that they promised me a chance at advancement.' He started as a tool and die maker at the Volkswagen factory on June 1, 1939. A third member of this group is Kurt Hocke, today a chauffeur at the Volkswagenwerk in Wolfsburg (his calling card reads, 'Call me "Mike" if you like'). Hocke was a thirty-year-old unemployed cabinet-maker in Chicago when he was recruited by the German consul in that city. Times had been tough for Hocke. He and the German-American girl he had married in 1934 lived in a tiny flat near Wrigley Field with their daughter and his adopted son. 'We had to steal coal during the Depression,' he says. He was dissatisfied and wanted to better their lot. Then the offer came from the German consul, who had addressed a pro-Nazi German-American club in Chicago called 'Friends of the New Germany', of which Hocke was a member. For workers like Hocke, the New Germany was not too generous. No moving expenses were paid, although Hocke spent only four hundred dollars for ship's tickets for himself, his wife, and two children. 'When I reported to Berlin,' he says, 'I told them I'd rather stay there than work at the Volkswagen plant, but they raised quite a fuss. So I reported to work at VW in February 1939.'

The vast enterprise, however, still seemed illusory to many in 1937, when Ferdinand Porsche visited the United States. A German Embassy press attaché in Washington was quoted at the time as saying, 'The Volkswagen really ought to be called "Christ", because everyone talks about Him without ever having seen Him.' The sceptical and blasphemous aide was promptly recalled by an embarrassed German Foreign Office. The time for jokes was over.

On both his 1936 and 1937 trips, Ferdinand Porsche had visited Roosevelt Raceway in Westbury, Long Island. On October 12, 1936, he saw Tazio Nuvolari win the race; now, on July 5, 1937, the victory went to Germany's Bernd Rosemeyer, who drove his rear-engined Auto-Union car at an average speed of 82·56 mph, covering the 90 laps in a fraction over 3 hours, 38 minutes, beating Nuvolari by 17 miles per hour. Rosemeyer won the cheers of 75,000 fans—and $22,100 in prize money. The 1937 race has been called 'probably the most spectacular automobile marathon ever witnessed in [the USA]' and was an important milestone in Porsche's continuing race career.

His reputation in this field was soaring throughout the 1930's, for even as he was perfecting his small car, he designed and developed some of the greatest competitive racing cars Europe has ever seen. After decades of French and Italian dominance, Porsche's cars brought Germany unquestioned supremacy and launched a battle between the two German giants which continued until World War II broke out. Porsche was the Auto-Union 'general'; his rear-engined 'P-car' created a sensation. Alfa-Romeo dropped to the background. The final success was attained in 1937 when the Germans produced two cars, each of which could reach over 200 miles per hour: the 650-hp Mercedes W125 and the 545-hp Porsche-designed Auto-Union C-type Grand Prix cars.[1]

Germany, like Alfa-Romeo and Bugatti, also developed great drivers, among them Rudolf Caracciola, Hans Stuck and Bernd Rosemeyer. The latter, a favourite of Porsche, was killed on the Autobahn at the age of twenty-seven while straining to set a new record in his Auto-Union car on January 28, 1938. He was determined to better both his own record of 223·9 mph and Caracciola's 268·3 mph. 'Some said there was a sudden boisterous gust of wind,' write Markmann and Sherwin. 'Others swore a front tire was wrenched from Rosemeyer's Auto-Union. Most said it was both. Travelling at tremendous speed [over 266 mph] the car skidded 80 yards, somersaulted twice and was thrown 200 yards through the air. Rosemeyer was hurled out in midflight and landed in an embankment. He died instantly.'

The tremendous horsepower built into these small cars is significant; the racing seasons of the mid-1930s were tailor-made for Porsche. As was noted before, the rules for Formula 1 races had been changed, specifically to reduce the dangerous speeds at Grand Prix races. Yet it was precisely the high-powered, lightweight racing car which had fascinated Porsche ever since he had initially grappled with the problem in the Sascha car a decade earlier. Heading the Auto-Union team, he realised its fullest potential.

1. Four great Porsche Auto-Union racers:
1934 P-car (Type 'A'): 295 bhp, 16-cylinder V engine (4500, later 6000, rpm): 265·96 cu. in. engine displacement; 7-to-1 compression ratio; front and rear independent torsion-bar suspension; 1628 lb. weight.
1935 P-car (Type 'B'): engine displacement increased to 301·95 cu. in.; bhp boosted to 375 at 4800 rpm; compression ratio raised to 8·95-to-1.
1936 P-car (Type 'C'): engine displacement raised to 366·61 cu. in.; bhp boosted to 520 at 5000 rpm; compression ratio increased to 9·2-to-1.
1937 P-car (Type 'C', modified): engine displacement raised again to 386·13 cu. in., and bhp boosted once more, to 545 at 500 rpm.

After his return to Germany, Porsche and others of the Volkswagen Development Company devoted themselves to completing their plans for the actual manufacture of the people's car.[1]

A factory had to be built and fully equipped and a suitable site had to be found for such an enterprise. It was also a problem to find workers to construct the factory (much less build cars), for the Third Reich's labour force was busily building for war. Other problems existed, even financial ones. While the German Labour Front had vast funds at its disposal, these of course could not be given over completely to this car. The solution was ingenious. It involved the KdF, a subsidiary organisation of the German Labour Front.

The German Labour Front (DAF), established by Hitler to maintain industrial peace and indoctrinate the workers, had in fact turned into a repressive pro-management organisation without the slightest resemblance to a labour union. It was responsible only to the State and to the Party and it prohibited strikes and other 'unruly' demonstrations. Its leader was a former chemist, Dr. Robert Ley, a notorious alcoholic, who had become Gauleiter of the party organisation in Cologne.

Upon accepting the job of DAF boss, Ley promised 'to restore absolute leadership to the natural leader of a factory—that is, the employer. . . . Only the employer can decide. Many employers have for years had to call for the "master in the house". Now they are once again to be the "master in the house".'

This was in full accord with the Nazi law governing labour-management relations, the so-called Charter of Labour of January 20, 1934, which proclaimed the employer as 'leader of the enterprise' and his workers as the 'following' (*Gefolgschaft*). 'The leader of the enterprise makes the decisions for the employees and labourers in all matters concerning the enterprise,' the Charter stated, and he was charged with caring for their 'well-being', without of course any back-talk from them.

For the benefactions from the German Labour Front the worker paid dues which enriched Robert Ley's coffers by about 800 million marks a year. Of this, 10 per cent was allocated to a DAF organisa-

1. One man at the Porsche Bureau who had an artistic streak was at this time making plans for something which was to last as long as the Volkswagen—and a lot longer than any of the Nazi plans then being concocted. He was Engine Designer Francis Xavier Reimspiess who in 1937–8 produced the famous 'VW' emblem (letters one above the other, enclosed in a circle) without ever being asked to do so. Reimspiess showed his design to Ferdinand Porsche and Porsche was impressed: he even gave Reimspiess a 100-mark bonus for it on the next payday. In subsequent years, Reimspiess's original design was embroidered with gear-teeth and other decorative elements, but after the war was again used as originally designed.

tion called Strength-Through-Joy (*Kraft-durch-Freude*, or KdF), which organised all recreation, travel, sport, and leisure-time activities. It offered workers bargain cruises and packaged holidays, inexpensive tickets to concerts, theatre and opera, and worked into many of these activities heavy doses of Nazi indoctrination.[1]

Kdf, then, had an income of about 80 million marks a year. Furthermore, accounting was secret and the funds could be spent as the Party liked; it amounted, in short, to a slush-fund.[2] Now, was not Hitler's *Volksauto* a car meant for the German worker and, therefore, basically a concern of the Labour Front? Furthermore, Hitler had said at the 1934 Motor Show that it was to be 'the source of yet-unknown happiness to them on Sundays and holidays'—and this made the car clearly a matter of concern to the Strength-Through-Joy organisation.

The matter was decided: KdF would sponsor the people's car. An ingenious 5-mark-weekly layaway plan was devised and on August 1, 1938, Ley announced the scheme to the German worker in a speech at Cologne.

This small car, Ley said, is 'the greatest social work of all time and all countries. The *Volksauto* is the Führer's very own work. The Führer lives and works with this as his pet idea.' As for the plant, he said it would become the 'materilisation in stone and iron of the idea of class education, settlement work, national health, and the beauty of work.' From a start of 150,000 cars a year, the plant was soon to boost production to 1,500,000 annually.

Moreover, Ley said, 'It is the Führer's will that within a few years no less than 6,000,000 Volkswagens will be on German roads. In ten years' time there will be no working person in Germany who does not own a "people's car".'

The price of the Volkswagen had by this time been boosted from Hitler's originally stipulated 900 marks to 990. But was even 990 marks the true price? This remained in doubt. Ley had claimed at one time that the 990-mark price included insurance and even garage and maintenance costs;[3] at another time he referred vaguely to the fact that 'of course, we shall attempt to find rational solutions

1. KdF holidays, Germans used to say, were occasions during which girls daily lost strength through joy.

2. In November, 1934, Admiral Raeder was told by Adolf Hitler not to worry about the costs of the new programme to build up the German Navy. In case of need, Hitler said, he would get Ley to put 120 to 150 million marks at the Navy's disposal from the funds of the German Labour Front.

3. If this were true, the New York *Times* noted on August 2, 1938, then 'the actual part payment on the car figures out to only 2·90 marks weekly [of the 5 marks paid in] . . . On that basis, the real cost of the *Volksauto* will amount to only 574·20 marks—or $230 . . .'

to the problems of garaging, repair shops, and replacement parts'. In point of fact, the Volkswagen contract, as we shall see, did not commit the state to any specific price for the car; it also specified that the cost of insurance for the first two years would be charged to the purchaser. The *Frankfurter Zeitung*, then the only paper to mention this contradiction, estimated insurance to add up to a total of 200 marks for the two-year period. In actuality, it appeared that the Volkswagen would cost the purchaser a total of 1190 marks, not 990. The New York *Times* commented on this on October 16, 1938:

. . . it appears that every successive announcement raises the effective prices of the *Volksauto* just a notch above the previous announcement. The original statement was that the price of 990 marks included insurance for two years, garage charges and the cost of periodic overhauling, so that the net price of the car would come to only about 574·20 marks, or $230. But according to the latest calculations, the effective price of the limousine is as follows:

Basic price at factory	990 marks
Two years' insurance	200 marks
Delivery cost, average	50 marks
Total	1,240 marks

These prices are valid only for members of the Labor Front; others must pay in addition to the regulation price the Labor Front dues fitting their income. The delivery charges may be saved by driving the car home from the factory, to which special buses will transport purchasers, but the insurance premium has become an extra charge and there is no further talk of free garage or overhauling. Nor is there any guarantee: the buyer buys on trust.

How much would it cost the average German to run? A German émigré, Joachim Haniel, in 1938 estimated the total at between 75 and 125 marks a month. Writing in *Neues Tagebuch*, a Paris weekly put out by liberal German émigrés, Haniel calculates this as follows. At 27 miles per gallon, he writes, the average owner might consume 25 gallons a month, at a cost of 40 marks. In addition, he would have to pay approximately 10 marks a month insurance once the first two years had passed; 20 to 30 marks garage rental in large cities, and the unavoidable expense of oil, tyres, repairs, parts, etc. Few Germans, Haniel says, could afford this 75 to 125 marks and certainly 'not the Germans whom Ley likes to address, those earning from 160 to 500 marks a month'. While Haniel's figures seem high (few VW owners would garage their cars), the breakdown of costs indicates some expenses which had to be faced. Still, as the New York *Times* of October 16, 1938, pointed out, several million workers earned about 2000 marks a year and a good proportion could, there-fore, afford a *Volksauto* at 990 marks, 'especially when it can be paid for under the special installment plan announced by the Labor Front'.

The installment plan was in actuality a gigantic layaway scheme. William Shirer refers to it as 'Dr. Ley's ingenious plan [whereby] the workers themselves should furnish the capital by means of what came to be known as a "pay-before-you-get-it" installment plan—five marks a week, or if a worker thought he could afford it, ten or fifteen marks a week'.

Under this gigantic layaway plan, 336,668 Germans eventually put aside 280 million marks. In postwar years, these 'savers' came to haunt Volkswagen management.

Subscription offices were opened in all Labour Front head-quarters, while specially appointed agents received subscriptions from workers in large industrial plants. A hard-sell campaign was immediately inaugurated. Germans who earned from 200 to 300 marks a month were to take up individual subscriptions; those earning less were asked to join with friends in group subscriptions.

Openïng such a 'layaway' account was tantamount to placing an order for a Volkswagen. The extraordinary contract was weighted heavily in favour of the State. It neither mentioned price nor even obligated the State to deliver a Volkswagen once the last payment had been made. The regulations are worth quoting here in full. (Italics are mine.)

RULES GOVERNING APPLICATION FOR A VOLKSWAGEN SAVINGS BOOK

1. The original Volkswagen savings book will be issued by the agent in the applicant's place of residence or work against payment of a fee of 1 mark. The book is made out in the name of the applicant and *neither it nor the rights it confers are transferable*. Acceptance of the savings book is equivalent to placement of an order for delivery of a Volkswagen, subject to the rules herein set forth.

2. Current instalment dues are payable at offices of Labour Front or the Strength-Through-Joy organisation which carry Volkswagen savings stamps. No liability is assumed for payments unless they are made against the immediate exchange of savings stamps in the amount of the payment. At least one stamp in the value of 5 marks is to be pasted in the book each week, such stamp to be cancelled by the holder by writing the date of purchase thereon. A special premium must be paid in the case of open cars and cabrio-limousines [i.e., convertibles and sunroof models].

3. Each car carries limited insurance against collision and public liability for a period of two years from the time the car leaves the plant, *the cost of such insurance to be charged against the purchaser*.

4. Payments must be made at the designated places of payment by the purchaser, though collectors may be employed.
5. When all the spaces in the savings book have been filled with stamps, the book is to be promptly turned in at the regional Strength-Through-Joy office in exchange for a new book. After the start of production an order number will be issued through the nearest *Gau* office. The final savings book is to be turned in at the Strength-Through-Joy office *in exchange for a certificate of ownership*. Lost or misplaced savings books cannot be replaced.
6. For reasons of technical improvement and consequent lowering in the price of the Volkswagen, *no interest will be paid on paid-in savings*.
7. Until further notice, the Volkswagen will be produced in a deep blue-grey finish.
8. *Volkswagen contracts are non-cancellable*. In exceptional cases the Strength-Through-Joy *Gau* office may authorise cancellation. *In such cases a fee amounting to 20 per cent of the payments made will be retained*.
9. Inquiries should be directed to the nearest office listed in this leaflet.
10. In case of change of residence the savings book must be submitted for correction to the agent who originally issued it.
11. Tampering with the savings book is punishable by law.
12. Applications for issuance of a savings book may be denied without reason.
13. No supplementary agreements not embodied in these rules shall be binding.
14. In case of legal disputes the courts of the city of Berlin shall have the jurisdiction.

The fact that paid-in savings accumulated no interest is less surprising today than when Haniel noted it in 1938 as being especially outrageous; the 'layaway' Christmas Clubs of US banks operate similarly today. The nastiest part of the contract was its non-cancellable and non-transferable nature. Workers who missed an obligatory weekly payment or who decided they could no longer afford to make any payments risked losing every single mark they had put into the scheme. The state might in exceptional cases permit cancellation, but it was under no obligation to do so and would in any event confiscate 20 per cent of the paid-in sum. Because contracts were non-transferable, they could not be used as collateral; in effect the payment books had no intrinsic value whatever, except for the purchase of a Volkswagen. The state was not even committed to coming up with a Volkswagen once all payments had been made, it was merely obligated to deliver 'a certificate of ownership'. This certificate included an order number, entitling the purchaser to a car—once a car had been produced.

At the rate of 5 marks a week, it would take a 'saver' four years and seven months to pay in the required 1190 marks. And then he would only become *eligible* for the car. It is not too far-fetched to suppose that he might have to wait another four or five years before delivery could be made if he were assigned a high number.

There naturally arose a widespread belief that the Volkswagen scheme was a plan to defraud the German people. Writing shortly after the Volkswagen plant was dedicated, the émigré Haniel concluded that 'the 500–750 million marks annually to be collected is the true meaning of the Volkswagen plant . . . The production of automobiles, which it conceivably may undertake some time in the future, is merely a sideline. With its halls, machines and warehouses, it is in essence the gigantic backdrop for the world's biggest instalment swindle.' Shirer also refers to it as a 'swindle' and notes, 'Tens of millions of marks were paid in by the German wage earners, not a pfennig of which was ever to be refunded.'

It seems, however, that in this case at least, the Nazis were *not* out to defraud. The idea that Hitler—who dealt in far greater sums—would construct so elaborate a plan to cheat workers out of a few million marks is doubtful. We have seen how the car-enthusiast dictator was interested in the VW and in motorisation. As for the cash paid in by the workers, that was actually deposited by the KdF organisation in the 'Bank of German Labour' in Berlin and was intact when Berlin was conquered. The 280,000,000 marks were seized by the invading Russians.

That Hitler was dead serious about building his car may also be deduced from other data. After the war, a US Strategic Bombing Survey team pointed out that 'the start of the war found the plant's management as well as the authorities in Berlin unprepared for utilisation of the plant in the war effort. The German government expected a short war and accordingly decided to keep the plant intact for postwar production of automobiles. This is supported by the fact that the plant remained virtually idle, its 1941 production representing only 20–25% of the plant's capabilities. During the entire course of the war the plant never produced more than 50 per cent of its capacity.'

It is clear the Nazi regime *did* intend to build Volkswagens. What has led many persons to conclude that the plan was fraudulent may partly be due to a lack of knowledge of its history, as well as a belief that *all* Nazi schemes were suspect. Further, the plan appeared bizarre and grandiose and the idea that 'every German worker' would own a car in ten years seemed absurd. Nevertheless, Hitler had now committed himself for four years to a Volkswagen. He would brook no opposition to any of his plans, however inflated. The Volkswagen scheme had gained momentum. No one could call a halt to it. Hesitation was tantamount to economic sabotage. It was heresy to doubt the Führer's will. Also, who could doubt the plan's eventual success, if Hitler was prepared to underwrite the costs, subsidise the company, and make up all losses?

Dr. Bodo Lafferentz, an economist turned administrator and Ley's aide in KdF's Travel, Excursions, and Holiday Bureau, meanwhile hunted for a suitable location for the plant. The site was to be about twenty square miles in size, near transportation facilities, close to sources of raw materials and yet not too close to Germany's western boundaries. Under consideration were several possible locations: the Weser River Valley, the Mannheim industrial area, the Fürsten-walde region near Berlin, a site near Regensburg, and another near Stendal on the Elbe River. All were rejected for reasons of congestion or distance from raw materials.

Lafferentz commandeered a light plane so that he could fly over the other proposed regions and find a place with 'Lebensraum' for the factory; in congested Germany, that would be quite a trick.

Lafferentz's interest increasingly centred on the Lüneburger Heide, a heath which stretches from north of Hanover and Bruns-wick to the moor and marsh country beyond the Autobahn from Bremen to Hamburg. It is a lonely region, thinly populated, with ancient villages which still retain the qualities of another world, full of the rustic homeliness of simpler days.

Lafferentz, however, was less interested in the peaceful villages than in the open spaces. From the plane, it seemed perfect for the purpose he had in mind; perhaps he was not aware that below lay a mosquito-infested swamp. Below also lay Schloss Wolfsburg, the fourteenth-century castle belonging to Count Werner von der Schulenburg, built on lands granted his ancestor Ritter (Knight) von Bartensleben by Emperor Lothair II in 1135. The grant rewarded his defence of the area against the Slavs, and the lands had in succeeding generations been held successfully against all comers.

Of these landlords, it was written in 1584: 'In particular the von Schulenburgs and the von Bartenslebens were the true captains of men . . . the noble lord Otho took the field against the proud Junkers . . . Nor was any of them strong enough to confront the proud young lion. But he routed them again and again . . .' Ironically, his lands were fated to fall before the assaults of such a one as Robert Ley.[1]

On the morning of September 15, 1937, a number of events puzzled Count Werner von der Schulenburg. His gamekeeper came across a stranger wandering around his lands and the man explained that he had recently flown over the area and was now examining its beauty on foot. Then the Fallersleben village school-teacher came bicycling to the castle to tell the count that he had just encountered a caravan of official cars parked on a nearby bridge. People were peering at the countryside and discussing it among themselves. Within a short while, this mysterious caravan was seen near the castle. No sooner had the cars disappeared than the count received an agitated telephone call from the mistress of the neighbouring Mörse estate. She had been out riding that morning and encountered a Maybach limousine in the forests belonging to Herr von der Wense, another neighbour. She approached the man seated beside the chauffeur and told him that no one was permitted to enter these lands without express authorisation, whereupon she was smilingly told: 'My dear lady, *I* am allowed to drive anywhere my car is able to carry me!' She was outraged.

The mystery was cleared up after lunch. An innkeeper in Fallersleben who had served lunch to some of the official delegation made it his business to overhear their conversation and conveyed his findings to Count Schulenburg. These men, he said, were not here in connection with the planned Autobahn, as had been suspected, but in connection with *a new city*, one which threatened not only the existing lands, but their very homes, perhaps the entire nearby village of Hesslingen.

Official confirmation soon came. Dr. Bodo Lafferentz—the very man who could drive 'anywhere' his car could take him—informed

1. The von der Schulenburgs, forced to surrender to the Nazis in 1937, were to prove themselves 'proud lions' in later years. Count Friederich Werner v.d.S., whom Shirer terms 'an honest, decent German of the old school', served as ambassador to Russia from 1934 to 1941. He had worked honestly to improve Russo-German relations, was respected in Moscow, and was never informed of German plans to invade the USSR, an event which caught him completely by surprise. He later joined the July 20, 1944, plot to kill Adolf Hitler. Count Friederich Dietloff v.d.S. joined the Nazis in 1932 and became deputy police president of Berlin in 1937. However, he soon became an active anti-Nazi and joined General Halder's stillborn plot to overthrow Hitler in September 1938. He resigned from the Nazi Party in 1940, and also became involved in the 1944 conspiracy to assassinate Hitler. Both men—the former sixty-nine and the latter forty-two years of age—were murdered by the Gestapo in late 1944. The wife of Count Werner v.d.S., who was resident in the castle in 1937, met an ironic end: driving a Volkswagen near the VW plant in 1951, she died after crashing into a petrol station on the very land her family had surrendered in 1937. Her castle is today being restored and transformed into a municipal art centre. Count Werner, still living, no longer occupies it.

the count that two-thirds of his ancient lands were to be surrendered 'for an important national project'. Compensation was offered.

The count fumed and was not interested in assurances of payment. He decided to resist. He knew that private reasons would never prevail and so he decided to undermine the effort through official agencies. The count and his countess moved to Berlin's Eden Hotel to direct their offensive more effectively.

The Minister for Church Affairs, a devoted Nazi named Hanns Kerrl, had grown up in Fallersleben and was a boyhood friend of Count Schulenburg. In addition to his main duties, Kerrl was also head of the Bureau for Regional Planning, an office directly responsible to Adolf Hitler himself. The count reached Kerrl immediately, but Kerrl was unable or unwilling to help his old friend. He tried to comfort him by saying that he was being asked to surrender only 7600 morgen (approximately 5000 acres) of the required 15,000 morgen. The rest would be commandeered from Herr Gebhard von der Wense, who would give up 2500 morgen, and from twenty-six other smaller landowners, who would make up the balance.[1]

Years later, Heinz Nordhoff spoke of Fallersleben as a place 'of which no one would ever have heard, had it not been that a Herr [August Heinrich] Hoffmann had lived here once, who wrote a poem which was later used as the text for the national anthem'. Nordhoff, addressing the Wolfsburg city council in 1963, on the twenty-fifth anniversary of the plant's founding, ventured the opinion that the real reason for the site's selection lay in Kerrl's civic pride. It is, he said, a 'quite unheroic' reason, 'despite the fact that the heroic enjoyed such high prestige in those days'.

Whatever the reasons for the basic decision, the count continued to resist. His family, after all, had owned these properties for over five hundred years, and he was not to be put off his lands so easily.

His arguments convinced the Ministry of Transport. It reported to the government that the site would overload existing railway facilities and would prove too much of a burden for the important Mittelland Canal which flowed through the area. The count convinced the Forestry Department that the ancient oaks on the property were worth preserving. He even convinced the Luftwaffe that the planned site would prove a ridiculously easy target for

1. Von der Wense was ruined by these and subsequent events. He bought land in Mecklenburg with the money received for his land in the Fallersleben area, but this was lost to the Russians at the end of the war. Back home, the only land he owned was the family graveyard. He took a job with the postwar Volkswagenwerk as a guide, touring visitors around the plant. His younger son also works for the company today.

enemy planes and that the open countryside, the industrial complex
to be erected, the railway lines, and the canal would prove irresistible
to bombers. Finally, he rallied the aid of the mosquitoes and made it
known that the proposed location was an insect paradise, unfit for
human habitation. (Joseph Werner recalls his first sight of the proposed factory area, towards the end of 1937, a few months after he
had arrived from the US to work with Porsche in Stuttgart. 'It was a
sandy field and didn't look like it would support a factory,' he recalls.
'No private company would have wasted money building there.')

Despite the importunities of Transport, Forestry, Air Force, and
insect specialists, the Party leadership was adamant. Lafferentz and
Ley won out.[1] As for the mosquitoes, an appropriate specialist was
sent to Fallersleben from the Reich Institute for Soil, Water, and Air
Pollution to inspect the area and offer recommendations. The man
examined the region carefully, then reported: 'Under no circumstances must you drain the water meadows of the stream valleys, because this would destroy the breeding grounds. A unique opportunity
to study about 70 of the most interesting gnat species would be lost!'
This scholarly gentleman's misplaced scientific curiosity was throttled.
He was permitted to select and mount the more interesting species, and
then the Third Reich moved exterminators into the insect paradise.

Finally, in January 1938, all opposition ceased. Papers transferring
the land to the State were drawn up and signed. Albert Speer, the
talented and outspoken thirty-three-year-old Minister for Arma-
ment and War Production, was charged with the construction of the
plant. Speer himself was busy with grandiose plans for rebuilding
Berlin into a city called Germania, a magnificent centre of the expanding Nazi empire. He looked around for an architect to whom he
could entrust the job of planning not only the factory near Fallersleben, but also an *Autostadt* (motor-car city) to house the 90,000
people who would be brought (from where no one knew) to the site.[2]
Speer remembered a young Austrian architect, Peter Koller, an international prizewinner whom he had met whilst lecturing in Berlin. He
found him working in obscurity in the Augsburg regional planning
office and offered him at thirty a chance to be top man at Fallersleben.

Koller threw himself into the task enthusiastically, evolving

1. There reportedly was a meeting in Berlin to argue all positions. After heated discussion,
which took some time, Kerrl produced a paper containing the news that Hitler himself had decided
in favour of Fallersleben. After that there was no point in pursuing the matter further. The delegation from the Forestry Administration, which objected to the destruction of centuries-old oaks,
left the room muttering, 'You could have notified us of *that* on a postcard!'

2. Plans called for 12,000 workers in each of two shifts. The families of these 24,000 would
bring the population to 90,000.

Ferdinand Porsche, 1875–1951

The 1937 Volkswagen prototype. A rear window was added before the 1938 KdF-Wagen appeared

The 1945 Volkswagen, identical to the 1938 KdF-Wagen

KdF-Wagens on display at the dedication ceremony of the factory's cornerstone, May 26, 1938

(Hans Pusen, Coppenbrügge-Salzburg)

Hitler watches whilst masons finish the cornerstone

(Hans Pusen, Coppenbrügge-Salzburg)

The KdF-Wagen
factory under
construction,
1938–39

elaborate plans. The mile-long factory and a tall administration building would lie along one back of the Mittelland Canal, while the city itself would reach out from the other shore. Vast blocks of flats and two-family houses would shelter the *Kleinauto* workers and their families; parks, hotels, market places, and broad boulevards to rival Berlin's would beautify the site. At the centre would be a cultural core, the site of theatres, public halls, palaces of culture, government and Nazi Party buildings. It was to be, as Ley put it, 'a materialisation in stone and iron' of Hitler's grandiose visions, 'proof' of what National Socialism could produce.

These plans were worked out 'bombastically, of course, as was the custom in those days', Heinz Nordhoff noted in his 1963 address to the city council. They were 'singular in that the emphasis lay in the subordination of the town to the factory, the latter being planned as the centre of all life. Such symbolic overestimation of the value of work was in line with the German Labour Front.'

The public got its first glance at the plans for the city at the 1938 Berlin Motor Show, where a model of Peter Koller's town was put on display. Hitler, as usual, opened the show. The New York *Times* correspondent referred to him as seeming somewhat pale, but vigorous enough to thump the rostrum for twenty minutes. The Führer emphatically announced that 'we soon will build the cheapest car in the world'. He was followed by Propaganda Minister Goebbels, who reviewed the gains made by motorists under Nazism. In 1932, he said, Germany had 548,700 passenger cars; by 1937 there were 1,108,500. Before Hitler, there had been only one car per 40 inhabitants; after Hitler, one for every 24.[1] The atmosphere was generally optimistic. Construction of the plant, it was announced, would begin immediately.

A month later, Hitler invaded Austria and annexed that nation. Even in Vienna, he could not resist throwing out the lure of the *Volksauto*. This German car, he told the Viennese, 'will also make a wish come true, a wish harboured by so many hard-working under-paid Austrian people'.

In Germany there was a good deal of activity at Fallersleben. The town planners filed their preliminary drawings and government inspectors came to the site to review them on the spot. Some of these bureaucrats were apparently unaware of what had been decided and they took a strictly official view of the project. 'The regulation relating to building in the open countryside applies here,' they snapped.

1. Goebbels was, as always, exaggerating. As late as 1939, there was only one automobile for every 49 Germans.

'It doesn't permit houses with more than three stories.' With this they dismissed Koller's plans. The Koller crowd insisted that the government had decided to build a major city on this open field, but were told that the officials had no information about this in their files in Berlin. 'Very well,' said the planners. 'We withdraw our applications to build a town.' The bureaucrats triumphantly went on their way. The next day construction started behind their backs.

Elsewhere, others were just as confused. Two of Koller's engineers went to the Reich Transport Ministry in February 1938, and asked casually for a railroad station for 'a city of 100,000 people which we're building near Fallersleben'. The functionary who heard their request nodded gravely to humour them and later dismissed them from his mind as two lunatics, the sort of cranks whom hard-working officials must occasionally endure.

The dedication of the cornerstone was scheduled for May 26, 1938. It was a busy week in May for Adolf Hitler, seven days which had given Europe its worst war scare in twenty years. It became clear that Hitler, who had just annexed Austria without a shot being fired, was planning boldly to seize Czechoslovakia as well. His troops were stationed all along that nation's frontiers and Nazi propagandists launched a hysterical barrage of accusations against the Czechs, who allegedly were persecuting Sudeten Germans within their borders. On May 20, the Czechs became alarmed enough to mobilise their reserves. The French, treaty-bound to aid them, sent a stiff warning to Hitler not to attack. The British followed with a reminder to the Führer that they in turn were treaty-bound to France, and the Soviets declared they would assist the Czechs if Hitler invaded.

Events were moving rapidly and presumably the last thing pressing on Adolf Hitler's mind was the cornerstone ceremony to which his aides had committed him some time before. On May 22, the Führer was forced to stall for time, to reassure the Czechs of his 'peaceful intent'. In actuality, he had, on April 21, ordered the High Command of the Armed Forces (OKW) to prepare plans for a Czech campaign; these had been submitted to him in mid-May and Hitler was now furious that information about their existence had apparently leaked out and he was meeting unaccustomed opposition.[1]

And it was in the very midst of this turbulent May crisis, with the

1. By May 30, his anger over having to give such humiliating assurances to the Czechs, whom he called 'subhumans', would reach such a point that he was to order the OKW to plan for an even speedier invasion, by October 1. In the intemperate covering letter, he stated, 'It is my unalterable decision to smash Czechoslovakia by military action in the near future.'

Führer's blood aboil and armour rolling all over Europe, that he was scheduled to attend a cornerstone-laying ceremony for reasons of public relations. All the grandiose plans for the car must have sounded uninteresting to him, for now there was conquest on his mind, not a little car for the German worker to enjoy on holidays. Those who saw him at the ceremony thought he seemed strangely silent and distracted.

4

The War Years

On Ascension Thursday, May 26, 1938, Adolf Hitler laid the cornerstone of the Volkswagen factory near Fallersleben, Lower Saxony. He had arrived by special express train from Munich, accompanied by Reichsleiter Alfred Rosenberg, the Nazi Party ideologist, Sepp Dietrich, an SS Obergruppenführer, and Jakob Werlin. At the Fallersleben railway station, he was greeted by Robert Ley; Bodo Lafferentz; Heinrich Himmler; Viktor Lutze, head of the SA (storm troops); Minister Hanns Kerrl; and Ferdinand Porsche. The party left the station in a column of cars and drove to the construction site along streets garlanded with Party flags and banners. They drove to the top of the Klieversberg, a hill which commanded a view of the countryside. It was 1 pm and the day was a gloriously sunny one.

An elaborate structure with 60-foot-high swastika banners had been erected at the Klieversberg, overlooking a brick court. At 12.40 pm, as Adolf Hitler and his entourage made their way to the site from the railway station, trumpet blasts called the celebrants to attention. Three hundred standards of the SA, the NSKK (National Socialist Motorists Corps), Hitler Youth, Labour Front, and SS were marched up to the tribunal and placed in position. Honour guards from the army, air force, and the SS Junker School at Brunswick came to attention. The 600 guests of honour and 150 reporters who occupied the tribunal became hushed as the column of cars approached. Altogether, 70,000 people had been assembled. They came by car, by bus, and by twenty-eight special trains. Two chartered buses from Stuttgart had brought the employees of the Porsche Bureau to the site. A special section had been set aside for them. Karl Rabe, Porsche's chief designer, spotted the RDA's Wilhelm Vorwig in the crowd and invited him to join the Porsche group.

At 1.15 pm, Adolf Hitler pulled up in his big Mercedes-Benz limousine. 'Drummers and trumpeters of the Hitler Youth, stationed on the tribunal, raise their instruments,' wrote the *Braunschweiger Tageszeitung* on the next day. 'A wave of "Heils" breaks over the tightly packed mass of people. Commands are shouted, a march is sounded, and the Führer's standard is raised beside the cornerstone. Fanfares and the roll of drums are heard.' Hitler stepped from his car, reviewed the honour guards and received a bouquet of flowers from a little girl. On the podium, he acknowledged the greetings of other dignitaries, including Artillery General Wilhelm Keitel, the Army chief of staff, and NSKK-leader Hühnlein. 'Seventy thousand people raise their hands in greeting, for the Führer is here!' the Brunswick reporter said. The construction of the plant, he wrote, 'is an act of such gigantic proportions as to be without parallel in the entire history of mankind'.

Certainly the ceremonies at least were impressive, even if the construction of the factory would never outshine the Seven Wonders of the World. The scene glittered with uniforms and with the traditional costumes of the 3000 construction workers who had been given the day off to attend the festivities, bricklayers in white with black top hats, carpenters in black velvet and corduroy. Those from the Porsche Bureau felt conspicuous in civilian clothes, reports Ferry Porsche, who was there with his father. Count and Countess Werner von der Schulenburg, who had been invited along with the twenty-seven other dispossessed landowners, mingled among the guests and later left outraged because Hitler failed to mention the patriotic sacrifices of the property owners on whose lands the factory and its city were to be built.

Robert Ley opened the ceremonies. 'My Führer!' he said, 'what has been started here—this factory and everything which will come of it—is fundamentally and singularly your work, my Führer! Your great idea and your great faith taught us that man develops himself only through work and that deeds, rather than words and phrases, represent socialism, and that man benefits only from that which he has won through work. . . . This Volkswagen factory is one of your own dearest works. We know how you thought of giving the German people a good but inexpensive motor-car even before you came to power and how you have ever since imbued with new strength all those designers and others who laboured on this car!'

Ley was referring to a little legend about Hitler which was being propagated with energy. Jakob Werlin, writing in the May 26 issue of Berlin's *Völkischer Beobachter*, the organ of the Nazi Party, had mentioned it again. He claims he once drove with Hitler on a cold rainy night long before Hitler came to power, and says they encountered a motor-cyclist on the highway. The man was huddled over his handlebars, wet, trembling with cold, and pitiable. According to the story, Hitler turned to Werlin and said, 'If I were in a position to do so, I'd like more than anything to give every one of these people a car as a present.'

Bodo Lafferentz stepped to the podium. An extraordinarily tall man, he towered over the others on the rostrum as he reported to his leader. The KdF, he said, had decided to allocate an immediate 50,000,000 marks for the construction of the factory and was meeting 'every conceivable requirement' set by Dr. Porsche, despite 'enormous difficulties'. The car, he added, would be a 'pricing miracle' at 990 marks. (The New York *Times* on May 27 agreed, noting that 'the cheapest German car now costs almost twice as much'.) Lafferentz mentioned the customers which his organisation planned to sign up. 'The guaranteed demand for the gigantic production insures that the price of the car need not be raised; it posed a unique and heavy challenge which only the German Labour Front could meet.'

Then Lafferentz pointed to the surrounding countryside. 'Over there,' he said, 'we shall build our beautiful city which, when completed, will house ninety thousand inhabitants. The lovely wooded green landscape offers an opportunity for a superb urban development, so that the city which will be built here will rank among the most beautiful in the entire world.'

There was of course nothing 'over there' for Hitler to see except scenery. A day or so earlier, there had been great excitement over the possibility that Hitler might visit the non-existent city after laying his cornerstone at the factory across the Mittelland Canal. Working overtime, the planners marked out the proposed main streets with white lines, so that the Führer might at least visualise the skeleton of the town. At the last moment, however, one of the officials had second thoughts about the markings and ordered them all removed. 'The entire landscape is ruined!' he raged. By May 26, the plans again existed only on paper.

Then Adolf Hitler delivered his speech. He grasped the rostrum with both hands and reminisced:

'When I came to power in 1933, I saw one problem that had to be tackled at once—the problem of motorisation. In this sphere, Germany was behind everyone else. The output of private cars in

Germany had reached the laughable figure of forty-six thousand a year.[1] And the first step towards putting an end to this was to do away with the idea that a motor car is an article of luxury . . .

'The factors which compel persons to seek out cheaper products are simple and sober ones. Those who find it possible to buy expensive items will do so in any case! The broad masses, however, cannot do so. It is for these broad masses that this car has been built. It is to meet the transportation requirements of these masses and it is to bring them joy! . . .'

Hitler was trying to reassure the German car industry, with which the VW seemed likely to compete unfairly. He had always insisted that the car would *not* steal customers from established manufacturers, but would reach those who could not become buyers of the more expensive cars. It would also, he claimed, stimulate an interest in motoring and ultimately prompt those who later could afford it to buy bigger cars. His prediction proved accurate, but only after the war.

'This car,' Hitler concluded, 'shall carry the name of the organisation which works hardest to provide the broadest masses of our people with joy and, therefore, with strength. It shall be called the "KdF-Wagen"! I undertake the laying of the cornerstone in the name of the German people! This factory shall arise out of the strength of the entire German people and it shall serve the happiness of the German people!'

And so the automobile was named 'Strength-Through-Joy-Car'. Ferry Porsche says the name was a complete surprise to both his father and himself. 'We were horrified,' he says. 'My father commented that we'd never be able to sell the car abroad with such a name.' Joseph Werner had the same reaction. 'What American would buy a car called "Strength-Through-Joy-Wagen"?' he asked himself. Of course no one, except obdurate Nazis, ever called it that. The general public continued to call it 'Volkswagen', as did the regulations governing the layaway plan; the factory, then as now, was called the Volkswagenwerk, although advertising brochures and such other printed materials as the savings-stamp book called it the 'KdF-Wagen'.[2]

1. After Hitler eliminated the unpopular automobile tax in 1933 to spur motorisation, passenger car production rose sharply. Figures for 1934–9—*including, however, deliveries to the growing armed forces—1934:* 144,542; *1935:* 205,233; *1936:* 240,530; *1937:* 267,910; *1938:* 289,108; *1939:* 250,788. Of thirty-five car manufacturers, four dominated the industry and accounted for 64 per cent of total sales. These were Adam Opel, owned by General Motors (30 per cent of total sales); Auto-Union (14·5 per cent); Ford (10·7 per cent); and Daimler-Benz (9·2 per cent).

2. Today, the Volkswagen company is understandably interested in making the point that 'Volkswagen' was *not* Hitler's name for the car. It became the official name only after the war.

When the ceremonies ended, Hitler seated himself in one of the three 'KdF-Wagens' which Ferry Porsche and two others had driven from Stuttgart for the ceremony, then had Ferry drive him back to the Fallersleben railway station in the car, eschewing for once his Mercedes.

On the next day, the New York *Times* reported that the car would serve another purpose besides bringing joy to Germans: 'Hitler declared that if the German people spent all their money on foodstuffs, some of which Germany does not have, the result would be a "catastrophe". Therefore, he said, the nation's purchases of cheap new motor-cars will do much to check over-development of the demand for foodstuffs.' It was, in other words, to drain off at least 20 marks a month in disposable income and thus contribute to economic self-sufficiency for the nation. As matters developed, Hitler almost did achieve self-sufficiency in food production; Shirer says the Nazis reached 83 per cent of this goal.

The local press also reported the speech of a certain Dr. Glehn, representing the workers' city about to be built. He felt called upon to issue lofty sentiments to the effect that 'here labour's noble ethic, the primal source of life-affirmative emotions, shall find convincing expression'. It was phraseology typical of what VW's postwar head, Heinz Nordhoff, has called the Nazis' 'symbolic overestimation of the value of work'.

The correspondent of the Hanover *Anzeiger*, equally enraptured, wrote:

'A world is being built. The fist of a cyclops has seized the clear Lower Saxon landscape. But it is a modern cyclops, one who understands the concept of the beauty of work. . . . One looks from the ceremonial square out over the canal at the softly swaying forested heights. It is there that the German Reich shall bed down the most modern and beautiful workers' city. . . . Happy people, who will find their homes there!'

The first to move in were not to be Germans, however, but Italians. Mussolini sent Hitler three thousand of his unemployed construction workers, accompanied by Tullio Cianetti, Robert Ley's Italian counterpart. They were quartered in wooden barracks clustered about an A-frame community building called Cianetti Hall. 'Chianti bottle and dagger ruled,' *Der Spiegel* wrote years later. 'And the crocodile whip in the wooden watch tower of the SS guards . . . the first girls pregnant with the babies of Mussolini's unemployed began to appear . . .'

German companies in the construction, metals, machine tool and car industries were now ordered to free some of their work force for the plant and for the construction of the workers' city. These also found themselves in wooden barracks. In requisitioning them, the Nazi Party demonstrated just how ruthlessly it was prepared to operate in furthering this plan to which the Führer had committed himself for so many years.[1]

It seemed as though Hitler's experiment in true 'national socialism' might succeed. The layaway plan eliminated middlemen, dealers, distributors, and others usually necessary to the motor-car industry. Customers were even to pick up their cars at the plant, where a gallery was to be built from which they might watch their KdF-Wagen roll off the assembly line. The entire resources of Joseph Goebbels's Ministry of Propaganda and Public Enlightenment, which controlled all media of communication, were at the car's disposal. This amounted to an unlimited advertising budget. One of the first promotional efforts made by the Nazis on behalf of the car— an almost *Life*-size multi-page, illustrated hand-out entitled *Your KdF-Wagen*—is interesting as an example of advertising techniques employed at the time. Neither colour photography nor slick paper was utilised, although the same cannot be said of the language employed by the Nazi copywriter, whose breathless prose was very slick and colourful indeed.

'The baggage space of the car,' the brochure promised, 'is especially roomy. It is completely sufficient for four to five people even on long trips. Behind the back seat, there is room enough for many large handbags or grips, together with smaller pieces of luggage such as typewriters, gramophones, bathing clothes, and so on. Under the front hood, blankets or a medium-size suitcase may be accommodated along with rucksacks . . .

'All windows are very large, including the rear window, which is also made of glass . . .'

The copy then goes on to compare the KdF-Wagen with Porsche's Auto-Union racing cars. Stating that Porsche 'drew largely on his experience in building racing cars' when he designed the KdF-Wagen, the copywriter says that a comparison between the two may

1. Postwar Germany's news magazine *Der Spiegel* comments that such plants tended to keep their best workers and sent only expendables to the Volkswagenwerk. This Nazi levy is an example of the regime's arbitrary actions towards German private enterprise. Another curious example appears in the Nazi sales brochure for the KdF-Wagen. After citing the fringe benefits enjoyed by workers at the KdF car plant, it urged other German workers to demand comparable benefits of their employers.

seem 'peculiar' but that 'the technical man finds many parallels'. The brochure points out that the suspension and weight distribution of both the KdF-Wagen and the Auto-Union racers were similar, as were the axles. Not only would an owner have the satisfaction of driving a 23·5-bhp relation of Porsche's 545-hp P-car, but of being the envy of everyone. Becoming positively rhapsodic beneath a headline reading 'Enthusiasm wherever it shows itself', the KdF writer said: 'It makes no difference where the cars go: wherever they are recognised, one sees beaming faces and, when they come to a halt, they are immediately surrounded by a great mass of people. Everyone is amazed at the miracle car. All are enthusiastic about the pleasing, smart lines, and the solid construction.'

Soon the 1350-metre (1476-yard) front of the factory began to rise to half its finished height. Hitler promised it would be bigger than the Ford plant in Michigan and would outproduce it as well.[1] A New York *Times* editorial clucked that 'Adolf Hitler's KdF-Wagen . . . will leave much to be desired' in the way of American-style comfort, but added that Porsche 'is an engineer of such high standing in Germany that its practicability can hardly be doubted'. A later article (July 3, 1938) claimed the car was already nicknamed 'the Baby Hitler'. It also referred to the fact that Germany's shortage of raw materials was 'so bad that sardine cans may no longer have steel openers attached', and claimed that the first 200,000 KdF-Wagens would have bodies requiring 'only 10,000 tons of inexpensive plastic material and so little iron and steel as not to matter at all', as well as Buna (German synthetic rubber) tyres.

Construction of Germany's vast 'Westwall' fortifications, which faced France's Maginot Line, was launched as a crash programme in July 1938. Virtually overnight, most of the construction crews building the workers' city vanished, shunted over to this priority task. Peter Koller's blueprint for 'one of the most beautiful cities in the entire world' was rolled up at least until September.

When that month came, there again did not seem much point in starting up energetically. Now construction materials were rationed. Work moved slowly; a year after the dedication hoopla, only one building, a home for unmarried workers, had been completed. Then in September 1939 came war. Construction slowed still further. By December 1941, when all new civilian housing units were halted by decree, only 2358 flats (less than 10 per cent of those projected) had been completed and for the remainder of the war, wooden bar-

1. Today's postwar VW plant, vastly enlarged, is indeed the world's largest motor-car factory.

racks had to serve as substitutes. The workers' city, which the Nazis referred to as the *Stadt des KdF-Wagens*, bore no resemblance then to the city of Wolfsburg as it exists today. As for its name, some people called it '*die Autostadt*' ('the automobile city'), while others made do with the clumsy Nazi name for it. Not until June 1945, when its city administration renamed it, would it bear the name of the Schulenburg castle, Schloss Wolfsburg. As a matter of fact, it was not certain before the war that the castle would survive Peter Koller's urban development. As it turned out in postwar years, it did, and in the changed atmosphere, Count Werner was even to proclaim that 'the Volkswagen plant and the Volkswagen city will carry the name Wolfsburg forward into the future'.

In the late summer of 1938, Porsche was asked to open the Great German Mountain Prize auto race (*Grosser Bergpreis von Deutschland*) in a Volkswagen. The scene was the Hochalpenstrasse (high Alpine road) on Austria's highest mountain, the Grossglockner. Tens of thousands of onlookers had their first look at the car on this occasion and Bodo Lafferentz hoped that the nationwide publicity would excite their interest in his layaway scheme. Porsche, accompanied by his son Ferry, drove the twisting, tortuous 13-kilometre (approximately 8-mile) mountain road, which rose 1240 metres (4068 feet), in just 21 minutes, 44 seconds. A technical journalist evaluated the performance: cars with far more powerful engines, he said, 'require an average of 25 minutes for the run, if indeed they do not boil over and come to a complete halt. The KdF-Wagen took this climb as though it were child's play . . .'

On August 3, 1938 the New York *Times* reported the Nazis 'jubilant' as queues formed early in front of KdF offices a day after Robert Ley had publicly announced his five-mark-a-week layaway scheme in his speech at Cologne. A little more than three months later, the newspaper reported that payments of five marks *monthly* would now be accepted to stimulate Volkswagen sales, especially among young people. At that rate, the paper noted, it would take sixteen years to complete a purchase! The KdF promotional brochure makes mention of the monthly payment scheme, adding that the company 'reserves the right' to increase the rate of savings to five marks weekly if the young people involved made more money later. So far, a somewhat disappointing 150,000 applications had been received. The New York *Times* said 'the international crisis was blamed for lack of interest as savers feel insecure'. By the war's end, the 'KdF-savers', as they came to be called, never totalled more than

336,668, most of whom had opened their accounts before 1940.[1] The number may seem large, but it represents a seven-year (1938–1945) total and raises the question of what Hitler would do with the remainder of the 1,500,000 'KdF-Wagens' he planned to produce each year.

At the Berlin Motor Show in February 1939, Adolf Hitler lent himself once more to the task of publicising his car. *Time* magazine on February 27 of that year commented on the car's birth tremors: '... for the second time in a year, Adolf Hitler posed alongside a gleaming sample of his $396 Strength Through Joy flivver. Well did he know, but nothing did he say about the wretchedly slow progress in production of the *Volkswagen*, which was conceived more than five years ago, but will not be on the market until 1940 . . .'

Porsche commuted between his Bureau in Stuttgart and his job in Wolfsburg, overseeing the construction of his plant. He settled down in 'a wooden, four-room bungalow built in the middle of the forest where the Volkswagen factory was to be erected', his son Ferry reminisced later. 'My father did not wish to direct its construction from afar; he wanted to be there while the plant was growing.'

Despite the pressure, there remained time for relaxation. He loved the cinema and sometimes, on Saturdays and Sundays, saw several films each day. In summer, Porsche liked to fish or sail and he owned his own boat. These were days of personal triumph, best shared with those who contributed to it. At the height of his career, Porsche celebrated in the simple backwoods manner of a man from Maffersdorf, Bohemia.

'Around the hut there was excellent hunting,' Ferry says, 'and from time to time my father came along. Carrying the gun on his shoulder, he tried to find mushrooms. "I am somehow sorry for the deer," he said.

'He often took . . . his collaborators . . . along to the "hut". And in the evening, dinner—preferably goulash, a highly spiced Hungarian goulash—was served to a large number of people. My father liked strongly flavoured dishes. And his engineers, who were not very partial to them, had to put up with it and resorted to drinking large quantities of beer. Evenings of this kind were always very pleasant and people were apt to start telling stories. However, whatever subject was touched on initially, it was always merely a question

1. Hitler's analysis of the VW market and his claim that the car would not steal away customers of companies producing other cars proved accurate: questionnaires filled out by KdF-savers showed that 70 per cent had never owned a car; of the remainder, 40,000 were motor-cyclists (90 per cent of whom did not own a heavy motor-cycle comparable in price to the VW). More than half, says the KdF-Wagen brochure, earned less than 300 marks monthly.

of time until the talk finally turned to technical matters. Technical matters appeared to us a kind of focal point of the whole world.'

Nazi Germany honoured its leading designer in 1938 with its own equivalent of the Nobel Prize. Hitler refused to have anything to do with the Swedish awards ever since the 1935 Nobel Peace Prize was awarded to Carl von Ossietzky, a pacifist editor who died in a Nazi concentration camp on May 4, 1938. In 1937, he established his own National Culture Prize. On September 6, 1938, Porsche won it for his work on the Volkswagen. Other 1938 winners were Ernst Heinkel, for his bombers; Willy Messerschmitt, for his fighters; and Dr. Fritz Todt for his Autobahnen.[1] Dr. Goebbels announced the prizes and Adolf Hitler delivered an anti-Semitic harangue.

From November 9 to December 21, 1938, Karl Rabe, Joseph Werner, and Otto Dyckhoff toured the United States again, to buy additional American machines for the factory. 'The atmosphere in America had changed,' Werner remembers. 'The night we left was the *Kristallnacht*, when the Nazis began to accelerate the persecution of the Jews. I remember that German offices in New York were picketed when we arrived.' They were able nevertheless to do business with American manufacturers and their expedition proved successful.

'At the beginning of the war,' Heinz Nordhoff reminisced in his speech marking the plant's twenty-fifth anniversary, 'when construction of both city and factory was halted, the plant had been only partially completed. . . . [it] never passed the improvisation stage during its first five years. . . .' By the time it shifted over to war production, only 210 KdF-Wagens had been built; these had not even been constructed at the factory, but elsewhere, and all went to Nazi bureaus or officials. Not one was sold to a KdF-saver or any other 'little German'.

Discouraged and exhausted, Koller, the builder of Wolfsburg, gave up and joined the Wehrmacht. He was sent to Russia, fought, was captured in 1944, and landed in a Soviet prison camp for the remainder of the war. He could not have imagined it then, but he would eventually complete his city.

Despite—or due to—the totalitarian nature of the Third Reich, confusion and lack of standardisation characterised its war production. Virtually every German car manufacturer produced his own

1. Todt—who also built the Westwall—was killed mysteriously in an accident after a February 1942 conference with Hitler, during which differences were aired. He was an engineer with whom Porsche worked smoothly during World War II, and was succeeded as war production chief by the boy wonder Speer, an architect who, Porsche felt, knew little about technical matters and with whom Porsche feuded bitterly.

model of car for the armed forces and it was not until 1944 that even
an attempt at standardisation was made. The models selected were
two motor-cycles, one passenger car, and nine lorries. The only
passenger car manufacturer chosen was the Volkswagenwerk. This
plant was singled out because the vehicle it produced was one of the
finest to be manufactured anywhere during World War II.

Porsche had been asked to adapt the Volkswagen for military use.
He boosted horsepower to 25 and engine displacement to 1·13 litres,
redesigned its body, increased its road clearance, but kept it light and
manœuvrable. It was a strange-looking vehicle, meriting its name of
Kübelwagen ('bucket-car'): an open, almost square car, with the
familiar VW slanting front, on which a spare tyre was mounted.
First produced in 1940, its air-cooled engine proved impervious to
both African heat and Russian cold and its good traction kept it
moving where other cars stuck, spinning their wheels in the snow,
sand or mud.

The Reich Government, each year more and more enthusiastic
about Ferdinand Porsche's designs, in 1940 saw to it that an honorary professorship was added to his doctorates. At the suggestion of
the Nazi minister of education, Stuttgart University promoted the
designer to Professor Dr. h.c. Ferdinand Porsche.

Elsewhere, however, the professor's designs were less popular. One
of the reasons it took so long for the Kübelwagen to be approved by
the German Army as its basic vehicle was the pressure exerted by the
car manufacturers, each having his own stake in continuing production
for the Army. None wanted the state-run VW plant to become
exclusive producer of military passenger cars. Carl Borgward, head
of the motor-manufacturing company which bore his name, for
example, was head of war production in Northern Germany, and in
charge of all military vehicles manufacture in Lower Saxony.
Standardisation in favour of the Kübelwagen might have put him
out of business.

Another wartime model of the VW was the amphibious Schwimmwagen or Schwimmkübel. Its sealed body, equipped with a retract-
able propeller, was completely waterproof. So navigable was it that
a committee of the Weapons Bureau (*Heereswaffenamt*) seriously
tried to get Porsche to equip it with coloured lights to starboard and
port, to conform with international navigation rules. Displacing
1131 cubic centimetres, this model generated 30 brake horsepower.

The square Kübelwagen bodies were manufactured in Berlin; the
chassis were built in one section of the Volkswagen plant, while other

parts of the plant produced a number of other war implements, such as mines and parts for the Ju-88 bomber. Towards the end of the war, the plant briefly was engaged in assembling V-1 flying bombs as well. One of its more prosaic tasks during the war years was to build 1,500,000 primitive stoves by means of which the freezing German troops on the Russian front could warm themselves.

Then came the Allied raids. The factory was completely unprepared for them. It had never been built for war. Lying uncamouflaged in the open countryside, it was a beacon alongside the Mittelland Canal, its massive rectangular buildings seeming to invite bombers. Allied pilots had only to look for the colossus beside the silvery ribbon of water and they could not miss. It was just as the German Air Force warned in 1937, when Count von der Schulenburg attempted to use this argument to save his land.

The factory was not even equipped with subterranean air-raid shelters. It had no basement in which the workers might seek refuge because it was built on a swamp. When the alarm came, the only place to go was into bunkers built on the ground floor. Just before the war started, an air defence general had protested the plant's construction as inadequate for war requirements. The general wanted to scatter the plant through neighbouring forests, to hide its buildings from view. Porsche argued that this would be impossible. The general had held things up and Porsche, exasperated, had hurried to see Adolf Hitler on the Obersalzberg, to settle the matter.

'Am I mistaken?' he reportedly asked Hitler. 'Am I to build a Volkswagen or an armoured car? A car for peace or a car for war?'

'I believe,' Hitler answered huffily, 'we spoke exclusively of the Volkswagen.'

'And may I assume that the plant at Fallersleben is being built for that KdF-Wagen?'

'I gave you the assignment for the Volkswagen!' Hitler answered. 'I think it is clear that everything else follows from that.'

Porsche returned to the plant site and told those who warned of war and bombing raids, 'Please, you go to the Obersalzburg!'

No one, of course, went, and in time the bombers came. Otto Hoehne and Joseph Werner had been expecting them all along. 'Most of us who had come over from America felt the war was lost for Germany the moment the United States entered it,' Hoehne says. 'We tried to explain to those who had not worked in America that it might take US mass-production a while to get mobilised but, once it did, it would inundate us. We were resented for our gloomy predictions.'

Joseph Werner says the factory air-raid warden kept insisting for a long while that bombers would never come. 'The factory is not strategically important,' the warden assured everybody. Then, as Werner recalls it, he changed his mind one day at the very beginning of April 1944. He said he thought 'something would happen very soon'. His premonition proved correct; the factory underwent its first air raid on April 8.[1] Other raids followed over the next five months and did considerable damage. The raids were part of a concerted Allied attempt to knock out the entire German car industry.

It is interesting to note that one particular bomb, which landed between the power plant's two turbines, could have had very far-reaching effects. It was a dud and was deactivated and removed by British troops after the end of the war. Had it exploded, however, it would have destroyed those turbines and, with them, Volkswagen's entire postwar future. The plant depended on power generated by the turbines and replacements for these were impossible to obtain in Germany shortly after the war. Detonation of that single bomb would have meant that no further work would have been possible in the plant and probably no effort would have been made to start the Volkswagenwerk up again.

After the war, the bomb damage throughout Germany was examined by a United States Strategic Bombing Survey team, whose members included George W. Ball and Paul H. Nitze, later respectively Under Secretary of State and Secretary of the Navy in John F. Kennedy's and Lyndon B. Johnson's administrations. A total of 2,700,000 tons of bombs was dropped against Germany, 72 per cent of this number after July 1, 1944. German civilian casualties totalled 300,000 dead and 780,000 seriously wounded from raids alone. Despite this, Germany actually increased production during the months of the heaviest Allied air attacks.

Surveying the damage which bombings had caused the Volks-

1. That day, between 40 and 50 aircraft approached from the southeast and dropped approximately 500 high-explosive, 1000 twenty-pound, and 400 to 500 incendiary bombs. The raid lasted only four minutes, from 2.15 to 2.19 pm. There was little damage, although 13 workers were killed and 40 were wounded. On April 29, at 11.19 am a pilotless British bomber crashed into Hall 1, destroying various roofs and the floor of the hall. Three heavier raids followed. On June 20, 1944, 90 bombers, accompanied by 30 fighters, attacked the plant from 9.04 to 9.14 am, dropping 500 high-explosive bombs, 180 of which found their target, as well as 130 incendiaries, 32 of which hit buildings. Result: 27 workers killed, 93 wounded, and some damage to all buildings. On June 29, 65 aircraft attacked from 9.39 am to 9.41 am, with approximately 350 high-explosive and incendiary bombs, killing 14 persons, and considerably damaging the plant, town buildings, and the prisoner-of-war camp. The last raid occurred between 1.30 and 1.40 pm on August 5, with 80 aircraft dropping 300 high-explosive and incendiary bombs, as well as doing a good deal of damage to the assembly plant, kitchens, streets and barracks. These daylight raids were all conducted by US bombers; the RAF, which did not bomb the Volkswagenwerk, handled night missions. The pilotless British bomber mentioned above remains a mystery.

wagenwerk, the team found that 20·2 per cent of the total floor area was completely destroyed, 13·6 per cent was heavily damaged, and 20·9 per cent was superficially damaged. Floor area rendered un- usable due to total or heavy damage amounted to 33·8 per cent, or 1,859,417 square feet. As for the 2476 machines which the plant con- tained, more than 20 per cent were damaged in the raids, about half this number totally destroyed.

The company claims that at least 60 per cent of the plant was destroyed and Heinz Nordhoff personally says that destruction was, in effect, total. Mere measurement of damaged floor area proves nothing, he says, for the destruction of one area often puts ten others out of business. In a sense, the factory after the bombings was like a decapitated man who, because his torso and limbs are intact, is regarded as only partially disabled.

The Volkswagenwerk, as noted, never produced even nearly at capacity during the entire war. Production of military vehicles was, on the whole, remarkably small. Most sources claim the plant pro- duced 55,000 Kübelwagens and 15,000 Schwimmwagens from 1940 to 1945; the US Strategic Bombing Survey says production never came to more than 48,548.

After the raids, production dropped to about 25 per cent of the previous average. In October 1944, it rose again to 1380 units and by January 1945 it had climbed to 2030. In February 1945 all raw material allocations were stopped because of the critical war situa- tion and output plummeted to its lowest level.

Why was production so very low? The capacity of just the first unit of the factory was originally to be 150,000 cars per year; to achieve that, the Reich had invested more than 215 million marks from 1938 on. For all those millions, *Hitler received in five years as many vehicles as the plant today turns out in less than two weeks!*

The Strategic Bombing Survey claims that 'No experienced or qualified men of the calibre required were put in charge of all operations. It was chiefly a political plant.' But this does not com- pletely stand up under examination. Ferdinand Porsche himself was in full charge both at the factory and at Stuttgart throughout the war; while he was away, his son-in-law, Dr. Anton Piëch, represented him at Wolfsburg, while Ferry Porsche was deputised in Stuttgart. Other experienced members of the Porsche Bureau team were active at the factory during these years. There were plenty of qualified men. The answer is more complex.

Plant management and even the authorities in Berlin were unprepared at the onset of the war to use the factory for the war effort. Expecting a quick victory, authorities hesitated to shift the plant over to war production, preferring to wait until peace-time KdF-Wagens could be produced. The plant, says the USSBS, 'remained virtually idle, its 1941 production representing only 20–25 per cent of its capabilities'.

There were other reasons. What was to have been the 'most modern motor-car factory in the world' had in actuality become an Oriental bazaar of war matériel manufacture and the plant which had been conceived of and built as one enormous unit had been broken up into a host of small factories lodged under one roof. Most halls worked on different projects. Lack of intelligent planning and much disorganisation in Berlin, together with that confusion which is always generated by totalitarian bureaucracies, never allowed the plant to be operated as a modern mass-production facility. Otto Hoehne remembers it as 'chaos'.

'It was amazing how few concrete plans there were,' he says. 'Only when it came to aircraft manufacture, there had been a great deal of planning—too much of it, as a matter of fact, with too many planners on the payroll, for this was regarded as a glamour industry at the time and every engineer seemed to want to work in it. But as for utilising those sections of the factory which were not engaged in working for the aircraft industry, there seemed to be no plans at all, nor did anyone seem to have any clear idea as to how the factory facilities might be used to full advantage.'

Yet another factor may have been a human one. Today, the factory is manned by free men; in World War II, two-thirds of its workers were slaves. The labour force increased more than 600 per cent, from 2732 in 1939 to 17,365 in 1944; the vast majority were foreign prisoners. Some were Russian and Polish prisoners of war, most were forced labourers from France, Belgium, and Holland, and others were court-martialled German soldiers sentenced to work at the plant. While treatment of the prisoners at Wolfsburg appears to have been better than elsewhere in Nazi Germany, it is a fact that many of those who arrived there were half-starved. When one contingent of emaciated Russians arrived, Ferdinand Porsche was outraged at their condition. He had them photographed and then took the picture to the Führer's headquarters, the Wolfsschanze at Rastenburg, East Prussia. He protested to Hitler that he could not get such men to work effectively. Hitler, apparently wishing to keep his favourite designer happy and productive, ordered improvements.

Eventually, prisoners were fed by the factory's own farms and food became decent enough, notes Ferry Porsche, for the local Nazi officials to complain that prisoners were being 'pampered'.

Ferdinand Porsche could not always keep an eye on things at the factory. Ferry Porsche remembers his father as being almost constantly on the road throughout the war, travelling between Stuttgart, Berlin, the 'KdF-Wagen City', Paris and points east. He always tried to spend at least two days a week at the Porsche Bureau in Stuttgart, where his staff had by 1940 increased to 291 (from 23 in 1933). There and in the Nibelungen Works south of Linz, Austria, Porsche designed a succession of tanks and other military vehicles, for which he was lavishly honoured by the Third Reich. At the height of its activity, in 1943, the Bureau had a staff of 600.

Throughout this period, Porsche dealt with Armaments Minister Albert Speer. Animosity developed between the two men, and Speer finally had Porsche kicked upstairs by naming him Reich Armaments Councillor (Reichsrüstungsrat), head of a council which never met. In the autumn of 1944, upon Speer's insistence, Porsche moved his Bureau to Austria. As his new headquarters, Porsche chose a small woodworking factory in Gmünd, near his summer home in Zell am See.

The Hitlerian Götterdämmerung was beginning. Production had virtually ceased at Wolfsburg. Now Hitler ordered that nothing was to survive him. On March 18, 1945, an alarmed Albert Speer pleaded with the increasingly irrational Führer: 'We must do everything to maintain, even if only in a most primitive manner, a basis for the existence of the nation. . . . We have no right at this stage of the war to carry out demolitions which might affect the life of the people. We have the duty of leaving to the nation every possibility to insure its reconstruction in the distant future. . . .'

Hitler replied: 'If the war is lost, the nation will also perish . . . because this nation will have proved to be the weaker one and the future will belong solely to the stronger eastern nation [Russia]. Besides, those who will remain after the battle are only the inferior ones . . .'

As the end hastened, Berlin ordered the transfer of all machinery from the Volkswagenwerk to mines in Longwy to protect it from future air raids which never came. Longwy lies in an iron-mining and metallurgical district near the Belgian and Luxembourg borders; the mine shafts were enlarged to house the equipment. A train took the first two hundred machines to the new location, and they were installed just in time to be captured by advancing American soldiers.

After the transport left the Volkswagenwerk, Porsche listened to the passionate arguments of the plant's chief inspector. This official railed against the decision to move the machines into 'damp caves', pleading that Porsche stop the transfer. The machinery, he said, should be scattered throughout the surrounding countryside: engines into a potato-dehydration plant at Neindorf, motor parts into a barracks in the forests at Soltau, front ends and steering mechanisms into a barn at Fellersleben, and light machinery into Lüneberg. The heavy presses could remain where they were. Assembly might continue at the plant as well. Such a move, he stressed, would ensure the post-war future of the VW. 'We will save the machines which we need if we are *ever* to build your car,' he told Porsche.

It was already too late to halt the first transport to Longwy, but Porsche decided to save the rest. His decision—although he could not have suspected it—did indeed prove crucial to the car and the company. Had the factory lacked machines in the immediate post-war years, it is certain that there would not now be a Volkswagen or a Volkswagen company.

As American armour rolled within ten miles of the plant, another precaution was taken for the future. Vital parts were removed from those machines still in the plant, packed into crates, and hidden in the conduits carrying electric cables underneath the factory.

At 8.45 pm on April 10, 1945, the sirens in Wolfsburg sounded a warning that tanks were approaching the city. At 9 pm, the sirens warned of an air raid. Neither materialised. American armour had indeed reached nearby Fallersleben, but the Americans did not come to the factory. They could not conquer Wolfsburg, because Wolfsburg did not appear on their maps. The town was too new.

Polish, Russian, French, Belgian, and Dutch forced labourers waited in their barracks. Their SS guards had fled;[1] German soldiers and Nazi city officials burned or buried their uniforms and records, or drowned them in the Mittelland Canal. By 11 pm, the decision was reached not to defend the town. The *Volkssturm*—that 'army' of old men and young boys whom the Nazis had assembled into a rabble of 'home-guards'—disbanded.

When it became apparent that their jailers were gone and their liberators were not about to appear to establish order, some of the prisoners broke loose. They sacked the executives' homes in the town and turned on the factory. Chaos reigned in the unguarded halls and offices of the administration building, although the

1. Mönnich (in his book, *Die Autostadt*) says Germans derisively referred to a 'National Socialist Escape Organisation' (NS-Fluchtorganisation).

machines in the plant itself, many of which remained manned by German workers, were left untouched. 'Every telephone had been torn from the walls,' *Time* later reported, 'every typewriter had been sledgehammered to junk, every file and record had been scattered and burned.' Even the dental office was reduced to dust.

At the railway station, the prisoners swarmed over a freight train, tore apart its contents, and captured, along with guns, sugar and flour, several crates of costumes belonging to a troupe of actors. Powdered, painted, and costumed, the exhilarated looters marched on. Soon they liberated a cache of schnapps and, roaring drunk, threatened to burn the town. They were joined by Germans anxious to get in on the pillage.

Most of the prisoners, however, remained in their barracks for the time being, somewhat dazed by their freedom. It nevertheless became clear that large-scale disorders would result if the town remained without authorities for much longer. Late that night, the factory's chief inspector, Rudolf Brörmann, accompanied by a colleague, drove to Fallersleben to urge the Americans to occupy Wolfsburg before rioting broke out in full force. They returned without success.

On the next morning, April 11, Pastor Antonius Holling, then Roman Catholic chaplain of the German Army's punitive battalion attached to the plant, determined to try where Brörmann had failed. 'Because I do not speak English,' he told me, 'I went to the forced labourers' camp and asked the French priest there, who did speak English, to accompany me. Although he himself had been a prisoner, he was just as afraid as I was of what might happen if another night went by without law and order. He agreed to go and we drove off in an abandoned German Army ambulance. When we arrived, we found that the US occupation 'army' consisted of eleven men and one young lieutenant. We explained our situation and the lieutenant was impressed by the fact that we corroborated what Brörmann had said the night before, by the fact that we were both priests, and by the testimony of the Frenchman. Then I told him that he should hurry, because there were about 20 American children in Wolfsburg who needed protection. He looked incredulous, so I explained that these were the US-born children of German-American engineers whom Dr. Porsche had brought to Germany before the war.' The lieutenant cranked at his field telephone. That same day, twenty Sherman tanks and two hundred US soldiers arrived. The Americans posted signs saying that looters would be executed on the spot.

5

The Years of Improvisation

Hitler's Germany was dead, and so, it would seem, was the Volkswagen. For six years, Hitler had prepared for war; for six more years, Germans had fought that war, and now their nation lay prostrate and torn apart. The war had cost Germany 3,500,000 battle dead and more than 1,128,000,000,000 marks; little was left. Germany had been crushed by enemies restored by men and machines from across the Atlantic. The limits of Nazi Germany's human and material capacity were reached in 1941–42 at a time when her foes were just beginning to mobilise their own strength. The very American factories whose productivity and efficiency Porsche so much admired poured out a torrent of war material which engulfed the overtaxed, comparatively antiquated, and largely inefficient war machine of this totalitarian state.

'When elephants clash, the grass gets trampled,' says an ancient proverb, and World War II not only crushed Ferdinand Porsche's honourable and long-fought-for vision of a car for Everyman, it crushed Porsche himself. It smashed his factory and what there was of his small town, much of it now a sea of mud and wooden barracks in which thousands lived wretchedly, often ten to a room. Along the canal his colossus of a factory stood crippled, its roof gone, its halls shattered, its interior battered behind windowless walls, its machines idle and corroding in six inches of water.

The fate of the various participants in the drama of Porsche's shattered dream differed. Hitler had killed himself; Albert Speer, who claims to have tried unsuccessfully to do that job for his Führer (by introducing poison gas into the ventilation system of Hitler's Chancellery), was captured. For his part in the war, Speer drew a twenty-year sentence which ended, finally, on October 1, 1966. Robert Ley, whose German Labour Front played so prominent a role in the development of the KdF-Wagen, escaped death at Nuremberg by hanging himself in his cell, from rags tied to a toilet pipe. He had earlier presented his American captors with a memorandum urging that Germany become part of the USA, that the US should adopt a 'non-anti-Semitic' form of National Socialism, and that Ley himself should be put in charge of the scheme, directing it from Nuremberg Prison. After that, he wrote to Henry Ford, reminding him of his connections with the Volkswagen factory, and applying for a job with Ford Motor Company on the basis of his 'extensive motor-car experience'. A short while later, he lost his nerve completely, stuffed his mouth with his underwear so as to silence his death rattle, jammed cloth into his ears and nostrils, and hanged himself. When Hermann Goering (who was later to commit suicide himself) heard of it, he said: 'Thank God! He would only have been a disgrace to us!'

The fate of Dr. Bodo Lafferentz, Ley's aide, is another matter and provides an interesting insight into Nazi society. He was, according to Dr. Volkmar Köhler, 'an extraordinarily intelligent manager, and expert at the adroit use of official connections, less a Nazi than a man who used the Nazi era to his own advantage'. Lafferentz married into the family of Richard Wagner, had many artistic and musical friends and, in his capacity with the KdF, organised popular German Army tours of Bayreuth, home of the Wagner festivals. As nominal Hauptgeschäftsleiter (general manager) of the Volkswagenwerk throughout the war years, Lafferentz not only represented management, but also the workers and the government itself, by virtue of the post he held in the government's German Labour Front. He was, Köhler remarks, 'the very embodiment of the *Führerprinzip* (leadership principle), for he needed only to meet with himself to make decisions from whatever point of view he wished: labour, management, or regime'. During the war, Lafferentz found the factory too confining for his entrepreneurial nature. He formed another company, also with DAF funds, called the Research and Development Company (Gesellschaft für Forschung und Entwicklung). Like many other such creations, this created a great many service-exempt jobs, presumably benefiting Lafferentz's very large circle of friends and acquaintances. The company engaged in Utopian research of a most visionary nature. One major if ill-starred project, for example, was the development of a small wind-powered electric generator, named a *Volkswindkraftwerk* ('people's wind power plant'), which was to electrify the Russian farms which the Nazis hoped to settle with German farmers west of the Ural Mountains. These farms, which of course never materialised, were to be protected from 'the barbarous Asiatic hordes' by Ural Mountain forts manned by SS men, who were supposed to be aided in case of attack by the armed pioneer-farmers themselves. Another project was to bombard US coastal cities with rockets, fired from cigar-shaped containers which Lafferentz's company was designing. These were to be towed to America by German submarines. When the war ended all these plans, Lafferentz fled south and settled near Lake Constance.

Up north, near Fallersleben in Lower Saxony, lay a town un-marked on the conquerors' maps. In spring of 1945, it did not even have a name, for the use of 'City of the Strength-Through-Joy Car' had become, to say the least, unfashionable, and no one had named the city Wolfsburg yet. In it, an epidemic of despair, fear, hunger and violence raged. Former slave labourers, freed prisoners of war, displaced persons, and escapees from the Russian Zone of Occupa-tion, which lay five miles east, jammed the town. The Volkswagen-werk, or what was left of it, was now a 'prize of war' and lay idle, awaiting the pleasure of its conquerors. These changed and Ameri-cans were replaced by British forces in the early summer of 1945. A unit of the Royal Electrical and Mechanical Engineers (REME) arrived and set up a repair shop for British Army vehicles within the factory; in August, Major Ivan Hirst was placed in charge of this facility. The plant itself had been marked down for dismantling and was under the authority of Colonel C. R. Radclyffe, CBE, DSO, who was in charge of all motor vehicle production in the British Zone, and under Major John P. C. Macgregor, his deputy for Lower Saxony. Victors and vanquished concerned themselves only with maintaining health and safety in the area. No one spoke of the future; indeed few could conceive of one. It was a time when the Morgen-thau Plan, which intended to turn industrial Germany into a pasture, was still being spoken of as a possibility.

The few German workers in the factory sloshed through the shin-deep water, trying their best to clean up the debris with their hands. They brought back to the plant the machines which had been dis-persed and hidden before the surrender, and began to put them into working order. Before the British were aware of it, they had made two complete cars with one surviving heavy press. It was, however, not one of these which triggered off the production start. Major Hirst says that the car which launched the postwar boom in beetles had been a Nazi KdF-Wagen.

'One of the few VWs that had been built at the beginning of the war was sprayed khaki green and driven to HQ 21 Army Group as a demonstration model,' Hirst reports in the April 1962 REME *Journal*. 'The resulting order for the first batch of saloons was taken as the signal to go ahead.' And so, as Heinz Nordhoff was to remark later, 'by one of the ironic jokes history is sometimes tempted to produce, it was the Occupation Powers who, after unconditional surrender, brought Hitler's dream into reality.'

The British were delighted with these cars and with the Kübelwagens which the workers began to hand-tool for them. They had come to know and respect these vehicles in Africa, where they had out-performed easily overheated and heavier British and American vehicles; there the going rate for one Kübelwagen was two Jeeps. They were especially welcome to the British occupation forces, for the United Kingdom was not then supplying its soldiers with enough cars, using its output instead to try to build up its peacetime market.

The Americans had placed Rudolf Brörmann in charge of the plant; he was the former chief engineer who had approached them on April 10, pleading for help for Wolfsburg. The British confirmed him in his post.

One of the first production Volkswagens was then sent to England with the suggestion that it might be well for Britain to take over the plant and produce this remarkable little car themselves. In Britain, however, the enthusiasm of the military was not shared by the automotive 'experts'. The car was too ugly, bizarre, noisy, and flimsy. It was a mere toy which was not to be taken seriously, something which even the Germans would not want once present shortages were overcome. A British commission visited Wolfsburg to inspect the ruins. Its members were displeased by the sight of the workers tramping through the debris, and recommended that the plant be dismantled and razed. Headed by Lord Rootes, then Sir William, the commission predicted that the factory would collapse of its own inertia within two years. Certainly it was nothing in which the British auto industry was interested, even as gratis war booty.

Said the commission: 'The vehicle does not meet the fundamental technical requirements of a motor-car. As regards performance and design it is quite unattractive to the average motor-car buyer. It is too ugly and too noisy . . . a type of car like this will remain popular for two or three years, if that. To build the car commercially would be a completely uneconomic enterprise. . . .' The commission predicted that—if Germans produced the VW—'it would mean no undue economic competition on the world market against British products'.

Today, of course, that early comment on the Volkswagen and its future evokes groans or supercilious smiles, depending on the nationality and orientation of those reminded of it. The years since this British commission made this judgment have proven it wrong to a degree and an extent inconceivable at the time. The 'inroads' the VW has made in Volkswagenwerk's largest export-market, the United States, will be detailed later, and the same holds true, as shall be seen, even in other countries, some of them Commonwealth members. Yet it should be remembered that this negative judgment regarding the Volkswagen, as well as this prediction that it would never succeed in attracting customers, made very good sense indeed at that time: it was not short-sightedness that rendered this verdict, but sound business acumen. What did *not* make sense at all at the time was any thought that the car might be a great success; those, like Major Hirst, who were convinced of its future then were enthusiasts, not practical businessmen. The post-war German news magazine, *Der Spiegel*, which also evaluated the British 'death-sentence', came to the same conclusion: the prophets of gloom and doom were right, it said, and the only thing wrong with them was that they did not see that this 'ugly, bizarre, noisy and flimsy' motor-car could be made into something very fine indeed. Even had they seen this potential of improvement, it might not have seemed worth while at the time—as, indeed, it did not seem worth while to Americans like Henry Ford II and Ernest Breech.

Refugees from East Germany and the territories handed over to Poland poured into the area, settling in nearby camps, and gravitating towards the Volkswagenwerk. The British found themselves with a mile-long white elephant on their hands and a large number of people who expected help from them. The plant was the only source of work; something had to be done. They decided to start the plant operating again, at least temporarily.

British Army trucks started bringing in Ruhr coal for the plant. By the end of 1945, six thousand workers had produced 1785 Volkswagens. Half of these workers, said *Time*, 'were cleaning up rubble; the others were virtually handtooling [the cars] . . . Falling bricks were a constant menace; live wires lay tangled in the mess.' Just getting raw materials for the cars and the basic necessities for the workers proved an enormous problem. It was solved in part at least by means of barter.

'We traded cars for steel in the Ruhr, for food, shoes, and clothing,' says Joseph Werner. 'We even traded with the British Army to get tyres. Sometimes we exchanged new cars for these commodities, sometimes overhauled ones, sometimes a wartime Kübelwagen or two. Occasionally we obtained food from Switzerland by sending a car down with a driver. We'd pay the driver five bananas and a few oranges to make the trip and he'd come back with packages of food and other necessities in exchange for the car.' Barter was necessary at the time, for the one mark per hour the workers were being paid on the average bought next to nothing in 1945, except on ration cards (and these, for example, provided a family with an eighth of a pound of cheese per month). Werner remembers eating little but bread and potatoes in Wolfsburg at the time. 'I'd travel to my relatives all the way to Munich on weekends,' he says, 'just to get a decent meal.'

Wing Commander Richard H. Berryman, OBE, had been put in charge of production at the factory, as Technical Liaison Officer. 'The supply of material got so bad,' he says, 'that we had a fleet of small vans and trucks going to all sources of supply, picking up twenty, thirty, or fifty of whatever we needed and bringing it back just to keep the place going. At times we'd have as many as a hundred cars on the floor with no wheels or tyres or glass, waiting for further supplies.'

Not only were the British officers at the VW factory plagued by shortages, but their customers faced the same problem. Fritz Fricke, in charge of maintenance at a British motor pool in nearby Celle, remembers that he needed spare parts desperately for his fleet of forty British Army Volkswagens. 'I happened to have heard that the British in Wolfsburg wanted one hundred 100-watt light bulbs at the time, so I approached my own major and asked him for a supply. I told him they were extremely valuable then and that they'd command a good price on the black market. When I finally convinced him we badly needed the spares for our VWs, he let me have the 100 bulbs. I took them to the British at the VW factory. "Here they are," I said. "They're worth a lot on the black market." But the British officer said: "Oh, we don't want them for the black market! We need them for our recreation room—we want to hang them above our billiards tables." I pulled out my list of motor-car parts, the officer filled the order, and I gave him his bulbs.'

Much barter had to be done secretly, for while many of the officers in Wolfsburg saw the need for this illegal business, others in head-quarters far distant were very disturbed at talk of such trade. Many vehicles, therefore, were simply 'lost in delivery' and never turned up again. What turned up instead was steel for the factory and food for its workers.

In August 1946, the British reorganised the management and re-placed Rudolf Brörmann, with whom they had difficulty working, with Dr. Hermann Münch, a tractable Berlin industrial lawyer selected largely because he was postwar custodian of all German Labour Front properties. Eventually, Otto Hoehne was made pro-duction chief. 'He got his first paycheck from me,' says Berryman. 'He did a wonderful job.' Julius Paulsen, then purchasing agent, was another of the German executives Berryman singles out for special credit. 'It is due to his efforts in getting materials that the factory was able to keep going.' Somehow, the factory seemed actually to be moving ahead. Its employees grew in number. In April 1945, the month the war ended for Wolfsburg, the factory had 450 workers; a month later, it had 1105; by December 1945, there were 6033, and by August 1946, the number had risen to 7951. In 1946, these workers produced 10,020 cars.

These, and the 1785 produced in 1945, were the first true 'civilian' Volkswagens, although all had gone to the British military and other occupation forces. 'Up until the end of the war, not a single Volks-wagen, in today's sense of the term, had been produced in the Wolfs-burg factory,' says Nordhoff. 'The few sedans that had been made were custom-built at Daimler-Benz for the cream of the Nazi hierarchy at a cost per unit similar to that of a Rolls-Royce.'

As the ten thousandth VW was turned out in October 1946, it was the focal point of what one writer called a 'pathetic celebration'. Across its windscreen, the workers had placed signs reading: 'Better and tastier food, or there will be many things we won't forget!' and '10,000 cars and nothing in the stomach—who can stand that?' (*Mehr und schmackhafteres Essen, sonst können wir vieles nicht vergessen! 10,000 Wagen, nichts im Magen, wer kan das vertragen?*)

Now things were getting worse. Production in 1947 fell to 8987. 'The vultures,' reminisced Nordhoff later on, 'began to circle over town and factory. Everything seemed hopeless.' The mark was worthless; the index of industrial production in Germany had crashed to 40.[1] It was hardly a sensible time to build a car; it was a time, Konrad Adenauer said, when 'every German would have been lucky to get a new suit every 40 years, a new shirt every 10 years, and a pair of socks every four years'.

1. 1936=100.

That year, Wing Commander Berryman, on leave in London, telephoned Sir William Rootes at the latter's Devonshire House office in Piccadilly and asked for an appointment, reminding him of the days before 1942 when they had met, working at the Ministry of Supply.

'I went over to see him and his brother Reginald,' Berryman reported in the series of articles about him which Britain's *Safer Motoring* magazine published. 'I told them all about the VW's construction and the production problems that had been overcome. I said that I had tried to break up the VW on numerous occasions in "destruction tests" over the most atrocious roads, and that I had failed to destroy the car, and had proved to my own satisfaction that it was exceptionally durable and practical. I told the Rootes brothers that I thought the Volkswagenwerk was a gold mine waiting to be exploited, and I suggested that the whole place could be bought for reparations at a comparatively low figure—a few million pounds maybe.

'They listened to what I had to say, then Sir William told me that he had had one of the Volkswagen cars tested by his own staff and that it did not come up to expectations and was considered to have not much future . . .' Years later, at a London Motor Show, Berryman happened to encounter Rootes again. 'I wish I had listened to you a bit more the time we last met,' Sir William said.

There was one more occasion on which Berryman tried to interest the British in the VW, showing it to an old RAF acquaintance then running a British factory. Berryman reports: 'They were interested in the body construction, but after a careful examination they decided they could not learn anything from it.'

This remarkable inability to learn anything from Porsche's remarkable design repeatedly saved the Volkswagen for the Germans. Even the Australians, Berryman says, turned it down. In February 1947, he met members of the Australian Reparations Commission in Antwerp, but the meeting proved fruitless. Berryman regrets it, for he says he had been 'promised the job of Production Manager if the Australian VW plan had come off'. (The Australian VW company operating today was established six years later, as will be reported in Chapter 10.)

While all these conversations went on, more practical matters had to be settled at the plant. Entire trainloads of coal were side-tracked to the factory to keep its heart—the power plant—alive, and more bartered Volkswagens found their way into the hands of co-operative railway officers. Major Hirst, by now a great enthusiast for the car and its factory, protected it ferociously, even against interfering British authorities. At one time, a British company demanded the return of two British machines and Hirst wrote them back: 'I know the machines are needed in Britain, but we need them even more badly here!' According to his driver, 'Mike' Hocke, Major Hirst once told him: 'This factory belongs to the German people and I'm here to see they get it.' Hocke, who returned to Wolfsburg as a discharged POW after wartime military service in Italy, says Major Hirst was so fond of his Volkswagen that for three months after Hocke arrived, he would not let himself be chauffeured. 'He wanted to be behind the wheel himself,' says Hocke.

Hirst's fondness seems to have been shared by the other British officers, all of whom were especially enthusiastic about the amphibious VW 'Jeep', the Schwimmwagen. They would hold games in which they would run it off the wharves into the Mittelland Canal at 40 miles per hour, hitting the water with a great splash and then driving the cars úp and down the canal. The amphibian, as a matter of fact, has been credited by Major Macgregor as saving the factory at one time.in its turbulent early years.

As he tells the story, there was no sheet metal large enough at the time to make the roof and doors of the VW of one piece. Smaller sheets were used and a seam ran across the bonnet and the doors to join them. (Macgregor says they tested these cars by rolling them over, and every fiftieth car or so would be dropped upside down, to see if the seam held.)

To make this seam, they needed a butt welder, which they finally found down in the Ruhr industrial area of Germany. This was a machine the Germans had seized in France during the war, and teams of French officers were then running around conquered Germany trying to locate machinery of this kind for repatriation. 'They were crawling all over the place,' Macgregor says. Knowing the French must be after this butt welder which was hard to replace at the time, the British quickly grabbed it, along with those Germans who knew from where it had come, and brought both machinery and men to Wolfsburg, to set them to work and keep the machine from the French.

Early one morning, two French officers showed up in Wolfsburg. They had heard of the machine and wanted to inspect it. The razzle-dazzle treatment they received at the hands of the resourceful British shows with what ferocity the latter protected their plant, and just how determined they were to see it in effective operation.

Major Macgregor says he and Berryman greeted the two Frenchmen cordially and invited them to the REME officers' mess, located
in the building which, later, became the Volkswagen's first Guest
House. So cordial was this inter-Allied discussion that the French
were half-drunk by noon, having been liberally provided with brandy
by the two British officers. After several hours' drinking, Macgregor
and Berryman put their guests into one of the Schimmwagens and,
chauffeuring them, charged along the bank of the Mittelland Canal.
'Then we suddenly swerved off the embankment and into the water,
flying out over the surface at top speed before we landed smack in
the canal,' Macgregor says. 'We gave the Frenchmen quite a wild
ride in the water too, and then the bilge tank plug just happened to
come out and our vehicle just happened to sink. Those two Frenchmen were getting a good ducking, what with Berryman and I thrash-
ing about a bit and shoving them under every now and then. We
prudently had a rescue vehicle standing nearby and hauled them out
after a while, dried them off, and got them into dry British uniforms.'
    They warmed the two visitors with more brandy but noticed that
they were getting 'a little nasty now'. Berryman offered to show them
the factory. 'He gave them quite a tour in one of the regular Volkswagens,' Macgregor says, 'skidding about corners and even tearing
through the building at 40 mph. By this time, the Frenchmen were
insisting even more strongly that they must see their machine, but of
course they were quite drunk and dizzy, which is what we wanted,
and we had gained some valuable time.'
    A machine was finally presented for their inspection. It was a
mockup, designed to look like a butt welder, but clearly not theirs.
Disappointed, the Frenchmen left town. Had they been soberer,
they might have been curious about the tarpaulin-covered object
standing next to the mockup they were shown. There, a few feet away
from them and hidden under canvas, was their butt welder. If they
had seen and confiscated it, the factory would have had to shut down
production.
    The years of 1945, 1946, and 1947 were years of improvisation and
ingenuity for the British in Wolfsburg, years of sacrifice and hard
work for the Germans at the plant, and fateful ones for the 'Wolfsburg Motor Works', as the Volkswagenwerk was then also being
called. Had this handful of British officers not engaged themselves so
daringly for the factory and its workers, there could never have been
a VW today. Inevitably, the factory would have decayed or been
dismantled. Despite their dedication, hard work, and self-sacrifice,

the German Volkswagen executives there at the time would have been powerless to save the plant in those years, had they stood alone. Fortunately, they did not, nor were they in the hands of victors seeking to exploit them.

Porsche knew little of all these events at Wolfsburg. When the war ended he was far away, at Gmünd, Austria. There he was briefly and politely questioned by a British technical commission and a guard placed in front of his house, less to watch him than to protect him against marauders.

In July 1945 he was ordered to Frankfurt in the American Zone, to be interrogated further along with others prominent in the Third Reich. Because of his advanced age (he was now seventy), Porsche was allowed to drive to Frankfurt in his own car, accompanied by his chauffeur, Josef Goldinger, who had served him since 1908. He spent three months in the 'Dustbin', a castle outside the city. Another prisoner in the Dustbin was Albert Speer who, despite his wartime differences with Porsche, defended the old man energetically and said it was ridiculous to interrogate Porsche about political matters of which he knew nothing.

Porsche was well treated and upon release was permitted to return a free man to Zell am See, Austria, where he had his home near his workshop in Gmünd. On his drive back, he stopped by Stuttgart to visit the former offices of the Porsche Bureau, quarters which were now occupied by Americans. He was rebuffed sharply and the US commander was not willing to let him enter the building. Porsche left deeply hurt, politically naïve as always.

In Gmünd and in Zell am See, Porsche and his colleagues set up shop, repairing cars used by occupation troops. They even designed and manufactured wheelbarrows and small wagons. Karl Rabe, his chief designer, worked in Gmünd in the British Zone, while Porsche worked in Zell am See in the American Zone; neither could visit the other because interzonal passes were not issued to Germans in mid-1945.

In November an event of far-reaching importance to Porsche occurred. A French officer, accompanied by a former Porsche engineer, approached the designer with an invitation to visit French headquarters in Baden-Baden, where a French technical commission waited to offer him an 'interesting assignment'.

Porsche, extremely cautious, finally agreed to go to Germany if Ferry could precede him to conduct preliminary negotiations and then report back. In Baden-Baden, a Colonel Meffre, in charge of French Zone industry, explained to Ferry that France's Minister of Industry, Marcel Paul, wanted to invite his father to build a true 'people's car' for the French Government. The chassis was to be identical to the Volkswagen's, since the French were satisfied with its technical excellence, but the body was to be redesigned to give the car 'a typical French look'.

Ferry hurried back to Austria to report. The offer seemed bona fide and the terms acceptable. Exhilarated that his talents were once more in demand, Ferdinand Porsche went to the spa in Germany's French Zone on November 16, 1945, looking forward to the exciting new turn his life was taking. He was, of course, aware that some Volkswagens were being produced, but undoubtedly he believed that the Wolfsburg plant was doomed and about to be dismantled. He had been given to understand that the British were offering the factory to France and that the French wanted to have a French version of the car built and tested before they accepted the plant. He had been told that preparations to dismantle and ship the plant to France were already under way in Wolfsburg and that the French also wanted Porsche's help in assembling it again. It was understandable that he should have believed this, for the factory did indeed stand on the dismantling lists in 1945, having been classified as a munitions plant because of its wartime production of bombs and V-1 flying bombs. After so many years of heartbreaking work on the car and seeing his 25-year dream shattered by war, Porsche must have been doubly convinced that only governmental sponsorship would ever get his car built.

In Baden-Baden, the negotiations with the French commission went smoothly. The officer who had invited Porsche, a Monsieur Lecomte, headed the French delegation. Ferry Porsche assisted his father for he spoke French. Porsche's son-in-law, Dr. Anton Piëch, was also there. Finally, an agreement was reached over a champagne breakfast. Then Porsche was asked to wait two days while Paris was consulted.

The Germans waited in comfort over the weekend, well supplied with food and drink in the beautiful resort. On Saturday, December 15, 1945, while they were still awaiting word of Paris's reaction to the terms, some French officers whom they had never seen before entered Lecomte's quarters, the villa Bella Vista, in which they were living— and summarily arrested them. The officers were from the Sûreté. Porsche, Ferry, and Piëch were placed in a crowded cell block in

Baden-Baden's former SS prison. Lecomte, completely surprised at this new development, later drove to Gmünd to assure Porsche's daughter, Louise Piëch, that he had nothing to do with the arrest of her father, husband, or brother. He said he would do what he could to free the three men.

When Porsche was finally informed of the charges which had been brought against him, he learned that his enemies were again executives of big motor companies, this time French ones.

The 'French VW' scheme had apparently been concocted by left-wing French politicians, including Marcel Paul. French car manufacturers, however, were determined to kill any such idea in its cradle despite the dangers involved. Louis Renault had been arrested by the French government on charges of collaborating with the Germans during the war, and his company had been seized and nationalised. There are many who believe Renault was innocent and that he was arrested only to permit the left-wing government of the day to grab his company. Renault died in prison and has still not been exonerated, although several Germans who knew of his activities during the German occupation of France assured me that Renault never co-operated willingly, but resisted the Germans as best he could. The example of Renault was a constant reminder to the French car makers. The French VW plan was a comparable threat. They wanted to save their companies and would not countenance a competing, government-backed car. The fact that the designer of this car was a German supplied them with the ammunition to sabotage the scheme. And so, Jean Pierre Peugeot charged Porsche with war crimes.

It was not difficult to make such an allegation in 1945–46, and it was likely to be believed, no matter which German stood accused. It was an atmosphere which encouraged mischief; arrest immediately followed a charge, and trial could be postponed indefinitely.

Specifically, Porsche was charged with violation of the Hague Convention governing the treatment of war prisoners, with being guilty of disciplinary reprisals against French workers at the Peugeot plant during World War II, and with responsibility for or complicity in deportations from France. The Peugeot plant was under the direction of the Wolfsburg VW factory during World War II, and it is true that Porsche regularly consulted with Peugeot's engineers and technicians in France. He had of course nothing to do with repressions or deportations. He had been there purely in a technical capacity, and so it would be proven two years later, when he was completely exonerated of all charges. Ferry Porsche recalls three specific instances in which his father had actually aided the Frenchmen from Peugeot. Once, when the Nazis proposed to deport Peugeot workers to Wolfsburg, Ferdinand Porsche effectively resisted this move, arguing that people work better when they are close to their own homes. Another time, Porsche stopped the Nazis from arresting Peugeot directors after an act of sabotage had occurred in the plant. Jean Pierre Peugeot himself visited Wolfsburg during the war and on that occasion Porsche saved him from arrest by the Gestapo. He intervened and arranged for Peugeot's safe return to Paris.

It now seemed as though the French Volkswagen scheme had been effectively defeated. Porsche sat in prison along with his son and his son-in-law, and Lecomte fretted helplessly. It was at this point that Ghislaine Kaes, Porsche's loyal secretary, turned up.

Kaes had always been a British subject and this finally got him in trouble with the Nazis. Ferdinand Porsche could not have cared less about Kaes's citizenship; in fact, Kaes remembers, Porsche never once mentioned it during all the years of their association. (After the war started, Porsche did, however, know that Kaes listened illegally to the 9 pm BBC newscast from London, and he would occasionally ask him what had been said.) Throughout these war years in Germany, Kaes said, 'I felt as if I was on the wrong boat and couldn't get the captain to change his course.' On February 9, 1944, the Nazis finally arrested him and sent him to the Eastern Front in a German Army punishment battalion. He was wounded in East Prussia, fighting the advancing Red Army, and was shipped to a hospital in Denmark, then still under German occupation. 'On May 5, 1945,' Kaes says, 'I saw the British flag flying over Copenhagen.' Enthusiastically, if naïvely, he rushed to British headquarters, 'to report', as he put it, but they refused to see him or to believe that he was a British subject. Instead, they turned him over to Danish resistance fighters who first took him to Hellerup where they pressed a pistol against the back of his neck and told him to prepare for death. At the last moment, a Danish officer stopped the execution and Kaes was shipped off to prison. He was released after a short while and began working for a British unit. Because of his wartime presence in Germany, Kaes was tried for treason. The court acquitted him, and he was freed. Then he rushed to Gmünd 'to find the Herr Professor', and from there to Baden-Baden, where he finally found him in prison.

'I was able to get meals in to him,' Kaes says. 'He'd ask me for some soup or a Schnitzel and I'd get it to him the next day. A woman in town cooked for me. Each day I had to bribe the guard 20 marks to get in the prison and another 20 to get out again.' After a while Porsche asked Kaes to get him better quarters by claiming his eyes needed treatment. The ruse succeeded and the designer was transferred to a hospital, Kaes meeting him at the prison and carrying his suitcases for him to his new quarters.

Throughout this period Ghislaine Kaes lived with Lecomte at the Bella Vista. Lecomte, still obsessed with the desire to build a French Volkswagen, told Kaes to go the the British Zone of Austria and get the blueprints of the car so that Lecomte could get them to Paris. He warned him that Porsche would be killed unless he agreed to do so. 'It was a bluff,' Kaes told me, 'but I had no choice. I went to the professor to ask him what I should do. He suggested I notify the British liaison officer in Baden-Baden and so I sneaked over there one night under cover of darkness and talked to a British captain. There was a brigadier in the room as well, who listened attentively and said nothing. The captain wanted to know all about the Frenchmen involved in this plan, what they had told us, where their offices were, even what their telephone numbers were. I had all this in my notebook of course. Then they told me to co-operate fully with Lecomte for the time being. They thanked me for informing them of the plan and assured me that nothing would happen to me as a result.'

While Porsche still lay in his Baden-Baden hospital bed, his son Ferry was transferred in March 1946 to the Hotel Sonnenberg in Rippoldsau, a Black Forest spa. There he was well treated, for the French also wanted Ferry, who already had a reputation as a brilliant designer, to work for them. Ferry refused, saying he could not design anything while he was still a prisoner. Besides, he emphasised, his only thoughts were with his father and his family. Then the French insisted they wanted the VW blueprints, and Ferry supplied Kaes with a car in which to drive to Gmünd. This was a special four-wheel-drive Kübelwagen, with a regular VW passenger body, which went under the special name of Kommandeurswagen. Lecomte supplied the petrol and funds and joined Kaes in the car. They drove off on March 17, 1946, and, after picking up necessary papers at Innsbruck, arrived at Gmünd in the British Zone of Austria late on the evening of the nineteenth.

'After Lecomte had gone to bed,' Kaes told me, 'I sat down with Mrs. Piëch and Karl Rabe to try and find a solution to this problem.

Rabe insisted that he was responsible to the British and did not feel free to hand over any blueprints to the French. They told me to report the matter to the officers at British headquarters in Klagenfurth, 60 kilometres away. I drove there the next day without Lecomte and spoke with a British major in the Field Security Service. He listened to me for a long while and then ordered me not to turn anything over to the French—and to tell Lecomte that this was the decision of British headquarters. I was worried about what Lecomte would do, either to me or to the professor, when he found out, so when I returned I told him that the British had discovered his plans by themselves.'

Lecomte did not believe this and suspected that Kaes had informed. He ordered Kaes to take the blueprints into the French Zone of Austria, carrying them over the Alpine mountain passes on foot. He also wanted machinery from the workshop and said he would arrange to have that transported out of the British Zone.

Lecomte was now prepared to move rapidly and the situation was becoming critical. Once again, Kaes consulted with Rabe and Mrs. Piëch and on Thursday, March 23, again drove to British headquarters in Klagenfurth. As a result, the British sent a soldier to Gmünd by motor-cycle that very night, to order Lecomte to report to Klagenfurth at 10 am the next day. Lecomte accused Kaes of treachery, then ordered him to come along on this trip.

'Lecomte wanted to arrive in Klagenfurth ahead of time, so as to meet with the French liaison officer there before we reported to British headquarters,' Kaes says, 'but this was one time the Volkswagen failed to make it. I was determined to arrive at ten sharp and I made sure I had to stop several times to get the "failing" engine running again.'

They arrived in Klagenfurth just in time for their appointment with the British. Lecomte reported to them, while Kaes waited on a bench near the French headquarters which Lecomte now wanted to visit after he was finished with the British. After a while, Kaes saw two officers emerge from British headquarters and march over to the French offices. He did not know it, but they were looking for him. Not finding him there, they returned to British headquarters and, after another fifteen minutes, emerged once more, this time with Lecomte between them. Lecomte led them to Kaes, seated on the park bench. Suddenly he broke away from his companions and dashed towards Kaes. 'Quick, give me your notebook!' he said. He referred to the diary which contained the particulars of the French authorities at Baden-Baden. Kaes refused to obey. In a moment, the two British officers reached the bench and ordered Kaes to accompany them. 'I gave Lecomte the car keys so he could go wherever he wanted,' Kaes says. 'I found out later he had been ordered out of the British Zone within twenty-four hours.'

British M.I.5 intelligence officers now began interrogating Kaes for a week, six hours a day, and then put him in the state prison at Langenfurth. 'I was in there without charges,' Kaes says bitterly. 'The British told me it was for my own protection—apparently they meant from the French. If you ask me, there was no sense in it at all. Besides, they broke the promises they made to me in Baden-Baden.' After four weeks, Kaes was transferred to the Federaun Internment Camp outside Villach, twenty miles west of Klagenfurth, where he was kept another sixty days. Then he was released without explanation. By that time, Ferdinand Porsche and Dr. Piëch had been taken to Paris. 'Lecomte was behind that,' Ferry Porsche says. 'He probably thought that, if he could get my father to Paris, he might still salvage his French VW scheme. Besides, having my father in France as a prisoner represented cheap labour.'

The two men were placed in attic rooms in Louis Renault's villa, where they stayed until the spring of 1947. Periodically, they met French engineers and were consulted on various problems. 'My father made no basic alterations in the Renault 4CV car,' Ferry says, referring to the many reports that this motor-car was redesigned by Porsche while he was in France. 'The car existed before he arrived there. My father made some suggestions regarding its faulty weight distribution, but made no important changes.' Ferry says that the design of the Renault 4CV had been suggested by a Daimler-Benz engineer during the war, while Renault worked for Daimler-Benz.

In the spring of 1947, Porsche and Piëch were handcuffed and transported to an ancient, unheated dungeon at Dijon. There they remained until the end of July, under circumstances so wretched that they broke the aged Dr. Porsche's health. Their only friend was a German Benedictine priest who visited them in their cells.

Then the French decided the two men could be released on 500,000 francs bail each. Although it was almost impossible for a German to raise that sum before the 1948 currency reform, Ferry Porsche managed it. Freed from Rippoldsau at the end of July 1946, Ferry designed a racing car for Italy's Cisitalia firm to raise the bail money. For this piece of work and others, he received about $62,000, more than enough to cover the bail. Two Frenchmen, Raymond Sommer, the Grand Prix driver, and Charles Faroux, a motoring correspondent, gave him valuable assistance. While Faroux got food packages to Porsche, Sommer served as middle-man between Cisitalia and the French, for Ferry himself could not transfer funds directly. On August 1, 1947, Porsche and Piëche were released. Thus the designer had paid with almost two years of his life for his close association with Adolf Hitler and the National Socialist regime.

It is obvious that Porsche had benefited by the Nazi regime and that his racing cars and Volkswagen brought prestige to the Third Reich. Yet he had not been a Nazi Party member, even nominally, perhaps simply because he was totally absorbed in his work and politically uninterested. Also, he faced the world of politics with great naïveté. He has been criticised for not being 'political' enough and for bolstering Nazi prestige indirectly by his continued activity. As Herbert Quint sees it: 'Simply because Ferdinand Porsche worked in the Third Reich . . . he gave [it] the opportunity of saying: see here, this man works wholeheartedly for us, with all his strength; this man stands on our side; how can anyone, therefore, have doubts about our state, if such outstanding men like Ferdinand Porsche obviously support it?'

Porsche seemed oblivious to such considerations. Under Hitler, as before, he gathered in honours and medals, always hurrying from the tedious ceremonies back to the drawing board. He worked under Germany's post-World War I Weimer Republic, oblivious to the forces fighting to destroy or preserve it. He turned down Stalin's offer largely because he dreaded homesickness; he did not seem to give a thought to the aggressive and totalitarian nature of the Soviet regime. To Porsche, a state was only a place in which to work and politics concerned him only in so far as they impinged upon that work. While he served the Nazi state, the facts are that Porsche was *not* guilty of war crimes or of involvement in deportations. His record was more than just scrupulously correct; it was humane. He judged a man only by whether he was talented and a hard worker, or whether he produced 'manure' and was therefore to be ignored. Porsche seemed temperamentally incapable of accepting Nazi notions about racially superior or racially inferior persons. Despite the fact that it was dangerous for him to do so, he retained Alfred Rosenberger, a Jew, as his foreign sales representative until World War II ended all foreign business. His protection of Kaes during the war and his aid to Peugeot, his directors and his staff also showed his humanity and courage.

Porsche's tragedy lay in the fact that the world had changed. 'Could he, the unpolitical one, grasp what is meant by . . . "totalitarian state"?' Herbert Quint asks. 'Could he grasp the fact that it is impossible to be apolitical in a totalitarian state?' Apparently not. It is perhaps unfortunate that in today's increasingly political world, it is not enough for a man to have lived a good life. Our times demand a political morality as well as a personal one, particularly of the highly placed.

For those who feel he should have been punished, there is the fact of his harsh imprisonment. Baden-Baden, Paris, and Dijon deprived him not only of his freedom but of his health as well. After returning to Austria, Porsche was finally permitted to re-enter Germany in 1949. At the end of September 1950, Ferry drove him to the Volkswagenwerk in Wolfsburg, where he spent a day talking with Heinz Nordhoff and technicians about the future development of the car. On the road to Wolfsburg and back, Ferdinand Porsche saw his dream fulfilled: the Autobahnen seemed filled with Volkswagens. Ferry remembers that his father was very much moved. 'He had to pull himself together not to start crying,' Ferry says. It had, after all, been a long time. There had been so many disappointments, so many short-lived successes.

Shortly after he returned from Wolfsburg, his health collapsed. Circulatory troubles plagued him and he began to sink. Before he died, there were two more occasions to delight him. Although the French never returned Porsche's half-million francs bail, a French court acquitted him of all war-crimes charges. Then, on September 5, 1950, he was honoured at a seventy-fifth birthday party given by old friends and acquaintances. Drivers who had played an important role in his racing days attended. The parking lot outside the hall was filled with Volkswagens and with the new Porsche sports cars. The old man was elated and his friends joyful. They did not realise that he had so little time to live.

He died on January 30, 1951. His son and daughter called for the Benedictine friar who had tended him at Dijon and it was this priest who read the burial service.

6

Nordhoff and the New Beginning

IN 1948 it would have been hard for anyone to believe that Volkswagen would within a few years become one of the world's largest car manufacturers, after General Motors, Ford, and Chrysler. Before the currency reform launched German recovery, what little life there was in Wolfsburg centred upon the plant's miniscule production. Even then, its future remained very much in doubt, for it was still classified as war booty. The car itself seemed a sorry reminder of Nazism to almost everyone. To foreigners and many Germans, it was a shabby product of a noxious past; to others, it was a galling reminder of Hitler's failure, here as elsewhere.

The two protagonists in the Volkswagen story were both out of the picture. Hitler, who had seized upon Porsche's dreams and designs for his own reasons, was dead. The designer, who had struggled since the early 1920s to see the car born, was an old, sick man in 1948. Who was there now to pick up the pieces of his vision? At that time, there was no one.

Dr. Hermann Münch, the industrial lawyer whom the British had placed in charge of the plant, was not much interested in the car or its future. He did not understand the car business and presumably cared little for it. His might be called a 'caretaker administration' devoted to maintaining jobs; Münch himself was grateful that he had a good job at a time when any work was welcome.

As for the workers at the Volkswagenwerk, only the few who had been there before the war remembered Porsche's dream. The majority were homeless, drifting refugees, living in a ramshackle town and working in a plant which might shut down for good any day. All were waiting, less for someone to take charge than for the economic situation to change.

In 1947 it was the end of an era for the Volkswagen. All connection with the past had been broken and no fresh start seemed likely.

The car might still be encumbered with the Nazi image, had it not been for the fact that the KdF-Wagen was such a monumental flop. Though it is hard to conceive, the Volkswagenwerk at Wolfsburg never built a VW production model until after Germany's defeat. The first prototypes and the ones which followed were hand-tooled in Stuttgart. A very few Volkswagens were put together at the Wolfsburg plant during the war for the personal use of Ley, Lafferentz and other Nazi Party and government officials. But these were made by hand, as it were, outside the course of regular production. The Kübelwagens and Schwimmwagens produced during the war, while modifications of the VW, were not models of the car Porsche had planned for the civilian population and cannot be considered Volkswagens. Hitler at any rate might never have made a success of this car, even if history had given him the chance. Only 336,668 Germans signed up to buy the car from 1938 to 1945, despite the hoopla and pressure which assailed the ears of millions. Most of the sober populace chose to be prudent, for wages were low in Nazi Germany. Hitler would never have put ten million Germans into KdF-Wagens, as he boasted, nor would he ever have found a market for the 1,500,000 cars his plant was supposed to produce each year.

His arbitrary price of 990 marks could not allow the company to buy new machinery or to expand. The Nazis had plans to obtain such funds by selling the car abroad at a higher price, but these were vague. The factory could have 'succeeded' only as part of a socialised economy, and it is probable that many National Socialists considered it a pilot effort of this kind. German private enterprise survived because of the brief life of Hitler's regime; had it lasted longer, the State would almost certainly have taken over more and more. Manipulating prices and costs, it might have produced a Volkswagen under socialistic conditions, subsidising the company for political reasons. Still, there were other basic flaws in the Nazi plan. They expected, for example, to produce 1·5 million VWs with 30,000 workers, yet today's modern, highly automated plant has only recently reached that production figure and has needed more than three times as many workers to do so. The fact is, of course, that there is little use in speculating about what *might* have happened, nor would the car's fate matter any more than the fate of Porsche's Austria model or, for that matter, Ford's Edsel. The Volkswagen is a phenomenon not only because of what it is technically, but also because of what it has become commercially. It is simply not enough to design a great car. That car must be produced in enough numbers to matter and to affect events. It must then be placed in the hands of an organisation energetic and imaginative enough to build a world-wide market against enormous odds, and must eventually be entrusted to a global network of salesmen capable of turning it into a success. The man under whom all this was accomplished is Heinz Nordhoff.

He was, in some ways, a most unlikely man to do all this. What previous association he had had with the VW caused him to dislike it. He had been inside one only once before he took the job of building it; after the war, a friend once drove him to a railway station in a beetle. Yet he had never driven the Volkswagen itself. He had never seen the inside of the factory. He was no visionary like Porsche, nor is he likely to be remembered for his technical achievements, though they are many. He is instead an American-style (and American-trained) industrial manager placed in charge of a product he at first despised. Today the press calls him 'the master magician of the Volkswagen miracle', yet there is little of the theatrical in his technique. Like sawing a woman in half, once explained, it seems easy.

The success Nordhoff achieved is, of course, apparent to any American used to turnpikes bristling with beetles or to US suburban shopping centres aswarm with bugs. It is apparent to any who visit Wolfsburg, a teeming, uncompleted and heavily damaged village at the war's end, which Nordhoff helped transform into a city exceeding even the youthful dreams of Peter Koller. It is apparent at the sight of the company's other huge German plants in Kassel, Hanover, Brunswick, and Emden, which have, along with the main factory in Wolfsburg, produced 12,000,000 VWs and more, and helped make the beetle the largest-selling single model of a motor-car in the world. Volkswagens are today manufactured in VW factories all over the world: in Australia, South Africa, Mexico, and Brazil, as well as in the Federal Republic of Germany. Volkswagens are assembled outside Germany as well: in Belgium, the Philippines, Venezuela, Uruguay, Paraguay, New Zealand, and in the Republic of Ireland. And, where they are neither manufactured nor assembled, it is certain that German-built VWs are imported and sold, for the beetle and the VW models which have more recently been produced alongside it are without a doubt the world's most truly international motor-cars today.

It has been estimated that at least a quarter of a million persons the world over earn their living by building, transporting, distributing, selling, servicing and—yes, also—repairing Volkswagens, and that these 250,000 support as many as 1,000,000 family members. When one adds to this figure of 1,250,000 all the personnel of service and supply organisations who derive at least part of their incomes from orders placed by Volkswagen, and all those whom Volkswagen employees themselves help support through purchases of their own, the figures become impossible to compile—and almost impossible to imagine. The economic and social benefits poured forth from a huge undertaking like this are staggering. They not only accrue to company shareholders (and VW today has more of these than any corporation except AT&T), but to entire cities (such as Wolfsburg), for as a company like this spends money to earn money, its contribution to economies the world over is immeasurable and by no means abstract. What a motor-car industry can mean to a country like Brazil which never had one; what an inexpensive car can mean to a man setting out in a business of his own; what a well-paid job can mean in places where jobs are scarce and well-paid jobs are scarcer— all this is considerable, and its impact is human. The homeowner in Wolfsburg who today enjoys prosperity and security after living in this city when there was hope for neither can perhaps best be understood in the United States by those Americans who suffered through the unemployment of the Great Depression before they ever met the Affluent Society.

The achievement, it has been said, is Nordhoff's, and many who know the company claim it is a 'one-man show'. Yet this claim of course bears only a limited relation to the truth. What this one man, Heinz Nordhoff, did in fact show was that he knew how to judge other men and attract them to his team. He also had a few tricks up his sleeve, the kind not every industrialist is willing to use. One key trick was integrity; another was a policy of being honest about his car. In an age when many another manufacturer regards potential customers as knuckleheads, those are pretty sneaky weapons. Especially since they worked.

The new era for Volkswagen started at the beginning of 1948 and was launched with an argument. On January 2, Dr. Hermann Münch admitted Heinz Nordhoff to his office, believing that he had come to head production. 'No,' Nordhoff told him, 'I've been put in charge. I'm replacing you.'

Münch could not believe his ears and refused to budge. Nordhoff suggested they telephone Colonel Radclyffe, who had given Nordhoff his assignment. Because Münch hesitated, Nordhoff made the call himself. 'I told Radclyffe I'd be obliged if he'd straighten Dr. Münch out, so I could get to work,' Nordhoff recalls. Münch then talked to Radclyffe also. After hanging up, he said he still wasn't sure he'd been replaced, because Radclyffe had told him to 'iron things out between yourselves'. When Nordhoff heard that, he once more called the Colonel. 'I can't work under these conditions,' he said. 'Either make a clearcut decision or count me out!' This time, Radclyffe agreed to tell Münch he was through and Münch left, quite shattered. 'It was one of the most painful episodes in my life,' Nordhoff told me, 'but it was necessary.'

Münch was not the only one who did not welcome Nordhoff's arrival; Major Hirst reportedly also had his reservations. Many who knew him believe he may have wished to become head of the Volkswagenwerk himself, as much for love of the car as for reasons of personal advancement, but that Colonel Radclyffe was determined to choose 'a good production man'. The one he chose was Nordhoff and Hirst may well have resented his authority, though he had played a part in selecting him. Hirst knew a man like Nordhoff was badly needed, for the factory at the end of 1947 had reached a low point, despite the fact that it had produced almost 20,000 Volkswagens since the end of the war. As Hirst points out in his *REME Journal* account, almost every single one of these cars had gone to the Occupation Forces or to individual members of these forces. There could be little future in this, nor was the factory in any way producing at even the capacity it might have attained then, had an experienced automobile executive headed it. Radclyffe, realising this, searched for one. Nordhoff's name was suggested to him by the Association of Automobile Manufacturers, successor organisation of the RDA, which Radclyffe had helped form.

Who was this Nordhoff, whom *Time* described as 'a compact (5 ft. 10½ in., 165 lb.) man with the steady eyes of a production whiz and the courtly manners of a diplomat'? The war's end in 1945 found Heinz Nordhoff just another homeless, jobless refugee, one among millions dispossessed by the advance of Communism, scraping along on starvation rations. At forty-six, he was no longer a young man and it seemed to him that his most productive years had passed, for the future looked empty of promise.

He was born on January 6, 1899, the second of three sons of an employee of a small bank in Hildesheim. He was christened Heinrich (later also using its variant, Heinz). In 1910–11, the bank failed. Johannes Nordhoff and Heinz's mother, Ottilie Lauenstein-Nordhoff,

lost every penny they owned. Penniless, they moved to Berlin, where
Heinz's father found employment at a small insurance firm and
where he worked his way up to become one of the firm's two directors, 'through unbelievably hard work', as his son recalls with pride.
Heinz was enrolled in a technical high school, for by this time he
had already decided on a career in mechanical engineering. At first
his interest was in ships, but this shifted later on (though his taste for
the sea is still lively and is attested to by ship models in his suite of
offices today). Then came World War I. Despite his youth, he served
in the Army as a private and was wounded in both knees. On his
discharge he went back to school and later to a university. In 1927
he graduated as a certified mechanical engineer from the Berlin-
Charlottenburg Technische Hochschule, or technical university.

Upon graduation, Nordhoff worked on airplane designs at BMW,
the Bavarian Motor Works (Bayerische Motoren-Werke) and soon
developed an even greater interest in automobiles and in the possibility of a future in the growing automobile industry. Looking
around, he became increasingly aware of the fact that 'there existed
an overabundance of technical ideas and construction designs in the
manufacturing field', as one writer puts it. He saw that management
seemed to offer the best opportunity for growth and he decided to
enter automotive production and sales.

He wrote to the Nash company in the United States and, for a
while, it looked as though he might get a job there. Then came the
1929 crash and his hopes were dashed. He was told that there was
not even enough work for Americans. Nordhoff looked elsewhere,
still convinced that an American company would be the place in
which to learn the motor-car business. In Germany, the obvious
choice was Adam Opel, which had just been acquired by General
Motors.

'He was soon confronted—and impressed—by American casual-
ness and fast action,' says *Time*. 'Appearing for an interview,
Nordhoff found his prospective boss in bed with a hangover. When
could Nordhoff start work? In a couple of months, said Nordhoff.
Said the American: "Come next week." '

At the Opel plant in Ruesselsheim, Nordhoff was given the un-
inspiring job of writing service manuals, but a year later was put in
charge of the company's customer service organisation, a stepping-
off point for management jobs. It is typical of the man that he almost
always worked seven days a week and that he spent his vacations on
Opel's production line. The company, spotting his potential, sent

him to the United States to soak up Detroit marketing and production techniques. 'Work was not a duty at Opel,' Nordhoff recalls. 'It
was a sporting event to show what you could do.' In this atmosphere,
his abilities developed and he was soon 'forged into an efficient
successful automaker by General Motors', as one reporter put it. In
1936, he became a member of the Opel board of directors and, from
this position, took a hard look at Hitler's plans for a Volkswagen.
He didn't like what he saw.

Those were not happy days for Adam Opel and his men. The
company itself intended to produce a *Kleinauto*, but Hitler was trying
to frustrate these plans. The dictator's snub of the venerable Geheimrat von Opel at the Berlin Motor Show was an insult to the boss and
a rebuff to the company which Opel management men could not
easily overlook. It festered in many of them until it produced, as it
did in Heinz Nordhoff, a strong dislike of 'that car of Hitler's'.

In 1939 Nordhoff was sent to Berlin, and in 1942 he took charge
of the company's nearby Brandenburg lorry factory, the largest in
Europe, which produced four thousand units per month. By that
time, of course, the Opel factories had been seized by the Nazi
authorities. 'Despite bombings, shortages, and personal privation,
he produced heavy trucks,' wrote Charles Barnard in *True* magazine.
'Whatever was going on down at the people's car ranch at Schulenburg's swampy acres, was no concern to him in those days—except
as it might be the butt of a motor manufacturer's private joke. . . .'

Nordhoff took his family with him to the new job in Berlin. In
1933, he had married his childhood sweetheart, Charlotte Fassunge,
and in the course of time they had two daughters. (Both are today
involved with Volkswagen, each after her own fashion. The elder,
Barbara, has worked for VW for several years, now lives in New
York City and works in the public relations department of Volks-
wagen of America, Inc. Her sister, Elisabeth, forged a Porsche–VW–
Nordhoff dynasty in 1959, by marrying Ernst Piëch, oldest son of
Ferdinand Porsche's daughter Louise Piëch.) Nordhoff worked at
Brandenburg until almost the very end of the war.

Nordhoff's wife and daughters had been evacuated from Berlin in
1944 to escape the heavy bombings and were now living in one room
of a large hilltop house in the Harz Mountains. As the end of the war
drew near, Nordhoff contracted pneumonia and the cellar life which
the day-and-night air raids demanded made it worse. He was ordered
out of the city to recuperate and joined his family in the Harz.

The last days of the war were approaching when Nordhoff had

fully recovered and he was now anxious to return to Berlin. 'He didn't want his workers to face the end of the war alone,' Barbara Nordhoff says. 'He knew there would be chaos there, so he made plans to get back and help as best he could. Mother pleaded with him not to go and he promised to sleep on it. The next morning, he and Mother went for a long walk along the ridge of the mountain. Because he had always hunted, he customarily carried binoculars with him, and did so that day too. While he and Mother were debating his return to Berlin, they saw clouds of dust rising in the distance. Father trained his binoculars on the dust and saw that these were American troops, advancing on the area. Thank God they came, for it meant he couldn't go back to Berlin. They had cut him off. If the troops hadn't come and he had decided to go, he would have had to drive by night with no lights on his car and that would have been very dangerous. He might also have never come back. He probably would have suffered the fate of the other Opel executives who were still in Berlin. They were deported to Russia and have never been heard of since.'

From their mountaintop, they watched the battle raging below, as the American troops advanced through the valley and met the German defenders in the hills. 'We knew the war was over and thought it was foolish for them to continue fighting,' Barbara says, 'but it was terrible to see anyway. They were our countrymen, after all, and we were watching them being killed.' A short while later, an American unit pulled up in front of the house and a US Army command post was set up in the living room. 'Because Father knew American-style English from his years with GM,' Barbara recalls, 'the American commander invited him down to the living room, where he could watch the progress of the battle on a map spread across a card table. I was twelve years old then and I can remember hearing them talk in a language I didn't understand at all. I was ill at the time, and an American Army doctor looked after me.'

Once the battles were over, Heinz Nordhoff made plans to get back to work again. Because his own plant was now in the Soviet Zone of Occupation, he felt he should report for duty at Opel headquarters in Ruesselsheim, near Frankfurt/Main, in the US Zone. He was able to locate a charcoal-powered van and he and Barbara made the trip west together with a driver. There, he deposited her with friends and returned to the Harz to fetch his wife and other daughter. By the time he reached them, the American troops had left and no one knew to whom the mountain area would fall. (As it turned out, most

Production of the Kübelwagen reaches 1000 in 1940

The amphibious Schwimmkübel with snorkel and propeller

Above: Soldiers and civilians watch barracks burn after an air raid in 1944, damaging plant and housing. *Below:* Bomb damage to the factory, 1944. Note the wrecked aircraft wings, produced at the plant in World War II, in the bottom right-hand corner

Major Hirst (*left foreground*) talking to Rudolph Brörmann, with his back to the camera, while Brörmann was production chief, 1945–46

British officers and VW workers celebrate a milestone. W/Cdr. Berryman, Major Hirst and Rudolph Brörmann are on the right

The 10,000th VW comes off the production line in 1946, covered with workers' scrawled demands for more and better food

Above: Porsche (*centre*) sees the first turbine started at the factory in 1939. The tall man behind him is Bodo Lafferentz. *Below:* Ten years later (*on the right*) Ludwig Erhard, former Chancellor of West Germany and Economics Minister at the time this photograph was taken, talking to Colonel C. R. Radclyffe (*centre*) during the 1949 ceremonies which officially returned the Volkswagenwerk to the Germans. Heinz Nordhoff is second from the left of the region ended up being assigned to the Soviets.) The trip back to Ruesselsheim was frightening, because they could not be sure which troops were occupying the area. They drove fast and used only back roads so as to avoid a possible encounter with the Soviets. They knew what all of them would face at the hands of Red Army soldiers.

Reunited in Ruesselsheim, all four Nordhoffs lived together in one hotel room, until they were given a small flat and Nordhoff was set to work at Opel. 'It was obvious, however, that they were just keeping him busy,' Barbara says, 'and he was very unhappy. He doesn't like being a fifth wheel.' Shortly thereafter, the American occupation authorities charged everyone in their Zone who had served in a supervisory capacity with being a Nazi and Nordhoff was out of a job. Then came an offer from Hamburg and, leaving his family behind so that they would at least be certain of a place in which to live, he travelled north into the British Zone. There the widow of an old friend who owned an Opel dealership had asked him to manage what was left of the business. And so it was that the former general manager of Europe's largest lorry factory and the future head of Germany's largest industrial enterprise began work running a small repair shop. He was grateful for the job at that, because just staying alive and providing for a family was a job in itself at the time.

In late 1947, Colonel Radclyffe contacted him and offered him the job of running the Volkswagenwerk. Nordhoff met the Colonel in Minden and told him he felt loyal to GM and still expected that he would be called back; he was therefore not interested. Radclyffe, however, insisted he think it over and return for another talk and Nordhoff urged the Colonel to cable a friend of Nordhoff's at GM in Detroit, to find out what the chances were of his getting back again.

The day before he returned to meet Radclyffe a second time, Nordhoff received a letter from US Military Government, declaring that persons in Nordhoff's category (former executives) would never be able to work again in the American Zone except as manual labourers. 'It was probably a routine announcement,' Nordhoff said, 'but the coincidence of its arriving the day before I was to meet Radclyffe helped decide my fate.'

When Nordhoff arrived at the Colonel's office, Radclyffe handed him a letter from Detroit. It was evasive and Nordhoff felt certain he could never go back to GM. When he got through reading it, he tossed over the letter he had received from US Military Government and he and Radclyffe had a good laugh. 'Well, I'm ready,' Nordhoff said. Radclyffe asked him whether there were any conditions he wanted set.

'I have only one,' Heinz Nordhoff answered. 'I want no interference from any side.'

'Does that mean the British as well?' Radclyffe asked.

'It means the British first of all!' Nordhoff answered.

'All right,' Colonel Radclyffe replied. 'You have a free hand.'

During Christmas week, 1947, Frank Novotny of the Press Department at the 'Wolfsburg Motor Works' received a telephone call at his home from Dr. Münch. 'Herr Nordhoff is in my office,' Münch said. 'Would you please come down and tell him some things about the factory?' Münch sent over his car and Novotny was driven to his first encounter with Nordhoff. They talked about an hour and Nordhoff asked countless questions about the people at the plant and about the factory itself. 'All this time, Münch said nothing,' Novotny reports. 'But I don't think he was worried about being thrown out, because he was not only general manager but also the German trustee for the plant and he expected to continue at least in the latter capacity.' (Aside from Münch, the trustees were all British. At Nordhoff's later insistence, trustees lost their authority and, eventually, the trustee system was abolished entirely.)

The bushy-browed, portly and short executive whom Heinz Nordhoff was meeting for the first time that day was one of several of those there already who would later play key roles in the development of the company. Julius Paulsen, who has headed purchasing at the factory ever since 1943, was then desperately, ingeniously, and ultimately successfully, searching for materials to buy for the plant. Hans Hiemenz, who had joined VW in 1940 and who had been in charge of finances since 1942, was also there at the time, playing another vital part in the company's lean 'British years'. It was his task to re-establish the company's credits and financial standing at a time when no one knew who owned the plant or even how long it might remain functioning. Otto Hoehne and Joseph Werner of the 'German-American contingent' were there also, of course. Two others who played major roles in the immediate postwar years and who were to play even larger roles under Heinz Nordhoff's management were the late Dr. Karl Feuereissen, who headed Volkswagen sales and service until he died (at work) in June 1955, and Wilhelm Steinmeier, now retired, who in those years was Otto Hoehne's boss, in charge of production at the Wolfsburg plant. It was in 1946 that

Steinmeier received a letter from the British, asking him whether he might be interested in heading production at the Volkswagenwerk; he thought it over for a month and then accepted, 'never thinking I'd remain so long with VW', he later said. 'The conditions under which we worked were unbelievable,' he reports. 'The worst thing of course was this shortage of materials. We could get them only through barter and Julius Paulsen even had it figured out that one car was worth a four weeks' supply of steel.' Steinmeier later rose to deputy general manager (*stellvertretender Geschäftsführer*) of the company and retired at the start of 1962, when he reached the age of seventy. By that time, Otto Hoehne had already succeeded him as production chief.

The achievement of Dr. Karl Feuereissen defies a brief description, for the 'Volkswagen miracle' that took place in the Nordhoff era resulted in large part from the efforts of this singular and dedicated man. He provided the 'missing link' in the corporation, for while the car and a factory which could be repaired and modernised did exist at war's end, the Volkswagenwerk had not a single dealer anywhere. It had no sales or service organisation, within Germany or outside it; no parts depots or policies; no shipping or transportation facilities. The factory could manufacture cars, but there was no one to get these to customers, nor anyone to sell, service, or repair the cars once they had been bought. Setting up a worldwide network from absolute scratch was Feuereissen's job. He brought to it a passionate and lifelong interest in motor vehicles, derived from an association with the industry which dated back to 1924, when he took charge of sporting activities for the German motor-cycle drivers' association of the time. This led to a post with the German Automobile Club, the ADAC, and in time brought him to the attention of Baron K. D. von Oertzen of Auto-Union, who had met him at races throughout Europe. In 1935, von Oertzen offered Feuereissen, then thirty-eight years old, the job of running an Auto-Union racing team—a job which led to Feuereissen's close and abiding friendship with the top aces of the era, as well as with the designer of Auto-Union's racing cars, Ferdinand Porsche. Feuereissen, who had been a flight lieutenant in World War I, served as a major with the Luftwaffe during World War II, but in 1944 he was released, at Porsche's request, to serve VW at its offices in Berlin. It was there that the end of the war caught him and, after a time as a farm labourer in East Germany, Feuereissen joined the millions of refugees streaming west. It was only natural that he would head for Wolfsburg and, once there, go immediately to work. It did not bother him that there seemed to be no future here; Feuereissen had a Germanic faith that work for its own sake was rewarding enough. He set up a tiny office made of cardboard walls, in the large hall which is now the lunchroom of the factory's Sector I, and began to plan marketing strategy. What ultimately came out of this workshop was an incredible worldwide organisation which today encompasses more than 2000 VW service facilities within West Germany and more than 6000 outside it, and which today has made the Volkswagenwerk the largest exporter of motor vehicles in the world. It was also Feuereissen's task to begin VW advertising, sales promotion, product publicity, and merchandising; it was he who helped give VW the distinct 'style' for which it has since become known. When he was laid to rest in Wolfsburg's Forest cemetery, his funeral was attended by thousands from near and far away who either had known him for a decade in Wolfsburg or for twenty or more years in the industry. The loss to the company was severe. Expressing his own shock and dismay at the sudden, unexpected death of the fifty-eight-year-old executive, Nordhoff said: 'It will be a long time before I know for certain that I can't any longer find my way out of a difficult situation by saying, "I'll have to talk this one over with Feuereissen . . ." '

Of these early veterans, some deceased, some retired, many still very much on the job at VW, Hiemenz, Hoehne, Novotny, and Paulsen are today members of the company Vorstand. All of them and, indeed, all of the others who lived through those early years have sagas of frustration and achievement of their own to tell, for World War II and the immediate postwar years shaped turbulent destinies even for those who might have preferred tranquillity. It is impossible here to tell even a representative sampling of such stories, but one brief personal account in any case requires recounting, for it in its own way mirrors the chaos of the 1945–48 period, as well as helps to introduce the new era about to begin. It concerns Frank Novotny, the man who met Heinz Nordhoff at Christmastime, 1947, in Dr. Münch's office. Novotny is today in charge of a host of activities at the company, running not only public relations, but community, governmental and industrial relations as well. 'He is the kind of man who always lands on his feet,' one reporter remarked, and what must have attracted Heinz Nordhoff early to this executive is a certain 'American style' he has about him, a way of doing business with which Nordhoff had become familiar at GM's Opel. One VW executive explains it this way: 'When Nordhoff took over, he met a lot of people at the plant who were completely dispirited. The ones to whom he gravitated were, naturally, those who had not let the times destroy them. Novotny was one of these. He got things done.'

Just how enterprising he proved himself may be seen from events in his life immediately after the war's end. 1945 found him and his wife in their home town of Prague; there and in Vienna, Novotny had a prospering export-import business of his own. As the Russians approached the city, Novotny sent his wife west, to the very Harz Mountains where Nordhoff and his own family were waiting out the end of the war. Mrs. Novotny arrived at nearby Fallersleben an hour before the American Army rolled in and never did get to the mountain retreat. Instead, she settled in nearby Wolfsburg.

Frank Novotny stayed on in Czechoslovakia for two months after the Soviets entered Prague and then set out for Blankenburg in the Harz Mountains, where he expected to find his wife. There a friend told him she had heard his wife had gone to Wolfsburg, and Novotny set out in his car once more. He reached a narrow river and found the Russians on his side of the bridge, letting no one cross, and American soldiers on the far end. Novotny thought fast and reached into his wallet, pulling out a wrinkled honorary press card he had been given on a 1933 visit to Chicago and which he had kept more or less as a souvenir ever since. He called out to the Americans that he was a war correspondent whom the Russians were trying to detain and one of the GIs responded by crossing the river to look at Novotny's card. 'Oh, you're from Chicago,' the soldier said. 'You're a gangster!'

'I certainly am!' Novotny answered in English. The reply seemed to satisfy the soldier that Novotny really did come from Chicago and he persuaded the Russians to let him pass and cross the river.

The wrinkled old press credentials saved the day for Novotny several more times before he reached Wolfsburg and on one occasion provided him with fuel for his car. Novotny had flashed his card to some British soldiers and told them he was an American correspondent trying to do a story about a nearby Nazi concentration camp. The British unit filled up his car and the soldiers waved him on. Finally, Novotny arrived in Wolfsburg. It was summer of 1945 and Novotny surveyed the scene to determine how an enterprising man could make a living there.

As it turned out, his knowledge of English proved invaluable. On one occasion, he saved a farmer from being executed by the British for possessing two guns, and out of gratitude the farmer allowed Novotny unlimited amounts of foodstuffs. After a while, Novotny had established himself with the British as a sort of counsel and negotiator for farmers throughout the area who needed to deal with the Occupation Forces.

Strolling in the woods or walking the streets of Wolfsburg, he used to encounter Dr. Münch frequently, and before long the two men began to pass the time of day. 'Münch often complained that newspapers were attacking the VW,' Novotny reports, 'and when he brought the subject up again one day in 1946, I asked whether he didn't have someone who provided the newspapers with information and in general handled press relations.' Münch remarked that he didn't have such a person on the staff, and after a while, he asked if Novotny might like to take the job.

Four weeks after this conversation, Novotny wrote the words 'Press Bureau' on a piece of paper and put it up outside his new office door in the VW factory. About an hour later, Major Hirst came by and said that he had noticed the sign. 'You ought to change the wording to read "Public Relations",' Hirst suggested. The paper was removed, reworded, and put up again. It is a safe bet that this scrap of paper made the Volkswagenwerk the first postwar German factory to have a public relations department of its own. It is today also the only German enterprise of major consequence to have a public relations executive on its Vorstand.

Novotny, who had been prosperous in Czechoslovakia, now told Münch that he wanted 2000 marks a month in pay, which caused some consternation, as the highest salary in the plant at the time was 1000 marks. Novotny thereupon agreed to work for nothing until they could agree on what his work would be. 'I'd been doing all right and didn't need the money,' he explains. 'I worked from June to December 1946 for nothing, but after everyone there insisted I had to be paid, we finally settled on 850 marks a month, retroactive to the time I started.'

The times are also mirrored in the experiences of Joseph Werner, who until the war's end headed chassis, motor, and transmission production at the VW factory. He had left Wolfsburg by 1947—for good, he thought. At the end of the war, he had gone to Austria to work with Ferdinand Porsche and had returned to Wolfsburg's chaotic conditions some time later. But the nearby Russians constantly harrassed the town and the atmosphere was charged with tension and fear. Wing Commander Berryman reports that all the British officers in 1945 and 1946 kept cars constantly waiting outside whatever building they might be at, ready to jump in and get out if the Russians decided to take over the city. Werner, like the British, also had a car at the ready. Finally, he and his wife had enough of the uncertain atmosphere and left, hoping to get to the United States, but an American consul in Munich told them they had no chance at all. The outer office was jammed with displaced persons and Jewish refugees. 'They come first,' the consul said. Then, one day in 1947, while Werner was sitting on a bench in Munich, passing time, two British officers pulled up in a Volkswagen and asked him to return. After thinking it over for a while, he decided to go back after all. He and his wife had been living off CARE packages sent by friends in America; these contained cigarettes which, at the time, could buy almost anything. But he was anxious to find work again. Since 1959, he has headed the company's transporter and engine works in Hanover.

'I had never even heard of Nordhoff before he started on the job,' Werner says, 'but I remember being impressed with him during those first days, watching him as he walked around the plant and talked to the workers. He was encouraging them—one might say appealing to them—to stay on the job. I don't know whether he really believed in the Volkswagen's future at the time, but he sounded convincing.'

Nordhoff did more than come to work: he moved in, bag and baggage. For six months, he lived inside the factory, separated from his family. He slept on a cot in a room near his office. At night, he says, he 'was kept awake by the sound of rats racing through the empty plant searching for scraps of food'. He was not living in the factory because of dedication, he says, but simply because no suitable quarters were available in town. Still, his night-and-day presence at the plant had a psychological effect on the largely demoralised work force.

'I had to start from scratch in the real sense of the word,' Nordhoff has said. 'Seven thousand workers were painfully producing at the rate of a mere 6000 cars a year—provided it did not rain too much. Most of the roof and all the windows of the factory had been destroyed. Pools of stagnant water were under foot . . .

'When I came to Wolfsburg, I was as poor as a churchmouse . . . I was hungry too, and about 60 pounds under my present weight. All the people I met in the factory were not only as poor and hungry as myself, they were desperate and without hope. Nobody belonged to Wolfsburg . . . and what remained was only a torso, abandoned after its founder had proved to be the greatest flop in our history and a criminal in every sense of the word . . .

'It was really an overwhelming undertaking to make these people believe in their future at a time when one Chesterfield cigarette had three times the value in buying power of one hour of hard work. They had to be convinced that there was a future which could be won only by themselves. It could be won only by the hard work of creating something of value.'

The size of the job Nordhoff faced in reassuring the workers can be seen from the way today's production chief, Otto Hoehne, describes the times. 'There were many days on which I came to work with shaky knees and an empty stomach,' he says. 'And at the end of the day, my knees would be even shakier and my stomach emptier. That winter the assembly line workers stood in water up over their ankles when it rained. Some of them had to work outside and were protected only by a makeshift sheet-metal "roof". We had to keep fires burning near the machines so the hydraulic fluid wouldn't freeze.'

On one of his very first days on the job, Heinz Nordhoff showed Frank Novotny a speech he wanted to deliver over the plant's public address system. It was largely political and fiercely anti-Nazi; clearly Nordhoff wanted to get a lot of sentiments off his chest. Novotny, however, convinced him otherwise. No matter how much he agreed with Nordhoff, he convinced him that a pep talk would be better, because after all, some of the workers might well resent a political talk like that. Nordhoff acquiesced. He admitted he was more interested in winning over the workers than in lecturing them about the past.

'His arrival had a tremendous impact,' recalls Günter Hellman, later Volkswagen parts manager for Canada, who started out in Wolfsburg in 1945. 'Everybody was in a rut before Nordhoff came. We had no food or materials to speak of and no one had any real idea where we were heading. When Nordhoff came and took charge, he just quietly got everything moving. It wasn't anything specific that he did which changed the atmosphere. You just felt his presence, felt he was there and had taken firm command.'

'One of the first things Nordhoff did,' says Otto Hoehne, 'was to survey world markets and plan a global service organisation. No one had even thought that way before!'

Not only was a service organisation being built, but a sales organisation was being developed as well. Nordhoff—'a great organiser', as Novotny describes him—set up a table of organisation and assigned duties all around. The production department, the finance department and the personnel department were formalised and the latter was charged as much with finding food for the workers as with finding the workers themselves. A purchasing department was represented on the board and Nordhoff insisted immediately upon an inspection department as well, showing that he meant business about quality production even then.

Despite all the activity, Nordhoff himself felt too little was being done. 'After two months, I knew things could not continue this way,' he says. 'There was an air of desperation and confusion. No one even knew how many hours it took to build a car, but it must have been 300 or 400.'

He decided to be brutally frank to the workers and had them all assemble in one of the large halls of the plant.

'He spoke,' says *Der Spiegel*, 'in a dry, even, effortless tone. But his sentences were honed to a sharp, ironic point. He did not rely on gestures or grimaces. Even as his eyes swept round the hall, they seemed to rest on an imaginary point. A self-confident, somewhat malicious smile tugged down the corners of his mouth whenever he paused.'

Nordhoff addressed the workers as partners in the enterprise. The approach was realistic and not patronising, for Nordhoff and his workers *were* in fact 'partners'. Nordhoff represented neither stockholders nor a board of directors, for the company's status had not been clarified at the time and it literally belonged to no one. The only interest to be served, therefore, was that of the work force. Nordhoff felt himself part of that. He had no contract, no assured future. In every way, he and his workers were in the same position. And so, he felt, he could afford to be frank and tough.

'For the first time in its history,' he told them, 'the Volkswagenwerk will this year have to face the necessity of standing on its own feet. It is up to us to make this largest of all German motor-car factories a decisive factor for Germany's peacetime economy.'

He then discussed how he proposed to go about doing this. He pointed out that it now took the workers as much as four hundred hours of labour to produce a car. 'If we continue in this manner, we shall not continue for long,' he said. 'We must reach one hundred hours per car!'

A muffled groan swept through the ranks of workers, followed by laughter. 'They all thought I was crazy,' Nordhoff says, 'but they began working harder.'

That speech helped change the climate. The workers could see that they finally had a boss who knew the car business. 'Somehow,' said one who remembers the period, 'you could feel Nordhoff's presence almost at once. There was a new spirit that was contagious. I had worked here under Dr. Münch. Whenever one of the British officers wanted to talk with Münch, he would say, "Go tell Münch I want to see him in my office." And I would deliver the message and Münch would hurry over to get his orders. In those days, any young British lieutenant was more important around here than Münch. There was a picture of King George in every office. Then, when Nordhoff came, it changed. I remember the day when Major Hirst said to me, "Go tell Nordhoff I want to see him . . . No, never mind, I'll go to his office myself. . . ." '

There was other evidence of the newly independent spirit. Nordhoff had two signs removed: one on a parking lot which said, 'For British Officers Only', and another, outside the plant, which said, in English, 'Wolfsburg Motor Works'. He replaced the latter with a German sign: VOLKSWAGENWERK. The significance of this act was not lost on his workers.

Nordhoff recalls that he changed those signs on his very first day in the job or immediately afterwards. 'A friend had driven me to the Volkswagen factory on my first day,' Nordhoff says, 'but he refused to drive me further than the canal. The factory grounds were in such bad shape that he was afraid his car would never survive if he tried to drive me all the way to the headquarters building. I remember thinking when I first saw the factory that it looked just as it must have looked after the last bomb had exploded in it; then, on the way in, I saw those British signs and made a mental note to have them taken down. Later, when I asked my secretary to have that done, several people were afraid I would bring down the wrath of the British on us, but as it turned out, they let it pass without comment.'

It might be noted in this connection that signs reading 'Volkswagenwerk' were really unlikely to outrage the British, for they themselves employed the designation 'Volkswagenwerk GmbH' in official correspondence, using it either interchangeably with or in addition to their own 'Wolfsburg Motor Works'. Volkswagenwerk GmbH, incidentally, was the name of the company which had been set up to manufacture the KdF-Wagen before the war, and it continued on as the name of the postwar company until public ownership transformed that into a corporation with the name of Volkswagenwerk AG.[1]

Nordhoff himself provides the background for the story regarding Major Hirst's summons to the new company general manager. On the day he took command, he says, Nordhoff received a telephone call from Major Hirst. 'He asked me to come to his office,' Nordhoff recalls, 'and I knew then that this was the crucial moment for me to show I was in charge and was not to be marched about. So I told Major Hirst that I was busy just then, but that *he* could come to see me in *my* office at eleven o'clock. When he agreed, I knew I was truly in command here.'

Now Nordhoff also was beginning to have some hope. Soon after he came to the plant, he test-drove the VW for the first time. 'The "repulsive Porsche-Invention" . . . was not just another small car,' he discovered. 'It had definite features which were greatly desirable and not found in cars of comparable size.' The Volkswagen he had despised now seemed to him 'an extraordinarily amazing motor-car with a special personality [and] unlimited possibilities'. With this realisation came a new enthusiasm for the job. By the end of 1950, he would be able to say with less braggadocio than confidence: 'It is my life's aim to make this plant into the greatest car factory in Europe!'

With pride, he reminisces: 'This was a time of political extremists and gangsters, but it was also a time when faith, and willingness, through hard work, to build rather than destroy, made possible the miracle that is Wolfsburg. In this respect, the job of reinstalling hope and confidence in the hearts of desperate people was a much more difficult task than getting a line of presses back in operation. But somebody had to show them the way, and that I did.'

Yet there was—in addition to the countless other difficulties—one

1. A word about German corporate terminology may be helpful. The initials *GmbH* stand for *Gesellschaft mit beschränkter Haftung* or 'limited liability company', while AG stands for *Aktien-gesellschaft* (literally 'stock company'), or a corporation owned by shareholders. Two other German terms, employed in all 'AG' corporations such as today's Volkswagenwerk, require explanation. One is *Aufsichtsrat* and the other *Vorstand*. The former corresponds to a board of directors more or less as it is known elsewhere; it is two-thirds composed of shareholder represen-tatives (including in VW's case the Federal Republic of Germany and the *Land*, or state, of Lower Saxony) and one-third of labour. The Vorstand, with whose members we are here more concerned, are referred to often as 'a 'board of management', but perhaps may better be compared to a cor-porate 'executive committee'. The head of the corporation serves as the Vorstand chairman and the various Vorstand members are either in charge of departments or divisions of the enterprise, or have sundry other responsibilities. Membership in this executive committee introduces an executive into a corporation's top ranks and the title he has is that of *Vorstandsmitglied*, or Vorstand member. (The title *Prokurist* signifies an officer who can act in the name of the corporation. A member of the Vorstand, while he is of course an officer also, abandons use of any Prokurist title he may have had, once he reaches executive committee rank.)

more factor beyond his control which he had to face. In 1948, a little more than two months after Nordhoff took charge, the British decided to make one last attempt to give the plant away, this time to Henry Ford II.

The meeting with Ford and his executives, still keenly remembered by Nordhoff, took place in an 'Allies-only' hotel in Cologne in March 1948, and he recalls needing special authorisation to attend. Breech's evaluation of the plant as 'not worth a damn' saved the day.

One other incident is worth recording in connection with attempts to give the Volkswagenwerk away. In mid-1948, the Soviets expressed their 'willingness' to take the Volkswagenwerk off the hands of the British authorities. By this time, however, the British were planning to turn the company over to the West German authorities, who were forming a central government for the British, French, and American Zones of Occupation. (The formal transfer occurred on October 8, 1949.) Relations between the Western powers and the Soviets had already cooled drastically, and the Berlin Blockade had begun in June. Despite this, the Soviets offered a plan whereby they could take the factory over 'conveniently'. Since Wolfsburg lies just five miles west of the Soviet Zone border, the Russians suggested that the boundary be shifted just this small distance, so as to place both plant and town inside East Germany. The offer was firmly declined. Town and factory would remain in the Free World. Now Nordhoff could really get to work.

7

The Years of Fulfilment

GERMANY was beginning to stir again. The changed climate of the Cold War forced the Western Allies to reassess their policies toward the vanquished foe. Military government retreated into the background or changed to mufti. Germans began to rule themselves again. The nation's industry, flattened more by defeat than by wartime bombings, was once more set into motion.

'The year 1948,' says the Bonn government, 'will be recorded in German history as the pivotal point in the postwar economy of the present Federal Republic. Two almost simultaneous developments served to lift the economy out of the morass: the currency reform of June 20 and the advent of American Marshall Plan aid.' Eventually, this aid was to total more than 14,000 million marks.

Overnight, 170,000 million Reichsmarks in banks and in circulation shrivelled to about 10,000 million new Deutsche marks (or 'D-marks'). Combined with the US aid, the new hard currency stabilised the economy and provided it with a basis for growth. A free-enterprise economy was established, and Heinz Nordhoff believes it was this lifting of restrictions on industry that was even more responsible for the subsequent growth of the West German economy than was the currency reform itself. 'We at VW never asked for Marshall aid,' he says, 'because we felt we didn't need it. We were, however, indirect beneficiaries of this aid, because many of our suppliers received it and were thereby able to raise the quality of the products they sold us.'

The psychological boost which the lifting of restrictions provided started business of all kinds moving again. Germans with things to sell—farmers at first, manufacturers later—did so, sure of the value of the new paper money, which was pegged at 4·20 to the dollar.[1]

1. As of September 1949; today it stands at slightly less than four to the dollar and 11·11 to the pound.

Shops which had remained empty for years now began to fill up again. The cigarette-economy was snuffed out. It finally made sense again to manufacture. For the Volkswagenwerk, the times meant that an attempt could now be made to sell to Germans and not just to produce for the occupation forces. For Nordhoff, it meant that he might actually have a business to run, not just a factory.

Ultimately, Major Hirst left Wolfsburg altogether and the remaining British moved out slowly thereafter, unit by unit. 'After a few months,' says Heinz Nordhoff, 'I had the place to myself.'

And what a place it was! The factory buildings were a shambles; the turnover of workers was almost as great as in 1946 (and it was 100 per cent then); the makeshift town would have to be built if Nordhoff were ever to attract—and hold—competent help; the company had no dealers, no salesmen, no sales organisation— virtually nothing. Worst of all, there was no cash.

Amazingly, there was also no cost-accounting system. Under Dr. Münch, the plant had no accurate idea of what it cost to produce a Volkswagen—and, indeed, the cost of one sedan often bore little relation to the cost of the next. Nordhoff quickly corrected this basic flaw in the system.

He needed money to do the rest. He had no one to turn to and no foreign country helped him. The German government, as he remarked later, didn't even notice the Volkswagenwerk until it found to its surprise that VW had become the biggest taxpayer in the state of Lower Saxony. Bankers remained as horrified of the VW as they had been whenever Ferdinand Porsche talked to them of a 'people's car'.

Nordhoff tried to introduce the VW in the United States in order to raise hard currency. An emissary went to the States in 1948; Nordhoff himself followed in 1949. When both attempts failed, he realised that 'we would have to make our own way in the world without a source of American dollars'.[1]

The week of the currency reform proved critical for the company —and resulted in the only occasion on which Nordhoff ever borrowed money for the Volkswagenwerk. The currency reform had cut Volkswagenwerk's cash on hand to 62,000 of the new marks. 'Our 7000 workers needed between 300,000 and 500,000 DM to be paid,' Nordhoff says, 'and we had only five days in which to raise that sum.' He did not want to ask his workers to wait two weeks until sales supplied the new funds; he felt it was essential they be paid on time,

1. For this visit and the story of VWs growth in the USA, see Chapters 11–13.

or they might lose what faith they had in the new currency. He telephoned some of the dealers and distributors who had already been appointed by Dr. Feuereissen and asked them for a short-term loan, to be repaid in two weeks. The day before pay-day, they arrived, cash in hand. One of them, company historians recall, showed up with a suitcase full of money, which popped open upon arrival. 'Notes to the value of 175,000 D-mark were blown merrily over the place—an enormous fortune, a rare sight indeed,' reported VW *Informationen*, a company magazine. 'Even Croesus would not have caused more excitement . . .'

By late 1948 the Volkswagenwerk had established the beginnings of a good distributor-and-dealer organisation. It was the only German motor manufacturing company to be functioning this soon after the end of the war; its 'head start' enabled it to sign up many motor dealers who earlier had handled other makes. Some, like those who had handled the now-defunct Adler, were looking for another car to sell; others, such as BMW and Auto-Union dealers, were also ready then to sign up with VW. Now that people had the new currency with which to buy, they began to sell.

Gradually, cash reserves grew. This was quickly followed by a demand for higher wages. Faced with this demand—which he feared would jeopardise the company's growing financial strength—Nordhoff in 1949 decided again to talk tough and be frank with his workers.

'If we kill the cow on whose milk we want to live later, just because it has fattened up a little—as we are advised to do by those who want to make the people happy—then we shall have no future, we shall go to the dogs, the whole lot of us, and our grandchildren will curse us because we did not think of them, but only of the present.'

He instituted a policy—which continues—of reporting completely and regularly to his entire work-force. It was, and remains, an unusual policy for Germany—and, indeed, for industry in general. It seemed to Nordhoff an essential one, however, if he were to obtain his workers' full co-operation, even to the extent of having them voluntarily defer requests for wage increases. He addresses his 'fellow workers' (as he calls them) every three months and circulates bulletins to them as well. Orally and on paper, he spells out the company's financial position and its prospects in plain language and blunt words. The news for the most part has been good ever since he started his quarterly meetings, but the honesty of the approach also tided the company over the first difficult years of extreme hardship.

Despite the austerity and the poor living conditions many of the workers had to endure in those years, morale at the plant was high, for pride in workmanship had begun. The atmosphere is recalled by Guenter Kittel, today VW vice-president for parts in the USA, who then worked in Wolfsburg as a packer in the parts department. 'The workers took a real pride in the idea of helping the words "Made in Germany" stand for top craftsmanship once again,' he says, 'and the strict and rigid inspection procedure initiated in those years helped to give them this feeling. There was also pride in working in this plant, because Volkswagenwerk paid higher wages than anyone else in manufacturing in West Germany, and jobs in Wolfsburg were at a premium at the time.' A freeze had been put on employment in order to keep costs down, because money was needed for reinvestment purposes. Heinz Nordhoff today notes with pride that Volkswagen has earned every Pfennig of its own money through reinvestments and sales. The same policy of reinvesting earnings, it should be noted, was followed in other segments of German industry and contributed in great part to the German 'economic miracle'. In the ten years following 1948, the country's gross national product and level of industrial production rose sharply, surpassing 1936 levels; by 1958, West Germany's aggregate G.N.P. stood 77 per cent higher than in 1936 and manufactured goods 116 per cent higher. This was achieved by a nation-wide practice of each year reinvesting 23 to 25 per cent of the G.N.P. into maintenance and expansion of plant and equipment.

The future which Nordhoff saw in those early years seemed implausible to many at the plant. The immediate present loomed large; the problem of providing food for the workers and of setting the plant in order seemed the biggest immediate concern to the average worker. Cash, now available through the modest start in sales, made an effort in both directions possible. Nordhoff opened up kitchens and provided his workers with one meal a day, a meal that may well have been the most nourishing one of the day for them. Factory farms, beside the plant buildings, cash purchases, and cars bartered for food, helped make this possible. Hungry men, Nordhoff knew, could not do much of anything.

As money trickled in, the factory was repaired and enlarged. More than three million square feet of plant and offices were rebuilt; another four hundred thousand square feet of factory space was created after Nordhoff reshuffled machinery and placed the huge assembly line under one roof, where it belonged from the very start.

He was beginning to reconstruct the plant along the 'American' lines envisioned by Ferdinand Porsche, for he, like the designer, had been on pilgrimages to Detroit.

At the end of 1948, so much was still destroyed in West Germany that a German magazine felt called upon to cheer its readers with the unexpected news emerging from Wolfsburg.

'So much now lies in ruins and ashes,' the *Stern* said, 'but the Volkswagen factory is still standing. What is more important, however, about 8,000 men are working again. On the average, a new Volkswagen leaves the conveyor belt once every three and a half minutes.'[1]

The editors pointed out that 'sceptics' regard the VW as the private property of the 'Occupying Powers'; *Stern* said 'readers will be astonished to hear that [their] current requirements . . . are comparatively small.' During the three months from September to November 1948, only 300 VWs went to the occupation authorities, while 2154 Volkswagens were produced in October alone. Of these, 1270 were sold to Germans and the rest were exported. 'At the moment,' *Stern* added, 'there is a waiting list of 15,000 for Volkswagens in Germany. And about 7000 export orders are outstanding.'

Publications issued by the Volkswagenwerk reflect the company's attitude toward its past. While they refer to these days as a time 'of almost forgotten sorrows', those times, nevertheless, lent a romance to the company's resurgence which today's prosperity cannot supply. There is in these almost nostalgic references the same note so often struck in histories of American towns and industrial enterprises, the note of pride in the early and then-hated hardships, the wistful backward glance at a pioneering atmosphere, the blushing acknowledgment of an early, embarrassing poverty. Indeed, many newsmen referred to Wolfsburg in those days as having a 'gold rush' atmosphere. The company says they did so unkindly, to denigrate the town and its factory, but it is clear in retrospect that they may have been right. There was in Wolfsburg in those years, along with the makeshift buildings and mud streets, a sense of great things about to happen, an awareness that any day now the town might hit pay dirt.

Writing about the city in 1961, the company (a real town booster) contrasted its 3000 lamp-posts with 1948, when 'there were only 20 along the concrete road which terminated abruptly and became meadows and fields'. In those days, a Wolfsburg bus passenger was

---

1. Contrasted with one every eight seconds today (calculated at actual working time, that is, two shifts during a five-day week).

wise to take along an umbrella, 'since the cardboard roof could not stand up to the continuous rain'. Then, too, there were only two and a half miles of 'tenth-rate' road.

'The huge pot-holes made every trip an endurance test for drivers . . . the workshop proprietors would rub their hands in glee at the number of cars that would turn up damaged. From 1952 onwards, drivers were spared these horrors, for the Braunschweiger Strasse was completed.' (To mark that occasion, the town bought the road gang and the guests of honour each a cigar and a glass of beer.)

Across the Mittelland Canal, the factory recovered slowly. It was 'about as efficient at producing cars as a starving man would be at his job', the company notes. Cars were being manufactured at the miserable rate of 78 a day. They were transported out of the plant by 'two old wheezy low-powered diesel locomotives built long before the war', together with 'second-hand track of rather doubtful quality'. Signals wouldn't work, and whatever did had to be worked by hand.

Nevertheless, production chief Steinmeier managed to coax 19,244 Volkswagens out of the plant by the end of 1948. It wasn't much, but it was ten thousand more than the previous year and clearly the beginning of an uphill climb. When the year-end figures were announced, workers began to realise that the plant might after all have a real future with this new man Nordhoff around.

'Gradually, painfully,' Charles Barnard writes, 'like a man with no credit rating and nobody to borrow from, Nordhoff earned his own working capital by selling cars; he bought the machinery he needed—and even set aside a little money . . . as a sort of "pretend dividend". In this period, Nordhoff ruled Volkswagen with such an iron hand that he was often called autocratic and dictatorial; money men were critical that Nordhoff made all his decisions in "splendid isolation" and that even his *opinions* represented final authority in Wolfsburg. To the bankers and other critics Nordhoff snapped a reply: "When we began, without any capital, to build the first cars here, and we needed help urgently, no one—no country or bank—as much as lifted a finger." '

If Nordhoff was an autocrat then, it seems today that an autocrat was just what this sick car company needed. 'When I assumed the responsibility of putting this wrecked factory into high volume production,' Nordhoff says, 'the car itself was still "full of bugs". It was really what you call an "ugly duckling". As usual, I had the dubious benefit of a great many well-intentioned advisers.'

The Volkswagen of those days, he says, was noisy and badly sprung; its upholstery and paint job left much to be desired, and the life of its engine was short. The pressure Nordhoff underwent to abandon the design was terrific, as he and several of his executives recall. It came from everywhere and continued for years; it originated from within the Volkswagenwerk's own ranks and from outside them. One Swiss dealer, for example, warned Nordhoff in the early 1950s that he would not be able to keep on selling this same model, year after year, in a country as sophisticated about cars as Switzerland, and he placed great pressure on Nordhoff to redesign the car.

In most cases, those demanding changes demanded only 'sheet-metal changes', not fundamental improvements within the car itself. Yet tests had shown that the slightest sheet-metal change affected the fundamental design radically and raised costs sharply. In one such test, for example, the bonnet was raised a fraction to allow for more luggage room; the result was that the redesigned VW now needed more horsepower to maintain a given cruising speed. It became ever more apparent that Porsche's bug-shape design had been carefully worked to call for the very minimum of sheet metal, thus guaranteeing low cost. It further became apparent that changing the outside would have made the car appear grotesque on its present chassis.

Nordhoff resisted all the pressure and rejected all the 'advice'. He, too, wanted to improve the car—but only 'organically', from the inside out, without touching the basically sound Porsche design. 'Most of all,' he recalls, 'I wanted to obtain better-quality materials to put inside the car, specifically for the engine, so as to keep it from breaking down so early.' At the time, Nordhoff was offering a gold watch and sending a personal letter of congratulations to any VW owner who had driven his car 60,000 miles. This policy has had to be discontinued, because that number of miles is no longer an achievement of note for a VW, thanks largely to the fact that Nordhoff in those early years had stood firm against the crowd which wanted outer changes first.

'Perhaps I was too busy to listen,' he says, 'and in any case, I myself knew exactly what to do. . . . I brushed away all temptation to change model and design. In any sound design there are almost unlimited possibilities—and this certainly was a sound one. I see no sense in starting anew every few years with the same teething troubles, making obsolete almost all the past. . . . Offering people an honest value, a product of the highest quality, with low original cost and incomparable resale value, appealed more to me than being driven around by a bunch of hysterical stylists trying to sell people something they really do not want to have . . .'

In 1951, Nordhoff hired a new chief engineer, Dr. Alfred Haesner, another former Opel man, to introduce improvements. Ultimately, a platoon of engineers and designers were employed full-time to knock every kink out of the car, as the company bettered it year after year. *Der Spiegel* claims that the 1953 and 1954 models, which resulted from the basic redesign, contained not a single screw which exactly corresponded to its Porsche-designed forerunner. Seen in this light, today's Volkswagen is the product of Nordhoff's redesign. But this 'redesign' was *organic*, not superficial.

Nordhoff did not just want to keep the plant above water in order to provide jobs for needy Wolfsburgers; he wanted to plan on a larger scale and think much more in terms of the future than did the British authorities who had given him his job. His mind surveyed the Europe of the first postwar years. It was clear to him that there was indeed 'fire in the ashes'. He did not question the future of Europe, including Germany. He sensed, at a time when some thought him a dizzy optimist, that this reborn Europe would be prosperous as it had never been. Such a Europe would need cars, but certainly not luxury cars which devour enormous quantities of petrol and groan under their loads of chrome.[1] Nordhoff saw that Europe required *transport*—and transport in numbers never before conceived of on that continent.

He began to prod output. His tactic, *Time* noted in 1954, was one of 'pressure-vacuum production'. Materials poured into the plant, while produced cars vanished from it immediately. 'The combination of large stocks of material on the inside and no reserve of cars on the outside . . . exerts a psychological pressure on workers to produce faster,' Nordhoff explains. 'In six months,' *Time* added, 'production almost tripled, to 1800 cars a month; by mid-1949, Nordhoff had so much faith in his product that he arbitrarily ordered production doubled.' The reaction in the plant was one of incredulity, even among some executives who could hardly be numbered among the congenital doubters. 'I remember a meeting back in 1949,' says Otto Hoehne, 'when Nordhoff ordered us to change over from one hundred cars a day to four hundred. Nobody said a word, but after-

---

1. Inevitably, though, prosperity brought a cry for luxury cars as well. The extremity in ostentation today is the 'Grosser Mercedes' at 60,000 marks, the longest car in the world, 200 of which were ordered in 1963 by the nabobs of Dusseldorf before the model was even in production.

wards, as we were walking out of the meeting, Wilhelm Steinmeier poked me in the ribs with his elbow and said, "Where does he think he's going to sell those cars? He'll never do it, I tell you, never!" '

In May 1949, the plant produced the 50,000th postwar Volkswagen. To celebrate, Nordhoff asked the kitchen personnel to make a special effort. The account of the festivities has a somewhat poignant air, as well as an earthy ending.

'The cooks,' according to VW *Informationen*, 'worried themselves stiff about what to put on the menu—then a gift of food from Switzerland came quite out of the blue: real coffee and flour. We had noodles (which were actually white in colour), goulash and coffee and cakes to follow. . . . We had to drink the coffee out of paper cups as no china ones were available, but that didn't lessen the enjoyment, at least not at first. But there was nevertheless a sting in the tail (and how!) when countless members of the staff had to go to see the company doctor—all suffering from stomachache, colic, and diarrhoea. Reason for the trouble—the paper cups had been impregnated with paraffin. . . .'

By July, the magazine reports, the kitchen still had problems. 'July 1st, 1949, and in the Hall 3 dining room the umbrellas were up —so that the serving ladies did not get wet, or the food watered down. It was raining like hell. The building had never entirely recovered from what the heavens had had to offer on a previous occasion and the makeshift repairs just could not stand up to the heavy downpour of rain. The bomb damage to the southern part of the factory had been too great.'

At the end of Nordhoff's second year, the factory produced its first eight trucks. Overall production in 1949 totalled 46,154 VWs and the plant was now turning out 185 vehicles a day.

Other German car companies were starting up as well. In 1946 Volkswagen's 9878 sedans represented 99·7 per cent of all cars manufactured in West Germany that year; by the end of 1948, VWs represented 64·6 per cent of the total, and by the end of 1949, VWs 46,154 vehicles comprised 50 per cent of all cars made in West Germany. Still, no company was moving as rapidly as was the Volkswagenwerk, nor was any company thinking on as large a scale.The company's export programme had begun, at a time when other German motor-car manufacturers concentrated almost exclusively on their domestic market.

The VW dealer organisation, which Nordhoff vowed would

'provide the best service in the world', was beginning to take shape. By this time, more than 200 dealers were scattered throughout West Germany; almost 8000 mechanics worked in more than 200 service stations and repair shops.

The eight commercial vehicles produced at the end of 1949 were delivery vans, as were all the ones exhibited in March 1950, when Volkswagen officially introduced its 'Transporters'. As far as the company was concerned, these vehicles were to 'revolutionise the truck industry', but it admits that 'the reception that greeted these 30 vehicles was slightly less than spectacular. In fact, the truck world viewed the project with scepticism, and for good reason. Here was a truck designed with no preconceived ideas, no outmoded traditions to follow, no existing tools and dies.'

Just as Ferdinand Porsche had discarded all preconceptions about what a small car should be like (merely a scaled-down big car), so Nordhoff and his postwar designers insisted on producing a commercial vehicle from scratch, with an eye only on quality and service and not on what might be expected. Nordhoff blazed a trail, one which would eventually be followed by other manufacturers, including several in America, after it was apparent how successful VW's strange-looking, box-shaped, rear-engined vans and 'trucks' could be.

Ferdinand Porsche had actually designed a VW van before the war, and prototypes had been built for testing. This vehicle in no way resembles today's VW Transporters; it was simply an adaptation of the familiar VW sedan. It never saw production.

To call Volkswagen's commercial vehicles 'trucks' is somewhat misleading. Officially, the company refers to them as 'Type II' vehicles, and they include not just commercial vehicles of all types and styles, but also what America has come to know as the Volkswagen station wagon. This latter is called the Microbus in Europe, a far better name for it, but one which, it was felt, would not have endeared it to the US public.

The Microbus station wagon is really just the familiar VW van dressed in its Sunday best—a Transporter to which have been added 21 windows, a sunroof, chrome, and a comfortable, passenger-style interior. It is a remarkable vehicle, hardly bigger than the little sedan, but holding nine passengers and/or as much paraphernalia as imaginative stowing can provide. (One Brazilian rancher regularly gets more than twenty calves into his.) This Microbus and other Type II vehicles rapidly followed the original delivery van into regular production. In October 1951, for example, a VW ambulance was produced and a year later a fire prevention vehicle; while few of these are built, they provide interesting evidence of the versatility of the basic design. One of the most popular adaptations is the Microbus as holiday 'camper' or 'caravan', with any number of specialist firms providing customised interiors.

The 100,000th vehicle in this series left the Volkswagen plant in October 1954; by the end of that year, Wolfsburg had reached an annual total of 202,174 passenger cars and 40,000 Transporters. Capacity had not yet been reached even within the existing facilities; the factory could readily produce more than a quarter of a million units annually (and was shortly to do so), but Nordhoff was once more planning a bigger future and preparing for it in advance, despite the cautionary advice of many.

Already, the 'mother plant' in Wolfsburg had available to it a small factory in nearby Brunswick, built in 1938 as a 'Vorwerk' to the Wolfsburg installation and meant then to supply the main plant with parts and training facilities. Running this for nine months during the war had provided Otto Hoehne with his 'first big break', as he recalls it, for it allowed him to show management then what he was capable of doing when handed enlarged responsibilities.

Now Nordhoff decided to put up an entirely new factory along modern postwar lines—and the job of building it and getting it started fell again to Otto Hoehne. After a review of 'presentations' by three hundred German mayors, the community of Stöcken, a suburb of nearby Hanover, forty-seven miles from Wolfsburg, was decided upon. Hanover would allow for easy communication but lay far enough away to ensure that Wolfsburg itself would not be overtaxed; further, it had twenty thousand unemployed workers and the new factory there would prove a shot in the arm for the entire Lower Saxon region, in which both Wolfsburg and Hanover lie.

Dr. Carl Horst Hahn, who joined the company in 1954 as Heinz Nordhoff's personal assistant, recalls that there was in that year no rigid plan concerning the construction of the Hanover plant.[1] 'We didn't even have a detailed budget for it,' he reports. 'Nordhoff farmed Otto Hoehne out to build the factory and get it going. Hoehne added whatever was needed to it as he went along and of course soon had it running as smoothly as a Swiss watch.'

1. Hahn, today the Volkswagenwerk Vorstand member in charge of worldwide sales and service, headed VW in the USA from 1959 to 1965. His career is covered in greater detail in Chapter 12.

The first commercial vehicles rolled off the Hanover assembly line in March 1956, only fourteen months after the decision to build had been reached. Under Joseph Werner's direction since 1959, production has climbed from an initial 247 vans and station wagons to more than 800 daily. Today the Hanover installation also manufactures all VW engines. It employs 23,000 workers, covers 250 acres of ground, and contains 85 acres covered with buildings.[1]

Nordhoff has sold more than 1,500,000 VW Type II since he produced the first eight in 1949; the total represents almost 10 per cent of Volkswagen's overall production. Despite the initial scepticism, the VW commercial vehicles proved so dependable and so versatile that within less than a year, the Transporter had become the best-selling commercial vehicle in its class in Germany. Sales rose year after year, as new customers were found for a design which adapted itself to a surprising variety of needs.

On January 5, 1960, Nordhoff addressed his truck salesmen after they had sold 121,453 Transporters the previous year. His talk provides an insight into the earliest period of Transporter manufacture, as well as an example of Nordhoff-style prodding.

'There simply does not exist any reason,' he said, 'why truck sales should be good in one country and poor in a neighbouring country. I know this isn't an easy business to get, but I repeat what I said two years ago—that the really big period for the Transporter hasn't even arrived yet. He who is smart will take his chances now, to prepare himself. I've asked our sales department for years whether we shouldn't enlarge Hanover's capacity. I know that I've been tiresome about this, but I now ask again with increasing urgency, for it takes us at least two years to implement such a decision. . . .'

He drew attention to Europe's industrial growth, which by then was in full swing, and to the fact that it could not continue without trucks. He urged his salesmen to draw the necessary conclusions from this. As for other companies' trucks and vans in the same price and weight range, he said, 'the VW Transporter still has no real competition'.

Then he looked back at the early days to remind his listeners how easy it is to miscalculate. He told them that when he decided years ago to boost Transporter production from 40 to 60 a day, he was urged to reconsider, because no market allegedly existed for so many

---

1. The Brunswick plant's 5500 workers today produce front axle units for both the Wolfsburg and Hanover assembly lines. The smallest of the VW complex of factories, it contains 18·3 acres of buildings on a 50·4-acre site.

trucks. 'Today,' he said, 'we produce 530 a day and I'm certain that even this isn't enough! . . . We must move ahead,' he concluded, 'not in a wild kind of optimism . . . but with the courage to do what has never been tried before, to take what the Americans call a calculated risk. . . .' Transporter sales spurted up from about 120,000 that year to more than 180,000 in 1962.

Heinz Nordhoff did not only talk of calculated risks, he took them as well. The introduction of the VW Karmann-Ghia coupé was one example. Volkswagen's relationship with the Wilhelm Karmann company at 49 Neulandstrasse in Osnabrück, Germany, dates back to 1949, when Karmann, an accomplished coachbuilder, began to produce a limited quantity of Volkswagen convertibles. In 1955, Nordhoff assigned that company the task of producing bodies for the 'Volkswagen in an Italian sports jacket', as a VW advertisement describes the Karmann-Ghia. The K-G bodies were designed by Ghia of Turin, Italy, and Ghia's styling, in accordance with VW policy, has remained constant since introduced.

All Volkswagen convertible bodies are assembled and all Karmann-Ghia body parts are today produced at the Osnabrück factory, while VW's Wolfsburg plant delivers to it all the required chassis, including engines and transmissions. Hand-welded, hand-sanded, hand-padded and hand-sewn, the K-G receives the kind of personalised attention which the VW plant at Wolfsburg is not equipped to provide. The car immediately became popular and in its first four years sales rose from 500 to 6000 a year. By September 1961, sales were so good and production was so efficient that, after studying his lower costs, Nordhoff passed the savings on to his customers by lowering the Karmann-Ghia's price.[1]

Shortly after he opened the Hanover plant, Nordhoff added another factory to the VW network, this one in Kassel, an industrial centre in Hesse, along the Munich–Hanover Autobahn. There, another 11,000 workers today manufacture transmissions, truck and van front ends, VW replacement parts, and also recondition Volkswagen engines and components. The factory extends over 411 acres and has 60 acres of roofed production area. The original Kassel plant was not built by the company; it existed before the war and was

1. In addition to VW convertibles and K-G's, the Karmann company today also produces all hardtop Porsches. This car, which Ferry Porsche and his staff designed just after the end of the war, is not connected in any way with the Volkswagenwerk. The Porsche company, now headed by Ferry, still operates out of the Porschestrasse in the Stuttgart suburb of Zuffenhausen. Income from sales of the VW helped put this company in business because Nordhoff chose to continue paying Porsche and his heirs a royalty. Relations are close all around and the Porsche Bureau continues to serve Volkswagen as consulting engineers.

almost completely destroyed in the heavy air raids which Kassel endured during World War II. Nordhoff had it repaired, expanded, and modernised. In 1958 he sent 25 workers there from Wolfsburg to start production. By the end of two years, the new set of factory buildings had been built and there were 9000 workers reconditioning 10,000 engines and 3000 axles a month.

As fast as the company grew—and as hard as Nordhoff pushed— it could not grow fast enough to suit him. By the mid-1950's, it had spawned two huge offspring in Hanover and Kassel and the parent plant at Wolfsburg as well as the small Brunswick factory had both grown and been modernised as well. Daily output rose from 312 in 1950 to more than 1000 in 1955 and, as production and sales grew, so did the cash position. Nordhoff now was able to buy more machinery.

Today, 40 per cent of the body presses used in Wolfsburg are US-built, as is all the ring- and pinion-gear-cutting machinery. For many years, the company bought large quantities of American steel, magnesium, and aluminium as well. In recent years, US steel prices became prohibitive and VW reduced its purchases sharply. Europe today produces steel which meets VW's high standards at prices lower than United States manufacturers'. On the other hand, VW purchases of American tyres have recently become significant; under a new contract, it buys 500,000 tyres a year from the Goodyear Tyre and Rubber Company. The Volkswagenwerk today is also the world's largest consumer of magnesium; its foundry uses about 35,000 tons a year, one-fifth of the Free World's production.

Three months after the dawn of the 'Soaring Sixties', in March 1960, Heinz Nordhoff reviewed the company's situation. Sales had jumped from 90,000 to 697,000 vehicles a year during the ten years that had passed and plans for 1960 called for 817,000.[1] Speaking in Switzerland on March 9, 1960, Nordhoff referred to the nagging disparity between the supply and demand of VWs. To that date, the company had never been able to meet the astounding demand for its vehicles, despite all the measures it took.

'We decided two years ago,' Nordhoff said, 'to do something decisive to normalise the relationship. In 1959, we invested 500 million D-marks and boosted production by 1000 Volkswagens per day to 3000 per day. In 1960, we once again invested 5000 million D-marks and in January boosted production by 100 VWs per day.

1. Sales proved again to exceed predictions. VW produced 865,858 vehicles in 1960.

In February, by another 100 per day, and in March, once again by 100 per day. By the end of 1960 we shall produce 4000 Volkswagens daily. Then we believe we shall have reached a balance between supply and demand, so that we can finally deliver Volkswagens to customers without a waiting period. . . .' The company, he noted, employed 54,000 workers. It had an income *per worker* of 62,000 D-marks. More than a third of all cars in West Germany were Volkswagens by 1960.

The vast investment programme of the late 1950s to which Nordhoff referred was, says Carl Hahn, 'a turning point' for the Volkswagenwerk. 'No one thought it possible to sell so many motorcars,' Hahn recalls, 'but when the big US market for imported small cars developed in 1959, Volkswagen was ready for it and best able to supply it.' The size of VW's investments in those years astounded almost everyone, Hahn remembers. 'One of Nordhoff's best friends even said to him, after a board meeting called to discuss them: "This is nonsense! You'll just get yourself in trouble!" and one of West Germany's most prominent motor manufacturers made speeches warning against manufacturers who were "overinvesting". There was no doubt whom he meant. But Nordhoff has a sure instinct about just how far he can go. He never butts his head against a wall; he just manages to walk through a door in the wall which no one else sees.'

A year later, on December 5, 1961, Volkswagen production had reached the 5,000,000 point. It had been fourteen years since Nordhoff accepted Colonel Radclyffe's offer to head the shattered and demoralised plant; as this occasion rolled around, Nordhoff took a moment to recollect the past. He presented the flower-bedecked 5,000,000th beetle to the International Red Cross, and noted the achievements over the past fourteen years. It was, he remarked, just fourteen days after he had joined the company in 1948 that the 20,000th Volkswagen had rolled off the assembly line.[1] 'We have good reason to be proud,' Nordhoff continued, for the Volkswagen is 'a symbol of one of the biggest industrial successes ever reached . . . the result of hard, unremitting work and of diligent attention to a correctly set goal.'

Nordhoff defined that goal and, in doing so, summarised VW's philosophy:

1. Intervening anniversaries: the 500,000th VW was produced on July 3, 1953; the 1,000,000th on August 5, 1955; the 2,000,000th on December 28, 1957; the 3,000,000th on August 25, 1959; the 4,000,000th on November 9, 1960.

'. . . to develop one model of car to its highest technical excellence;
'. . . to dedicate ourselves to the attainment of the highest quality;
'. . . to destroy the notion that such high quality can only be attained at high prices;
'. . . to subordinate technological considerations to human ones;
'. . . to give the car the highest value and to build it so that it retains that value; and
'. . . to build up an enterprise which belongs to its workers more than any other industrial concern in the world.'

In honour of the 5,000,000th VW, the Bavarian State Mint issued gold and silver coins commemorating the occasion; they bore a profile of the car on one side and of Nordhoff on the other. The Volkswagenwerk had already become West Germany's leading industrial enterprise, with sales totalling more than 5,600 million marks. That year, it was also the world's *third* largest motor-car manufacturer, after GM and Ford, a position it held until 1963, when Chrysler recovered and also acquired sales of the Simca. ('Since then,' as a VW executive puts it, 'we're in fourth place, unless Chrysler has a bad year. Then we move back up to the number three position.')

Six months after the 5,000,000th VW was produced, Nordhoff warned that profits must keep pace with production, for the postwar boom 'stemming essentially from postwar needs cannot continue to go up and up . . . without reacting sharply.' Nordhoff well knew that Volkswagen was riding the crest of that boom and was troubled by one result of the continuing disparity between supply and demand. The urgent necessity of closing that gap had forced the company into ever-increasing investments. By 1961, the amount laid out for automated and other late-model equipment was, he said, 'enormous'.

Two years earlier at Geneva he expressed the belief that the 1,000,000,000 D-marks invested between 1958 and 1960 would push the plant over the hump. This did not happen. 'Despite a present daily production of 4600 vehicles, the demand still cannot be met, making further large expenditures necessary,' Nordhoff said. He was in the unusual position of bemoaning the staggering demand for his product, but with good reason. A shortage of trained workers plagued management and importing foreign workers did not prove a total solution. Furthermore, it was harder to keep costs down everywhere. 'This situation,' Nordhoff said, 'subjects us to the utmost strain, forces us to keep our organisation tight, efficient, and highly effective.'

The Wolfsburg plant by the early 1960's was enormous. It housed 10,000 production machines and covered 10·8 million square feet in roofed area alone—more space (about 270 acres) than all the houses of Wolfsburg combined. Daily production had skyrocketed to 5091 and the plant employed 43,578 workers, about seven times as many as in 1948, when Nordhoff took over. The two 'wheezy old locomotives' of that earlier day had long since been replaced; today, the VW grounds include 31·2 miles of railroad track, with 25 tracks side-by-side at one point, plus 21·9 miles of paved roads. Its continuous flow conveyor lines now total about 110 miles, long enough to reach from Wolfsburg, right through the Russian Zone, all the way to Berlin. By 1962, Heinz Nordhoff had spent 2,700 million marks on factory expansion alone, had brought sales to 6,400 million marks and had seen VW's share of the ever-growing West German car market reach 34·5 per cent of the total number of passenger cars and 42·3 per cent of all commercial vehicles below 2750 pounds capacity.

His constant prodding had paid off. Over and over again, he had pressed his people to work harder, cut costs, avoid complacency and the accumulation of corporate fat. The man whom 'General Motors had forged into an efficient car maker' proved also to be a steely-eyed administrator and a fiery sales manager.

'We shall some day speak of the Golden Fifties,' he warned his salesmen in January 1960. 'We are now moving away from them and we must recognise that fact and use the time given us. The wheel of history never turns back! Whatever opportunities you miss today will never return! The new year will have 366 days this time; every day, we will cross one off—and soon there will be only four left. No power of heaven or earth will bring those days back. Let us use this time, as long as we are free to do so, as we are now, and as we shall still be for a few years. . . .' He was speaking of the fact that markets were still unusually receptive, Volkswagen's sales, by and large, were easy, and the company's growth was constant and rapid. Yet he knew that there were specific traps into which a highly successful enterprise can fall—the psychological dangers of complacency and smugness.

He never stopped trying to intensify the enthusiasm and sense of urgency of his men, to make them feel a dread of a lost opportunity. He tried to keep watch over everything: the plant itself, its offices, the offices of dealers and distributors, and the repair shops. His questions were incessant and his demands those of a perfectionist. During a January 1960 staff meeting, he warned of 'bureaucratic departmental thinking', of 'indecisiveness and hesitancy'. He urged his executives and dealers to make certain their organisations were 'lean, wiry, and productive'.

'We must never become lazy or sink into deadly patterns of thought,' he said. 'We must never become bureaucrats or administrators—that would be the end of our success!' On this occasion, he pressed his executives to read *Parkinson's Law*, which describes the growth of unproductive bureaucracies. ('That unique book,' he said, 'will open your eyes.') 'We want to remain salesmen and engineers,' he said. 'Every one of us must prove daily, through initiative, action, and hard work, that he is the right man in the right job.'

Volkswagen was growing older, he warned, and young people had to be brought up fast to positions of authority. He still worries about this problem and about those who in turn worry about being replaced by younger men. 'I know how afraid people are, and I also know the noise they make claiming there aren't young people available,' he told his men. 'There is a contradiction here which should stimulate you to some reflection.' Blisteringly, he contrasted the modern, automated factory with its administrative offices. 'Antiquated thinking is big here and missed opportunities are legion!'

In his impatience with incompetence, Nordhoff resembles Ferdinand Porsche; neither could countenance mediocrity and each drove himself hard to set an example. Nordhoff remembered his first six months at the rat-infested plant, when he lived in his office and worked seven days a week; he was determined that what he had built up would not be choked to death in a wrangle of memoranda and a proliferation of offices. This spirit has largely proved infectious and continuing VW successes seem due in large measure to this psychological momentum which Nordhoff has created, as well as to his ability to recognise, employ, and promote men who approximate his own drive and flexibility.

As the annual rate of production has climbed over the years, Volkswagen anniversaries keep moving closer together. It took five and a half years to build the first million Volkswagens; it took a total of fourteen years to build the first five million, but the second five million were produced in only three and a half. The tenth millionth Volkswagen rolled off the Wolfsburg assembly line in September 1965, while the Frankfurt Motor Show was taking place in Frankfurt/ Main, West Germany, and closed-circuit television brought the event to a room in Frankfurt where several hundred Motor Show reporters and editors from the world over had assembled. I myself was there and watched these journalists spontaneously burst into prolonged applause as the 10,000,000th came down the line in Hall No. 1 of the Wolfsburg plant. The accolade, however deserved, struck me as unusual, for such journalists are generally cynical about the companies whose affairs they report to the world and one does not often see them cheering corporate achievements. Yet there was no doubt about it on this day: they shared the feeling of pride and understood the sense of fulfilment which must have filled Heinz Nordhoff as he stood among them in that room, watching the distant ceremonies projected on to the huge TV screen there. 'It's an incredible achievement,' one of them said later. 'I think everyone here feels it, because there's something about the VW that captures the imagination. There isn't another motor-car that's got as much romance to it, except maybe the old Model T.'

The romance today is apparent only to those who know the full history, for as the decade of the 1960s draws slowly to a close, the Volkswagenwerk seems to the casual observer a coldly efficient corporate enterprise, rather than a place of personal triumph and fulfilment. Highly automated equipment throbs in halls wherein workers once laboured ankle-deep in rain water; management consultant firms today advise where once seat-of-the-pants decisions were enough; a small army of market statisticians plot graphs and sales projections, and computers issue forth their chilly pronunciamentos. Behind the tall office building at the northeast corner of the Wolfsburg factory sprawls an ever-growing complex of buildings, housing the earsplitting production plant and the hushed spaces of support services such as technical development and marketing. The Volkswagenwerk factory area in Wolfsburg today continues to be concentrated in the same position along the canal, but this and its frontage are all that remains today to remind one of the pre-war factory; behind that mile-long façade there now sprawls a colossus *three times* as large as the plant which Ferdinand Porsche saw on his last visit to Wolfsburg before his death.

Everything at VW has of course over the years grown bigger, more grandiose, more expansive, more complex, and far more organised and structured than it was earlier. Today, the company has even entered into a relationship with Mercedes-Benz wherein both work co-operatively in many areas, including research, and VW has also bought control of Auto-Union GmbH, adding this company's Audi to its own expanding line of cars. Another large VW factory, at Emden, today helps supply the demand for the new model

SMALL WONDER

VWs which Heinz Nordhoff launched in the 1960s, to broaden the product line his company can offer its customers, and still more factories elsewhere in the world manufacture and assemble Volkswagens as well. VW's total production today exceeds 1,600,000 per year and more than one million of these were exported in 1966.

This achievement tends to overawe a visitor coming for the first time to the home of Heinz Nordhoff. One tends to encounter the leading industrialist of any country filled with certain preconceptions and expecting a certain stereotype, no matter what one may have heard of the man in advance. Writers who are acquainted with businessmen and industry executives in the United States and elsewhere learn from the experience of many encounters with such men that the business world moulds them into a handful of well-defined types. One expects perhaps the executive who is a chilly corporate machine which has successfully slaughtered its individuality in the struggle with faceless organisation men, or perhaps expects the frequently encountered 'self-made man' who blusteringly boasts of having majored in Sharp Dealings in some sleazy 'school of hard knocks'. Certainly one has learned to expect that the top industrialist's world begins and ends in the executive suite, and one has encountered a host who are filled either with contempt or condescension for the world of art and intellect, or who patronisingly act their 'patron', at the prompting of public relations counsellors. And so it was with considerably more than curiosity that I discussed Heinz Nordhoff with those who have known him long and well and formed my own impressions during many hours in Heinz Nordhoff's home and office over the past several years. These are now difficult to sort out, for while it is a simple matter to describe a lesser man, it is a larger task to describe a man whose giant size seems to derive from an inner simplicity.

As for the preconceptions, Nordhoff tends to destroy them gently on one's first visit to his home. Walking there, one passes along a winding, tree-lined street of modest, two-storey 'executive-row' homes, until one comes to where the road curves back again towards the Steimkerberg guest house (the very building which once served as the British REME mess). At this curve of the road stands Nordhoff's home, a somewhat larger, but quite unpretentious, L-shaped house; one is struck by the fact that it might belong in the United States to a middle-echelon executive, and it bears not the slightest resemblance to the huge homes, mansions, and estates which American manufac-

turers inhabit in Westchester or Fairfield Counties, Grosse Point or
Bloomfield Hills, or in the North Shore suburbs of Chicago. Either
Heinz Nordhoff or his wife usually answers the doorbell here, takes
the visitor's coat and ushers him into the living room. Immediately
one is struck by the scent and sight of flowers; by paintings, sculp-
ture, and other objets d'art, and by a profusion of books—a great
many in English—which litter a table beside the chair in which
Nordhoff seats himself. A visitor's glance at one of these books, or
his indication that he is familiar with a title here, is enough to start
this motor-car executive talking at length about any of a variety of
subjects, whether it be the politics of medieval France or of today's
Germany, Eastern philosophy or the sociology of the West, a recent
New Yorker short story or the current Munich theatre. Nordhoff
speaks quietly, in an almost hushed voice; one recognises it as the
tone of a man who does not need to raise his voice for attention. As
the conversation continues, one notes that Nordhoff has an easy
familiarity with a surprising array of subjects and that a visitor with
preconceptions soon finds himself quickly put in his cultural place.
Wine is poured and Nordhoff now earnestly discusses the character
of the vintage, expressing satisfaction with it or disappointment with
another; he flatters his visitor by disarmingly assuming that, of
course, his guest has an equal understanding of the merits of these
wines. As one begins to hunt for a term capturing a first impression
of this man, there comes to mind a word which one uses seldom in
today's age of sound and fury: one is struck by Nordhoff's *gracious-
ness*. He does not offer compliments, nor does he say or do anything
which might be calculated to put a visitor at ease, but he flatters his
visitors nevertheless by placing them completely on his own level.
There is in this nothing that seems affected, nor have I noted the
slightest suggestion of condescension or superiority in the man,
though I had been alert for it, for Nordhoff has been criticised as
'arrogant'. He simply puts his visitors at ease by paying them the
irresistible compliment of assuming they are honourable, intelligent,
and cultivated men; he flatters them further by being utterly and
disarmingly frank with them. No matter the subject, Nordhoff offers
his observations in a way that makes clear he does not have advisers
who suggest what views he 'ought to' express. One asks Nordhoff,
for example, to explain a recent reshuffle of management in a competitive company; he replies at length and offers a detailed, informed
and dispassionate appraisal of the strengths and weaknesses in the
men and forces involved. As the evening progresses, one adds an-

other word to one's lexicon regarding Nordhoff, and it is *detachment*.
Now one begins to understand whence his reputation for 'arrogance'
derives; dispassionate and detached men are often mistakenly
thought to have a superior air. One senses Nordhoff has learned from
life to be surprised at very little which events and men may offer and
that looking back on his career he sees not only the highs of achievement, but regards with detached equanimity the frustrations and
difficulties through which he has had to pass. He may be—and is—
impatient in details, but has won a reputation for regarding important and far-reaching matters with detachment and objectivity; one
notes from his conversation that he has the natural tolerance of a man
who either was born, or grew to be, philosophically inclined, and one
is reminded again of Carl Hahn's statement that Nordhoff never
butts his head against walls.

'He always has time for important things,' says Carl Hahn.
'When you sit down with him, he never ends the conversation after
fifteen minutes, nor does he set any arbitrary time limits at all. He'll
give you as much as two or three hours. And throughout that time,
you have his undivided attention. Everything is quiet and there are
never any phone calls interrupting, and at the end of your talk he
gives you the feeling that it's wonderful of you to have helped him
spend the afternoon—as though he had been worried about how it
would have gone, if you hadn't arrived.'

Reporters have also noted in Heinz Nordhoff a slight mischievous
instinct and the ability to be cynically realistic about himself and
others. He has seen more than his share of human weakness and
knows that people can be motivated by a man who knows these
weaknesses. His detachment extends to himself; in his darkest days,
he loathed looking back in anger or self-pity. 'The future begins
when you cut every tie with the lost past,' he said when he took over
the factory.

Just as he demands the right to a private life for himself, he eschews
paternalism towards his workers. 'We have a rule here,' he says, 'that
when a man crosses the bridge over the canal [which separates the
factory from the town], then his life is his own.' He adds, with
characteristic cynicism: 'Why shouldn't they be free to be fools if
they wish? All I want to do for these people is to create the conditions for a decent life—but not to interfere with that life. The
minute the factory becomes a landlord as well as employer, then
the worker is no longer a free man—he is a slave.'

One man who knew Heinz Nordhoff almost forty years ago is

John Eschenlohr, now chairman of the board of VW Canada Ltd. and for years general service manager of that company. He worked with Nordhoff in the Opel service department in 1929, and it is interesting to note his recollections of Germany's greatest industrialist when he was starting his career. 'Nordhoff was a very detached fellow even then,' Eschenlohr says. 'He sometimes threw delightful parties and he knew all the good jokes, but he never liked to just go out and drink with the boys. He was very ambitious and much addicted to the fine arts and that sort of thing.'

'I have never seen another German industrialist,' says Carl Hahn, 'or any industrialist for that matter, who is as diversified in his interests as Nordhoff is. His mind ranges from roses to hunting to painting to orchids and from there on almost infinitely. Part of this can be attributed, of course, to his wide and constant reading, which keeps his mind active and open to many ideas.'

If one asks him about these interests, one learns that flowers, art and literature are neither Nordhoff 'hobbies' nor the cultural affectations a successful industrialist might cultivate in his later years, but that they are the important avocations of a cultivated man. Nordhoff proves knowledgeable in a host of fields and he puts his knowledge to practical use. He cultivates his own orchids and tends his own flower gardens; he collects paintings and has tried his own hand at the art, and he is an insatiable reader who seems as well-informed about the Napoleonic Code as he is about his car or the Common Market. He reads widely in English and receives *Time*, the *New Yorker*, and the *Wall Street Journal* regularly. He learned English, which he speaks fluently with a soft German accent, while with Opel, 'reading *Automotive Industries*', he says. He knows classical Greek as well as Latin, his company's publicists proclaim proudly. (They go so far as to claim he 'reads ancient manuscripts with the ease of an American reading a detective story'). 'I find there are more books which interest me published in English than in German,' Nordhoff says, 'and I go through more of them today than I ever did, reading late into the night.' On a 1963 visit to the United States, he bought a handful of historical books, among them Alan Moorehead's *The White Nile* and *The Blue Nile* and *Eichmann in Jerusalem* by Hannah Arendt. He had of course read the news reports of Eichmann's trial, but wanted to study the record once more in a comprehensive book. Unlike many Germans one meets, he does not hesitate to face the past and to keep it alive. 'You cannot make the past go away,' he has said, 'by turning your back on it or

refusing to look at it.' Characteristically, he decided upon reading
the history of the Eichmann trial in Jerusalem that he would buy a
dozen copies of the book and mail them to German acquaintances
who even today will not or cannot believe that all this horror was
wrought by their fellow Germans during the Nazi era. 'I think all
Germans should know about this and that they must face these facts,'
he says. 'The horror of it is overwhelming and reading this record of
Nazi atrocities will make them understand why there are people
who are not only anti-Nazi, but anti-German.'

His 'missionary zeal' in sending out books to 'educate' others is
characteristic of the way all his interests express themselves.

His interest in fine arts, for example, extends from home to office
to the community in which he lives. Visits to the Far East have
resulted in a collection of Japanese brush paintings and statues of
the Buddha, now set in his home among German baroque wood
carvings and an original Renoir. Persian carpets and statues from the
Far East also add a note of dignified opulence to his offices. He has
been the guiding light behind Wolfsburg's artistic life, originating
the company's biennial art exhibit, a major cultural event in the
town, which has drawn 500,000 visitors. One recent show covered
120 years of French art and included 237 works on loan from 64
collections throughout the world. In 1967, a six-week show brought
a priceless 129-piece collection of Van Goghs to the city.

His interest in the performing arts also expresses itself in the same
way. Once a year, he brings the Berlin Philharmonic to Wolfsburg,
and his daughter Barbara remembers the first such concert, conducted by the famed Wilhelm Furtwängler. A large hall, originally constructed as a factory kitchen, but later used as a testing and experimental facility, was set aside for the purpose. It has tiled walls and
ordinarily poor acoustics; the moment, however, it is filled with
three thousand people, its acoustics are excellent. When Furtwängler encountered it for the first time he could not have known
this and it is therefore understandable that he baulked at conducting
there. Not only would the acoustics be terrible, he said, but the
workers probably wouldn't appreciate the music. Finally, he was
persuaded to conduct anyway, but did so with many reservations, as
Barbara Nordhoff remembers it. 'I think Furtwängler thought the
workers would probably applaud in the middle of the concert,' she
says, 'but you could hear a pin drop when there was a pause, and
at the end, there was so much applause that Furtwängler claimed he
had never heard the like. "I wish I could play for your workers every

day," he told Nordhoff afterwards. As it turned out, he was able to come only once more before he died.' Since then, a number of other halls in Wolfsburg have been looked into as possible replacements for the hall now housing testing equipment, but none has been found with the same excellent acoustics. Today's conductor of the Berlin Philharmonic, Herbert von Karajan, refuses to conduct anywhere in Wolfsburg except in that 'tiled kitchen'.

Nordhoff also has arranged for theatrical companies to come to the Volkswagen city. 'Nowadays most leading plays are performed in Wolfsburg,' Barbara says, 'and I think we have one of the most sophisticated and critical theatre audiences in Germany. In the beginning, we used to go and see whatever was being offered in town, but so many companies come here nowadays that we are much more selective.'

Heinz Nordhoff's interest in gardening is also not only a hobby but part of his orientation toward nature, part of a view of life which shows itself in the spacious green areas which are scattered throughout Wolfsburg. It is also reflected in other hobbies such as big game hunting, which he used to pursue each year in Africa, but with camera as much as with gun. These were not the big safaris which are usually arranged for executives of comparable stature: motorised caravans with all the luxuries and amenities of life in London or New York. Nordhoff ventured out alone, accompanied only by a native guide, and they carried little, living off what they could find or hunt locally. 'We knew the general area in which he was travelling,' Barbara Nordhoff says, 'but we had no idea of his exact whereabouts until he emerged a month later. He usually came home with a wretched stomach—the result of unbelievable food—but well rested.' He also came back from many of these trips with film footage of professional calibre. 'He could get a job with any film company in Germany if he wanted to,' Barbara claims. So far, his films are only for close friends and business associates. He filmed, for instance, Angkor Wat, the ancient jungle temple of Cambodia, near Angkor Thom, the old capital of the Khmers, and prepared a narration, using ancient Eastern texts. Heinz Nordhoff's interest in motion pictures prompted him over the years to commission a series of award-winning documentaries for the Volkswagenwerk. Produced by Konstantin Kalser's Marathon International Productions, New York City, these have won prizes at international film festivals such as those held at Venice and Edinburgh. Kalser, who has won an 'Oscar' for documentaries, told me that at first he had no idea

Nordhoff was an amateur film-maker. 'I saw that movie of his on Angkor Wat after we started working for Volkswagenwerk,' Kalser told me, 'and I can assure you that I'd never have signed a contract to produce a film for this company if I'd seen that movie earlier. It's absolutely first-rate and I would have been worried about getting too much professional criticism from him.' As it turned out, it was precisely Nordhoff's professionally amateur interest in photography which led him *not* to interfere with the Kalser camera crews. His only stipulation has been that the films must be entirely non-commercial, with no direct 'product publicity' worked into them. To be sure, the documentaries deal with matters of vital concern to Volkswagenwerk, but they are of broader significance as well. Automation, foreign trade and international communications are subjects which have been chosen and one recent film, entitled *The Way of a Ship*, reminded audiences that the bulk of the world's international cargo, even in the jet age, is carried by freighter. The low-key script was written by the author of *The Cruel Sea*, Nicholas Montserrat, and what public relations benefit the company may derive directly from the film stems from the fact that some of the ships shown are part of Volkswagenwerk's fleet of time-charter vessels.

Heinz Nordhoff's wife and daughters share a fierce sort of pride in his accomplishments and catholicity of tastes. 'We have a game we used to play, called "trying to corner Daddy",' says Barbara Nordhoff. 'We tried to stump him but rarely succeeded.' When she and her sister Elisabeth lived at home they would look up various subjects in reference books and challenge their father with them. 'It seems he's always able to offer some information about almost anything,' she reports, 'whether it's Telstar or the latest Paris fashion. He even has wonderful taste in clothes. He bought me my first evening dress, selecting it by himself, and it was exactly the style and colour that proved perfect for me.'

It is clear from her comments that family ties are close. Nordhoff's wife and daughters have shared with him not only the executive life in Berlin during the war, when he headed the Brandenburg Opel plant, but also the years of poverty, joblessness, and crowded rooms after the end of World War II. These years of adversity had their effect. Barbara Nordhoff recalls the time in 1948 when the mother and daughters came to Wolfsburg for the first time. Their father had moved out of the factory after having camped in his office for six months and had sent for them. 'When we arrived after a drive of about seven hours,' she remembers, 'the driver took us into a very nice quiet street with one-family houses along it and I remember thinking that maybe we would have a home like one of these some day. Then the driver stopped in front of one of them and said, "This is your home", and out came Daddy. He had somehow managed to get some furnishings and when Mother saw the house, she just broke into tears. She had so geared herself for a life of poverty that it was too much for her.'

His wife is a slender, elegant lady who has devoted herself to her husband's interests exclusively, now that her children are no longer at home. She has an unostentatious way, drives a standard Volkswagen sedan, and can be seen walking home alone from market. The Nordhoffs' lack of ostentation may be natural, but it also proves to be good employee relations, and Nordhoff has won his workers' admiration by buying a beetle on the same terms as do the rest of them. (This is his wife's car; Nordhoff, like other VW executives, drives a company car.)

The life of poverty has, of course, ended, and the man whom the American occupation authorities had promised a life only as an unskilled labourer has since risen to high position and achieved considerable honours. He is an honorary citizen of São Paulo, Brazil (home of VWs Brazilian subsidiary), an honorary citizen of the State of Texas and Wolfsburg's only 'Freeman'. The Brunswick Institute of Technology awarded him an honorary professorship and doctorate in engineering and he lectures there periodically on industrial relations. As a result, he is addressed as Professor Nordhoff in Germany. Berlin Technical University conferred upon him the unusual rank of honorary senator and the West German government awarded him with its highest civilian medal, the Great Federal Cross of Merit with Stars (Grosses Bundes-Verdienstkreuz mit Sternen). The Vatican, which takes pride in him as an outstanding Roman Catholic layman, has also given him awards, first making him a Knight of the Order of the Holy Sepulchre in Jerusalem and, more recently, presenting him with the Medal of St. Gregory (Gregorius Orden). In London in 1967, he became the first non-British motor industry leader to be awarded the coveted Lord Wakefield Gold Medal for outstanding contributions to motor industry development.

'I have to be careful what I think sometimes,' Nordhoff admits. 'Some other man might not have done what I have done—it's true. Volkswagen could have failed. Even I must admit that. And, had another man failed, people would have said: "Well, naturally it wouldn't work. No one could make it work. Nothing Hitler ever started ever came to a good end. The VW was just a mad scheme. No wonder it failed." '

The fact that he has succeeded has made him somewhat of a legend in West Germany. Charles Barnard wrote in *True* that Nordhoff's fellow countrymen regard him sometimes as 'a new Nordic superman' and Nordhoff admits there have been friends who have urged him to enter public life. 'Some people told me they thought it would be a good thing if I got into politics,' he says, 'but I'm too busy to give any thought to it.' Further, he reminded me that industrialists do not always prove to be well suited for political life. 'Remember what happened to Charlie Wilson,' he said, referring to the General Motors president who was appointed Defence Secretary in Dwight D. Eisenhower's first cabinet. He knows that his own industrial eminence would make him, as it has already done, the target of much sniping and criticism.

Yet Nordhoff's political views remain significant even if not given practical scope, for they are after all those of the man who heads the largest corporation in Europe's leading industrial nation, West Germany, and become by extension the views of Germany's most powerful industrialist. These views were given partial expression in an Alexander Graham Bell lecture on communications he delivered at the Boston University School of Business Administration in October 1962. Here Nordhoff spoke of his deep-felt belief in closer Free World ties. 'We must be ready to think about uniting the western world of the Atlantic Community,' he said. 'Otherwise, time will begin to work against us. Time is not on our side. It is on the side of the enemy. The man on the street is ready for unity. He is ready in France, and he is ready in Germany, where the problems of national self-interest are worsened by one thousand years of history. We in Europe know that you are equally ready here in America, where with the flexibility and eagerness of youth, concepts of international thinking come more readily.' He spoke of the Marshall Plan as 'the first important step toward unification of Europe' and called it 'history's greatest act of community unselfishness, a massive example of democratic generosity'. He again expressed concern over the 'protectionist thinking of certain high-tariff groups' in the European Common Market and denounced the idea that the Common Market might form a 'Third Force' in the world today. Its members, he said, must 'share everything—not only with its members, but also with those outside its ranks.'

He made his own commitment clear. 'In this area,' he said, 'the liberal thinking of the United States is an outstanding example to the world. Tariffs here are low. The policies of your government during the Eisenhower and Kennedy Administrations show clearly that the majority of Americans favour this attitude. *So do I.* And so do *many* others in Europe.'[1] Nordhoff shows himself to be a liberal committed to free trade, international co-operation, and even Atlantic union. His views are important in Germany, for they are heard attentively.

Although Nordhoff disavows any interest in actively participating in German politics, he is, however, outspoken in his views. For years, he was disappointed in Germany's politicians. Neither the Social-Democratic Party nor the Christian Democratic Union told the German people the truth about their situation. Nordhoff says. 'The truth is that we and all Europe are utterly dependent on the United States,' he states. 'But no one will tell the public that.' While he is hopeful about the future of German democracy, there is a note of pessimism as well. He quoted Heinrich Heine to me—*Denk' ich an Deutschland in der Nacht, dann bin ich um den Schlaf gebracht* (If I think of Germany during the night, then my sleep is ruined). He feels that Germany may have recovered too fast after the war, that prosperity may have come too easily to the German people. 'They all think that it should always be a boom period,' he says, 'and I do not know what they will do if it ever stops. Perhaps they will think there is something basically wrong with the system.'

For the time being, Nordhoff is content to continue building cars. A general drop in West German motor-car sales, which affected all manufacturers in 1966–7, had its effects on VW as well. (Though not as badly, perhaps, since one million out of the 1,600,000 Volkswagens produced in 1966 were *export* models.) Characteristically, Nordhoff faced the 'slump' with equanimity—and found at least one solution. He produced an economy model Volkswagen, a beetle with the basic 1200 cc engine but with less luxury than had been added over the years; it proved an instant success. The VW, after all, is unmatched transportation within its price range and those West Germans newly anxious to economise welcomed the bargain beetle.

This slump may be the last, or one of the last, critical situations through which Heinz Nordhoff will have to guide the company. He has announced his retirement on December 31, 1968, when Dr. Kurt Lotz, a newcomer to Volkswagen, is to take his place as head of the

1. Italics are Nordhoff's, as provided in a reprint of his address published in 1962 by Boston University Press.

company; until that date, Dr. Lotz will work as Nordhoff's deputy. Born 1912, Lotz's spectacular rise in industry matches West Germany's own post-war industrial boom. War's end found Major Lotz, then 33, desperately needing work to support his family; he found it first on a farm, as a labourer, paid in sausages. In early 1946, he took what was then a daring step: he turned down the well-fed life on a farm to take a minor post in industry, in the expectation that, sooner or later, the gamble might pay off. The office-job was with the German branch of a Swiss-owned company, Brown, Boveri & Cie, and the gamble did indeed pay handsomely. Nine years after he joined Brown, Boveri, he was named a director; in 1957, he was *Sprecher des Vorstande* or spokesman of the management committee; a year later, at the age of 45, he was named managing director of the company's Mannheim German operations, or *Generaldirektor*. In announcing Nordhoff's decision to retire after more than 20 years at the Volkswagenwerk's helm, the board requested he continue thereafter to furnish advice and counsel. Perhaps he shall; certainly, he is not the man to be content with reminiscing about the past. He has pointed out that, while there are more than one hundred million people who own cars, hundreds of millions more do not yet own one. They are not likely, he believes, to want a big car at first. He is convinced that VW's 1·5-litre range will have an enormous future as this market opens up. 'We still have many arrows in our quiver,' he once said. 'We are prepared. We cannot build as many cars as mankind needs. And if the worst comes to the worst, the last car to be bought will be a Volkswagen.'

8

From Wolfsburg, with Love

THE beetle and the beetle's 'big brothers' are today less German than they are international, for they are not merely exported to other countries but are in several cases built there as well. Those who buy Volkswagens in Brazil, for example, do not buy a product of 'fine German craftsmanship' at all, for the VWs sold there are almost entirely made on Brazilian materials, in Brazil, and by Brazilian workers. Their cars are products of the craftsmanship of their fellow countrymen. The same may be said of a number of other places far away from Wolsburg, for VWs manufactured in Australia, South Africa, and Mexico are similarly largely of local origin; in some places, the 'local content' of the car runs 60 per cent, in others more than ninety. In each, however, the aim and the direction is towards producing a car that is almost 100 per cent made locally. Today, there are VW manufacturing plants in the nations mentioned above; elsewhere, local assembly plants put together VWs shipped 'completely knocked-down' (CKD) from Wolfsburg; in other places, as in Britain and the United States, they are imported 'built-up', ready for sale. Volkswagens may be bought today in more countries than are represented at the United Nations and Germany's Volkswagenwerk is today the world's largest exporter of motor vehicles.

Probably the very first foreigner to buy VWs from Wolfsburg for import on a commercial basis was Ben Pon, an extroverted, snuff-sniffing, ebullient Hollander who had tried unsuccessfully, in 1948, to interest the US in beetles. These, however, were not the first VWs to leave the Wolfsburg factory for foreign climes; before Pon came the occupation powers. In 1946, French soldiers accompanied a military train load of 3000 VWs sent to France, and the very first beetles to leave the factory for foreign countries were very likely the fifty which were picked up by the Red Army in March 1946. Wing Commander Berryman recalls that the British contingent at the

Volkswagenwerk entertained two Soviet officers in its mess, while the fifty young Red Army 'chauffeurs' accompanying them were being taught how to drive cars.

Ben Pon, on the other hand, knew how to drive—and had even driven in a VW before the VW factory had ever been built. In 1938, he and his father had read of the German plans to build the factory in Lower Saxony and Ben Pon travelled to Fallersleben to try to get the Dutch franchise for the car. He met Porsche (he even presented him with ten thousand tulip bulbs for his cottage garden near the factory site), then travelled to 'Gezuvor' headquarters in Berlin, where he talked with Porsche and Robert Ley. The Nazis actually assigned him the Dutch franchise then and Ferdinand Porsche, 'wearing brocaded felt slippers', as Pon recalls, drove him around the Berlin Autobahn 'Ring' in a beetle. 'It was terribly noisy,' Pon says, echoing the sentiments of almost everyone, 'but I liked the basic design.'

A year later, the roar of guns had drowned out the noise of the car. Ben Pon reports he developed a 'violent hatred' of the Germans, and that, when the war was over, he wanted nothing to do with the VW any more. Briefly, he says, he tried to get the franchise for a US car; when this failed, his father persuaded him to try for the VW again. The elder man pointed out that, through old ties with GM's Opel, the family had a link with Germany that could not be denied. 'He told me not to be a fool and said we might as well do business with Germany again,' Pon reports.

Temporarily commissioned a full colonel in the Dutch Army, Pon made his way to Wolfsburg, hoping to impress the British officers who were then running the plant. 'I covered my chest with phony ribbons I'd made myself, got a Dutch corporal as a chauffeur for an old Mercedes, and drove into Germany in high style, puffing a cigar and waving at passers-by,' Pon says.

When this theatrical officer pulled in to Wolfsburg, he met Major Hirst and Hermann Münch, but preferred to pose as a high-ranking Dutch officer on a friendly inspection tour, rather than as anyone soliciting a franchise. Then Colonel Radclyffe asked to see him and, hearing that he had been in the motor business, asked him to help 'break a few bottlenecks'. These, of course, concerned the shortage of materials, and Pon was asked to trade cars for steel. In October 1947, Ben Pon bought six VWs to resell in Holland. 'They were,' he says, 'the first civilian sales of VWs.' As it turned out, he got only five beetles, as the sixth broke down on the makeshift assembly line.

Pon hired five drivers and took the cars back by road to Amersfoort, Holland, his home town. From this modest beginning, Pon's VW import operation, its headquarters still in Amersfoort, has grown to a network of three hundred dealers, importing more than fifty thousand VWs a year. Holland is Wolfsburg's second biggest import country, surpassed only by the USA. Other major markets for VW in 1966 were Austria, with 38,000; Sweden, 37,000; Belgium, 30,000; Great Britain, 28,000; and Switzerland, 27,000.

Other countries followed Holland's lead in obtaining franchises, once Nordhoff had come to the factory. Denmark, Switzerland, Sweden, Belgium, and Luxembourg came next, and then the pattern was set; franchise after franchise was assigned, as the company's policy of global exporting developed.

The size of this export programme today is impressive. The number of VWs sold to world markets outside Germany in 1966 passed one million, the total number exported to date is in excess of seven million; and well over five hundred thousand VWs have been manufactured abroad. Heading world-wide sales and service for VW is Dr. Carl H. Hahn, a member of the Volkswagenwerk's Vorstand, and heading export sales since the start of 1967 is Dr. R. M. Mummerts, who replaced Manuel Hinke, now retired. To handle this worldwide traffic, the Volkswagenwerk has had to go into the shipping business as well, and today it has more than sixty-five freighters under long leases or 'time-charter'. Just to supply the American demand for VWs, one of these ships arrives at a US port almost every single day of the year, returning to Europe loaded with American and Canadian coal, timber, grain, and other products. I was aboard Captain Rolf Lüning's 15,500-ton M/S *Carl Trautwein* as the process of discharging VWs took place in New Jersey; it took less than 24 hours to unload more than a thousand VWs and to be under way again. The Volkswagens are stacked in such ships as gently as chocolate-covered creams in multilevel candy boxes; as each deck is emptied, the pontoons which form it are lifted away, exposing another level of goodies. When the bottom has been reached and all decks have been cleared away, a hold for coal or wheat stands ready to receive its cargo. Speed is of the essence, says B. A. Hoeger, head of the Traffic Department of the US Volkswagen organisation, for a cargo-load of more than fifteen hundred Volkswagens must be ready for American distributors and dealers as rapidly as possible, to cut pier costs.

This international traffic, it has been pointed out to Americans, is not just two-way only in that ships return to Germany loaded with products imported by that country. The American products these ships bring back are minuscule when one considers what impact sales of VWs in America have on a larger scale. VWs are Germany's biggest export to the United States; they provide the wherewithal which allows Germany to buy from the USA. In 1965, West Germany bought US goods valued at 9,200,000,000 marks while sales to the US were valued at 5,600,000,000 marks.

While the beetle's success in the United States has been spectacular, its success elsewhere has been even greater, at least in terms of 'percentage of the market'. In Brazil, for example, the Volkswagen enjoys the same position that General Motors enjoys in the USA: more than every second car sold there is a VW!

The man who has made the VW a 100 per cent Brazilian commodity is a German who has himself become a Brazilian citizen: Dr. F. W. Schultz-Wenck, a slim, handsome, greying executive in his fifties, with the air of a man who seems equally at home on a polo field as a production line. He established 'Volkswagen do Brasil S.A.' on March 23, 1953, and started production of Brazilian Volkswagens four years later. Between 1953 and 1957, the company assembled VWs from imported parts, selling a little more than 2800. Today, about eleven thousand Brazilians work in the VW plant at São Bernardo do Campo, and in 1966 produced 95,000 vehicles. Schultz-Wenck's organisation sells 62 per cent of all passenger cars sold in Brazil and 42 per cent of Brazil's total motor-vehicle production. Here Volkswagen has provided a motor-car industry to a nation that never had one before and, in the process, helped prove that a VW produced elsewhere than in Wolfsburg can be just exactly as good as a Volkswagen which Germans make. Recently, a merger of this company and Vemag, third-largest motor-car maker in Brazil, created a large manufacturing consortium. A VW-designed and Vemag-produced car is planned for 1969.

VWs have been built not only in Brazil but in other countries as well. Another nation in the Western Hemisphere which manufactures VWs is Mexico, where Hans Barschkis, head of Volkswagen de Mexico, has sold more than fifty thousand cars; interest in the car is mounting so rapidly in that country that Barschkis expects to sell another fifty thousand in just a third the time it took him to sell the first batch. Today, well over 60 per cent of the materials in the Mexican VWs he produces in Xalostoc is of local origin and provides work for almost 2000 local citizens.

Two other VW-manufacturing nations are Australia and the Republic of South Africa. More than a quarter of a million VWs have been sold in the former country and more than 150,000 in the latter.

The story of the growth of Volkswagen in the United Kingdom and the stories of its development in Australia and South Africa are told in the two chapters immediately following. The rise of Volkswagen of America Inc. follows these accounts; because the USA today is Volkswagenwerk's biggest export market and second-largest customer (after West Germany), proportionately more space has been allocated to tell this story.

The importance of VW's success in the export market lies in just a few points. For one, the global success proves the universality of the Volkswagen design. It shows that this car has adapted itself to all sorts of local conditions and uniquely local needs: that it is a useful vehicle not only in crowded London or New York streets, but also in African jungles or Australian mountains. For another, it proves that this design is one which lends itself to manufacture and service from Germany to New Zealand, any place in the world. There are today thousands of Volkswagen dealers and service centres the world over; by and large, all adhere to the high standards set globally by Wolfsburg. By and large also, VW executives credit the success of their cars to these high standards. Manuel Hinke, the big gruff Bolivian-born German who for years headed the Volkswagenwerk's Export Department, gives major credit to VW's worldwide insistence on service first, sales second. (He points out that VW goes so far as to maintain service facilities in Moscow, where no VWs are sold, explaining that these are attached to the West German Embassy in the Soviet capital just to make sure each diplomatic VW is treated in Moscow as it would be back home.)

The car itself, or the service provided for it—which, then, can be assigned more credit? As we shall see, many VW executives, importers, distributors and dealers claim not any one of these can be credited with the 'Volkswagen miracle'; the truth, they say, lies in a combination of good product, good service, and good organisation. Yet what I have found so particularly pleasant about VW's organisation and about its service facilities is that I have not needed to encounter them often with my own Volkswagen. It may be nice to know VW's mechanics are experts in servicing their cars, but it is surely far better to enjoy the feeling that one will encounter them mostly at lubrication and inspection time. Looked at in this way, the success of the VW traces back to a unique integrity of manufacture. That this can be and is being maintained at a current rate of well over 1,500,000 cars a year is nothing short of amazing. Yet countless trials and the reports of countless independent motor journalists attest that this is so. Those who question it need only follow the advice that another car manufacturer once used: 'Ask the man who owns one.' There are now more than twelve million to choose from, all over the world.

Up the Mall, Full Throttle!

BACK in the year 1953, when Volkswagen's brush with Britain began, the company had a peculiar way of convincing potential customers of the unique virtues of a beetle. A salesman would take a prospect out for a demonstration drive and head for the Mall in London. 'We'd tear down that Mall, career around Victoria as tightly as we could a couple of times, sometimes even hit the kerb at forty miles per hour, and then race the car up the Mall, full throttle,' one salesman recalls. That hard-driving approach convinced many a sceptical Briton and sold a few cars, but it did not over the years prove enough to pull the British VW organisation into the twentieth century. Britain's automobile industry—or, at any rate, the marketing end of it—was a 'cottage industry' in 1953 and would remain so for a long time; far more drastic measures than careening around Victoria would be needed to pull it out of the Victorian age. That Volkswagen played a major role in this development is one of the most fascinating aspects of the story of how the Beetle invaded Britain.

The start wasn't easy. Volkswagen executives in 1953 needed to grow hides as thick as elephant-skins and cultivate the patience of saints: they faced strong anti-German sentiment as well as a general reluctance then to buy otherwise than British.

These sentiments continued to exist for many years, steadily shrinking all the time. Britain's moves towards Europe and the simple passage of years helped create a British market that is increasingly sophisticated and internationally minded. Volkswagens are today an accepted part of the British motoring scene, popular with their owners and praised by the press. Well over a quarter million VWs are on British roads today and their numbers are increasing at an accelerating pace. It is just for this very reason that the early years and growing pains of the British VW organisation are worth looking at and recording.

The start, birth-pains and development of VW in the United Kingdom was shot full of unique problems and obstacles. Consider, first of all, that Great Britain is virtually the seed-bed of the small car. It was in the United Kingdom that the small car was first developed and later perfected; Britain in the early 1950's produced more small cars than any other nation in the world, except West Germany. As we shall see in later chapters, the job of selling a small car in the United States of America was facilitated by the fact that the Americans grew tired of huge cars in the 1950's; a ready market for smaller cars suddenly and explosively developed and importers—primarily Volkswagen—filled it. In West Germany, as we have seen, the VW captured the bulk of the motor-car market at a time when other manufacturers were not yet ready to compete. In Britain, however, the situation was 100 per cent different. A successful small-car producing industry existed and, in order to compete in the UK, Volkswagen had to battle uphill all the way. Over the years, that battle was made steeper and stiffer by the introduction of high Customs duties, surcharges, taxes—and, lately, by the West German revaluation of the D-Mark. That it succeeded as well as it did in the face of such obstacles is testimony to those VW dealers and corporate executives who transformed adversity into success. The car they sell may be German, many of the techniques used to sell it may be American (or 'international'), but the dogged stance and the determination seem to an American author to be typically British.

Heinz Nordhoff's relations with Colonel C. R. Radclyffe and with other British occupation officers and officials had been very cordial; whenever he spoke of the British, he spoke with admiration for what he called 'British fairness'. He also was aware of the fact that anti-German sentiment remained relatively strong in Britain in the early 1950's; for both of these reasons, he came to the decision that 'if Volkswagen is ever to succeed in Britain, it must be a British company, under British management.'

Yet the man he appointed was, paradoxically, not British, but Irish. Stephen O'Flaherty of Dublin had met Nordhoff shortly after he became head of the Wolfsburg plant in 1948 and, by the early 1950's, O'Flaherty had started a Volkswagen import (and, eventually, assembly) operation, Volkswagen Distributors Limited of Long Mile Road, Dublin. (His son, M. P. O'Flaherty, today serves as Managing Director.)

Until 1953, the Volkswagenwerk had not been represented in Britain by any full-time, large-scale concessionaire operation, partly due to import restrictions prevailing until then. In 1952, a limited and restricted import licence was granted an Englishman named A. John Colborne-Baber, but only for the purpose of supplying VWs and VW spare parts to Americans in the UK, most of them US Air Force personnel in Kent. When renegotiation of a licence came due at the end of 1952, O'Flaherty was first on the scene to request it. He was given the UK franchise on January 1, 1953 and incorporated a new company, Volkswagen Motors Limited, the name of the firm ever since.

He had evidently convinced Volkswagenwerk that what a British VW operation needed was a bit of the luck of the Irish but it soon became clear to him that it needed more than that. Extra cash was required and O'Flaherty obtained it by bringing in two partners, K. J. Dear and Stanley Grundy. By then, although almost six months had passed, Volkswagen Motors Limited still existed only on paper. It had neither staff, nor offices, nor cars. Hopefully, once it had these, it would find its dealers—and then, customers.

In June 1953, Stephen O'Flaherty set his company up in business at Inego Place, Bedford Street, London, in space given to him in his solicitor's offices. The first members of the staff were hired and, after a board meeting, introduced to the new Managing Director, K. J. Dear.

There wasn't much to manage at that time. There was hardly any cash; there was not even enough furniture to go round. 'We had only one chair in that solicitor's office,' said an early member of the VW contingent. 'The chap who came in first got it.'

In July, the company moved into quarters it could at least call its own, located above the Lotus showrooms in Regent Street, London. A few secretaries were added and the handful of executives began to plot their moves. Corporate chairman O'Flaherty, who needed to spend most of his time in Dublin, visited about once every fortnight.

Press notices regarding the formation of Volkswagen Motors Ltd. had brought in inquiries from prospective applicants for dealerships and distributorships. Anne Hilton, then private secretary to K. J. Dear, recalls the atmosphere:

'Sometimes we had six people sitting about our small eight-by-six foot office, waiting to be interviewed. We had a large file of correspondence from others who'd written in as well. Screening these was the main activity of the men; we girls were busy all day long just typing letters to applicants.'

Why so many applicants? One answer lay in the shortage of motor-cars then plaguing Britain. Being themselves short of cars to sell, British car distributors and dealers were anxious to add more lines of cars to their rosters. The British public was hungry for motor-cars and, being anxious to get one, tended to sign on to as many dealer waiting lists as possible, planning to buy the first car made available to them.

Another factor which helped build up VW's early distribution network was the failure of the Jowett automobile company in Bradford, Yorkshire. When Jowett folded, its dealers were left high and dry. Most of them ended up with Volkswagen Motors Limited and, by the 1960's, about a fourth of all VW dealers in the UK were Jowett veterans or casualties.

In July 1953, while VW executives in London were busy scanning prospective dealers, a long-distance call from Wolfsburg demanded to know how many cars the company was finally going to order.

'We all looked at each other blankly,' one man then on the VW payroll remembers. 'We hadn't had time to figure out any estimates, any costs, nor any detailed and precise figures. We had no facilities, no service department, no parts depot, not even a showroom. We knew we were up against it! What could we say to Wolfsburg? Should we order five vehicles, or ten?'

At that very moment, while they were trying to decide what to say, Stephen O'Flaherty walked into the office and the question was posed to him. 'Order two hundred!' O'Flaherty replied. His colleagues looked at him wide-eyed and thought he was mad.

The cars, each accompanied by £10 worth of spare parts, came in twenty at a time. New, larger quarters had been located on St. James's Street and these even included the needed showroom. As luck would have it, however, the first twenty cars came in before the company had moved. 'As we hadn't any proper facilities,' Anne Hilton recalls, 'we fitted the number plates down at the kerb in Regent Street.'

Still, it was a thrill to see their first cars. 'They looked wonderful, absolutely beautiful,' said one veteran. 'They were all in gleaming shiny black. Even the dockers remarked how fine they looked!'

The job of selling them fell to James J. Graydon, who replaced K. J. Dear as Managing Director in midsummer 1953 and who was to remain with the company in that position until his retirement in January 1968. The conditions he faced were primitive indeed.

Executive headquarters for Volkswagen Motors Limited consisted of a basement set of offices, beneath the ground-floor showroom on St. James's Street. Not only was Graydon in the basement, but he had to work alongside the spare parts, which were down there as well, along with a few cars not displayed at ground level. This continued until the end of 1953, when a spare parts depot of sorts was established in Davis Street, London W.1; that new depot—also inadequate—served the company for twelve months.

As the cars came in from Germany, they were turned over to distributors as fast as possible, so that the company might avoid the high dock storage fees. A basic distributor network had by now been set up and each member of it had been given rather easy conditions: a distributor had to agree to buy only four cars immediately, with 50 per cent of the price being paid upon placing the order; in addition he had to buy £100 worth of tools and £250 worth of spare parts.

'We kept the requirements low so as not to frighten off prospective distributors,' said one VW executive then dealing with them. 'Yet we offered them only a $16\frac{2}{3}$ per cent discount, as against the $17\frac{1}{2}$ to 20 per cent discounts British manufacturers were offering.' Still, the distributors signed; 70 per cent of British car production was then being earmarked for export, and they needed cars to sell within the United Kingdom.

The distributor network which J. J. Graydon was then putting together 'just happened'—which proved one of the weaknesses of the British VW organisation in years to come. It was built up entirely from among those who contacted VW rather from a group of men whom VW had gone out to find and select. One of Graydon's staff explained it this way: 'Volkswagen in Britain faced a far more difficult problem in building up a distribution network than did other VW importers in other countries. We had to write off the top five or six dealers and distributors in many towns simply because they couldn't join Volkswagen without losing their existing franchises. Therefore we had to rely on those who wrote to us or visited us after reading about us in the papers.'

A good many who joined the Volkswagen team in those early years did so because they were enthusiastic about the beetle, but some were downright rude, as an early VW executive recalls. Some prospects who had written Volkswagen Motors Limited would keep VW's men waiting an hour before seeing them; they'd then come out and sneer, 'Well, where's that weird little German car of yours?'

Others proved not rude, only sceptical. One prospect who had his doubts brought his aged father along for the demonstration drive.

With the old gentleman seated in the back seat and the prospective distributor seated beside the driver, the Volkswagen was taken out for a spin about the roads. VW's man who was at the wheel says he could see the prospect was losing interest. 'On a whim,' he reports, 'I swerved off the road and on to a bridle path. I drove up it at full speed, shaking up the old man in the back seat pretty badly, but demonstrating just how well a Volkswagen can perform.' The prospect signed up. 'If you had gone up that bridle path at less than full speed,' he said later, 'I'd have thought you were trying to hide something.'

Scepticism wasn't all that plagued the company in those years. Vandalism was another headache—and a costly one. A collection centre had been set up in High Meads, but by the time the cars had arrived there from Harwich, the port at which they were unloaded, a staggering 75 per cent of them were damaged. A company official says that this damage, inflicted while the cars were parked in railway yards overnight, was apparently caused by some of the railway workers who would pass along them, banging hammers or spanners against their doors. Such workers caused other problems: car batteries were placed in the cars upside-down after Customs inspection, with the result that acid leaked all over the floors.

In an attempt at remedying these and other problems, Volkswagen Motors Limited decided to charter a ship, the *Aphia*, which soon began to transport eighty vehicles at a time direct to London, where distributors picked them up as 'drive-aways'. (This was necessary because car transporters were not then available in the UK. The first six Austin and six Rootes car transporters, built in 1950, were used exclusively for export cars which were meant not to have any mileage on them; transporters for the domestic British market came into use only in 1955.)

When the spare-parts depot in Davis Street proved inadequate, the company acquired 50,000 square feet of unused railway sheds at Plaistow, London E.15. The move was conducted under terribly primitive conditions. 'Instead of trained help,' J. J. Graydon said, 'we had to hire a group of university students on holiday. When they got a load of spare parts to Plaistow, they just dumped them on the floor. It so infuriated our spare-parts manager that he quit.'

As well he might, one could add. Volkswagen in Britain was 'making do' in a makeshift manner, from the selection of its distributor and dealer network to the organisation of its depots. The highly professional, smoothly efficient manner in which Volkswagen operated in West Germany (and throughout the world) was hardly in evidence at all in the United Kingdom. Part of the reason is to be found in the weaknesses then within the British Volkswagen organisation itself; part of the reason stemmed from weaknesses within the entire British automobile industry. Management methods were often antiquated and amateurish; salaried salesmen 'deigned' to take orders for cars, not being threatened by commission-salesmen who would actually *sell*; fusty, dusty, and musty facilities demoralised automobile mechanics and contributed to sloppiness in repair work; team-work as well as pride in work well done were reduced by rigid distinctions between salaried employees and hourly-paid 'blue-collar' workers; in short, much of the British automobile industry was hopelessly behind the times. Volkswagen Motors Limited merely reflected the shortcomings of its sister British companies.

Still, the car itself sold itself. Only 945 Volkswagens had been bought in 1953; the next year, sales had quadrupled, to 3260. Although import licences continued to restrict sales sharply for several years, a gradual growth was visible. Between 1955 and 1957, sales hovered at slightly above the 5000 vehicles a year level, then rising to 7436 in 1958 and 9227 in 1959.

As the 1960's dawned, about 36,000 Volkswagens were to be seen on the roads of Britain. They did not seem quite so strange by that time. Volkswagen owners in the United Kingdom, like VW owners elsewhere, came to be enthusiastic salesmen for the company. Their attitude may perhaps be summed up by John Langley, who wrote of his early experiences, with a Volkswagen he'd bought, in the *Daily Telegraph*:

'More than ten years ago, when British small cars still had features such as rigid rear axles, "buzz-box" side-valve engines and three-speed gearboxes, I horrified friends in the motor industry by buying a Volkswagen. They were even more horrified when I liked it! Compared with most of its rivals of the time, the VW was fun to drive and a tireless performer . . .'

'You either hate or love a Volkswagen,' wrote Malcolm Withers in the *South Wales Echo*. 'It's a car that has generated more emotion than any other car since the Model T. Significantly, its . . . success is based on the same selling points as Henry Ford's brain-child—ruggedness, reliability, and value for money . . .'

His point is illustrated by an experience J. J. Graydon had at a London Motor Show. A Volkswagen owner asked to see Graydon; he wanted to complain that his beetle wasn't pulling quite as well as it used to. Graydon urged the man to have the car serviced and then, on parting with the disgruntled owner, asked him a final question. 'By the way,' he said, 'how many miles do you have on it?' As though that were beside the point, the owner replied, 'Eighty-two thousand.'

A car that can cover that many miles before beginning to act 'tired' develops a lot of consumer loyalty—a fact which one London daily newspaper learned to its dismay after publishing an article some years ago attacking the beetle. Rather than the one or two 'crank letters' the editors expected to receive, the paper was deluged with four thousand outraged letters from British VW owners.

The import licence system ended in 1958 but a temporary surcharge was imposed from 1964 to 1966. Lifting of the licensing system of course benefited Volkswagen and sales by 1959 had risen to 16,000 vehicles a year; that year, too, the 50,000th Volkswagen had been delivered to the United Kingdom—and fittingly presented as a gift to the widow of Colonel C. R. Radclyffe.

The person who presented that car on behalf of Volkswagen Motors Limited was Lord Brabazon of Tara, who became chairman of the company in 1957, as a result of a significant change in the company's fortunes. That year, Volkswagen Motors Ltd. had become part of the Thomas Tilling Limited 'family of firms', an industrial holding company with a variety of interests.

Lord Brabazon, a colourful personality in British industrial and sporting life, has since died; Kenneth Chapman replaced him for some time as chairman of Volkswagen Motors. (Mr. Chapman has since become Managing Director of Thomas Tillings; today, P. M. Meaney is chairman of Volkswagen Motors Limited.)

Thomas Tillings pursues a policy of non-interference with the companies it acquires; it places one of its senior executives into the company as chairman, but allows each of its companies full freedom of action, so long as its aims—growth and profitability among them—are fulfilled. Precisely these aims came into question in the late 1960's.

By 1966, there were about 200,000 Volkswagens on the roads of Britain and sales had reached about 28,000 vehicles a year; while this was success of a sort, it merely tended to accentuate the company's shortcomings. While unit sales seemed fine, Volkswagen Motors Limited needed badly to be overhauled if the aims of both the Wolfsburg factory and of Thomas Tillings were to be realised. To cite only one example, the company at that time had twenty-seven distributors and more than 400 dealers; each of the distributors were on different financial arrangements with the company and no uniform standards had been set up.

In early 1967, John Tyzack & Partners, management consultants retained by Tillings to study Volkswagen Motors Limited, recommended a complete restructuring of the company under a new managing director. Graydon, an enthusiastic archaeologist and Egyptologist, planned to retire in 1968 and helped in the search for his successor.

A chain of events far away was making that successor available. Alan M. Dix, an Englishman who had had a phenomenally successful career with VW in the United States, had resigned from the US company in July, 1967, after serving it as Group Vice-President (Operations). Manuel Hinke, the Volkswagenwerk's retired export chief, contacted Dix and asked him if he'd do a job for the Volkswagen importing company which his son, Manuel Hinke Jr., directed throughout the Caribbean. Once this job was completed in autumn of 1967, the Hinkes offered Dix a permanent position with VW in those sunny southern waters. The proposition was a tempting one and Dix flew to Frankfurt, Germany, to discuss it further with Manuel Hinke Jr., who happened to be there at that time. While in Frankfurt, Dix placed a social telephone call to London, to say hello to an old friend: James J. Graydon.

Graydon immediately countered the Hinkes' offer with one of his own: he needed to find a successor, he told Dix, and if Dix were interested, he ought to come to London to meet the Tillings people.

Anyone who knows Alan Dix could have predicted which offer he'd take. Not only would the British offer allow him to return home with his Scottish wife but, more importantly, it would allow him to become the number one man almost immediately. Dix, who is almost constitutionally unfitted for a subordinate role in any organisation, flew to London. There, both the Tillings and John Tyzack people met with him and, on 24 November 1967, named him Managing Director-Designate of the British VW company.

I met Alan Dix only a couple of days after he first arrived in London and recall being somewhat overwhelmed by the enormous drive and energy of this tall, powerfully built dynamo. His wife and three children were still in the United States at that time and Dix threw himself into the job of reorganising Volkswagen Motors with all the energy and enthusiasm at his command, working himself and his associates virtually around-the-clock. While still only Managing Director-Designate, he did a lightning tour of VW installations and facilities and prepared an exhaustive and detailed study for Tillings, recommending changes in every area of the company's operations. I recall from my earliest meetings with Dix how utterly appalled he was at what he found on his arrival in London and, at the same time, with what apparent delight he faced the enormous task of turning everything upside down. What troubled him most was that the tried methods which had worked so successfully for Volkswagen in almost all other countries had hardly been applied in the United Kingdom at all, not to speak of fundamental modern management methods applicable to any successful business. What the company seemed to need more than anything else was strong and decisive leadership, as well as rigorous application of the standards and systems which had made VW a success everywhere throughout the globe. 'The product is a good product and the system is a good system,' Dix said; as improvements on the product were the concern of the German VW factories, Dix addressed himself to the job of overhauling the system in the UK.

That VW system is one which Alan Dix has soaked up into his bones for twenty years. Born in Copenhagen as the son of the British Naval attaché in Denmark, Dix spent his childhood and early life there, escaping to Sweden from German occupied Denmark in 1943 and thence to Scotland by stowing away on a ship. He became a wartime R.A.F. Intelligence Officer, posted to a fighter squadron, and served until demobilised in 1947, when he joined BEA in Copenhagen for two years. From there, he went to East Africa, where his Volkswagen career began. In 1953, as sales manager to the Cooper Motor Corporation, the VW concessionaires, he personally won the gruelling East Africa Safari, driving a beetle. The following year, the hard-driving Dix became general manager of the Uganda operation and then, at the personal invitation of Heinz Nordhoff, underwent two years' training at Volkswagenwerk headquarters in Wolfsburg. That completed, he was sent to the United States, where the Volkswagen service-and-sales system was being perfected to such an extent that it has served as a model ever since for other VW operations elsewhere. After some time on the West Coast of the United States, Alan Dix joined Capitol Car Distributors, the VW distribution operation in Washington, D.C. in 1959, when it had a wholesale turnover of 6000 vehicles a year; by the time he became president of that company, he had helped raise sales to 37,000 vehicles a year. Capitol Car, which in 1959 was the second smallest distributorship in the United States, had grown phenomenally, with its dealers averaging a higher number of Volkswagens sold per dealer than the domestic car dealers' average. 'How healthy can you get?' Alan Dix pointed out in an interview with Britain's *Motor Trade Executive*, stressing that Volkswagen dealers in the United States sell more cars per dealership and make a higher profit than even Ford or General Motors dealers do. 'I would give ten years of my life to see that over here,' he added.

For a time, what with working around the clock, it almost seemed he was determined to make that morbid prediction come true. His appointment as Managing Director was confirmed on January 10, 1968 (Graydon retiring to Malta) and, on the very next day, Dix presented Thomas Tillings with his report and recommendations. Despite the fact that it involved an investment running into six figures Tillings gave Dix all he asked. They posed only one question: 'What happens if you fail to reach the targets you predict?' To which they got an answer typical of Alan Dix: 'Simple. You fire me!'

The situation Dix faced in the United Kingdom would require a book in itself to describe adequately. Briefly, however, some of the highpoints (or low points) can be spelled out as follows:

There was virtually no management whatever, for sixteen departmental managers had been reporting directly to Graydon, who was required to make decisions in every field, no one else having any authority. This inevitably delayed needed decisions or made it impossible for expertise to come to grip with problems; further, the morale of corporate executives was at rock-bottom, few of them being able to put into effect the policies they felt were required.

The importer (Volkswagen Motors Limited), far from setting standards for its distributors and dealers, had no effective control over them. Virtually every one of whom had separate and different financial arrangements with the company.

Dealer morale was as low as dealer apathy was high. Because Volkswagen Motors Limited failed to set standards, the twenty-seven distributors existing in Britain (versus only fourteen in the entire USA) treated their dealers in an arbitrary and often high-handed manner.

With few exceptions, Volkswagen facilities in the United Kingdom failed remotely to match the standards of quality elsewhere in the global .VW network. Headquarters was understaffed, poorly equipped, and largely uninformed of what was happening throughout the British VW dealerships. Distributors and dealers generally operated out of antiquated facilities; training standards for service and sales personnel were virtually non-existent; service standards had been neglected to such an extent that one was hard-pressed in Britain to find the equivalent of the typically modern, well-lit, almost antiseptically clean Volkswagen workshops encountered elsewhere. Because profits for the dealers were too low, they hesitated to invest additional funds in crucially needed improvements, nor was it made clear to them by headquarters what improvements were called for.

Volkswagen was being run in Britain like 'a cottage industry' and, says Dixon, 'could have slid either way at that time: up or down.' It is his way of pointing out that, had the company remained as it was, it would have inevitably slid downhill in the increasingly demanding and competitive marketplace of the 1970's; success on the other hand, could almost be assured as an inevitability if the methods, techniques, and standards applicable elsewhere were applied with speed, vigour and determination.

'There is not a single company in the British motor trade,' one VW executive states, 'which underwent a comparable experience: of one man shaking it up completely and turning it totally around, as Dix did. In fact, it took a lot of faith to join Dix when he first arrived, for the company could have failed and we could all have ended up losers, but the reorganisation not only worked, but was exhilarating.'

Less than exhilarating, to be sure, to the distributors, *all* of whom were phased out during 1968, or for the dealers whose numbers were slashed from over 400 to well under 300 as those who refused to meet Dix's standards were sacked or left. Headquarters too was reorganised from top to bottom; those in it who survived 'the purge' were often extremely bright young men who had never before been given an opportunity to demonstrate their abilities.

After interviewing seventy-five men, Alan Dix appointed five senior executives and then, in sharp contrast to the old system, gave them full responsibility for their divisions. Work standards were set by asking each executive, senior and junior, to write his own job-specifications, a system Dix considers to be essential for a host of reasons, one of them being that a man will tend to demand more of himself than another would, if he were writing the job-description for him. Two bulky volumes, detailing every aspect of management organisation, were produced in record time, telling every divisional, departmental and section chief his precise reponsibilities and targets. At the same time, similar manuals were prepared for every dealership, concerning every aspect of management, sales, service, advertising and promotion. Nothing was left to chance and the *Financial Times*, surveying Dix's changes with unabashed admiration, commented that 'the new dealer operation is being run with almost military precision.' Dix's 'recipe' for VW's success in the UK, the paper stated, was adapted from the US model, where 'a tough policy towards dealer standards, backed up by a meticulous attention to detail' made other European car importers 'appear slipshod in comparison.'

Driving his people as hard as he drove himself throughout this reorganisational period, Dix found, furnished, and staffed a completely new headquarters building within a record-breaking 100 days. Staff was vastly expanded so as to provide dealers with all the services to which other VW dealers elsewhere in the world are accustomed. An architectural department, for example, is busy changing the Volkswagen image from one end of Britain to the other, a job which will take some years, but which already has made impressive inroads. New dealers are queuing up for franchises today and all are required by contract to construct facilities along the lines this department specifies; older dealerships are being required to convert their premises to meet the new specifications—and are being provided with detailed drawings enabling them to do so. Investment on the part of the dealers is today being rewarded, as the more efficient dealers, those who adhere to headquarters' highest standards in sales, service and facilities, receive a higher discount on the vehicles and parts they purchase. Indeed, those dealers who refuse to meet Volkswagen Motors' standards today find themselves rather unsentimentally phased out of the network, after years of 'having gotten away with murder,' as one executive put it. In September 1970, the company announced that orders placed with British firms under the Buy British policy which Dix started for components and raw materials would run between £7–£10m that year.

The beneficiary of all these changes is, ultimately, the Volkswagen owner. As Dix's changes permeate every dealership in Britain, no longer will British Volkswagen owners need to put up with dirty facilities, indifferent workmen, gloomy reception areas, questionable standards—in short, with all the miseries which the British motor car owner in general has had to put up with in thousands of garages, whether belonging to VW, to domestic manufacturers, or to independents.

The familiar blue-and-white Volkswagen sign will in the future signal the same uniform, modern, brightly-lit and spotless facilities which Volkswagen owners have found on travels abroad; already, several score VW dealerships in the United Kingdom have come up to the highest company standards. As every Volkswagen mechanic today filters through a training course at company headquarters in Purley, Surrey, or at Doncaster, the company's Northern Region headquarters, the standards of mechanical work at dealerships is soaring as well, helped along by Volkswagen's revolutionary electronic Diagnosis system, which totally takes the guesswork out of car inspections. A VW insurance company and a VW car-rental operation are also in operation, to provide owners with additional and economical services geared specifically to their needs.

The product being a good product and the system being tried and true, it is small wonder that sales under the new management team have begun to soar. Data processing equipment can give Dix and his executives an immediate picture of dealer sales and inventories, of both vehicles and parts, allowing the company to move rapidly to correct shortcomings. Today, Volkswagen Motors Limited issues monthly sales figures and most months have shown a startling improvement over the same month the previous year. The gamble which Thomas Tillings took when it accepted Alan Dix's recommendations lock, stock, and barrel, has paid off. But then Dix never thought it a gamble at all. Volkswagen's success had everywhere been built on service first, sales afterwards, as well as on maintaining the highest management and operational standards. There was no reason why this 'system' shouldn't work in Britain. In fact, it has—and it has proved a model for many a British motor car manufacturer as well.

Beetles Enter Bush and Outback

THE plump little German lady heading for Antwerp in 1951 felt as
though she were heading into the future. Not surprisingly, there
didn't appear to be one in Germany that year. Soviet pressure on
Berlin continued, West Germany swarmed with millions of refugees,
and six years after the war few Germans felt sure of their position in
the world society. Those who occupied West Germany had not yet
fully accepted the Germans, as they have, by and large, today, as
allies and respected partners. The year 1951 began, as a matter of
fact, with sharp and inauspicious words. In Hamburg on New Year's
Day, British High Commissioner Sir Ivone Kirkpatrick charged the
Germans for allegedly still being interested in 'adventurous policies'
and claimed he had not found signs that, 'despite their weak position',
they wished to understand the views of others or harmonise their
policies with those of other nations. It was a strange comment to
make of a people hardly able to consider adventures and, in any case,
busy rebuilding democratic institutions and shattered industry. But
the comment underlined the fact that, in some quarters, a deep
distrust remained. To Therese Hanael, the future seemed clearly to
lie far away, and she sought it now in Australia, which was about as
far away as she could get.

She was going to rejoin her husband, Ted, from whom the war
had separated her in 1941, when he was sent to Australia to be
interned. Ted, Therese, and their son had lived in Persia; when Ted
was interned, she went home to Germany. After his release, Ted
Hanael looked about him at the vast Commonwealth in which he
found himself. He liked what he saw and liked even more the spirit
of growth and hope around him. He decided to stay and to couple his
future with Australia's. He saved enough to pay for the passage and
in 1951 sent for Therese. No doubt he also counted on her own
savings to help them in their new home.

When she arrived, he was dismayed, for it turned out that Therese had spent her savings, most imprudently, on a 1946 model Volkswagen, bought from a British officer in Germany. 'We needed so many things to get started again,' Ted says. 'We had so little, and the last thing we seemed to need was a car.'

That beetle may have been unwanted in 1951, but ten years later, things had changed. In 1961, it was the object of a four-month hunt. When it was found (still being used by Ted and Therese Hanael), it was 'bought back' by Volkswagen; in payment, the Hanaels received another prize car. A 1961 VW, the 100,000th Australian Volkswagen was presented to Mr. and Mrs. Hanael by the Premier of Victoria, the Hon. Sir Henry E. Bolte. As it turned out, Therese Hanael's 1946 beetle was the very first Volkswagen to land on Australian soil and zip along Australian roads. *Tasmanian Motor News*, reporting the ceremonies attending the swap, said: 'It might pay you to keep that old car for a while. . . . If you keep it long enough, someone may give you a new one in exchange for it one day.'

Surrendering his vintage bug, Ted Hanael said, 'Take good care of it: it's a good little car.' Reporters say his eyes were moist; he had, it was clear, long since overcome his misgivings. That 1946 beetle, now a museum-piece displayed by VW in Australia, had logged 105,000 miles and is the grand-daddy of the more than 250,000 VWs which have since been sold in the Commonwealth.

It is a huge country for so small a car. Australia is the world's biggest island (and its smallest and driest continent); more than one-third of its 2,974,581 square miles consists of desert or semi-desert, with an annual rainfall of 10 inches or less. Those Australians who had encountered Wolfsburg's *Kübelwagen* in the deserts of North Africa and had seen for themselves how it performed there perhaps had faith in a future for VW in Australia, but few others had. In 1951, the Hanael car must have seemed mighty queer; most Australians liked and relied on larger, more powerful cars, many of them US makes. The arduous conditions of the Australian 'outback' seemed to call for big cars and many of the small ones with which Australians were familiar had high-revving motors without stamina for long, continuous running. Local tastes and driving conditions seemed hostile to the beetle and the job facing those who wanted to sell VWs in Australia was one of first building public confidence, then building cars.

A German baron, K. D. von Oertzen by name, was one who did

Professor Heinrich Nordhoff

The VW factory at Wolfsburg today, largest single motor-car factory in the world. The smokestacks indicate the power plant.

Volkswagenwerk administrative building tower looms above the expanding skyline of Wolfsburg today

A consignment of Beetles being loaded at Emden for dispatch abroad.

M/S *Johann Schulte*, the world's largest car-carrying vessel and flagship of the growing world-wide Volkswagen fleet, nears a US port with a capacity load of 1750 new VWs.

The German M/V *Aphaia*, one of three Volkswagen ships which sails to Britain, discharging VWs for the British market. Largest ship to bring cars to Britain is the roll-on, roll-off M/V *Agenor*, with nearly 200 cars each journey.

Dr. Kurt Lotz, Chairman of
Volkswagenwerk A. G.

J. Stuart Perkins, President,
Volkswagen of America,
Incorporated

Alan M. Dix, Managing
Director of Volkswagen
Motors Limited.

have confidence—and he set about trying to build it in at least *one* Australian. The baron (the very one who had attended Porsche's 1934 meeting with Hitler) had been an unabashed Australiaphile ever since he first visited the Commonwealth and sniffed its air of opportunity. That was before the war, when he worked for Auto-Union; one of his Australian friends was Lionel R. V. Spencer of Melbourne, who had been granted the franchise for DKW cars at that time. In 1950, von Oertzen joined the Volkswagenwerk and two years later he persuaded Spencer to see Wolfsburg for himself. Spencer was impressed; so much so, that in October 1953, his company became Australian distributors, assigned not only to import Volkswagens, but to organise a pattern of distribution Down Under which would meet Wolfsburg's standards.

Regent Motors (Holdings) Ltd., Spencer's company, displayed the first Volkswagen imported by it in Melbourne on October 11, 1953. The car's reception may have been mixed, but Australians with a fine eye noticed a new note. One of these was Athol Yeomans, of *Wheels*. He recalls his first encounter, not with a VW, but with a VW news release.

'It was my first experience of VW press relations,' he reports, 'in fact my first direct contact with VW . . . There was no boasting, no exaggeration, no claims like "best", "newest" and so on. It was a breath of fresh air, that release, in stark contrast to those from American car factories. . . . I made a mental note that VW might be a car to try. . . .'

Another motor writer was Laurie Whitehead of *The Herald*, Melbourne. A few days after seeing Regent's first beetle, he wrote: 'The German Volkswagen offers the most serious challenge yet faced by British small to medium cars on the Australian market, trade leaders believe. When the Volkswagen made its debut in Melbourne last week, one remarked, "This is the nearest thing we've seen to a modern-age Ford T." He meant nothing derogatory. The compact, beetlebacked, rear-engined car offers just about everything needed by the owner with a small family. . . .'

By the year's end Wolfsburg had shipped to Australia thirty-one Volkswagens; another VW was shipped 'completely knocked down' (CKD). Plans were afoot not just to import beetles, but to assemble them locally.

The first steps meant to turn the little German car into an Australian citizen were taken in May–June, 1954, when Australian coach builders Martin and King Pty. Ltd., under contract to Regent

Motors, began assembling CKD Volkswagens at their plant in the Melbourne suburb of Clayton. By the end of 1954, Wolfsburg had shipped 3084 CKD vehicles (and 1286 'built up' ones) to Australia, Clayton had assembled 1385 sedans, and the motoring public had bought 1,746 Beetles and 299 Type II Commercials. This was a modest beginning indeed: the little beetle had 'captured' a tiny (1·2 per cent) share of the Australian sedan market and a minuscule (0·5 per cent) share of the commercial vehicle market.

A lot still had to be done to convince sceptical Australians that the VW was suited to a land whose lonely stretches seemed to swallow up a car as small as this. (One example: a road sign in the Northern Territory. One arm lists only two communities: '2½ miles to Katherine; 737 to Alice Springs.') Regent Motors General Manager Allan V. Gray decided to subject the Volkswagen to endurance trials so brutal that few would ever dream the beetle could survive, much less compete effectively.[1]

'The decision to subject our car to Australia's terribly demanding reliability trials no doubt seemed foolhardy at the time,' Allan Gray admitted afterwards. 'But it turned out to be one of the smartest moves we could have made.'

In the mid-1950s, Australian motoring enthusiasts watched in amazement (and amusement) as the beetle entered the field against cars twice its power (and twice its price). The trials, considered the world's severest tests of car and drivers, covered thousands of miles of Australia's unmade roads, led through the torrid north and over the wet, tortuous mountain roads of the southern Great Divide. As the winners of the 1955 Redex Trial (which included a horror stretch of 143 creek crossings in eighty-two miles) were announced, the amused smiles had disappeared and the amazement had doubled, for VWs had won both first and second place. Even the amazement disappeared over the next several years, for beetles were beating the big cars so regularly by then that hearing the winners announced was proving monotonous. In the 1956 Mobilgas Trial of 8745 miles, VWs came in first, third, fourth, and sixth. In the 1957 Ampol Trial of 6000 miles, VWs came in first and second; in the Mobilgas Rally of 10,738 miles, staged the same year, twenty of the fifty-two surviving vehicles were beetles and six of these had captured each of the first six places. Then, in the Mobilgas Trial of 1958, VWs came in first, second, fourth, and fifth.

1. Gray, until lately Managing Director of Volkswagen Australasia Ltd., had served with VW in Australia from the Regent Motors days through 1966.

Australians did more than watch now: they also began to buy. By 1959, the beetle had taken more than 10 per cent of the Australian sedan market (and six per cent of the commercial market). By year's end, almost 73,000 Volkswagens had been sold in Australia since 1954.

The Round Australia Trials ended shortly thereafter. Australians believe that Volkswagen's continuous success was responsible for doing them in. VW wins were so consistent during the years this event was held, that the results became a foregone conclusion, not only to its competitors, but to press and public as well. Since the end of the Round Australia Trials, the factory has not been active in trials and rallies, although many private individuals have continued to use VWs in such events. VW management turned to the task of making the most of success.

A new company had by this time been formed to handle the job. Created with both Australian and West German capital (the Volkswagenwerk in Wolfsburg owned 51 per cent of the shares), it was called Volkswagen (Australasia) Pty. Ltd. One of the first things it did was acquire the Clayton assembly plant from Martin and King and expand it, investing $A24,000,000 in it—and in the future.

Clayton became headquarters. As management explains the choice of this suburb, located fourteen miles from the financial heart of Melbourne, it offered good transport facilities, close-by suppliers, available workers and homes in which they could be housed. Additional land, abundant electric power, a stable and growth-minded State Government also existed, as well as the Martin and King facilities which would serve as a base.

Expansion of these had cost VW more than $A28,000,000 by 1960; a new press shop, third largest in Australia, alone cost $A10,000,000. As Volkswagen's investments in Australia grew, so did the number of Australian components in the cars themselves. The first locally produced components found their way into a VW assembled at Clayton in 1955; now, nearly 80 per cent of the VW 1200 and VW 1300 models is literally 'made in Australia'. This growth from an assembly plant to a full-scale manufacturing operation was helped along by a second, even larger, expansion programme begun in 1964. In that year Volkswagen (Australasia) Pty. Ltd. changed its name to Volkswagen Australasia Ltd. and its status to that of a public company; Volkswagenwerk AG in Wolfsburg had bought up the Australian-held shares and was now full parent to its Australasia subsidiary. With needed support from West Germany, a new

$A44,000,000 expansion programme was begun. The three-year effort involved will bring to Clayton a new VW engine manufacturing plant, a non-ferrous foundry, and a transmission-manufacturing plant, and increase the Australian content to 95 per cent.

The Volkswagen factory in Australia, says a VW publication in Wolfsburg, hardly differs, except for size, from the works in Germany. 'The same production level is maintained. . . . The same modern equipment was provided as is installed in the automobile firms in Europe and America. . . . The Australian Volkswagen factory is one of the most modern plants in the Southern Hemisphere. . . .'

The expansion programme has of course contributed to the economy generally. More than $A20,000,000 a year are spent buying from more than 1500 Australian suppliers. Speaking of this, one Senator called the investments 'a further manifestation of the confidence of the world in Australia' and providing 'an opportunity for further employment' as well as 'for Australia to increase further its . . . stature in the commerce of the world.'

The Australian subsidiary had indeed gone international. Noting in 1962 that Wolfsburg could meet only 85 per cent of the world demand for Volkswagens, it began to export on its own.

Australian-made Volkswagens and parts and accessories have since been exported to no fewer than twenty countries. The Clayton plant has exported vehicles worth more than $A2,000,000 over the three years between 1962 and 1965 and the rapid expansion of export sales volume resulted mainly from its having taken over the business of supplying the majority of VWs required in New Zealand. More than 2000 VW sedans a year are being shipped to New Zealand in CKD form by the Clayton, Victoria, plant and exports to that country have been maintained at the maximum permitted by New Zealand's import restrictions. Following New Zealand, other important 'importers' of Australian-made VWs are Papua/New Guinea, Fiji, the British Solomon Islands and Western Samoa.

'The future of Volkswagen in Australia,' management says, 'will be closely linked with the expanding trade between the Commonwealth and the developing nations of these areas.' Although Germany has been shipping VWs to these countries for years, the Australians compete with Wolfsburg for these markets.

The New Zealand operation, a major customer of the Clayton organisation, is a wholly-owned subsidiary of an all-New Zealand-owned holding company, Motor Holdings Ltd., whose Chairman is Joseph Noel Turner of Auckland. Called VW Motors (New Zealand)

Ltd., and starting as an early Jowett franchise-owner, it switched to VWs in December 1953 and began assembling locally, using CKD parts shipped from Wolfsburg. By April 1955 its 1000th Volkswagen had rolled off Otahuhu assembly lines; since then, the plant has grown and is now capable of assembling more than thirty-five cars a day. As noted, New Zealand also imports heavily from Australia and in 1963, for example, placed the largest single order ever received by Clayton up to that time, for one thousand VW 1200 de luxe sedans.

Unlike British fleet-owners, who have rarely used non-British cars, Australia's fleet-owners do buy Volkswagens. This may, of course, be due to the fact that the Clayton-produced VW is almost completely Australian in content; whatever the reason, a host of Commonwealth and State Government Departments are among VW customers and even the military have joined the ranks. The Australian Army in 1963 placed its first order, for forty-six bronze-green Microbuses, to be used as personnel carriers, and the Air Force that same year ordered sixteen Microbuses and sixteen double-door vans (golden yellow with white roofs), for use on RAAF stations. The Snowy Mountains Authority, which bought its first VW in October 1958, today owns more than a hundred.

One important recent anniversary celebrated by VW in Australia arrived in November 1964, when the 200,000th Australian-made VW came off the production line. Although sales have passed 250,000 since, sales efforts are pushed as though something were gaining on the beetle. Volkswagen's success has also directed the attention of other companies to the small car field. In 1961, BMC introduced the Morris 850 and followed with the Morris 1100 in 1964. Ford, whose Prefect and Anglia had competed unsuccessfully with Volkswagen, introduced the larger and more powerful Cortina. General Motors came up with the Vauxhall Viva and in 1963 the Japanese took a major step when the Toyota range of vehicles obtained dealer representation.[1]

As sales mounted into the highs reached in the 1960s, the company, its distributors, and its more than 300 dealers continued to dazzle Australia with razzle-dazzle promotions. In 1962, drivers Ray Christie, then thirty-six, and Joe Dunlop, then forty-two, challenged the nine-day record time in which a VW competitor

1. Beetle competitors in Australia today are the cars mentioned above. Japanese competition is increasing; VW 1500/1600s compete with GM's Holden, Ford's Falcon, Chrysler's Valiant, and the Toyota (as do VW station wagons). VW Type II Commercials compete against Holden, Falcon, Valiant, Toyota, Land-Rover, Morris and Commer.

sent a big six-cylinder model car around Australia. Melbourne business proprietor Christie, and Dunlop, a member of the Greensborough Police, took on the test in a VW Standard sedan (to prove it was as good as the De Luxe model). They completed the 8100-mile run in seven and a quarter days (168 hours). Between Perth and Ceduna (1400 miles) they *averaged* sixty miles per hour. Their only mishaps: two punctures (one caused by a horseshoe). In 1964, the same two men challenged their own record, this time using a VW 1500 sedan. Leaving the Southern Cross Hotel in Melbourne at one minute past midnight on Sunday, August 23, they slid smilingly into the same spot at 10.18 pm, Friday, August 28. Total elapsed mileage and time: 8044 miles; 5 days, 22 hours, 17 minutes. They claimed they could have done better if they hadn't caught a few hours of sleep in Mount Isa and in Geraldton while their car underwent routine servicing.

VW distributors and dealers in Australia like this sort of flamboyant touch. Although the initial distribution system, set up at first by Regent Motors, had been different, today's is company-controlled in the main, with Volkswagen (Distribution) Pty. Ltd. representing Volkswagen Australasia Limited in most of the Commonwealth.[1] Vast distances are covered, and the methods used to do so seem far advanced to anyone not accustomed to Thinking Big in the Australian manner. *VWA Review* expresses the problem, and one solution, when it reports that a 1965 Volkswagen was delivered from Perth to Derby aboard a DC–4 Cargomaster. This 'air mail, special delivery' beetle 'opens new prospects to VW owners in the north', Volkswagen Australasia stated. 'In this way, new cars can be delivered with only a few miles on the speedometer—those needed for dealer testing and driving to and from the airport at both ends.'

Some of the techniques dealers use to build the beetle's sales are already 'Volkslore'. One Osborne Park dealer in Western Australia, for example, took a 1965-model, three-week-old camel as a trade-in, crediting $A100 for the gangly creature. Hare Motors accepted with delight Cohuna (Vic.) dentist P. Clavin's 1949 Rolls-Bentley as a trade-in on a beetle, later sold it to be reconditioned by a Rolls enthusiast. Lanock Motors of Sydney startled Sydney Harboursiders in 1959, when it launched a standard VW beetle into Kogarah Bay

1. State managers run distribution in Victoria and Southern Riverina, New South Wales, South Australia and Northern Territory, and Western Australia. The only exception is Queensland and Northern Rivers of N.S.W., where VW Motors Pty. Ltd. acts as distributor. In New Zealand, distributor is VW Motors (New Zealand) Ltd.; in A.C.T. (Australian Capital Territory), Greg Cusack Pty. Ltd.; and in Papua–New Guinea, Rewo Motors Pty. Ltd. Other distributors exist in the New Hebrides, Fiji, Western Samoa, British Solomons, New Caledonia, and Tahiti.

on the final day of speedboat championships there. The driver encountered little traffic as he ploughed the car along at a steady five knots, for the championships had been delayed because of the rough weather. Yachtsmen admitted the car showed good stability despite the heavy swell and even made sharp turns (with the driver archly offering hand-signals). On subsequent occasions, Lanock sent its 'boatswagen' across the half-mile Middle Harbour stretch four times, with the car in water more than forty minutes on each occasion. The few modifications which needed to be made: a 10-by-8-inch propeller fitted behind the rear bumper, driven by the generator drive wheel at the rear of the crankshaft; a snorkel fitted to the exhaust, and some grease smeared on to standard dust seals. No rudder was required as the front wheels steered satisfactorily. Another VW agent, Burr Motors, of Mildura, 'sailed' a similar beetle across the Murray River, cheered on by thousands of spectators.

All this delights Australian and New Zealand VW enthusiasts, many of them enrolled in local VW clubs. Testing the car's economy is a popular club event; at a Seymour VW Club economy run, a 36-hp sedan racked up 58 mpg, while a VW 1500 stationwagon scored 44 mpg. At another event in Bendigo (Vic.), a club member returned a figure of 58·3 mpg. Such highs are of course abnormal, but the normal seems good enough for most owners. Richard Bayles of Bairnsdale (Vic.) is one; he reports that his new VW, measured over 3000 miles covered in three months, 'averaged 40·2 mpg and up to 45 mpg'. Bayles took his car to Cooma in the Snowy Mountains, where temperatures run to below 8°F. 'Snow, rocks, rain, dust, sun, mud, cold—all just don't seem to affect this car!' he says. 'This is more than I ever expected.'

To drive just this point home—that 'nothing' often seems to bother beetles—Volkswagen Australasia Limited have made a big promotion out of the standard VW 1200 sedan which spent a year in Antarctica, at Mawson Station, a lonely Australian scientific research headquarters on the coast of MacRobertson Land. Taken at the suggestion of the head of the research team from among hundreds which had come off Clayton's assembly line in December 1962, this ruby-red beetle was subjected to smothering snows and 125 mph winds, 'competing' against dog-teams and tracked vehicles ('Snow-tracs', 'Weasels' and 'Caterpillars'). The latter, however, proved slow, cumbersome and costly to operate, while the dogs had a restricted payload and range and could be driven successfully by one owner only. The beetle turned out to be perfect for running around the station and even up snow-covered hills which had proved difficult to climb on foot because of the sinking snow. Air-cooled, it never froze; tightly sealed, it was immune to the drifting snow (so fine a powder at Mawson that it blows through tack holes). The scientists called it their 'Red Terror'; back home, Volkswagen Australasia proudly called it 'Antarctica 1'. After its year was over, and it was replaced by 'Antarctica 2', Christie and Dunlop tanked it up and took it out to the 1964 BP Rally of South Eastern Australia, entering it against forty-two competitors. All leading automobile firms were represented in this rough-road 2000-mile event, VW by a dozen cars. Predictably perhaps, the Christie & Dunlop beetle, bearing number 32 and its 'Antarctica 1' licence plate, won first place.

The 'Volkstote' madness swept Australian campuses as well, surely final proof that VW had 'come of age' Down Under and that its enthusiasts had succumbed to Beetlemania. As we shall see, this had its start in the United States, but Australians can perhaps still claim the (unofficial) championship. The sport consists of carrying a standard VW 'beetle' a fixed distance, with any number of bearers permitted to participate, the only catch being that all who carried it must fit inside it for the run back to the starting-line. During 1965 Orientation Week, twelve brawny members of the Law Students' Society at Melbourne University made it in 31·6 seconds, claiming the world championship. West Australian University law students retaliated by breaking the record in 27·6 seconds. The championship next moved to Wright College students at the University of New England, in Armidale, who made the trip in 26·8 seconds. For a time, Volkswagen Australasia Limited issued an annual cash prize, donated to charity.

All this seems evidence that the Volkswagen has settled in pretty firmly, that it is part of the permanent scene in Australia. Yet the best evidence provided for that seems to this writer to be provided by two modern New South Wales graziers, Mrs. Pauline Falkiner of Haddon Rig and Mr. Bruce Magger of Nevertire, who use Volkswagens for droving on their properties. Mrs. Falkiner bought three VW 1200 sedans to replace Jeeps, which she regarded as too costly both in purchase-price and upkeep, and they are used daily both by her and by her overseers for checking stock, tanks, mills and fencing, and for the all-important contact and running of the stud ram sheds. Her VWs average 12,000 miles annually, while Mr. Magger's average 22,000 miles a year, his droving over a 16,000-acre property.

Magger carries several dogs inside the beetles—and one dog, who likes to rough it, on top of the roof.

Roughing it seems to be the way of many an Australian VW and two recent examples were provided by Australians who followed in the footsteps of two intrepid explorers, using Volkswagens to do so. Four men in a beetle recently drove 180 miles along the trek of explorer John Eyre, along the shores of the Great Australian Bight, to examine its suitability as a tourist route, covering a tortuous trail along which, at times, they averaged only five to seven miles an hour. Among the group were two members of the VW organisation, Narrogin's VW agent, Harry Smith, and Don Cuthbertson, service manager of Volkswagen (W.A.) Pty Ltd., accompanied by Perth journalist Harry Marris and a photographer.

Three young Sydney men recently took a beetle along the trail of explorer Charles Sturt, across the South Australian Stony Desert, described as one of the hottest and harshest areas in Australia, driving through temperatures of up to 130 and 140 degrees in the sun and negotiating their way over stones the size of footballs. Barry Lloyd, a Customs and shipping clerk; Stan Hopwood, a photographer, and Ron Maloney, manager of a bowling alley, used the VW that had earlier won Class A victory in the Armstrong 500 race (driven by Bill Ford and Barry Ferguson) and they covered areas in which, according to the local residents, only heavy trucks had ever been seen. This sort of terrain, suitable for rugged pioneers, has prompted Volkswagen Australasia Limited to pioneer as well, producing a particularly rugged Volkswagen for just such conditions. This vehicle, which resembles a slightly racier version of a Jeep, utilises most of the unique engineering principles that VW pioneered over the years. It has a ground clearance of twelve and a half inches and is designed to climb a sixty-degree slope in first gear. Its 1300 engine, its transmission housing, and its front axle are all protected from damage by rocks and tree stumps by strong steel plates. Special reinforcement has been built into the union between the front axle and the chassis frame. It has been provided with CV reduction gears and brakes. The side walls of the vehicle have built-in flotation chambers that will permit one person to tow or push it across streams too deep for effective wheel traction. The prototype has been extensively tested for over a year. It has been through the 'dead-heart' of Australia, on mountain roads and through all types of weather conditions. VW dealers have seen the vehicle and greeted it enthusiastically. It is easy to understand why: it is a new kind of

Volkswagen, a country vehicle designed in Australia, to meet unique Australian conditions. The company, which began selling it in 1967, expects it to be used for everything from kangaroo shooting to mustering cattle.

This vehicle, developed by VWA staff under the direction of Rudi Herzmer at the Clayton factory, is not the only 'product change' initiated by Volkswagen Australasia Limited. The last VW 1200 came off the Clayton line in November, 1966; since then, all beetles made in Australia have carried the 1300 cc engine. The beetle model previously known as the 'Standard' is now called the VW 1300 Custom and has better trim than the car it replaced. Other models now manufactured are the 1500 sedan, the 1500 'Squareback' (known in Germany and elsewhere as the 'Variant'), and the new 1600 Fastback. All commercial vehicles are now manufactured in Australia with the one-ton modifications.

These changes are only a few which have recently been introduced, due in large part by the management changes which took place within Volkswagen Australasia Limited in December, 1966, when Allan V. Gray was replaced as managing director and completed in March, 1967, when W. J. King retired as alternate chairman of the company.

The new Volkswagen team presented itself to its dealers for the first time at the start of February, 1967, when a National Dealer Convention took place in Melbourne, to which dealers from all over the Commonwealth were airlifted for the occasion by specially chartered planes. The men they met were four joint Managing Directors, each with a specific area of responsibility. John A. Cook (Director-Marketing) is a Canadian who came to Australia from Volkswagen Canada Limited as General Sales Manager during 1966; Dieter Korff (Director-Manufacturing) and Rudi Herzmer (Director-Inspection) are both Germans who have been with the Australian company for some years and are veterans of its operation; the fourth is Dr. Alfred F. Solzer (Director-Finance), who is both financial chief and organisational head of Volkswagen Australasia Limited and who is a German new to the Commonwealth.

These management changes, of course, created headlines and startled the Australian automobile industry. *The Canberra Times'* Motoring Editor, Leonard Ward, referred to them as 'a clean sweep' and a 'shock' move; the Business Editor of *The Australian* said it left the 'motor industry in a furore of speculation', while other papers regarded the business reasons for the change as less important than the fact that 'three Germans and a Canadian' had taken over 'from Australians'.

The 'furore' has pretty much died down since, as the reasons for this 'clean sweep' came to be more generally appreciated. Clearly, top Volkswagenwerk management did have reason to be concerned, as well as to take action. What it regarded as a number of basic mistakes in marketing, as well as in investment policies, had reduced the profitability of the Australian operation and had led to a drop in VW sales and share of the market, especially in the face of the growing competition already mentioned earlier. There was a feeling that much of the sales approach had been wrong for some time: that, in trying to compete with GM, Ford and Chrysler, management had mimicked them and had presented the Volkswagen in such a way that it began to look to the public as 'just another car', rather than what it really is, a motor-car which qualifies as unique transportation. As Jack Cook told the dealers' convention: 'We will not be suckered into playing the motor game the way US manufacturers have. We are here to sell transportation and intend to do just that.' (A by-product: VWA in 1967 again began actively competing in motor sports in Australia. A team of top drivers was assembled for this purpose and charged with entering VWs into major trials and rallies held in all States of Australia.)

The four joint Managing Directors are also members of the board of the Australian company, along with Dr. Carl H. Hahn, Otto Hoehne and Dr. Friedrich Thomee, all of top Wolfsburg management. Chairman of the Australian board continues to be Heinz Nordhoff.[1]

As the new management team began the job of boosting sales, share-of-market percentages, profits, and dividends, Patrick Hayes, editor of *Australian Motor Sports & Automobiles*, assessed that job and the new men themselves. 'Many readers told us,' he wrote, 'they were confused about the company and its cars . . . so were we.' An interview he conducted with Jack Cook helped dispel the doubts. Summing up, Hayes writes, 'With a car that was designed, as far as its basic construction is concerned, some 30 years ago, VW has a big job in front of it. But there will always be room for a car with reliable service and dealers dedicated to serving their customers as

1. Also introduced at the dealers' convention were four senior marketing executives: Mike Woods, Sales Manager; Gavin Shaw, Parts Manager; Bill Harvey, Public Relations Manager, and Peter Koeppen, Service Manager. Newly appointed State Managers for the company are: Rod Cameron (New South Wales); Jim Sawyer (Victoria); Ian Barr (South Australia); Howard Mumme (Western Australia), and Larry Byers (Queensland).

keenly after they have bought their car as their salesmen approached them beforehand.'

'What's happening at VW?' the magazine asks. 'No more confusion,' it replies. That, of course, cannot but be welcomed by Australians, a people who prefer performance to glitter. They seem to have a no-nonsense quality about them; no wonder that VW achievements in trials and tests impressed them so particularly. Yet, despite all that, there remains even in Australians room for a bit of sentimentality and that is something a beetle often evokes best, as witness the story of 'dear old 508,475'.

That was the pet name given his beetle by *Melbourne Sun* motoring writer Peter Livingstone and, in a way, symbolises the growth of VW's acceptance in Australia. The digits represent the chassis number of a used VW Livingstone had bought; it was built in Wolfsburg in spring 1953, before Regent Motors had even displayed its first Volkswagen. Genealogist Livingstone traced his car's history, sifting through the records of the Motor Registration Branch. 'I discovered I had become the fourteenth owner of dear old 508,475,' he says. 'The previous owners had chalked up between them 190,000 miles.' That's the equivalent of having Christie and Dunlop take the car around Australia about twenty-four times. Fascinated, Livingstone went even further in his explorations; he dug up the addresses of most of the car's former owners and contacted them. 'Not one,' he said, 'could find even one harsh word to say about the old bus. One of them wanted to buy it back on the spot out of sheer nostalgia.' To which many a VW-owner the world over will nod and say, 'Small wonder'.

Across the globe, lying more or less on the same parallels of latitude as Australia, there are those who don't like Volkswagens. Mostly, however, they seem to be elephants. This, at least, was the conclusion reached by Canadian tourist Peter Hollick, and his friend Ian Castleden, driving their VW Microbus through the Wankie Game Reserve in Rhodesia on July 6, 1965. Late that afternoon, they found the road suddenly blocked by a herd of elephants. They halted; then Hollick noticed a sudden movement to his left: a huge cow elephant, her calf at her side, had been startled by the Microbus. No doubt wishing to protect her calf, she turned and charged the 2535-pound vehicle. Hollick and Castleden beat a hasty retreat out the right-hand front door and into the bush. The elephant's enraged attack lasted ten seconds. She flipped the Microbus on to its side, then overturned it on to its roof, then again flipped it on to its side. When it was clear she had disabled the monster, the elephant stopped. The 'enemy' lay vanquished, with tusk-holes six inches in diameter throughout its steel sides and floor. Smugly, the cow returned to her calf, and, joining the departing herd, sauntered off as nonchalantly as an elephant can.

Hoping for a search party (for it was now getting dark), Hollick and Castleden built fires, switched on the headlights of their over-turned Microbus, and made a lot of noise to keep the animals at a distance. They spent quite a night, their sleep interrupted by new herds of elephants, as well as of buffalo and an occasional leopard. They discovered that their Microbus lay beside the trail to a water-ing-hole—a Piccadilly Circus as far as Game Reserves are con-cerned. Early next morning, passing motorists took them to a nearby station. The Game Ranger was shocked: this was the first attack in thirty-three years! He rounded up a team, accompanied Hollick and Castleden to their Microbus, righted it and recharged the battery, for this had been drained during the night's long vigil. Hollick and Castleden noted that their Microbus had been battered brutally. Predictably perhaps, it started straight away and, says Hollick, 'has run perfectly ever since'.

As the Game Ranger told Hollick, the hostile elephant must have come from elsewhere, Bechuanaland probably, for several hundred had recently migrated over to Rhodesia. The indigenous version, he assured him, was much friendlier. Perhaps even to Volkswagens, which today are surely as numerous in Africa as elephants, and much tamer.

The vast distances involved on this second-largest continent make the great stretches in Australia seem small. Crossing Africa from its northern Mediterranean coast to Cape Town, in the Republic of South Africa, one covers 5000 miles (and several VWs have done it); from west to east, the distance can be as much as 4700 miles. The roads on which one must travel exist in many cases only on maps or in the minds of governmental planners, and the terrain is brutal. Such conditions—which always and everywhere cause the Uninitiated to spurn Volkswagens—of course prove ideal for beetles. Those who know better in Africa buy VWs—and the customers are Africans as well as Europeans.

An example of the driving conditions encountered and the local enthusiasm for VWs is provided by a West German, Arno Beger of Hanover. Beger recently was one of a clutch of shutterbugs being chauffeured by Southern Cross Safaris, Nairobi, Kenya, a company that owns a fleet of forty red-and-white VW Microbuses. Riding in one of these, Beger after a while could not bear the grinding groans the driver caused the Microbus to make: he decided he'd teach him how to shift gears properly. The African chauffeur, however, just grinned. 'It's a very good car,' he reassured Beger. 'You can do everything with him. All he need is fuel, that's all.'

So confident was he that he carried neither reserve fuel nor spare parts, explaining that plenty of parts were available in VW work-shops; so fond was he of the bus he drove that he kept it spotless, washing it each morning before moving on. The safari covered quite a distance: 2500 miles, through Kenya, Uganda and Tanganyika, and 2000 of these were along game paths, not roads. Beger says the route led through jungle 'which lashes the vehicle on all sides, through elephant grass six foot high, through rivers and waterholes where the wheels disappear completely'. The worst hazards, however, seemed to him to be the unmade roads and sand tracks. 'I sometimes closed my eyes,' he remembers, 'and thought we'd never make it!'

But the VW *has* made it throughout most of Africa. Its biggest success has, of course, been in the Republic of South Africa, where there is a prosperous European community and where the VW is today the best-seller among *all* cars. Elsewhere on the Continent, however, the VW is also taking hold. VW General Importers R. T. Briscoe of Ghana report the population is 'car mad—particularly for the Volkswagen'. (It might be noted that only about 10 per cent of Ghana's 22,000 miles of roads are paved; experience has shown Ghanaians that VWs cover the other ninety reliably, if sometimes bouncingly.) In Lagos, capital of nearby Nigeria, to cite another example, VW Importers Mandilas and Karaberis have brought in so many Volkswagens that, when their 15,000th arrived in the early 1960s, the contribution these cars have made to the economy (as well as to the mobility) of Nigerians was noted over several pages of Lagos' 120,000-circulation *Daily Times*. Jackie Phillips, who owns three beetles for himself and his 'Society photographers' staff, suggests one reason for their popularity in the Nigerian capital. Lagos' street-scene is a crowded one and not every car can get through the traffic efficiently. 'The beetles start well, are extremely agile and so fast that I never get stuck,' he reports. Prince T. O. Fadina, owner of a transport company, is another Lagos enthusiast. He switched to VW Commercials after being disappointed with other makes. To his 'very great joy', he says, he found he saved money on parts and maintenance. When he needs service or repairs, he says, 'they are carefully carried out all over Nigeria, irrespective of which VW workshop you go to'. Far from Lagos, over in northeast Africa, lies the Somali Republic. In its capital, Mogadiscio, the police drive a fleet of beetles, and the authorities have even issued a postage stamp which shows a VW sedan. Honouring the Police Auxiliary, it shows two policewomen (though none existed), one seated behind the wheel of the car, the other standing beside it. VWs are part of the every-day street scene in Mogadiscio and compete briskly with traditional modes of transport, such as 1-hp donkey-carts.

Transportation traditions are, of course, not the only ones changing in today's Africa. Change, indeed, seems always to have been the rule, for even in the days of the Roman Empire, Pliny remarked, *Ex Africa semper aliquid novi* ('There is always something new from Africa'). The biggest and the newest is the growth of the Continent's manufacturing industry, and it is at its southernmost tip, in the Republic of South Africa, where that industry has been in existence longest, that this is seen best.

This Republic is today well into what has been called the third phase of its economic development. Before 1870 or thereabouts, there was little of the European influence in the interior except a lot of hardy pioneer farmers, 'trek boers', building a subsistence agriculture. The second phase came once the diamond, gold, and other extraction industries opened up. Phase three—that of *manufacturing*—began during World War I, although it was not until many years later that it grew to anywhere near its present proportions. Volkswagens in South Africa, a latecomer to the Republic's industry, provides a good case-study of economic development, for VW there has also gone through its phases, just as the nation has.

It all began in 1946, when the Municipality of Uitenhage sold fifty acres of land in the Zwartkops River Valley on the outskirts of town to a South African company which had been formed to assemble and distribute Studebaker motor-cars. Mel Brooks, a Studebaker vice-president, was released to accept the position of managing director. A short while later, work began on the site the company had bought, and by April 1947 a foundation had been laid and the first employees moved in—into a tin shanty on the grounds. In October, Brooks sailed from America to inspect progress; as he stepped off the *Robin Locksley* at Port Elizabeth, twenty-two miles away, his £300,000 plant was nearing completion.

In those months, the events taking place in Uitenhage and those unfolding at Wolfsburg ran somewhat parallel. At the end of 1947, when Uitenhage's Studebaker plant was getting ready for full production, the British officers who were running the show in Wolfsburg were getting ready to turn theirs over to Heinz Nordhoff. As 1948 began, full production started in Uitenhage, Heinz Nordhoff had taken over in Wolfsburg, and workers in both of the far-distant plants began to look into the future with anticipation. Yet here the parallel stops abruptly, for Mel Brooks was, of course, assembling Studebakers and it is doubtful that he gave much thought at the time to the trickle of beetles emerging from Lower Saxony.

Brooks' company was called South African Motor Assemblers and Distributors Ltd.; as the company's fortunes grew, it came to be best known by its initials, SAMAD, and until recently these stood for VW in South Africa. (Today the company is called Volkswagen of South Africa Ltd.) The addition of Austins to the Studebakers being assembled at Uitenhage was the first step in the company's growth; the second came with the arrival of the very man who later introduced VWs into Australia, Baron von Oertzen. By mid-1951, it was agreed that SAMAD would assemble beetles as well; the announcement was made in Uitenhage at a meeting between Mel Brooks, Nordhoff and Von Oertzen. Sufficient parts for 340 cars were shipped from Wolfsburg, and on August 31, 1951, the first VW to be produced in South Africa came off the final assembly line. By the end of that year, 312 had been produced, and in 1952, another 575. Wolfsburg's production expert Otto Hoehne, not yet on the Vorstand at the time, accompanied the initial shipment and stayed a month to advise and help out.

One of the 887 VWs built during these two years was bought by a Swede named Löfberg in Cape Town in 1952. Löfberg, who today lives on a farm near Modder River, C.P., knew VWs from Sweden, where they were popular even then. The Cape Town dealer, however, wasn't convinced. 'The salesman we spoke to,' Löfberg recalls, 'was a bit sceptical about whether or not they would ever be able to sell this queer kind of car, aircooled, engine at the back, and so on.' Mr. and Mrs. Löfberg assured the salesman it was a fine car, and then bought one from him. They drove it 115,000 miles in ten years and claim it performs 'the way it did when we bought it', Löfberg adding, 'That's nothing for a VW—this is a motor-car, not a fancy toy.'

Another who bought one of the first South African VWs is E. H.

Burri of Johannesburg. VW dealer G. K. Lindsay sold it to him on September 29, 1951, and *Rand Daily. Mail* headlined the sale, 'Delivery of First Volkswagen' (though its credentials as *the* first are still in question). 'The trip down,' says Burri, 'gave me a lot of pleasure, especially as no one had seen this beetle before. My biggest task was to explain why and how the engine was air-cooled.'

By 1956, Austin had built its own assembly plant near Cape Town and SAMAD, which had by then produced 15,000 Austins, ceased assembly of them. Now, for the first time, the beetle dominated the SAMAD production picture. In 1956, almost 3000 VWs were assembled, versus 1800 Studebakers.

In 1957, the *Eastern Province Herald* noted that German cars for the first time overhauled US cars in South African sales, due largely, it is said, to the 'increasing popularity in the Union of small cars such as the Volkswagen'. That year, the Swedish vessel *Victoria* brought in a record cargo of 1068 knocked-down and 131 fully built-up VWs to try to satisfy what the company was by then calling 'the insatiable demand' for the car. (Waiting time for a VW in South Africa in 1958: two to three *years*!)

Just how insatiable the demand for VWs had become may be seen from the.fact that the Volkswagen has been the best-seller in South Africa among *all* makes and sizes ever since 1957! The beetle, of course, benefited from the lifting of import restrictions in the mid-1950s and VW executives have always watched balefully for any signs that they would reappear. In 1958, these showed up; noting a speech given by Deputy Director of Imports Major W. Geach, the press said it contained hints 'that import control would be reimposed . . . only a month after the last relaxation of regulations'. It quoted Geach as saying, 'We intend to open the door to imports just a little —with emphasis on "little".'

Baron von Oertzen, speaking of imposed restrictions on August 14, 1958, said, 'I look with the greatest apprehension on all forms of government-controlled and planned economy such as is found in the totalitarian states.' He made these remarks at ceremonies marking the completion of a £500,000 investment programme at Uitenhage. The company by now found itself the third-largest automobile assembly works in the Republic and the end of both growth and investments was not in sight. Changes were being made: Volkswagenwerk in Wolfsburg had bought controlling interest in SAMAD in 1956, and SAMAD's new chairman, Baron von Oertzen, had settled down to live in South Africa. Managing Director Mel Brooks had died in 1958; SAMAD and its growth, said Von Oertzen, were the direct consequence 'of his rare vision and foresight and are a fitting monument to his beloved memory'. A new managing director was named; he was Roy T. Hurd, a Canadian also, who had joined the company originally as Mel Brooks' executive assistant.

In accordance with policies set by the Volkswagenwerk in Germany, the growth of production and sales at SAMAD was governed largely by the growth of the dealer network, for in South Africa as elsewhere, dealers showing the blue circle sign with the VW in it must meet unusually high standards. To assist them in doing so, SAMAD in 1958 set up another corporation, South African Motor Acceptance Corporation (Pty.) Ltd. (SAMAC for short), through which dealers could obtain financing for themselves and for their customers. Today, Volkswagen of South Africa's dealers number about 200 and are scattered throughout a marketing area of 800,000 square miles, in the Republic itself, in South-West Africa, and in Swaziland. To service them and keep standards high, the company maintains five regional offices staffed with regional managers, these in turn supported by a network of district managers and service and parts representatives. Mobile service schools back-stop training facilities in Johannesburg and Uitenhage. A warehouse, valued at 200,000 rand, was built in the early 1960s, so as to process the more than 1000 items ordered by dealers each day. 'It is the salesman who sells the first car,' as the company is fond of pointing out, 'but the workshop which sells the second.'

Reimposition of import restriction in 1961 hurt the company. As Roy Hurd stated on August 1, it cut production 'quite considerably'. Assembly of the beetle continued to run at peak, but the more costly VWs (Karmann-Ghias, Sunroof models, Stationwagons, De Luxe Microbuses, etc.) were no longer part of the production schedule. Still, SAMAD—as it was still known then—kept growing and, said Hurd, at a 'meteoric' rate. In December 1961, the 100,000th vehicle assembled at Uitenhage was produced and in 1963, Volkswagens outsold thirty-one other makes, showing almost twice as many sales as the next most-popular car in South Africa (the Cortina 1200). That year, it acquired forty-seven more acres, raising its total holding at Uitenhage from Mel Brooks' original 50 to 100.

By this time, new management changes had been made. Roy Hurd had relinquished his post in order to return home to Canada and a new managing director, A. B. ('Theuny') Theunissen, had taken over on August 15, 1962. Theunissen started energetically by racing around the entire marketing area by car and plane; a month after he took over, he had personally visited sixty towns in the Republic and before the end of the year, another twenty-four. Management was reorganised to cope with the changes which were yet to come.

The latest and most important change is a very fundamental one: from an assembly works, Volkswagen of South Africa is becoming a major vehicle manufacturing company. Acting to meet Governmental demands that 55 per cent of all manufactured models be of South African origin, it is engaged in a multi-million rand expansion programme on the Uitenhage site (by now almost 120 acres). At the end of 1965, the first completed floor frame for a VW 1200 beetle was produced entirely out of South African steel; in spring 1966, crankcases, cylinders, cylinder heads and flywheels were machined in the new machine shop and, shortly thereafter, work began on the production of similar components for the VW 1600 passenger car range. The company will go a step further than the Governmental regulation calls for; Theunissen predicts that at least 65 per cent of every car produced at Uitenhage will be 'made in South Africa'.

There are now more than 150,000 Volkswagens in the Republic and they and their owners have performed pretty much as has been the experience elsewhere. South African owners have joined together in VW Clubs; thirty-four students at the University of Orange Free State have packed themselves into a beetle for the photographers, and VWs have been winning rallies and trials as rapidly in the Republic as in Australia.[1]

One thing, however, seems unique—and that is the amazing number of VWs which are carried off by floods in Africa. A scattered sampling of news items provide these stories:

§The Reverend Carrol W. Eby of Kenya's Kaimosi Mission reports he was swept downstream in 1959. 'I drove my Volkswagen sedan over some of the worst roads in Africa,' he says, 'and in some places where there are no roads and no bridges. The Volkswagen is excellent *and will float*. I discovered this when I drove into a drift where the water was deeper than I expected and we floated downstream. It took a long time for much water to seep in at the doors. Finally a group of men carried the VW out of the stream.'

1. Some early events serving to popularise the car: In 1958, VWs won 1st, 2nd, 3rd, and 4th place in their class in the toughest motor rally in Africa, the Kenya Coronation Safari Rally (only half the competitors finished at all). Also in 1958, five of the seven cars finishing the African Endurance Championship were VWs (thirty-two started out over 1,500 miles of Angola and Congo); these captured 1st, 2nd, 3rd, 4th, and 6th places. In 1959's Congo Marathon Rally, only ten cars finished a non stop 1500-mile run which thirty-four had started. Of these ten, *seven* were VWs, which also won 1st, 2nd, and 3rd places.

§In 1961, Allan and Rita Esser, twenty-two and twenty-three years old, were returning to Johannesburg in their VW from a honeymoon in Durban. A few miles outside Standerton, they suddenly came upon a flooded river and encountered a three-foot wall of water bearing down on them. 'We resigned ourselves to certain death,' the newly-weds said later. 'But miraculously we did not overturn and were washed down the embankment right under the water. We later heard it was twenty feet deep. All the windows were closed and only the heating was open . . . the car was virtually airtight and we bobbed to the surface.'[1] Allan Esser climbed out of the window of the floating beetle, feet first, and, hanging on to the side, tried in vain to touch ground. As he clambered back, a little water entered through the open window. Leaning out now, he and his bride tried to grab willow branches as they were swept along. 'Then we realised,' they said, 'that if we did catch hold, the jolt might capsize the car. So we resigned ourselves to our little boat trip. . . .' The beetle carried them a thousand yards before it came to rest. They then tried flashing for help, but the headlights were under water. 'There was only one thing to do, and that was to wait,' they said. After four and a half hours, the police arrived, along with a farmer who pulled them out with a tractor. The only mark the storm left on the car was a small dent on the running board. Within two days they were back on the road.

§In 1962, E. D. W. de Klerk, of the Ousdhoorn Magistrates' Office, tried to cross the flooded Grobelaars River at about 8.30 am on August 22, when he discovered that the water over the causeway was too deep for him to get across. The stream immediately rushed over the beetle's bonnet and dragged the vehicle downstream. De Klerk and the two friends who were with him acted cool and confident. 'I immediately closed the windows and put the gears in neutral,' he says, 'and off we went in a foaming, eddying river.' After fifty yards, they collided with a tree. This impact threw the car back into the middle of the stream and then across to the other side. The beetle drifted on, for a total of 200 yards, without the wheels striking anything. Finally, it came to rest against a bridge. It was still bone-dry inside, as were its passengers. De Klerk and his friends climbed out through a window but, being unable to shut it again from the outside, watched as water now seeped in. After a while, the beetle sank. By the time an Army crane had pulled it out, damage was con-

1. The Essers thus provide the first 'VW Submarine' account, to be added to sundry 'Boats'- and 'Floats-wagen' stories which have been authenticated.

siderable. That experience, however, was enough for de Klerk. 'One thing stands out,' he says. 'I shall buy a Volkswagen again.'

§More recently, J. M. Gerber of Commercial Road, Port Elizabeth, credits his beetle with 'miraculously' saving the lives of everyone in his family. The Gerbers were driving home from Onderplaas, when they reached flooded Kouga River, near Joubertina. Halfway over the bridge, which they felt certain they could cross, they were swept into the rushing waters. 'It was an absolute nightmare,' Mr. Gerber says, 'and an absolute miracle we survived.' He reports his children were panic-stricken and he 'had to think and act quickly'. He opened a front window and managed to climb out, then tried to push the car to the riverbank but was instead pulled along after it. Suddenly, he lost hold. As he struggled to dry land, he watched in terror as his wife and four children were swept downstream. He ran along the edge of the river until the VW finally came to a halt in a bush, a full 900 yards from the bridge. Gerber courageously entered the river again and once more tried to drag his family to safety in the car. By this time, however, help had arrived; Mr. Gerber's brother, who had crossed the bridge safely in a truck and who had watched with horror as the VW was swept off, had raced ten miles to Kransfontein to get a cable, and was now back. One end of it was tied to a tree, the other to the car, and along it Gerber made five trips back and forth, carrying his children (nine, five, three, and two years old), and helping his wife, to safety. Shortly thereafter, a tractor pulled the car out, the Gerbers climbed in again and drove their beetle home.

It is of course on dry land that the watertight Volkswagen tends to perform to best advantage; in Africa, the very qualities which keep the bug afloat in roaring rivers often help it outperform other cars in difficult (if dry) terrain. Hans Kriess of Swakopmund, South-West Africa, drove his VW along the shifting and, in some places, towering sand dunes of the notorious Skeleton Coast, and through the treacherous Namib Desert, remarking afterwards, 'It is unbelievable what it stood up to.' Kriess carried a load of over 1000 pounds, yet averaged 23 mpg (versus 9 mpg averaged by an accompanying Land-Rover). 'The Volkswagen,' says Kriess, 'carried twenty-two gallons of extra petrol, emergency water rations, a complete camera outfit, a tent and all personal effects such as bedding, stretchers, cooking utensils, stores, etc. The car was a pretty old model which I had overhauled completely. Through all the 1600 miles of sand and mud along the Skeleton Coast and later through the Kaokoveld Mountains she did not give any trouble except for two punctures. Sometimes the airfilter was so clogged up with sand that it had to be cleaned twice a day.'

It seems to be just this kind of performance under gruelling conditions that has helped popularise the entire line of VW motor-cars in such rugged areas of the world as Australasia and Africa. Motoring writers and motor-car customers in densely populated, urbanised societies may look for something else: manœuvrability perhaps, speed, and ease in parking; hence the reputation of the VW (particularly the beetle) as a good 'second car' in cities like New York, London, or Munich. In such places, owners have come to rely so much on VWs in heavy traffic that they seem to think only beetle-maniacs cross continents in VWs. Africa and Australia prove them wrong. The fact that the VW has not only prevailed, but become a front-runner in continent-size conditions, reveals this as too narrow a view.

Volkswagen executives in Australia regard their Commonwealth as the toughest, most competitive automobile market in the world today; they point out that the VW competes there against an army of makes, from big Detroit models to efficient, small British and Japanese ones. Theunissen's experience in the Republic of South Africa is no different. His organisation also has had to place its cars in the ring with bigger, heavier, makes—as well as with many good small cars. Scepticism and even prejudice plagued VW in both places. Unlike the USA, where the beetle first became popular among the imported-car 'snob-set' before it proved its worth to the average man, the Volkswagen in Africa and Australia had to prove itself to the average man right off. For in both of these continents, people do not have any desire (and often not enough surplus income) to buy a car just because it's different. In both continents, motor editors who test-drive all makes of cars look first for performance, durability, quality, and economy, and then only for design. They have subjected each VW model, as it appeared, to trials and punishment matching the worst a local driver might encounter; they were quite prepared to turn thumbs down in print once they found something wrong. The beetle and its bigger brothers, however, have consistently amazed them. Their recommendations and, ultimately, the recommendations of owner-drivers, have made the Volkswagen the most popular make of motor-car in South Africa.

The accomplishment of the Australian and South African VW operations are quite remarkable, when one considers the short time it took their organisations to make the Volkswagen a success in their areas. Yet energy and dedication have built the VW miracle in many countries; the 'Wolfsburg' formula of success has been a shrewd mix of car and character. Given a motor-car the people want, all cne needs to make a big success of it is a lot of bright, hard-working people, the kind who don't cut corners. As we shall see in the succeeding chapters, it was this combination which opened the eyes of Detroit's Big Three.

Coals to Newcastle

Volkswagen's extraordinary success in the United States—that home of the chrome and bastion of big cars—was somewhat unexpected, even by Heinz Nordhoff. Today, the USA represents the Volkswagenwerk's second biggest market (after Germany) and its biggest overseas customer, with more than two and a half million VWs on US roads and the number growing at the rate of more than four hundred thousand a year. Yet VW had no preferential position when it first entered the American market and, indeed, made its bid for US sales late in the game. Britain's Rootes Motors was the first European car manufacturer to export seriously to the USA after World War II and a variety of other British, French, and German manufacturers sent cars over well before VW got going. Yet Volkswagen today is so far ahead of all foreign car competition that it has even skipped ahead of all US compact cars as well, and it shows no signs of slipping. Its sales may represent less than five per cent of total US car sales, but the car is far from lost in the crowd. It is recognised instantly by Americans who can't tell a Fiat from an M.G., a Saab from a Volvo, or even a Plymouth from a Ford.

The 'familiar line' handed out by Wolfsburg has become so very familiar indeed that few Americans are aware that virtually every one of the two and a half million VWs on their roads was bought in the comparatively few years which have elapsed since 1954. In the first nine years after the end of World War II, VWs were virtually unknown in the United States, except as weird-looking souvenirs which a handful of veterans of the US Army of Occupation had brought home from Germany. That the VW organisation which has been built up since then was built so quickly and effectively is amazing. The enormous achievement of constructing a network of distributors and dealers throughout fifty states has all the earmarks of having been started by means of a brilliantly conceived plan, of

carefully charted strategy, and of a high-powered organisation ready
to push it to fruition. Yet nothing, in actuality, could be further from
the truth.

It all started without much of a plan at all, with very little strategy,
and with no organisation to speak of. The success story of the VW in
the United States was written in the beginning by less than a score
of men, some of them American, some German (and one of them
British). Of the Americans, several became VW distributors; if they
seemed reckless at first in joining up, their recklessness has since
rewarded them by making them rich men. Of the Germans, a number
cruised around the country in VW trucks, preaching the gospel of
service at a time when there were virtually no VWs for mechanics to
look after. The man responsible for sending most of these men
round was one of the most colourful and remarkable individuals to
appear in the history of Volkswagen, a super-salesman possessed of
both demonic drive and courtly charm as well as a sure and personal
vision of what would some day come to pass. His name was Will
Van de Kamp. He and a few others built everything up in a few
years, starting from scratch. This is their story. Between its lines lies
a lesson for all other European motor-car manufacturers who were
so enormously outdistanced by VW in the USA.

Before Van de Kamp got started, however, the climate in the
United States was radically different. It was back in 1948 that Heinz
Nordhoff decided to make his first stab at selling VWs in the USA.
It was not so much that he needed the sales, for in that year (and all
succeeding years) he actually had more orders to fill than the factory
could meet, but what he did need was American machinery for
Wolfsburg. The way to buy it was with dollars and the way to get
these was to sell Volkswagens to persons owning the precious hard
currency.

The man he chose to make the first foray into the Land of the Big
Cars was big Ben Pon, the colourful Dutchman who had successfully
sold the German beetle to his fellow countrymen at a time when
anti-German sentiment ran high in Holland. If Pon could do that,
Nordhoff reasoned, he ought to be able to sell it to Americans.

Ben Pon brought to America the first VW 'officially' exported to
that country, travelling with it aboard the Holland-America Line's
M/S *Westerdam* and arriving in New York on January 17, 1949. No
sooner had the ship docked than Pon ran into trouble.

'An American friend of mine helped me stage a press conference
aboard the freighter,' Pon says. 'We got a lot of publicity—all of it

bad. I even tried calling the VW the "Victory Wagon" to take the curse off it, but the press referred to it only as "Hitler's car".'

Problems ashore were different, but no less maddening. Everyone whom Pon tried to enlist as a VW dealer turned it down. 'I drove the car to Massachusetts to see a Packard dealer,' Pon says, providing one example of the American reaction. 'I raced through a heavy snowstorm to get to him by 9 am. When I arrived at his home, he wouldn't even open the door. He just took one look at the car through the window and turned away in disgust!'

After three weeks in New York, Pon had begun to run out of money, for his government allowed him to spend only ten dollars a day. 'I had a big bill at the Roosevelt Hotel,' he says, 'and I couldn't meet it. So, in desperation, I sold the car and all the spare parts I had brought with me to a New York imported-car dealer for eight hundred dollars, just to pay that hotel bill.'

Pon reported the disappointing news to Nordhoff and also warned him that many European car-makers were sending cars into the US without establishing adequate service facilities. 'I felt we would kill the VW if we did the same,' he says. 'I felt we should not even try to sell the VW in the US before we could do a good job.'

Nordhoff was also disappointed at the news, for US sales and US dollars were badly needed. In late 1949, he flew across the ocean to check things out for himself.

Armed with a stack of photographs of his car, he arrived in New York City and took his place at US Customs. The Customs inspector opened his suitcase, picked up the bundle of pictures, and asked Nordhoff what these were. Told they were photographs of a German car Nordhoff hoped to sell, the inspector proved sceptical.

'No, this is no car,' Nordhoff quotes him as saying. 'I've never seen a car like this; these must be drawings or promotional artwork.' As such, he explained, they were subject to duty. Nordhoff tried in vain to convince the inspector that what he held in his hands were actual photographs. 'But it was all no use,' he remembers. The inspector refused to believe him and insisted that he pay ten or twelve dollars duty for them as advertising sketches. 'That hurt badly,' Nordhoff says, 'because I was allowed only fifteen dollars a day spending money.'

The trip, Nordhoff reports, proved 'an utter failure'. The Volkswagen again failed to impress a single American dealer. Not one believed the car could ever be sold in the United States. Newspapermen to whom Nordhoff took his case felt the same way. The

VW, they said, was hopeless as a marketable commodity in the USA. Nordhoff returned home discouraged. 'I realised then that we would have to make our own way in the world without a source of American dollars,' he says.

It was not surprising that the American dealers hesitated to handle the Volkswagen. This was a time when the American public, which had been starved for new cars during the war, clamoured for other kinds of vehicles. Detroit saw the trend coming: what the public seemed to want were heavy, wide, long, low cars; cars whose bumpers were festooned with the protruberances the trade came to call 'Dagmars'; cars with flaglike fins and chrome hugging each seam; cars with ever more powerful engines. Not only did the Volkswagen's design seem as out of date as that of the Tin Lizzie, but the press kept emphasising that the car's history was suspect as well. Wasn't its name a Nazi name? How could Nordhoff expect to sell 'Hitler's pet' to Americans four years after the war?

As it turned out, the Volkswagen did not prove to be out of date; it proved to be ahead of its time. Americans weren't ready for it yet. American interest in imported small cars began to climb in the mid-1950s and by then the car did not seem nearly so bizarre or objectionable. By the time Nordhoff made another try at the US market, the country was almost ready.

The first Volkswagen officially exported to the US, apart from Pon's 'display model', arrived there in 1950. To be sure, a few had come in before, brought home privately by American servicemen returning from duty in West Germany. Two were sold in 1949. In 1950, however, the company decided to make another formal try at the US market and appointed a New York foreign-car dealer named Max Hoffman exclusive VW importer and agent for the United States east of the Mississippi. Few people noticed the 330 Volkswagens he sold in 1950; they were lost among the 6,660,000 other cars Americans bought that year as well.

Max Hoffman, however, did not just sell Volkswagens; the beetle was more of a sideline to his main and more profitable business, that of selling a wide range of better-known foreign cars, many of these high-powered and high-priced ones such as Porsches and Jaguars. Hoffman's status as exclusive importer of many European makes meant that many Americans then entering the growing foreign-car field found themselves buying from Hoffman—and many of them also found themselves stuck with a funny little German car called the VW.

Typical of many were Carl and Oliver Schmidt of Chicago, two unrelated namesakes who had then joined forces to form Import Motors of Chicago, selling a line of foreign makes. When the Schmidts went to Hoffman to buy a Porsche, they found they got one more easily if they also bought a Volkswagen. 'Funny thing was,' Oliver Schmidt told me, 'we sold that first VW right away. Then, when we went back to buy more Porsches, and ended up again with more Volkswagens as well, we sold *those* beetles right off too. One day I came around to Hoffman for more cars. I was asked if I'd come to buy Porsches. "No," I said. "I just want you to sell me some VWs." ' Hoffman's Chicago warehouse was filled with quite a few; the Schmidts began selling them faster than they or Hoffman expected.

Thousands of miles away from the United States, another man who was to figure prominently in the history of VW in America was selling Volkswagens—to the Moroccans. This was Arthur Stanton, today the largest-volume VW distributor (for Connecticut, New Jersey, and New York), not only in the USA, but also throughout the entire world. In the late 1940s, Navy veteran Stanton found editorial life at Crown Publishers too restrictive for his entrepreneurial instincts and, together with his brother Frank and another friend, set up an export-import firm in Morocco. In 1948, their firm was appointed to distribute Chrysler products in that country and also developed into a large importer of virtually anything that showed promise. (Stanton at the time even bought an abandoned US Army camp in Italy, then rented a local arena for eighteen months to sell off its equipment, item by item.)

In 1949, just as Ben Pon was heading for the United States, Stanton and his colleagues decided they wanted a small car to sell to the North Africans. Two wartime VW Kübelwagens had been parked in one of their garages, and on the basis of the cars' performance, they decided to try to get the VW franchise for the area. Stanton went to see Heinz Nordhoff in Wolfsburg. He must have impressed the new head of VW, for he got his VW franchise and started to produce sales. 'Twelve months after we began handling Volkswagens in North Africa,' Stanton reports, 'we were selling fifteen hundred a year.'

That buyers for this odd-looking car could actually be found in the USA was becoming apparent to a few others. One was an American racing enthusiast by the name of John von Neumann; impressed by the Porsche VW concept, he early sensed the potential in the beetle and with his wife shuttled from Los Angeles by bus to Hoffman's New York headquarters, to return West in two VWs which they promptly sold to two more West Coast foreign-car enthusiasts, covering 7000 miles for each brace of beetles sold.

In Columbus, Ohio, a young World War II Air Force officer named Robert Fergus was another man who was buying cars from Max Hoffman. Fergus's Columbus Sports Car Company, formed in 1951, sold Morris, Austin and Jaguar cars—and soon VWs as well. Again the beetles were at first taken on reluctantly, to get the popular Jags. Two years later in Overland, Missouri, a veteran of the FBI and the Navy named George H. Capps opened a small-car dealership and got into the VW picture with a total starting inventory of six imported cars, two of them beetles.

Here and there, then, Americans *were* selling Volkswagens—one by one and in small quantities. Often they had bought them for resale with considerable reluctance, so as to expedite delivery of Porsches and Jaguars; although they frequently found that the low-priced VWs were outselling the high-priced sports cars, the business in beetles remained erratic and unorganised. Projected over the nation as a whole, sales by the end of 1953 (2173 VWs since 1950) totalled fewer than the number of counties in the United States; in short, despite these sales, VW was not making even the slightest inroads on the roads of that continent-sized US market.

Back in Wolfsburg, where this was being studied, the realisation grew that the patchwork Hoffman 'network' had to be dropped. Because John von Neumann was by 1953 selling enthusiastically and successfully along the Pacific Coast, VW that year appointed him Hoffman's counterpart west of the Mississippi and, as the end of that year approached, the Hoffman contract was cancelled completely.

'Hoffman was in general a very perceptive man,' says Stuart Perkins, the Englishman who heads Volkswagen in the United States, 'but somehow he just couldn't see the future in the VW.' Manuel Hinke, export chief of the Volkswagenwerk, agrees. 'We felt there was a potential that Hoffman would not recognise,' he says.

In point of fact, this seems hardly surprising, for few Americans looked upon the car as one which might truly become popular. Hoffman had then (and has now) a prosperous imported-car business; he was less 'Volkswagen's US importer' than an independent importer of a wide line of cars. Also, his responsibility ended at the 'wholesale level', once he had sold his beetles to dealers for resale elsewhere. He did not have to concern himself with what happened

to them later; neither did he have to have the long-range interests of
the VW company at heart. He was, after all, in business for himself,
not for the Volkswagenwerk.

That this, however, should prove intolerable for Wolfsburg is
clear if one recalls that, by 1953, Nordhoff had been on the job for
five years already and that, while the VW business in the USA was
tiny, it was elsewhere growing large indeed and very highly organised. VW's annual payroll in Wolfsburg had by the end of 1953
reached almost 120 million marks; total worldwide exports that
year had reached almost 70,000, and production had climbed to
close to 180,000 cars. Yet the number of VWs bought in the US, the
biggest car market in the world, was so tiny that year that Wolfsburg's production line could even then fill the entire US demand in
less than a day and a half.

Throughout much of the world, in short, VW was an efficiently
functioning and rapidly growing company, whose policies and distribution pattern had not only been set, but had already proved
themselves. It had established its networks of importers, distributors
and dealers, most of them devoting their efforts to selling VWs
exclusively; it had developed service and sales standards; had
worked up uniform service and repair facilities and procedures; had
determined methods of training mechanics and sales personnel; had
created a uniform appearance for VW showrooms and service
centres, and it had tested its policies in markets in Germany and
elsewhere, finding they worked. It also found that the United States in
1953 was a glaring contradiction of all that the company believed in.

A disorganised, superficial and slipshod network had evolved
from among dealers who sold VWs along with a host of other cars;
while some of these men were doing a fine job under the circumstances and could be retained in a later and better organisation, the
fact remained that all of them had to be re-evaluated by the company.
Those who might be reappointed had to be made familiar with VW
policies, aided in following them, and had to be provided with
direction and guidance, rather than just with cars. Already a VW
policy of moving into new territories by means of establishing 'service
first, sales second' had been developed throughout existing markets
and had proved essential to the car's success; people were clearly
buying Volkswagens not just because they were good cars, but because they were assured adequate service and parts facilities. It was
clear in 1953 that the continent-size US market needed such policies
—and lacked them.

Back in the field and well before the end of 1953, those who were selling the Hoffman-imported Volkswagens sensed that a major shake-up was due to come. Trade rumours and industry journals hinted that Hoffman's contract with VW was about to end. Several of his dealers decided not to wait, but to protect their interests by contacting Wolfsburg. Because they had until then dealt solely through Hoffman, they did not know whom to address in Germany.

Don Marsh, then manager of Fergus's Columbus Sports Car Company, was one of several who wrote to the 'sales department' in Wolfsburg; boldly, he asked not just for 'some territorial rights' but for everything east of the Mississippi. Oliver and Carl Schmidt, in Chicago, were two others who wrote the factory, also asking for a franchise to distribute VWs. Marsh got a letter in reply, advising him that a 'factory representative' would visit Columbus 'presently' to discuss the matter; other dealers, like the Schmidts, were left in suspense until the factory man actually showed up out of the blue. This suspense must have been keen among those who had successfully been selling beetles, for they were beginning to see the potential in the car, yet did not know what was brewing.

Certain plans were indeed being formulated. These had to be flexible, for the United States was virgin territory for VW. Almost no one with VW had first-hand experience of the demands this huge market might make. 'We didn't know too much about the United States,' Heinz Nordhoff has admitted. 'We just looked at a map and saw that the Mississippi River seemed a good dividing line, so we split the market at that point.'

Now the company decided to send two factory representatives to the USA, give them equal authority, and have them open up headquarters in New York and San Francisco respectively.

Geoffrey Lange, sent to the West Coast, was first to arrive. To a large extent, his 'beat' proved somewhat easier. For one thing (and for unknown reasons), the West Coast had caught fire for foreign cars earlier than the East; for another, von Neumann's enthusiasm for VWs had brought results. Lange, following John von Neumann's initiative, soon had matters in hand. Because Wolfsburg had decided on a policy of establishing distributorships largely according to state boundaries, and because states West of the Mississippi were larger than elsewhere, there were fewer distributorships to appoint. These were soon assigned.

An initially more complex situation prevailed east of the Mississippi, for sales had proved tougher there and the number of states and territories to be assigned was much larger. To handle the job, VW sent to New York a man who not only measured up to it, but who towered above it, Will Van de Kamp.

Van de Kamp was in his early forties when he arrived in the United States; tall and handsome, with hair greying at the temples, he struck Americans as having the formal, courtly manners of a European aristocrat and something of the dash of a fighter pilot. He appeared impeccable in Savile Row suits, a Homburg and furled umbrella and no one was ever to see him sloppily or even casually dressed; indeed, one person who once saw him on a weekend, working on his lawn, swears that even then he was dressed to the nines and wore pigskin 'work gloves'. As may be inferred, Van de Kamp was reserved, somewhat unbending, unfailingly 'correct'—but also overwhelmingly charming, whenever he wanted to be.

He arrived in New York towards the end of January 1954 and immediately started on a tour of his territory, intent on setting up the nucleus of his distributor and dealer network as quickly as possible. He was armed with a sheaf of letters which had been written to Wolfsburg by interested motor dealers, several of them members of the earlier Hoffman group. Among these letters were Marsh's letter from Columbus and the Schmidts' from Chicago.

He must have seemed very strange indeed, stepping out of airplanes in the towns of America's wheat and corn country, or travelling through New England and the South, much as a diplomat from the Court of St. James's visiting a land of Levi's and galluses, of shirt-sleeve conferences and 'just plain talk'. Yet the first impression he made was not the last, for there was underneath his mixture of correct formality and charm something else again. And it was this that did much to put VW on the map in the United States.

Will Van de Kamp was an evangelist, possessed of a near-fanatic missionary zeal, his catechism laid down by Wolfsburg. He believed passionately in the Volkswagen and in the truth, beauty, and justice of his company's policies; he never doubted for a second that Volkswagen would become a tremendous success in the United States; he regarded it as heresy for a dealer to believe in (much less sell) any other car but the VW, and he considered it his personal mission in life to infect others with his faith. With that confidence—and following his instructions, admonitions or suggestions to the letter—the men he would appoint could not help but succeed, and make VW succeed as well. Those who argued policies with him, those who questioned the methods he insisted upon, those who baulked at the 'VW way of doing things', were regarded by him as the not-yet-saved, the benighted whom it was his duty to convert. He did so mainly with the sheer force of his personality, his conviction and his expert knowledge; often he did so with his charm, sometimes with exasperated anger. 'Why do you make it so hard for me to like you?' he was soon to groan repeatedly at one stubborn distributor. 'If you will only stop arguing and do *exactly* as I say, I assure you, you will become a millionaire!'

'If ever a man ought to appear in the *Reader's Digest* as "My Most Unforgettable Character",' says Carl Schmidt, 'that man is Will Van de Kamp. He was one of those rare individuals one can never overlook, never ignore; he commanded every situation and everyone's attention, from the moment he entered a room. We met him for the first time in February; he had come to Chicago to choose a distributor from among about three applicants for the franchise. We had asked him for the states of Iowa, Indiana and Illinois; when he finally appointed us, he gave us only the latter two at first. He never told us *why* he picked us over the other applicants. I think he went on instinct largely.'

The experience of the Fergus brothers in Columbus, as well as of others, confirms the belief that Van de Kamp operated less on any notion of 'market research' than on what the Germans call *Fingerspitzengefühl*—sheer sensitive intuition. 'Van de Kamp met with us very briefly in Columbus at the end of January 1954,' says Robert Fergus. 'He'd received Don's letter to Wolfsburg and looked us over. Then, in mid-February, he asked us to meet him in Cleveland.'

Robert Fergus, his older brother John (a lawyer), and Don, Marsh drove to Cleveland on February 19 and used the trip to set up the three-way partnership they meant to offer Van de Kamp as his local distributorship. 'He'd already met with some pretty substantial and established businessmen who applied for the franchise,' John Fergus recalls, 'and we were up against some tough competition. We were young fellows, thirty-three, twenty-nine and twenty-one years old. He never really did tell us that day that he had chosen us; he just asked us to place our order, so we knew we were in business and we ordered seventeen beetles and three trucks.' At a later date, when they asked him just why he had picked them to be distributors for Ohio and Kentucky, Van de Kamp answered in deadly earnest and in his heavy German accent: 'I liked the sparkle in your eyes.'

If that sounds arch or questionable, it was nevertheless largely what Van de Kamp was looking for. He was searching out Americans who, by and large, were young, energetic, capable of flexibility and growth, able to devote enthusiasm and energy to the job, and who, he hoped, would trust his judgment completely. As he travelled throughout his territory, he tried to imbue each with his unshakable faith in the future of the Volkswagen.

He had that rare combination of vision and shortsightedness that achieves success through sheer determination. 'He had blinders on,' one distributor says. 'Van de Kamp simply could not see that what he was trying to do was just impossible! If you raised the possibility that the VW might fail in the US, Van de Kamp just scoffed at you. 'It's succeeding in Germany, isn't it?' he'd say. 'So it will succeed in America!' If you argued with him that conditions in the States were different, that there was "Detroit" to consider, he just stopped listening. He was completely uninterested in what Detroit was doing or how it was doing it. To him there was only *one* car—the Volkswagen—and only *one* way of doing things: the VW way!'

During that first year in the United States, Van de Kamp appointed eight of the ten VW distributors operating in his territory; Geoffrey Lange's own West Coast distributor organisation was also virtually complete by the end of that year. Although some states have been reassigned among distributors in the years since then, the pattern of distribution that was largely developed by Van de Kamp continues in force today.

A year after he had arrived in the United States, Van de Kamp could, therefore, look on the beginnings of a national network which to a very large extent he alone had created. Doing so, while at the same time periodically returning to Wolfsburg for discussions, was a tremendous achievement possible only for a man of boundless energy and determination.

'In the first year or so,' one distributor says, 'we'd see him every two or three weeks, sometimes more often than that. He'd come flying into town, lunch with us, and fly on to the next city. He was a gadfly, encouraging, pushing, checking, admonishing—and always infecting us with his complete and utter faith in this small car.'

He also tried to help them convey that faith to others. The distributors, after all, were responsible for appointing the 'sub-network' of dealers, for motivating and enthusing them, as well as for getting them to work in that special 'Volkswagen way' Van de Kamp in-

sisted upon. Doing so was quite a job, for inculcating faith in the
VW at that time was not easy.

Americans who drove Volkswagens in those early days had to have
thick skins. The somewhat more than two thousand VWs sold before
1954 has been joined by another 6614 sold during that year; sales
may have 'soared' in just twelve months, but it still remained a fact
that fewer than 9000 VWs were on US roads by 1955. American
owners therefore looked queer indeed. 'A lot of people thought they
resembled nuts,' writes Huston Horn in *Sports Illustrated*, 'and
they were rewarded for their courage by the sneers of other drivers
who regarded them with envy mixed with contempt.' The car itself
was regarded at best as a passing and minuscule fad and the VW
owner sloughed off as a faddist. Not only was this the attitude of
most American car drivers, but also of a small army of dealers. Any
number of VW distributors and dealers, reflecting today on the
brilliant stroke of genius (and sometimes luck) which led them to
throw in their lot with Volkswagen, have pointed out to me that they
each know several men in their towns who kick themselves each
morning for having said: 'Thanks, but no!' to Will Van de Kamp
in the early 1950's. Paul Lee, a one-time Chevrolet dealer who later
served for some years as a VW advertising man, was so convinced in
the early 1950's that VW was a crazy passing fad that when a friend
came to him and urged him to invest five thousand dollars and open
a Volkswagen agency with him, he talked his friend out of the whole
idea. 'There was just no reason to believe the car would last,' Lee
admits. He has since avoided his friend, who regards himself as 'a
thwarted millionaire'.

Simple mathematics show how big the job was, how many
sceptical Americans had somehow to be convinced that this car had
a future in America and a future too for a VW dealer. Today, the
Volkswagen organisation in the United States consists of about one
thousand dealers and annual sales are now at such a level that each
of these, on the national average, sells about three cars every two days,
yet Volkswagen has yet to make significant inroads into the *overall*
US car market, even if it has captured its price class. There are, in
short, still plenty of people to convert, even today. In 1954–55,
however, the number of potential US converts defied analysis and
reaching them demanded as rapid a build-up of Volkswagen dealerships as could be managed.

Doing so while maintaining high dealer standards was of course an
absurdly disproportionate job for one man, even if he now had dis-

tributors covering the field for him. Van de Kamp needed an organisation to help, yet almost everything in his psychological makeup resisted building one. He finally surrendered to the need, but he was never happy unless he did everything himself.

The first man he hired was a twenty-five-year-old Englishman named J. Stuart Perkins, who is today president of the entire Volkswagen operation in the United States. Perkins arrived in New York from VW in Toronto, Ontario, on February 14, 1955. 'We didn't have much,' he says. 'There were just the three of us—Van de Kamp, a secretary, and myself—operating out of a suite in the St. Moritz Hotel on Central Park South. We had to build everything from there.'

Next, Van de Kamp sent for three men from Germany—and their arrival underlined one of the company policies he was trying to drive home. Not one of the three was a salesman; all were service representatives. Three more arrived after some months, and in 1956, Wolfsburg sent over another twenty-six, to tour the country in specially built Volkswagen panel trucks, chock-full of tools, and to train mechanics in those dealerships that had already been appointed. At about the same time as the twenty-six arrived, two parts representatives came over, bringing the total service and parts contingent to thirty-four. Each had undergone a year's training in Wolfsburg, including instruction in the language and customs of the United States.

'We believed sales would come if we started with service,' Perkins says. 'There is nothing odd in the fact that we had thirty-four service and parts people touring the country while hardly any Volkswagens were being sold. When I was assistant service manager with VW in Canada, we didn't have a single sale. We didn't even have a single Volkswagen to show customers. We actually had to borrow one from a private owner in New York City for an exhibit in Canada. But we had more than thirty thousand dollars' worth of spare parts stocked, ready for the day when sales would come along!'

On April 19, 1955, Van de Kamp, Perkins, and the gradually growing staff moved out of their hotel suite into sixth-floor offices at 720 Fifth Avenue in New York City. A new corporation, Volkswagen of America, Inc. (VWoA), a wholly-owned subsidiary of the Volkswagenwerk in Wolfsburg, was established in 1956 and appointed sole VW importer for the United States.

Making Volkswagen of America sole importer immediately presented nightmares for the small staff. Until then, each distributor had, in effect, acted as his own importer, arranging for the arrival of the cars he needed. Now, all this fell on the new corporation. With what seems justifiable pride, Perkins remembers that the tiny company set up the kind of network of ports of entry in three weeks that usually takes much longer to establish. 'I confess I had no idea how to go about it at the time,' Perkins says. 'I simply called ships' brokers in a dozen ports, let them advise us, and soon we were in business. Wolfsburg helped us as best they could at long distance, but most of it was handled over the telephone from New York.'

Two more distributorships were appointed in 1955. In January, Riviera Motors Inc., of Oregon, was named; it now distributes throughout Alaska, Idaho, Montana, Oregon, and Washington. In July, Capitol Car Distributors Inc. was appointed and now represents Volkswagen in Maryland, North Carolina, Eastern Tennessee, Virginia, West Virginia, and the District of Columbia. Behind the latter organisation lies the story of a story.

The story in question was written by Blake Clark, a *Reader's Digest* roving editor, and it appeared in the February 1954 issue of that magazine. Entitled 'The Car That Built A City', it dealt with the VW and the town of Wolfsburg, and it reached the eyes of Will Van de Kamp just after he set foot in the United States. Van de Kamp was delighted with the valuable, unsolicited publicity and, after appointing a Washington foreign-car dealer named Jack Pry as his distributor in and around the nation's capital, he suggested to Pry that he give Clark twenty per cent of the Volkswagen end of his Capitol Car business as a gesture of appreciation for the nice article. Pry didn't mind doing so, for this concession was so small then as to be meaningless; he didn't even mind when Blake Clark, sniffing the winds of change faster than Pry did, bought thirty per cent more of it. Then the beetle's sales began to soar and Pry found that he had cut himself out of fifty per cent of a business moving into the millions of dollars. Eventually, VWoA had to move into the picture to correct an impossible situation. Pry's half-share in Capitol Car Distributors Inc. was bought out by the Schroeder-Rockefeller Bank in New York, which appointed a bank vice-president, James Madden, as chairman of the board. President and operating head today is Alan M. Dix, an experienced veteran of VW operations all the way from South Africa and Oregon to Wolfsburg itself. As for Blake Clark, he continues as a roving editor and serves the firm as chairman of the executive committee and vice-chairman of the board exemplifying in his own life the upbeat ending of a *Digest* 'Life in These United States' anecdote.

In 1955, plans were formulated to manufacture the Volkswagen in the US as well, and a Studebaker assembly plant in New Brunswick, New Jersey, was purchased. Six months and one day later, it was sold again and the plans were abandoned. Preliminary estimates had proved to be too low and it now became clear that the venture would cause the Volkswagenwerk to lose money. 'You don't have seats in your cars,' said one US supplier who boosted his estimates after a close look at the beetle. 'You have chairs.'

'The decision to sell,' says Dr. Carl H. Hahn, then a rising young man in the Wolfsburg export department who would soon be headed for larger jobs, 'was taken one afternoon in Germany by Professor Nordhoff himself. He never asked who obtained the inaccurate estimates, nor did he blame anyone. "Well," he said, "I made a mistake. Let's sell." '

Van de Kamp and his men continued to race all over their part of the country, interviewing prospective dealers and helping to appoint and train those who impressed them and their distributors. They had their problems with many. 'One of the first things we had to do,' remembers one veteran of these visits, 'was to get in there and have them clean up the dirt in their workshops. We wanted these to be neat and uniform—we had to convince them to get rid of pink and green shops—so that Volkswagen facilities could have the same single and recognisable image in the country that the car had. We wanted our workshops to be attractive and tidy, even to have flowers placed out front if possible, so as to make them really stand out from other dealerships.' A lot of American dealers thought they were crazy.

One Virginia dealer, who dated back to the Hoffman network, worked out of a dilapidated wooden building. 'The filth was indescribable,' says Edward Valentin, today VWoA's personnel chief. 'We found this man sitting behind a cluttered rolltop desk and repairing everything from motor-cycles right up on and down the line. We finally straightened both him and his place out. Another whose ways we finally changed was a New Hampshire dealer who used to dress like a beatnik and thought the whole VW idea was a big joke. He'd talk with customers while sitting cross-legged on the floor, as though he were in an artist's colony.'

Hans-Dieter Deiss, today with VW management in Wolfsburg, recalls another encounter, typical of many. Deiss, then a young service manager with Capitol Car, had driven to the address given for a 'VW dealership' near Washington, D.C., only to find a men's clothing store at the site. 'Sure we sell Volkswagens, mister,' the haberdasher said. 'Out back behind the store.' It turned out that the store owner found his 'dealership' an easy way to get cars cheaply for his friends. When he learned Deiss's identity and was threatened with cancellation, he pleaded for another week's time. 'You come back next week,' he said, 'and you'll see that everything will be the way you people want it.'

A week later, Deiss arrived to find a storefront with a VW sign above it close beside the haberdashery. A Volkswagen sedan was actually to be seen in the otherwise bare shop. Deiss wandered in and found a man standing in the empty rear 'store room', neatly dressed in a starched white coat. 'Who are you?' Deiss asked without identifying himself. The fellow turned around and smiled. 'Oh, heck,' he said. 'I don't really work here. I work across the street in that plant over there. Fellow just hired me for the day to stand around here because he's expecting some big shots from Germany to come in.'

Dealerships such as this were cancelled rapidly. Van de Kamp himself toured with a baleful eye. He walked into one Washington dealership and saw three salesmen in the showroom, one reading a newspaper in his shirt-sleeves. 'This is out!' the impeccable Van de Kamp announced to the dealer. 'You either straighten out that man or you fire him!'

There was no stopping this determined German. He neither took 'no' for an answer, nor could he regard anything as impossible. Stuart Perkins describes the harrowing way in which Van de Kamp would get himself airline tickets after his secretary had failed to get him on the particular flight which he insisted on using. 'Van de Kamp would just call the president of the airline and start in on the man in his heavy accent until he gave in,' Perkins says. 'Then afterwards, Van de Kamp would write him a charming letter, thanking him for his trouble, but also explaining that he did, after all, expect service, since he flew thousands of miles on that airline. The next time Van de Kamp wanted to fly, he'd just telephone the president directly and say, "Remember? You promised to help me next time I needed a ticket and I'm holding you to your word!" Of course the airline president had never made such a promise. He had never even answered Van de Kamp's letter. But Van de Kamp always got his tickets.'

Generally speaking, Van de Kamp got results by overwhelming the Americans he met. He did so, apparently, without artifice and completely naturally. With his commanding appearance, accent and suave manners he dominated every situation. No one ever forgot him.

'He would, for example, go into an elegant restaurant for the first time,' Stuart Perkins recalls with fascination, 'and the head-waiter, not recognising him, might say all tables had been reserved. Van de Kamp would ignore the remark or just proceed to enlighten the man. "I am Mr. Van de Kamp!" he would tell the head-waiter, spelling his name out carefully. "Van de Kamp—*from Volkswagen!*" Half the time, the head-waiters would not have understood him, but they did understand *one* thing: that one did not refuse this man. Van de Kamp always got his table—and they always remembered his name, even when he returned months later. There are restaurants I frequent today who still ask about him by name.'

'We were out to the theatre in New York City with Will Van de Kamp one evening,' John Fergus says, supplying another anecdote illustrative of this man's stubborn will to win. 'There were about four of us, with our wives. Van de Kamp wanted a taxi afterwards and it was no use arguing with him that we could walk the six or eight blocks to our restaurant, that he would never get a taxi in Manhattan when the theatres let out, and that he might as well join us. '*I* will get a taxi!' he said. Last thing we saw of him, as the rest of us started walking crosstown, he was standing in the middle of Eighth Avenue, with the cars streaming by on either side of him, waving his furled umbrella and occasionally even banging it on the sides of passing cabs. Then, just as we got to our destination about ten or fifteen minutes later, a taxi pulled up, with Will Van de Kamp inside. His umbrella was upright between his knees and his hands rested, folded, across its handle. He half-bowed to us through the window. "I *told* you I would get a taxi!" he said.'

Van de Kamp's determination absolutely overwhelmed, sometimes appalled, but always impressed. It was clear he was used to issuing orders and the combination of his often peremptory commands and of his equally enormous charm seemed often enough to get them obeyed. After one early distributor meeting, for example, Van de Kamp said, "Gentlemen, we will all now go to our rooms and clean up and then you will be my guests for cocktails and dinner!' One of the distributors objected that he had a train reservation for early that evening. Van de Kamp asked him if he couldn't get another reservation, but the man answered that nothing else was available. Whereupon Van de Kamp looked him straight in the eye and said: 'Your train leaves tomorrow morning!' The flabbergasted, but awed, distributor stayed for the evening.

'Never in my life,' says Perkins, whose task it often was to make Van de Kamp's directives more palatable to others, 'have I met a man like him! He could antagonise you and in the next moment charm you to the point where you forgot the slight you had received earlier. You could switch from hating to loving him in thirty seconds.

'His broken English and his heavy German accent insulated him from all criticism or objections,' Perkins continues. 'He simply never recognised them. The word "no" was never allowed. As for the market, he was such a fanatic believer in the Volkswagen that he paid no attention whatsoever to US car manufacturers or their methods. He never even discussed them. The issue was very simple: the Volkswagen had been a success elsewhere, so why shouldn't it be a success in the United States? The fact that the USA was the country of big cars didn't bother him. He would simply answer that point by saying: "Yes, but you don't understand. *This* is the Volkswagen!" He was absolutely blind and deaf to whatever criticism he might hear and he had this enormous personal horsepower and terrific force of personality with which to overcome it.'

Eventually, however, these characteristics of his did him in. As the end of 1958 approached, Van de Kamp was told by Wolfsburg that he should find himself an opportunity elsewhere. The remainder of his contract was compensated for by means of a large allocation of cars—representing a generous financial settlement, as well as a very powerful negotiating lever indeed.

For four years, Will Van de Kamp had poured out his energies and his enthusiasm into the job of laying the groundwork for the US Volkswagen network that exists today; why, then, the need for a change?

The answer lies less in any mysterious 'company politics' than in the changing situation VWoA and its parent company were now facing. Van de Kamp had been a freewheeling, intuitive operator, the typical 'one-man show', satisfied only when he knew personally everything that was going on and could do every job himself. The only 'management systems' he knew were his own and, instinctively, he distrusted those of others. His small staff had learned to live with both him and his methods and had even developed ways of getting round him, so as to establish some procedures and a semblance of a corporate organisation, but the fact remained that Will Van de Kamp was getting in the way of the very network he had built up. He considered this network *his* baby and he continued personally to mother (and, some say, smother) it after it had grown too big for that. Van de Kamp's time had passed him by, thanks to his own success.

It had been possible in 1954 for Van de Kamp to know almost everything about VW in the USA and to handle it all by himself; four years later, when sales had passed 100,000 a year, when 'his' distributors and their dealers were operating efficiently and growing rapidly, this was no longer the case. Van de Kamp found himself often in the dark and making mistakes; like an army platoon leader who suddenly finds himself a general, he was unhappy with staff-work and planning and still insisted on being in the front lines, personally leading the attack, rather than dealing through subordinates and building a team.

To be sure, his insistence on being in these front lines had its charming and amusing sides too. Once, when driving a VW along a motorway, at a time when very few Volkswagens were to be seen on American roads, Van de Kamp spotted a disabled beetle parked by the side of the highway. Without hesitating a moment, he zoomed in front of it, stopped, and leaped out to confront the distressed lady driver. 'How may I be of help?' he asked gallantly and, when the lady pointed to her car's flat tyre, Van de Kamp and the other VW executive with him immediately whipped off their jackets and changed it for her. After they were finished and Van de Kamp once more stood before her in his Homburg hat and immaculately tailored British suit, she thanked him and asked if she might pay him something for the trouble to which the two men had gone. In reply, Van de Kamp snapped his heels together, bowed, and presented her with his business card as head of VWoA. 'A pleasure, madam!' he said. 'Just typical Volkswagen service, nothing more!'

It was this kind of personal contact that he enjoyed and that the pressing need for a relatively impersonal organisation would deny him. It may have been a shortcoming of his that he apparently could not grow with his growing job, but surely it was a virtue and much to his credit that he had honourably worked himself out of that job. There is a time when his kind of pioneering enterprise no longer serves a need and managers have to take over. That time had come.

Van de Kamp now looked about him for the opportunity that might exist. A settlement had been arrived at with the factory and Van de Kamp wanted to remain with VW's US operation. He began to speak with distributors.

Some, however, weren't interested. Van de Kamp's dominating personality was perhaps at fault; while all the distributors appear to have liked and admired him, working with him full time and having him as a partner was another matter again.

Two who were not apprehensive about this were Oliver and Carl Schmidt of Import Motors of Chicago. Indeed, both profess to have been anxious to get Van de Kamp into their organisation.

'I couldn't think of a better man for us,' Carl Schmidt told me. 'We both liked him a great deal and respected him enormously. We were growing so fast then that we badly needed a man of his calibre. When he approached us, we were extremely interested in his talents.'

Van de Kamp joined them as executive vice-president and general manager of their VW distributorship and also bought a share in a Porsche dealership they owned.

Van de Kamp's relationship with VWoA had ended before 1958 was up and he formally joined Import Motors of Chicago in the early spring of 1959. That he apparently harboured few (if any) resentments was evidenced at the first 'post-Van de Kamp' VW distributor meeting, at which his successor was introduced to men Van de Kamp himself had largely appointed.

'To my amazement,' says Stuart Perkins, who was there, 'Will Van de Kamp attended this meeting, seated among the distributors, between Carl and Oliver Schmidt, and looking perfectly calm and comfortable. Another man might have waited a year before showing up in public "at the other side of the table", but not he! He was too big to be in any way embarrassed by the turn of events.'

If he looked cool and comfortable, that seemed to be how he felt. He and his wife, a charming and attractive German lady with whom he enjoyed a very close and devoted life, had moved into a handsome house in Illinois and could devote more of their energies than ever before to leisure and the cultivation of their own cultural interests.

Then, just six months after he had moved to Chicago, Van de Kamp was killed, in the early autumn of 1959, at the age of fifty. It happened while he was away in Germany, on business; he was driving a Porsche at night and, speeding over a rise on the Auto-bahn, he slammed into the rear end of a lorry he had apparently failed to see in time. He died instantly. He may have had some premonition of his death, for it was during that trip to Germany that he reportedly had for the first time in many years resumed contact with his family there. According to all reports, Will Van de Kamp actively avoided any contact with or discussion of his family members in Germany while he was at VWoA. The Van de Kamps had no children and it seemed as though his entire private world centred only on his wife. But just before he was killed, he reportedly had taken up that broken link again.

Stuart Perkins, his close associate for four years, happened to have been in Wolfsburg when it occurred and he attended the funeral. After the ceremony, Perkins noticed a German whom he had never before met and he introduced himself. The stranger told Perkins he had come to the funeral because he had been Van de Kamp's Luftwaffe squadron leader on the Russian front during World War II. 'You know,' the former fighter pilot said, 'Van de Kamp used to fly on my wing during the war. I came to rely on him. He was quite a man.'

Detroit Meets the Beetle

BACK in the summer of 1954, a twenty-seven-year-old German economist attached to the Office of European Economic Cooperation in Brussels had an idea regarding the 'Europeanisation' of the Continental car industry. At the suggestion of his father, a member of the Auto-Union board, he outlined the idea in a letter to Heinz Nordhoff, whom he had never met. The answer he got back in reply was disappointing.

The plan, Nordhoff wrote, wouldn't work, and he sketched out his reasons for thinking so, remarking, as an aside, that 'there are already a lot of international organisations like this and the one thing most of them seem to have in common is that they want to be headquartered in Paris'. But Nordhoff had liked the young economist's thinking and invited him to visit when he found himself in Wolfsburg.

This is just what Dr. Carl Horst Hahn did and, some time after doing so, he decided to stay. Nordhoff had invited Hahn to become his personal assistant and for a while he even lived at the Nordhoffs' home. 'I was also assigned a big office,' Hahn says, 'but there was no real work for me to do, because Nordhoff is so used to doing everything himself. I complained about this once or twice and, when nothing happened, I finally threatened to resign.' This provided the shock Hahn had wanted to administer and he was reassigned to the export department's sales promotion operation. In what time he had left from his new job, he also assisted Professor Nordhoff prepare his Brunswick University lectures. Hahn himself had been educated in Germany, Switzerland, France, Italy and England, and had received his doctorate from the University of Berne in 1952, his thesis being on European economic unification. The Nordhoff lectures were more practical—they tried to teach the students the hard facts of industrial life, to prepare them for business

—and while this work and that in the export department interested Hahn, he felt he wanted still more scope.

There were actually plans afoot that Hahn should manage VW's Canadian operation and that the man who had built up this market, Bernard Jansen, would take over in the United States now that Van de Kamp needed to be replaced. It was during this period that Nordhoff underwent his operation for ulcers at the Mayo Clinic and, using his visit to North America also to talk with Jansen, he found that this executive, now growing older, did not like the idea of being given the huge US assignment at his age.

On January 5, 1959, Carl Hahn returned from a skiing trip in Switzerland to find that he had immediate instructions to proceed to New York City with his boss, VW export chief Manuel Hinke. Nordhoff was waiting for them at the St. Regis Hotel, having been released from the Mayo Clinic. He told Hahn that he and Hinke would like him to take over the US operation; ever since Van de Kamp had left, VWoA had been without an official head man.

'Hahn was very uncertain about whether he could do a good job,' Nordhoff remembers.

'I was overawed,' Hahn admits.

The two men spent the entire day in the hotel. 'I wanted to give him some confidence and also explain what I wanted done here,' Nordhoff says. 'For decades, no one had believed that European cars could ever be a success in the United States. Then, after the war, the British showed that it could be done. I knew that we could do the same.' The talks were intense and strenuous for Heinz Nordhoff. 'I was so weak from my operation that we could only talk for an hour at a time before I'd have to rest for a bit,' he says.

'That day in the St. Regis,' Nordhoff reports, 'I told Hahn I wanted VW to have more dealers in the USA, fresh dealers, and dealers who would want to sell Volkswagens exclusively. We had not come into the US market to be a fifth wheel to the Big Three, nor did we want to be the seventeenth car in anyone's line! I suggested to him that he go after people who had no automobile franchises at all, because so many of the best dealers had been taken on by Detroit.'

Nordhoff urged Hahn to place even more emphasis on service. 'I had already been told by many to look at the British operation in the USA,' Nordhoff says. 'Much of their early successes had dissolved because they couldn't adequately service the cars they had sold. When we planned entering the US market, people kept telling us, "Be careful! Look at the British!" Well, I looked—and I learned a lesson!'

After Carl Hahn had been appointed head of the US operation, he and Manuel Hinke took a tour of the country to see for themselves. It was during this trip that they decided that the United States VW operation should no longer be 'split down the middle' at the Mississippi River, but that the country should be regarded as a unit. Gradually, they began to de-emphasise the West Coast operation and in 1962 it dissolved completely.

'After Van de Kamp had left and before Carl Hahn took over, we had gone through a period of considerable worry,' says Stuart Perkins, who was to serve as Hahn's sales manager and, later, as his assistant general manager. 'There were rumours that the factory was going to close down the whole US operation and work directly through dealers, so it was a relief to see that this had not come about. The first thing one noticed about Hahn was a completely refreshing approach. He could make a decision and have it followed through, because he had Nordhoff's complete confidence, which Van de Kamp never really enjoyed. Hahn immediately took to modern techniques. We got computers in and we got consultants to develop a training programme and to do essential research jobs for us. Hahn proved to be a slide-rule man, which is what we needed. He also proved fast in adapting to American ways and that contributed to his success in the United States.'

The creating of a real VWoA organisation, expansion of the dealer network, standardisation of service facilities, and modernisation of the entire network into an efficient and well-managed one occupied Hahn's tenure in office. Under him, also, marketing became a science for Volkswagen, advertising began, and standards of service and sales were raised.

'Our customers buy service along with the car as part of a single sales package,' says Hermann Bruns, until recently VWoA's vice-president for service and parts and today a leading executive in Wolfsburg. Another VW service specialist once put it this way: 'At Volkswagen, we feel that sales without service is a little like kissing your sister. It's very nice, but there's no future in it.' Far from permitting sales to grow in an ungoverned and uncontrollable manner, the company refuses, says Bruns, to 'let sales outpace the service facilities of a single dealer. His sales potential (the number of cars given him to sell) is increased only as his service potential grows. We also insist that each dealer maintain enough service facilities to care for *all* Volkswagens in his area for which service is demanded. Market studies show us just how large his facilities must be. We tell him, if you want to get something out of this business, you've got to put something into it.'

Distributors select dealer locations and, once approved by VWoA, choose a suitable applicant for the dealership. Again VWoA joins in the final say on each man. 'We set high standards as to buildings, working capital, personnel, equipment, and tooling,' a company executive says. 'We want our buildings to have a distinct Volkswagen look. Even the interior space distribution is standardised. And we insist on cleanliness everywhere, not just for the customers, but for the sake of the "grease-monkey", that much-neglected man whose image is so tarnished. We ask for attractive lunchrooms for the personnel, as well as locker rooms and showers.' Dealers receive complete blueprints and floor plans, down to the type of desk and desk lamp the company recommends. The company establishes various specifications, ranging from the smallest to the largest dealerships. It claims these save dealers about $5000 [£1783] in architects' fees alone. Still, it does not reject an applicant who owns adequate facilities, just because he will not rebuild to its specifications. It is expected, however, that the dealer will sooner or later abandon his present facilities and achieve that uniform look VW likes. In buildings alone, VW dealer investment totals about $30,000,000 [almost £11 million] and keeps rising each year.

New dealers must buy a large parts inventory from the distributor. The minimum parts and accessories inventory for the smallest dealer is worth $7000 [£2500] retail, representing three months' requirements. A minimum number of work stalls is also prescribed. The smallest dealer must have four work stalls, each two hundred square feet in size. Distributors maintain a minimum five-months' inventory. In practice they carry a good deal more. Yet these high requirements have proved invaluable. The company was never encumbered with the deadly 'lack of parts' stigma which other imported cars bore. 'American motor manufacturers think of service and parts as supporting the sales effort,' says Hermann Bruns. 'We disagree. They ought to be profitable operations in themselves and act as stabilising influences. A dealer ought to make a decent living from service and parts if market conditions fluctuate.' The dealers' parts business has proved to be profitable: it rose twelve-fold between 1956 and 1963.

'Twenty years ago General Motors and Ford did what we're doing,' says Hermann Bruns. 'But somewhere along the line they got sidetracked. They began to concentrate almost exclusively on sales. Then they tried to make up for their lack of service by advertising more. Ten years ago, Chevrolet had 11,000,000 cars on the road and today they have far more than twice that. But their number of work stalls hasn't increased at anywhere near the same rate. And Chevrolet isn't the only one. Much the same thing has happened to most of the Detroit manufacturers.'

At VW, service personnel are as much cared for as service facilities and training programmes for VW were started early. Today they exist in each distributorship, as permanent, full-fledged schools. Thousands of service and parts employees have attended them.

Dealers do not seem to mind the company's rigorous standards. The reason, as might be expected, lies in high sales and profits. Volkswagen dealers today vie with Chevrolet for first place among cars sold per dealer. The average VW dealer sells between three hundred and four hundred new cars a year, and many sell more. 'We can prove that our dealers make twice the average profits of any other car dealers in the US car industry, yet their profit margin per car is lower and their overhead is greater because of the big investments we require,' says Perkins. 'When you don't change the model each year, you can afford the extra costs. You can afford to modernise and meet our specifications. Today, eighty-five per cent of our dealers are in buildings less than four years old.'

The paradox between unusually high costs and top profits is resolved because VW dealers are not vexed with the built-in weaknesses plaguing their Detroit counterparts. First of all, the demand is still so high that some US customers still have to wait for delivery. This demand eliminates all need for discounts, rebates, price-cutting, and 'unloading' at the end of a year. VW dealers do not need to throw in extras, nor sell at cut-rate prices to clear out showrooms for next year's model. As a result almost one hundred per cent of the dealers obtain the full manufacturer suggested retail price for a Volkswagen. In addition, the car's constant design eliminates the need for new tools, new service facilities, or the retraining of service personnel. Dealers are also not stuck with obsolete parts and accessories.

Almost all dealers sell only the VW, a vital element in creating the success of VWoA. A very few (fifteen or twenty per cent) also sell Porsches; four dealers also sell Mercedes-Benzes. 'But we explained to them that product diversification doesn't mean more profits,' Perkins says. 'In America, you can't sell a high-powered car in the same showroom with a Volkswagen. Also, if you sell only one car, you can stock fewer parts. Most of our dealers agree.'

'We might have sold the first 50,000 or 70,000 Volkswagens on the basis of the car alone,' says Guenter Kittel, VWoA's vice-president for parts. 'But all sales after that were due to our organisation.' Kittel credits the product as first among the reasons for the success and believes the VW paint job is a big attraction. 'Only cars in the $5000-and-up category equal it,' he says.

Interest in foreign cars started rising sharply in the early 1950's. In 1955 (when VWoA planned its New Brunswick factory) Volkswagen sales reached 31,000, including 2000 Transporters. In 1956 sales jumped to 50,000 sedans and 5000 Transporters. Headquarters personnel reached fifty-four and moved to a small brick building in Englewood Cliffs, New Jersey, across the George Washington Bridge from New York City.

Sales ever since have been so good that Volkswagen in a certain sense occupies both first and second place among imported cars in the United States. This is because even VW's Transporters (Microbus station wagons and trucks) outsell all other foreign passenger makes. VW today also outsells all US compacts. A huge gulf exists between Volkswagen and the rest of the imported car market.

The gulf was widened after Detroit entered the small-car market. The peak year for imported cars in the United States was reached in 1959, with 614,131 sold. Of these, VW's leading share was 120,442 sedans and 30,159 Transporters. Then, when foreign car sales reached ten per cent of total US car sales, American manufacturers took notice. In 1960, they entered the market with their so-called compact cars.

Of this new competition, Carl Hahn said with delight: 'We no longer talk about the other imported motor-cars. . . . They are of minor concern to us. New names are mentioned now—names like Ford and General Motors. We are in the big league now.'

Heinz Nordhoff also appraised Detroit's entry into the small-car market in 1960, in an address to his German dealers and distributors. All US compacts, he said, 'are interesting vehicles, particularly the Corvair which closely followed our principles. They will all be successful, if perhaps not so completely and not so quickly as their creators had expected. Partly this is a question of time, partly of prices which in some cases are still too close to those of the bigger cars—and for many Americans the big car still has undoubted prestige-appeal, although it is becoming less and less fashionable to display one's wealth by the size of one's car.' In March 1960, Nordhoff spoke out again on the subject, at the opening of the International Automobile Salon in Geneva, Switzerland. He noted that American compacts had their 'well-earned and sensible success; their share of the market is even bigger than optimists hoped for, or feared, and I am completely convinced that this development will continue'. These cars would not hurt Volkswagen, he predicted accurately. He could not resist chiding Detroit for its rigidity. Despite 'scientifically advanced market research techniques' which predicted that 'it would no longer do to make cars always bigger, always more powerful, it took the example of European imports, particularly of the Volkswagen, to drive the point home to the US manufacturers'. His analysis was accurate: VW, as one writer noted that year, was 'the pacesetter'.

Introduction of Detroit's compact cars had a disastrous effect on most European imports, cutting sales in half, to 378,622 in 1961 and 339,160 in 1962. Only the VW survived, captured the bulk of the remaining foreign car market, and eventually outsold the compacts themselves. In 1960, 'year 1 of the Compact-Car Age', as one writer labels it, VW imported its 500,000th vehicle into the United States. A year later, forty-six per cent of all imports were VWs; dealers now totalled 500 and employees 8500.

Not only were compact cars having their effect, but a nasty 'buy-American' campaign had been launched nationally, especially in areas where steel companies were having difficulties. So ugly was it that one VW distributor's son actually was beaten up by his 'patriotically' motivated schoolmates and certain Midwestern employers had let it be known that workers driving foreign cars would not be permitted into the factory parking lots. That this campaign was as short-sighted as it proved unsuccessful may be seen from information already provided in Chapter 8, which deals with VW's worldwide exports and in which the impact of VW sales in and on the USA is also assessed. As for VWoA, its public relations department countered the campaign by pointing to 'the give and take' of world trade; as a matter of fact, a VW film with just that title was issued and has been shown on US television as an unsponsored public service film more often than any other similar production. A VW brochure, *Fair Exchange*, also made the point that, if Americans weren't buying such German products as the VW, Germany couldn't 'buy American' (which it does far more than the US 'buys German').

Such anti-import campaigns continue sporadically even today, especially in the Middle West, but, by and large, Volkswagen does not seem hurt by them. VW sales today run over 400,000 a year in the US and each year keep climbing.

The impact of the compacts began to lessen in 1963. By this time, VWoA had captured more than 69 per cent of the imported-car market. As for the compacts themselves, 'they got steadily more and more elaborate,' the New York *Times* reported. Tom McCahill, probably America's best-known popular motoring writer, put it this way: 'When compacts came out several years ago we predicted that the Michigan knotheads would soon be adding size and more power to these jobs and wouldn't stop until they became full-size cars again. They've almost made it.'

Heinz Nordhoff visited the United States in 1958 to receive the Elmer A. Sperry Medal on his own behalf, for his co-workers, and on behalf of Ferdinand Porsche posthumously. This considerable honour is bestowed from time to time by three American engineering societies to those who make significant contributions in transportation. Nordhoff was the first man ever to receive it for a car. Previously recipients had been Donald W. Douglas, the designer of the DC-3, 'workhorse of the air', and William Francis Gibbs, who designed the SS *United States*.

In 1962, Nordhoff returned to America to celebrate the millionth VW sold in the United States. In New York, he addressed a press conference and delivered himself of some predictions. 'The next twenty-five years will be the most significant in history for all those involved in the world's car industry,' he said. 'Despite achievements in space, the motor-car will continue as basic transportation for the world's millions. There are 127,000,000 motor vehicles in the world today. In the next twenty-five years, the number will double and perhaps triple.'

From New York, Nordhoff went to Detroit to the Motor Show. On October 22 he addressed the Detroit Economic Club on the subject of the Common Market, warning that high Common Market tariffs against the outside world 'protect obsolescence and inefficiency' and urging more trade between the US and Europe. The second obstacle to such trade, he noted, 'is the unpreparedness of many American firms in exporting'.

'This has been demonstrated to us during the last half year,' he said. 'Out of five hundred letters sent to companies in this country producing items and materials we could use, over half were not even answered. Another forty per cent were answered, but stated they were not interested. Only ten per cent seemed to want our business enough to respond positively to our letters.' Nordhoff was referring to a situation which continues to trouble business analysts.

Nordhoff was received enthusiastically at the Economic Club by virtually all of the US car industry leaders, some of who were Henry Ford II, GM's Chairman Frederic Donner and President John Gordon, Chrysler's Lynn Townsend, and American Motors President Roy Abernathy. In all, 750 leading motor manufacturers came to hear the man whose company had by then sold a million Americans the car which many of them had regarded as unsaleable. That evening, Henry Ford II introduced Nordhoff at the Automobile Manufacturers Association's biennial dinner as 'my good friend and great competitor'. Next morning, Nordhoff and his party visited the General Motors Technical Centre and toured its engineering, styling, and research departments. Afterwards they lunched with Henry Ford II and his top aides.

Leaving Detroit, Nordhoff visited VW's Canadian headquarters in Toronto, and from there went to Boston, where he gave the Alexander Graham Bell lecture on communications, on the occasion of the fiftieth anniversary of Boston University's School of Business Administration. Since then, Boston University has awarded Nordhoff his first American honorary doctorate.

In 1964, he called Carl Hahn back to Germany, to take charge of worldwide sales and service, the post which had been vacated a few years earlier through the sudden death of Dr. Karl Feuereissen and the accession of his successor, Fritz Frank, to the Auto-Union board. 'We take our promising men and send them out into the field to test them before we bring them home,' Nordhoff says. First a deputy member of the Vorstand and later a full member, Carl Hahn brought with him to his new post the experience of five years in the United States, the toughest car market of them all, as some manufacturers characterise it. Those five years have 'Americanised' him a good deal and while some members of the Volkswagen organisation in Germany have questioned the applicability of 'American' sales and service methods in Germany, many there and elsewhere in the worldwide VW empire like the infusion of fresh ideas from the States. One of these is Heinz Nordhoff himself. To him, Volkswagen is less a German product than an international commodity, and nationalities disappear when the product one sells is as unusual as is this car.

And so it was also no surprise that Stuart Perkins, an Englishman, was named to succeed Hahn as general manager of Volkswagen of America, Inc. Then in 1965, at the age of thirty-six, Perkins became president of this US subsidiary. The choice could not have been more logical. Perkins, who was the first man hired by Volkswagen in Canada, had come to New York to be the first man hired by VW in the USA; he had served as assistant to both Van de Kamp and Carl Hahn and he knew and was trusted by every one of the US distributors, as well as by many of their nearly one thousand VW dealers. He was a man with whom the distributors could work effectively and harmoniously; he knew their problems and considered them with understanding. No longer was it true, as one distributor had said of the Van de Kamp era, that working in the field for VW was a little like being a States' Rights champion and working for the Federal Government.

Stuart Perkins's quiet, soft-spoken and diplomatic manner seems well suited to dealing with such stresses as may arise. Under him, a continuing interchange of views and opinions has been instituted, with distributor executives attending seminars at VWoA headquarters and feeding it with their own suggestions and ideas. These, in turn, are fed back into the field after the experience and opinions of others have been added and evaluated. The result is a rising flow of information and ideas up and down the network.

The job of raising personnel standards (and salaries, to competitive US levels) also occupies Perkins's time as much as anything. VWoA no longer can afford to rely just on imported Germans or young American eager-beavers; it needs, more and more, experienced US motor industry men, and Perkins is trying to attract and hold them. An extremely advanced computerised data processing system throughout the entire Volkswagen organisation is being expanded constantly and is already, in this field at least, placing Volkswagen ahead of Detroit. The amount of expert information required by the maturing organisation is enormous and has a direct and vital role upon the profitability of each dealership. Perkins's aim is to make certain that these dealerships remain attractive and profitable, so that the network may continue to expand.

In addition also to the management of VWoA-owned distributorships in the USA, Perkins and his staff are responsible for VWoA's Carribbean Department, selling VWs in a host of sun-drenched islands.

The biggest job Perkins faces is, of course, to keep VW sales mounting in the USA. That's a job performed by his distributors and dealers: hence VWoA's concentration on aiding them and on performing a national marketing, as well as co-ordinating, service.

With 2,500,000 VWs already sold in the USA and annual sales adding 410,000 and more to that figure, Volkswagen's success in America can be called nothing short of phenomenal. This is all the more clear when one looks at the remaining entries in the race for American sales: the other cars imported, along with the VW, into the USA. Britain, which opened the market in the early years, cannot be said to have slipped: British makes have plummeted. Surveying 1966 figures of the 12 'leading' makes of imported cars competitive with Volkswagen, the British occupy 6th and 11th place, respectively held by Standard-Triumph which sold 15,442 cars (dropping 20·1 per cent from 1965) and by English Ford which rose 70·2 per cent but which sold only 8189 cars. Opel and Volvo hold the number two and three positions (with 32,044 and 24,696 respectively); neither sold even 10 per cent of Volkswagen's 410,000 volume.

The Sunday Times on April 23, 1967, stated that 'it is doubtful if UK car makers will ever regain the position they once held' and attributes this partially 'to nearsighted marketing tactics by British importers . . .' Reporting on recent inroads made in the US market by Japan's Datsun and Toyota motor-cars, it states that the Japanese 'used the same marketing tactics as America's own "Big Three" producers and Germany's Volkswagen. The tactics are simple: a car tailored to American tastes and American driving conditions; a large and powerful network of exclusive dealerships supported by an efficient network of regional parts distributorships; eschewal of repatriation of profits in favour of investments in local, regional and national advertising campaigns.'

British cars, by and large, *do* meet American tastes and driving conditions (though there is room for improvement); British car makers, however, have by and large failed to follow the other tactics mentioned. They have been satisfied to sell, paying little heed to the customer afterwards; as a result, customers pay little heed to them, and they seem to sell fewer cars each year. The Japanese have begun a huge, nation-wide dealer organisation, many selling either Datsun or Toyota exclusively; as a result, Datsun moved from 6th to 4th position in 1966 and Toyota leaped 257·6 per cent from 13th place to 5th. Still, their *combined* sales in 1966 (including Toyota's Land Cruiser) totalled only 40,496, less than 10 per cent of Volkswagen's.

But their move is in the right direction, their sales are gaining, and they have learned their lessons well. As a matter of fact, *The Sunday Times* quotes a Datsun official as saying: 'None of the foreign car makers except the German and Japanese has learned to sell in the US. The US isn't like Europe, where customers have to come to you because you're the only dealer around. Here you have to sell cars. They won't sell themselves.'

Not only marketing tactics have failed British car-makers in America: something far subtler helped do them in. I have spoken to any number of British executives who have succeeded in the USA about this: all bemoan the lack of professionalism they believe lies at the root of so many British commercial failures. Often one hears of lack of drive or lack of initiative, but almost always of amateurism. One top executive told me of his experience with a British motor-car maker selling in Canada; in his day, British salesmen would reply to a prospect's questions with a mumbled, 'Buy it, old boy, it's British!' He reported this to me in deadly earnest; he cited it as an example of amateurism. Those salesmen took no professional pride in selling—perhaps because many of their superiors took a superior attitude towards business in general. Why did they fail to offer sound technical reasons for buying the car they were supposed to sell? Because, this executive says, they were inadequately trained and many, incredibly, thought 'it's British' ought to be argument enough for any Canadian. It seems a shame, as there are so many better arguments for buying high-quality, superbly engineered British products.

The 'secret' of VW's success in the USA is no secret at all. As a matter of fact, it is one which Stuart Perkins is happy to hand out to all comers. Many of those who visit him are fellow-Britons, who see in him an Englishman who has successfully adapted himself to American needs. This adaptation (similar to that which helped Carl Hahn meet the challenges of the US market) has helped Perkins's career. Certainly he is a remarkably young man to run so large, important, far-flung, and ever-growing an enterprise. Barely out of his thirties, slim and medium height, he has none of that nervous drive which characterises so many young men who move up rapidly. What he has achieved, he accomplished by means of calm research and planning. He is horrified at the thought of unpremeditated action or decisions made before research has been completed. Typically, he had instituted a method by means of which VWoA works towards the future. Each job is 'programmed' so that each man knows exactly what portion of what job he is to have completed on each day. Stuart Perkins not only has a programme such as this for his own work, but he also knows the stage which each of his executives should have reached in theirs on any day. It keeps things moving. Perkins calls it an 'Action Programme', and it is just this that Volkswagen will need if it is to keep moving ahead in the years to come. Perkins intends to see it does.

13

A Matter of Taste

IN 1959, Volkswagen of America, Inc., began to advertise seriously
—humorously. 'What a happy day for Volkswagen it turned out to
be,' Huston Horn wrote in *Sports Illustrated*. 'Volkswagen ads have
won a list of prizes longer than an account executive's expense
account; they are talked about at cocktail parties, read aloud at the
office water cooler, analysed and dissected in college [i.e. university]
term papers . . .' *Sales Management* credits the advertising with
having 'identity and personality . . . like the Bug itself . . . Car and
campaign combine to stir comment and wisecracks out of all
proportion to the size of either.'

'The average American,' *Sales Management* said, 'may be somewhat confused by Comets, Corvairs, Darts, Falcons, Hawks, Larks,
Ramblers, Tempests, Valiants—not to mention such imports as
Austin-Healeys, Fiats, Jaguars, MGs, Mercedes-Benzes, Peugeots,
Renaults, Saabs, Triumphs and Volvos. But chances are he'll know
one little bug by its changeless shape, and even know that its engine
is rearward and air-cooled.'

Everyone in the USA, in short, seems to know Volkswagen's
advertisements—and to have a favourite one. There's the 'Think
Small' ad and the 'Lemon' headline, the 'Why Won't Your Wife Let
You Buy this Car?' ad for the Microbus stationwagon, the 'Ugly Is
Only Skin-deep' confession, and the ad which showed no car at all,
but which headlined beneath a blank space, 'We Don't Have Anything to Show You in Our New Models'. The list has become a long
one today and there are Americans who read Volkswagen ads in a
magazine before they get down to reading the editorial content itself.
Such people seem to have unbounded confidence in the high quality
of each ad and they expect to get a chuckle out of each one every time
a new ad appears. Suzanne Prefect, a teacher at Rye Centre School
in Rye, New Hampshire, gave expression to general attitudes, writ-

ing to Volkswagen of America, '. . . we all think you're tops in the advertising field. The kids "can't get over your genius" (in their words).'

They are not alone. The average American Volkswagen owner, said a firm of motivational researchers in a report to the company, regards Volkswagen advertisements as 'excellent, witty, sophisticated, delightful, truthful, to the point, informative, unique, cute . . .' The ebullience does not belong to the researchers; the adjectives were culled from interviews with Volkswagen owners.

Genius, Emerson said, is the quality of believing 'in your own thought . . . to believe that what is true for you in your own heart is true for all men.' If VW's advertising has the quality of genius, it derives from the company's decision to be true to itself and true to all men—to be, in short, honest in its advertising.

Will Van de Kamp didn't believe in advertising, preferring to use available funds to improve service. In 1958, however, the company placed a few ads via J. M. Mathes agency but nothing much came of this. The appearance of these ads and the appearance of ever-increasing numbers of Volkswagens on American streets, however, brought on the media representatives—that most persistent gaggle of salesmen ever to infest a corporate anteroom—to offer Volkswagen the pages of hundreds of American newspapers, magazines and trade journals, not to speak of billboards, radio commericals and television 'spots'. These salesmen had a hard time at Volkswagen, for the company's executives, knowing they were already far behind existing orders for their cars, often responded with, 'Who needs advertising?'

The atmosphere changed when Carl Hahn came to the United States, for he suspected that Volkswagen might indeed need advertising, not perhaps to spur the sales, but as a hedge against the future, for Detroit in 1959 had compact cars up their designers' sleeves. Further, distributors were now pressuring their company to advertise nationally and to backstop their own efforts. And so Carl Hahn and a few others began looking into the advertising agencies along Madison Avenue shortly after Hahn arrived in New York.

'This was my first exposure to American advertising executives,' Hahn says, 'and, frankly, I was terribly disappointed. We expected great things, but all we saw were presentations which showed Volkswagen ads which looked exactly like every other ad—an airline ad, cigarette ad, a toothpaste ad. The only difference was that, where the tube of toothpaste had been, they had placed a Volkswagen.'

It was hardly surprising, for much of American advertising had by the late 1950's become so banal and its promises so suspect that hardly anyone in the business seemed to have a good idea left. Pink-shirted copywriters who sipped cocktails were writing beer advertisements which were supposed to appeal to undershirted dockers who like their beer straight from the tin or bottle; agency art directors vied with each other, not to make their ads more effective, but to win prizes for their portfolios in New York Art Directors Club contests; and the management staffs of advertising agencies whipped the so-called creative group on, urging them 'to get down on all fours and look at the problem from the client's point of view'. As for the poor suffering public, they were referred to as 'The Great Unwashed' and regarded as a herd of nincompoops motivated not by quality, but by saturation advertising. In 1959, nothing much had changed from the situation Samuel Johnson described exactly two hundred years earlier in the *Idler*. 'Advertisements,' Dr. Johnson wrote, 'are now so numerous that they are very negligently perused, and it is there-fore become necessary to gain attention by magnificence of promise and by eloquence sometimes sublime and sometimes pathetick.'

'Pathetick' was the word all right for most US motor-car advertis-ing, and while responsible neither for that nor for its 'sublime' counterpart, I watched it being produced while serving a term at one of the medium-sized New York agencies Carl Hahn visited in early 1959. As secretary of this agency's 'plans board' (a group whose membership seemed to expand in proportion to the importance of the prospective client being confronted), I attended one of the presentations through which Hahn suffered four years before I ever thought of writing a book about the Volkswagen. With Hahn on that occasion as on most others were Manuel Hinke, a young German named Helmut Schmitz, and Arthur Stanton, if memory serves correctly. These four men, together with the company's advertising and public relations manager of the period, Scott Stewart, underwent the brunt of the agency assaults. In the smooth but ineffective attack I was privy to, there was an element of pathos. How could our Plans Board know what Carl Hahn was up to? Honesty in advertising? Our men expected, perhaps understandably, that VW wanted the same kind of malarky handed out that every other car manufacturer seemed to want, the same slippery use of meaningless but allegedly persuasive advertising terms, the same aura of glamour and sex. As one agency art director put it at the time, 'Car ads are all full of mansions, horses, surf, mountains, sunsets, chiseled chins, chic women, and caviar—anything but facts.'

It was not this agency which won the Volkswagen advertising account, nor for that matter was it any of those which put on elaborate presentations. In 1959, the account was split two ways, that for the beetles going to Doyle Dane Bernbach, and that for the Transporters going to Fuller & Smith & Ross.

Edward G. Russell, DDB vice-president and account supervisor for Volkswagen, tells the story of how Doyle Dane Bernbach was assigned the account. It began with the famed American fashion photographer Richard Avedon, who knew Russell's wife, a model. Avedon had just spent a weekend with his friend Arthur Stanton, who was a member of the VW distributor advertising committee, the very group which was urging VWoA to advertise nationally. Stanton had apparently asked Avedon who did the unusual ads for Ohrbach's, a New York City department store, and Avedon explained that Ohrbach's was the account which had put Doyle Dane Bernbach into business as an agency. One or two other agency names were mentioned by Avedon and Stanton began looking into them. He then hired DDB to do some ads for the distributorship he was just then starting. While they were working for Stanton's operation (then called Queensborough Motors, not World-Wide), they also made their presentation to the VWoA group. 'We didn't prepare anything special for them,' Bill Bernbach says. 'We just show prospects ads we've done for other clients. The only thing we try to "sell" them on is that we are advertising men and know our business. We told VW: "You know your business better than we'll ever know it. But *we* know advertising better than you do." '

'When that meeting was over,' Russell remembers, 'we had the feeling that Hahn thought of us as his kind of agency.' Then, however, trouble began, for the advertising trade press, a regular rumour factory, bruited about that 'Stanton's agency' had the VWoA account 'sewn up'.

'The other distributors didn't like that one bit,' Russell remembers. 'It looked as if Stanton were running the whole show. So Hahn and the others at VWoA continued to interview agencies and these, hearing we were "ahead", began knocking us. "Great artwork they produce at DDB," they'd say, "but they're weak on copy." '

Then Helmut Schmitz visited Russell, to check on DDB's ability to do sales promotional work as well. Schmitz had been assistant to the creative director in the Wolfsburg VW advertising department for a few years and, then in his mid-twenties, was sent to New York to be assistant advertising manager there. Quick, brilliant, and

creative on his own, he was just the type of client executive to annoy
an agency. 'When he walked in, I just happened to have a lot of ads
which were heavy on copy, as well as a lot of our sales promotional
stuff lying around,' says Russell. 'It was an eleventh-hour meeting.'

At about this time, a minor argument with major repercussions
arose around an ad which Doyle Dane Bernbach did for Arthur
Stanton's distributorship. It was intended for a full page of the New
York *Times* and featured the opening of Queensborough Motors.
Arthur Stanton approved the ad, but as a matter of courtesy to
VWoA, asked Russell to take it to New Jersey and show it to Schmitz
and Scott Stewart. They also liked the ad, but Schmitz had one
objection concerning the copy.

'The second sentence in the ad said something like "The fender
costs only so and so much to replace",' Russell says, 'and the third
sentence said that service was quick and easy. Schmitz's point was
that VWoA wanted to put the stress on service, rather than on
replacement parts, and that the third sentence should therefore come
ahead of the second.

'I disagreed,' Russell continues, 'because I felt we got the idea
across by mentioning the low price of the fender first and that it was
a logical progression from there to go on and speak about service,
once we had established the fact that parts were inexpensive.'

The matter was not resolved at that meeting, and a few days
later Arthur Stanton telephoned to ask if Russell would have breakfast with him, Hahn, and Manuel Hinke at the Plaza Hotel. 'Bring
that ad along,' Stanton told Russell. 'I want you to show it to them.'

'We had a very nice breakfast and didn't talk about advertising
too much,' Russell recalls, 'and then, when it came time to go over
that ad, we looked around for a place where we could discuss it
privately. We finally went into the Palm Court of the Plaza, which
isn't open for breakfast. It was rather dark in there and all the chairs
were piled up on the tables. We stepped over the ropes and cleared a
space on one of the tables and I was literally just taking the ad out
of its envelope when who comes racing in out of breath but Scott
Stewart and Helmut Schmitz. They'd heard that this was a breakfast
with the ad agency and felt they should be there too.

'Hahn asked them if they'd seen the ad and Schmitz answered that
he had and that he disagreed very strongly with it. That opening
remark started the two of us arguing for forty-five minutes!

'Well, it's very hard to talk about two sentences for three quarters
of an hour,' Russell says, 'and when we were both almost exhausted,

I told the group that I would go back and see what the writer had to say about it. If the writer agreed with the change, then we'd make it. If he didn't, I told them, we wouldn't change a line!

'When I got back to the agency, I went in to Bernbach's office and said, "Well, I either blew it or I got it!" '

The result was not that clear-cut after all. When Volkswagen of America chose two agencies instead of concentrating all their billings at once with DDB, it appeared to some at Doyle Dane Bernbach that Ed Russell had indeed 'blown it' at the Palm Court that morning. Some time later, however, Carl Hahn set the record straight. At a dinner in the VW Guest House in Wolfsburg, Germany, he told the DDB agency contingent:

'You know why I hired you people? When we had that breakfast in the Plaza, I'd already seen about four thousand agency people and I had decided that they were *all* a bunch of phonies. Then, after that breakfast and that argument, I had the feeling I'd finally met an honest man in this business and, if he were honest, he'd give us his best advice.'

The choice of both F&S&R and DDB seemed advisable to Volkswagen at the time. The former had an exceptionally good record in industrial advertising and so it seemed logical to give them the Commercial ads to do; the latter was regarded as highly creative—just the type of agency needed to implant the VW 'image' and to help popularise the beetle. Further, Hahn and the others at VWoA believed then that having two agencies would prompt each to compete with the other for excellence.

That first year, DDB was assigned $800,000 [approx. £285,400] to promote its passengers cars and F&S&R was given half that amount to advertise the Transporters. About a year later, in November 1960, the two-agency experiment had proved cumbersome and F&S&R's involvement ended. Doyle Dane Bernback has handled all aspects of Volkswagen advertising ever since.

'When we were awarded the account,' says William Bernbach, president of DDB, 'the first thing we did was go to the factory in Wolfsburg. A whole team of us went over there. We spent days talking to engineers, production men, executives, workers on the assembly line. We marched side by side with the molten metal that hardened into the engine, and kept going until every part was finally in its place. We watched finally as a man climbed behind the steering wheel, pumped the first life into the newborn bug and drove it we the line. We were immersed in the making of a Volkswagen and off knew what our theme had to be. We knew what distinguished this car. We knew what we had to tell the American public. . . . We had seen the quality of materials that were used. We had seen the almost incredible precautions taken to avoid mistakes. We had seen the costly system of inspection that turned back cars that would never have been turned down by the consumer. We had seen the impressive efficiency that resulted in such an unbelievably low price for such a quality product. We had seen the pride of craftsmanship in the worker that made him exceed even the high standards set for him. Yes, this was an honest car. We had found our selling proposition.'

Perhaps the first American to write of the Volkswagen as 'an honest car' is Arthur R. Railton. Writing in 1956, when he was Motoring Editor of *Popular Mechanics* magazine, he analysed the success of the VW in the USA. 'Never in the sales history of the motor-car,' he wrote in the magazine's 1957 *Cars Fact Book*, 'has so much been accomplished by what, at first glance, seems to be so little.' For four years, he said, he had been trying to find out what there is about this car that makes it sell. His answer: 'The Volkswagen sells because it is, more than anything else, an honest car. It doesn't pretend to be something it is not. Being an honest piece of machinery, it is one the owner can be proud of. Wherever he looks, he sees honest design and workmanship. There are no places where parts don't fit, where paint is thin, where trim is shoddy. There are no body rattles, no water leaks. Neither, of course, is there overstuffed, false luxury either. There is nothing about the car that is not sincere. One just can't imagine, for instance, a Volkswagen with a fake airo scoop or tailfins to make it look like an airplane in flight.' (Railton became so enthusiastic about VWs that he joined VWoA in 1960 as public relations manager, replacing Stewart, who opened a VW dealership in Erie, Pennsylvania. In 1965 Railton was named vice-president in charge of public relations.)

The 'honest car' not only had to have a selling proposition, but advertising guidelines as well. These were provided to the Doyle Dane Bernbach group early in the effort. They are today recognisable elements in all those VW ads which fascinate, amuse, bemuse, and incidentally motivate American readers.

DDB's copywriters and art directors found that Volkswagen executives like Hahn and Schmitz were actually serious about insisting on 'honest advertising'. But just what *was* honest advertising—and did VW's insistence upon it mean that most ads placed by others were *dis*honest?

A 'Floatswagen' enters the Swan River at Perth, Australia, as part of a Volkswagen promotion stunt, demonstrating the beetle's 'seaworthiness'. The 'amphibious' VW ploughed its way up river, equipped with only slight modifications: a snorkel tube and a propeller connected to the engine. The front wheels acted as rudders

Top: A 'model town' has evolved across the canal from Wolfsburg's VW factory. *Middle:* Castle Wolfsburg, today an art centre, contrasts sharply with the modern lines of new Wolfsburg. *Bottom left:* Separated by parklands, the town's several communities offer abundant recreational facilities. All homes receive heat and light from the factory power plant. *Bottom right:* Porschestrasse, main street of the city centre, bustles with high-quality shops and, of course, with worker-owned VWs

Workers on the continuous conveyor assembly line at Wolfsburg. A car rolls off the line every eight seconds.

Volkswagens go through the completely automated 'carousel' on the Wolfsburg production line. Huge sheets of metal go into the presses, and come out as motor-car body shells.

Britain's Ramsgate Distribution Centre storage warehouse covers three acres, and is the heart of the Volkswagen Motors Ltd. parts operation. A computer is used to speed up the supply of parts to customers.

The 1971 Super
Beetle.

The VW 1600
Fastback.

The VW 411, the
largest car in the
VW range, seen
here in the Variant
(Estate Car)
version. There is
also a VW 1600
Variant.

The (Type II) VW
Commercial or
'Transporter',
fitted out as the
VW Microbus, is
also available as a
van, truck or
Camper. (In the
U.S.A. the Microbus
is referred to as the
VW Stationwagon.)

'Everybody wants to be honest in their advertisements,' says Helmut Schmitz, 'and a lot of advertisers ask for honesty. But they never seem to take the plunge into a *real* honesty! Honesty isn't just a matter of giving people honest technical data—a lot of advertisers do that—but also of facing up to what people regard as your short-comings. One of our ads said our stationwagon [the Microbus] had "a face only a mother could love". Well, that's the way people felt about this vehicle, so why not face it?'

Carl Hahn also wanted no drawings or paintings of the cars, to make them look glamorous. 'We started using only photographs in all our ads and brochures,' Hahn says, 'because we believe the car itself looks beautiful.' He laughs as he uses that adjective, but does so defiantly. 'The beetle,' he says, 'is simply an acquired taste. Nobody likes oysters when he first tries them.' The ads, however, do not call the beetle 'beautiful', no matter what VW executives feel about it. 'Ugly is only skin-deep', a recent advertisement said, urging another look at the beetle's line.

As another example of VW 'honesty in advertising', there is the ad which showed three beetles, each with a different miles-per-gallon figure headlined beneath it. 'We simply admitted that there were people who only got twenty-four miles per gallon, that there were others who got thirty-two, and there were even some who got fifty,' says a company adman. By contrast, a popular Detroit 'compact' at the time advertised that it achieved thirty miles per gallon, although anyone who had ever driven it knew that this was the case only sometimes, and seldom.

The element of humour was also insisted upon. 'We wanted to be not only humorous, however, but also *human*,' Schmitz remembers. 'We felt that people would take us more seriously if we didn't take ourselves so seriously. We wanted to involve the reader in our ads, not lecture to him. We didn't mind having him argue back, just so long as he was involved. Then, in the last line, we'd try to give the ad a little lift, to make it very relaxing.' Says Bob Levenson, DDB writer on the account: 'The key to these ads is this person-to-person approach, one person talking to another person.'

One other initial rule which VWoA established was not to 'knock the competition'. 'Detroit,' says Carl Hahn, 'is part of America and we are here as guests. What could offend Detroit could easily offend other Americans.' Bob Levenson and Helmut Krone (DDB art director on the VW account) recall two proposed advertisements which never found their way into print because of this consideration.

Both dealt with Detroit's introduction of vans which aped the Volkswagen Transporter. One showed a Ford on one half of a double-page spread, with a Chevrolet on the other half. The headline: 'VW introduces two new models'. The other ad showed a picture of a group of white-coated Detroit engineers in a board room discussing a picture of a VW Commercial vehicle. The copy underneath: 'First thing we do is get this damned VW off it!' Even milder ads which involve Detroit cars have been killed for the same reason. 'One which we kicked aside,' says Helmut Krone, 'showed three compact cars—a Ford, a Chevy, and a VW—coming down the road together. The headline read, "There's room for all of us." We didn't do this ad because VW didn't want to be caught coming into the United States and then telling people who lived here that there was room for all of us.' Although comparisons have since been made with US cars, VW continues not to attack by name, as several other foreign car companies have done.

The 'biggest taboo' on the account, says Krone, 'is against lying and exaggeration'. Also, Volkswagen ads concentrate on one point per advertisement and do not attempt to cover the whole car. 'We want the ads to say something meaningful,' VW's admen insist. 'We don't want words like "The Quick One" or "The Car With Youthful Vigour" and fortunately DDB never even considered offering that sort of thing. These are meaningless words and no one reads them.'

In 1961–62, Volkswagen ran an ad which showed no picture at all. The space usually allocated for a photograph of the VW was left blank. Underneath was written: 'We don't have anything to show you in our new models'—making the point, of course, that the beetle's design remained the same. Stuart Perkins cleared the ad in his capacity as sales manager at the time, but Wolsburg was upset when they saw it in print. 'How can you buy all this expensive space and not show anything?' they asked. The ad, however, provides an interesting example of how such advertisements do indeed 'show readers something'. Dealers reported that this ad brought in more inquiries from potential customers than any other that had been run before. 'Show us those cars you wouldn't show in your ads,' they'd ask the dealers. Wolfsburg changed its mind.

The ads are not 'a matter of taste' in that some like VW advertising while others don't; they are a matter of taste in that they are tastefully executed, offering even the most technical data in a way which attracts readers, treats them as intelligent adults, and speaks frankly with them. Such advertisements motivate people, for they reflect the good taste which has been built into the car itself. Columnist William D. Tyler had this to say about Volkswagen's advertisements in a mid-1965 issue of *Advertising Age*:

'VW advertising is so much in a class by itself that it has almost removed itself from consideration by people in advertising.' Discussing the 'ten top ads,' Tyler says, 'by that I mean that whereas all other advertising is considered in a frame of competitive reference, Volkswagen's is not. It stands alone, and thus beyond critical comparisons. The excuse for excluding it from comparison with domestic car advertising is that our cars haven't the unusual features to talk about, and thus shouldn't be expected to live up to the VW standard.

'But all cars get painted, don't they? Consider what Volkswagen has done with this less than spectacular feature.' He quotes the DDB headline, 'After we paint the car we paint the paint'. 'You know what you are in for,' Tyler writes, 'but you keep on reading. . . . When did you last read such vivid writing on such a pedestrian (yet significant) subject? And, did you notice, there was hardly an adjective in the lot?'

Volkswagen of America does not approve every ad which Doyle Dane Bernbach proposes. The selection process is a constant one. The views of a number of department heads are solicited. Service and parts executives, for example, make certain that the ad is technically sound. Those in charge of dealer relations offer their views as well. Doyle Dane Bernbach does, however, have the option of asking for higher reviews if the ads are disapproved anywhere along the line. Occasional ads have reached Stuart Perkins after having been vetoed by VWoA executives involved at earlier stages. 'If you have no convictions about your ads,' says William Bernbach, 'then your ads can have no convictions either.'

'Cleverness for the sake of cleverness is the worst thing in the agency business,' Bill Bernbach says. 'When an agency gets preoccupied with the techniques of advertising, these get in the way of the message. It's not just words and pictures that talk to a reader. There's a feel and tone to a page. And these too were used in the VW ads to convey honesty. The layouts are utterly simple and plain and clean, the type classic and unadorned, the copy style factual and straightforward: subject, verb, object. Psychologically and creatively everything was done to make our selling proposition of honesty reach the consumer faster and with the greatest impact. We've had five writers on the account and I defy anyone to tell the difference in

Volkswagen copy over the years. Once the basic concept is evolved, then the right words follow.'

The ads have been called 'original, refreshing and effective'. Yet there is really nothing 'original' about the appearance of a VW advertisement. The company uses one large photograph in the standard position with headline and copy below. What is original and unusual about VW advertisements is that these advertisements actually do say something concrete.

Paul Lee, who had for several years been in VWoA's advertising department, was one of several who helped shape such early policies. He is no longer with Volkswagen of America and others are in charge of working with the agency. Before he left, he delivered himself of some complaints about motor dealer advertising in general and explained what VWoA tried to do about it. 'Most dealer advertising,' he said, 'is sheer drivel . . . the ultimate in bad taste, in dishonesty, and in bad advertising.' Dealers simply are not advertising men, Lee pointed out, and no one tells them what to do. VW early decided they would help their own dealers improve the quality of their local ads.

This effort was not always welcome at first, even in the ranks of the VW organisation in the field. Some VW dealers complained that the ads didn't say 'Buy one today!' To that, the company answered back that every one of these ads said precisely that—without saying it once. Gradually, Lee reported, dealers came to understand that soft-sell advertising like VW's is extremely hard-sell advertising after all. There was no need to offer discounts, free trips to Las Vegas, puff up the claims, put in higher mileage figures, or be dishonest in any way. The re-education process has, by and large, been successful. Today, many of the company's dealers and distributors watch the ads carefully and critically. One distributor advertising manager, for example, objected to an ad which claimed one could get thirty-two miles per gallon in a Volkswagen because a few of his customers had achieved only twenty-nine mpg, although VWoA's filing cabinets are full of case histories of drivers achieving fifty mpg. When others agreed with this ad manager, VWoA modified the line by adding, 'give or take a few miles depending on your driving habits'. Such care helps explain just what honest advertising demands.

'Honest advertising sells like crazy,' a company adman has said. 'Strangely enough, this honest advertising is called "creative" advertising. And the agencies who produce this type of work are called "creative agencies".'

'Properly practised, creativity *must* result in greater sales more economically achieved,' William Bernbach told the 1961 annual meeting of the American Association of Advertising Agencies. 'Properly practised, creativity can make one ad do the work of ten ... [it] can lift your claims out of the swamp of sameness and make them accepted, believed, persuasive, urgent. Is creativity some obscure, esoteric art form? Not on your life. It's the most practical thing a business man can employ ... [But] you've got to have something to be creative about.'

As to the question of what credit for the US advertising campaign should go to Doyle Dane Bernbach and what to Nordhoff and Carl Hahn, the answer is that Volkswagen's executives 'let the ads happen'. They did not interfere. Fortunately for DDB's creative group, such VW executives like Carl Hahn did not have too much experience in advertising when they began their campaign. They had no preconceptions and were simply looking for a different, honest, attention-getting approach. They were well aware of the fact that their budget could never compete with the budgets of Detroit's Big Three. 'We made a rule,' Hahn remembers, 'not to advertise when Detroit introduced its new models. While Detroit shot off its big guns and rockets, we didn't want to come in with our pistol. We decided to fire our pistol when it could be heard.' William Bernbach, whose unusual agency allows writers and art directors to work with no interference whatever from account supervisors or directors, regards Volkswagen as an unusual client. As for Hahn, Bernbach believes 'the company could not have picked a better man at the time'. Hahn was no advertising man, he says, but 'had an intuitive sense of what we were trying to do when we got started'.

Today, Volkswagen's ads in Germany have the same look they have in the United States. The same may be said of VW ads in much of the world, for even where other advertising agencies have been employed (as in the United Kingdom), it seems clear that much of their inspiration has come from the ads which are produced by DDB. After Helmut Schmitz left VWoA, he came to be creative director for Volkswagenwerk's advertising division in Wolfsburg, carrying to Lower Saxony the 'feel' of the ads produced in mid-Manhattan. He has since left Volkswagenwerk altogether, but his contribution to VW's advertising in Europe continues, for he now heads DDB's office in Düsseldorf. It has even affected other European advertisers. Schmitz's Düsseldorf DDB office handles VW in Germany and it was Schmitz who helped introduce colloquial

German into German VW ads, to the horror of many who felt advertisements should speak only the most formal parlour German. The effect has been sensational and VW ads in Germany actually have twice the readership of American ads for the car, because there the ads are so very unusual. In the USA, Starch readership surveys show that VW ads have twice the readership of any other automobile advertisement. 'This doubles the value of our advertising budget,' the company points out.

The danger of becoming 'too cute' worries VWoA as it does Doyle Dane Bernbach. Both feel it is their job to see that each ad makes a very specific point and isn't funny for the sake of humour alone. 'But we do like to be arresting,' a company adman says. 'Take our station-wagons ad, for example. We know perfectly well that no one's going to buy one of these wagons as a surprise for the family and then drive home and be cheered. It takes guts to buy one of our boxes. So we challenge the reader. We ask him frankly if he's man enough to own one. We dare him. We even ask if he's got the right kind of a wife for one of these.' Advertisements for VW station wagons, incidentally, are the only VW ads which consistently appear in colour.

Just how responsible are the ads for Volkswagen's growth in the United States? Many Americans tend to credit them for the company's success. Often those who do so drive what *Sales Management* magazine calls 'gadgeted Gas-Guzzling Dinosaurs' and encounter the merits of the 'bug' only through the pages of *Life* or *The New Yorker*. They tend to believe that the advertising created the car, rather than the other way around. Yet, as Arthur Railton noted in 1956 (before VW began advertising), the car sold 'without advertising, without big deals, without fat trade-in allowances and with only four hundred dealers'. The company does not believe it is the job of advertising to sell cars. 'That's the dealer's job,' its admen say. 'The job of advertising is to be read and to be believed. And there we've succeeded.'

The fact is that VW's advertising programme was launched to boost sales, not to create them. At no point in the company's history can one look at the VW sales curve and say with certainty, 'Here's where advertising stepped in.' The sales have risen steadily, and DDB and those droll ads have done their share. As Carl Hahn put it, 'We couldn't rely on word-of-mouth advertising after a certain period. Our campaign created a mass market for us. And Doyle Dan Bernbach's contribution was most significant. After all, it set the

tone of all VW ads, not just in America, but around the world.' Yet
there seems little doubt that, in addition to ads and salesmen, what
sold the Volkswagen to Americans was, and is, the Volkswagen and
its owners. As Railton wrote in 1956, 'Every VW owner is an enthusiastic salesman.' The product is exceptional. 'It is,' said Railton,
'a car that, despite its small engine and low power, feels alive. It is
nimble. It asks something from the driver. He and the car seem to
share a kinship. Volkswagen owners never baby their cars—they
drive them mercilessly. But the true Volkswagen owner never asks
the car to do something it can't. He shifts gears joyfully because of
respect for the car's limitations. There seems to be some of the feeling here that a cowboy has for his pony.' Mechanics, even those not
trained by VW, often have the same feeling for the car. They find it is
easy to deal with, easy to repair. Their respect for its workmanship
and the enthusiasm of the owners made the car a success even before
advertising began. The company's extraordinarily painstaking service
and parts policy was a vital ingredient as well. The advertising merely
had to reflect and convey the car's own integrity. To do so was a
challenge which probably few advertising agencies could have met.

William Bernbach agrees that it is the quality of the car which is
the key to VW's success in America. He also regards the company's
service facilities as an integral part of the total product, as does
VWoA itself. 'Our agency looks for good products to advertise,' he
told me. 'We've even had clients improve their products before we'd
handle them. Volkswagen was a great product right from the start.
We believe our contribution lies in the fact that we helped people
appreciate its merits. The car would have succeeded in any case, but
we accelerated its success.'

It is a different matter with the 'Microbus' VW station wagons
which, as both DDB and VWoA point out, had no appeal before an
advertising programme was developed for them. 'You couldn't give
that bus away to Americans,' Bernbach told me. 'We found that it
was women who were against it. They wouldn't let their husbands
buy them. So we faced the problem head on. One of our first ads was
headlined: "Why won't your wife let you buy this car?" By bringing
up the objections we had a chance to answer them.' The campaign
has succeeded beyond expectation.

'The key to Volkswagen's success is simple,' said Carl Hahn in
1961. 'An honest product aimed at satisfying a basic consumer need
will always sell. This universal truth . . . is our secret. And of course
it is no more original than it is secret. The VW beetle is a well-

engineered, reliable motor-car. It has engineering features still regarded as advanced by the rest of the motor industry and, we must add, still being copied. Yet its appearance is so unpretentious, so simple that it would be completely out of character for our advertising to be anything but direct and straightforward. By talking about our product in easily understood language, by describing what makes it the good, reliable motor-car it is, we appeal to buyers who have become disenchanted with superlatives and flights of fancy.'

'We just aim at being ourselves,' another VW executive adds. 'By talking plainly, we can't help but be original in our advertising.'

The impact of these ads on advertising generally has been substantial. Several advertisers have learned from VW and DDB that it pays to talk sense. Others simply want the identity, without the honesty. According to 'The Creative Man's Corner' in *Advertising Age*, its author was 'among the first to laud the Volkswagen advertising'. He added: 'We would also like to be among the first to suggest that it has led the advertising world down the wrong path. The great contribution of the Volkswagen advertising was that it called an ugly duckling an ugly duckling, got the basic sales resistance out of the way thereby, and then proceeded to sell the positive side of the picture. But not all products are Volkswagens. And we wonder how many advertisers who tell their agencies they want Volkswagen advertising own and drive a Volkswagen?'

American VW owners, who read VW ads religiously and regularly, seem to appreciate this advertising campaign more and more. There have been objections to the campaign, some experts arguing that it fails to motivate those who do not own Volkswagens to go out and buy one. The fact is, however, that one of the biggest functions of VW ads is to train Volkswagen's best salesmen—its present customers. 'Each ad provides our owners with additional information about their car,' says Stuart Perkins, 'so that they have more arguments to use in talking their car up. Americans who buy VWs like to be reconfirmed in their choice.' Motivational researchers have reported the same: 'The Volkswagen owner,' they said, 'is often put in the position of defending his choice of a foreign car and is looking for ways to do so. . . . [A VW ad] confirms owners in the feeling that they made a wise choice and gives them "narcissistic" enjoyment in that it compliments them on their choice of car.'

Some of the research interviews are interesting examples of American VW owners' reactions to their beetles. A New York tailor, for example, is quoted as saying:

'No doubt about it; I have a car that's working for me, not I for it. Now I spend $2.50 a week for fuel instead of the $7 I used to spend for even less driving. Sure it's less car, but then it's more for the money than what you get when you buy the bigger cars in the first place. And then every week you pay more and more for what? Just to get there. Well, we get there too! Sure, maybe it isn't as comfortable; anyone who says it rides as good as the big cars isn't looking at it right. When I'm old and comfort is important to me, then I'll buy for comfort. Maybe you think it's funny I should like a foreign car so much? Some people say you should buy American. Well, if we bought American only, what would happen to foreign trade?'

A cashier in his thirties claimed that 'owning a VW is like being in love. It's a member of the family. You don't hurt it or misuse it, yet you don't baby it either. We're fussier with this one than with any other car we've ever had.'

'At first I thought it looked like an anteater,' said the manager of a shoe store. 'But now that I own it, it begins to grow on me. Now I think it's an adorable car and it keeps on growing on me even more. Also, the looks are constant and I don't have to concern myself with being out of style.'

The interviewers asked Volkswagen owners what they thought a comparably priced US small car might look like. One owner, from Miami, answered: 'I'd expect it to be more stylish than the VW, with more cheesecake on it, and it would probably end up costing a lot more. They always say it'll cost less but by the time they get through with it, it's way out—three or four hundred dollars more than you expect to pay. They can't kid me.'

These attitudes have taught VWoA that the 'honesty' of the advertising must be carried over into its dealerships as well. Volkswagen salesmen could not afford to contradict by their words or behaviour the very ads which bring them prospects. VWoA sales training executives point out that the social prestige of an American motor-car salesman is in general very low in his community. 'We want ours to stand out,' one of them said. 'We don't look for the storytelling, back-slapping kind of salesman. We want one who is heavy on product knowledge and is sensitive towards his customers, so that he knows what the customer's needs are and can think in terms of those needs. Our men are taught to listen, not just talk!'

Listening is in some way the key to the selling effort, whether it is in the ads or in the showroom. The remoteness of the salesman and the ad agency writer or artist from those they are trying to reach is less a problem at VW than elsewhere. Volkswagen does not think of its customers as 'targets', or for that matter, as infantile. This is apparent in every American VW advertisement, each of which compliments the intelligence of the customer. It is apparent also in such minor details of VW showroom decoration as the general absence of cellophane tape, for VW has a rule that whatever is put up must be in a frame, not merely taped on the walls. This also is a matter of taste and as everyone who reads advertisements knows, VW has it. It is also a matter of intelligence. 'What I like about Doyle Dane Bernbach,' Carl Hahn has said, 'is that their copywriters and art directors look at the product when they are trying to think up an ad. They don't just sit and look out their window at the Empire State Building!' Nor, it might be added, at any 'Great Unwashed' out there.

14

Volkslore

ONE November day a few years ago, a raging flood swept Mrs. Mabel Stevenson's Volkswagen down Palmer Canyon, five miles outside Pomona, California. When the torrential rains had stopped, Mrs. Stevenson went to find her car. A wall of water five feet high had tumbled it down a stream bed for a quarter of a mile and it now lay in a graveyard of debris. 'Both doors opened at once,' she recalled later, 'and the interior was bone-dry and undamaged. All the windows were in perfect condition. I'm sure I could have ridden down the canyon in it and been perfectly all right. Neighbours who saw it on its journey told me it rode the waters like a little ship.'

The story of Mrs. Stevenson is part of what might be called the global 'Volkslore' of the car. In providing an amazing store of legendary exploits, the little VW is a sort of Paul Bunyan of Lilliput. Some of these exploits in Australia and South Africa have already been told; the US variety is similar, but carries a distinctly American flavour.

The fact that the VW floated down river comes, however, as no surprise to those who know the reasons for the car's seaworthiness: a flat, one-piece steel sheet completely seals and encloses the car's bottom and, as any owner knows, the car is so airtight that one is best advised to roll down a window before trying to shut the door. To prove the truth of an article's title ('The Beetle Does Float'), *Sports Illustrated* lowered a VW gingerly on to the water of Homosassa Springs, Florida, by crane; it remained on the surface for 29 minutes and 12 seconds.

'It's bad enough that some people think the VW should float,' says *Small World*, VWoA's customer magazine, which reaches 500,000 US owners each quarter. 'Worse still, others feel the engine should fly.' There are at least nine airplanes aloft which are powered by VW engines. None of these aircraft is produced by

Volkswagenwerk or under licence by the company. Indeed, the company takes an officially stern attitude toward them, although *Small World* could not resist commenting: 'Certainly the VW is aircooled and relatively light [and] would seem well-suited to use in a plane [but] we don't recommend the practice.' *Safer Motoring*, the independent British magazine for VW owners, showed photographs of one such plane, the Turbulent, at the White Waltham RAF station; in the cockpit, instructed by an RAF squadron leader, was Prince Philip, Duke of Edinburgh. He flew the plane for thirty-five minutes and apparently liked the experience. The Turbulent, according to the editors of *Safer Motoring*, 'is not generally known as a VW-powered job' but is 'undoubtedly the most economical plane in the world today.' It cruises at 80 to 85 miles per hour, gets 40 to 45 miles per gallon, and costs about £930. Other VW-powered airplanes include the Bébé Jodel, the Fournier RF-01, the Poussin, the Microplane, and the Pinocchio, all of them French, as well as the Tefft Molecule, Belgium's Tipsy Nipper, Yugoslavia's pursuit-like single seater, the CA-51, and another single seater designed by an American, Don Stuart of Michigan. Volkswagen industrial engines, adaptations of the automotive engine sold by the Volkswagenwerk, have also been used to operate an Alpine ski lift, a boat called the Davie Hydroglider, a hydrovane compressor, and a host of other machinery.

Such adaptations will come as no surprise to Volkswagen buffs who are readers of the many magazines issued for their entertainment. Several of these magazines are unconnected with the company and its importers, who publish a number of their own, such as *Small World* in the United States, *O Bom Senso* in Brazil, *De VW* in Holland, and others in Australia, South Africa, and elsewhere. In addition to Britain's *Safer Motoring*, other independent publications largely or entirely devoted to the VW but unsponsored by the VW company include *VW Autoist, Foreign Car Guide* and *Popular Imported Cars* in the US and *Gute Fahrt* in Germany. The editorial pages of such magazines are filled with uses to which VWs and their engines have been put, as well as with accomplishments newly recorded for the car.

Competing in VWs is one such use. While Heinz Nordhoff in 1962 commented that the Volkswagenwerk had no intention of launching a factory racing team, the fact is that many owners feel differently, and several VW organisations, such as in Australia and South Africa, have encouraged and sponsored VW entry.

The races, trials, and competitions described in Chapter 10 as taking place in Australia and South Africa are undertaken in stock Volkswagens, but the latest and most exciting 'VW racing' going on does not use these at all. The racers utilised are, instead, one-seaters consisting of a stock VW engine and transmission mounted on a tubular frame and covered with a lightweight fibreglass body. Unlike the VW beetle, these racers have their engines ahead of the rear axle and have replaced the rear torsion-bar suspension system with coil springs and shock absorbers. Their name: Formulae Vee (for Volkswagen) cars or, in German-speaking areas, 'Formel Vau'.

Formula Vee racing is relatively new and had its start at the annual Nassau Speed Week in the Bahamas. Because the Vee racers use ordinary VW parts, their upkeep is low. So is their price. One can buy Formula Vees either complete with new parts for about £800 in Britain or, in do-it-yourself kits which sell for anywhere from £325 to £425. Volkswagen Motors Ltd., London, offer both the Swedish Dolling and the US Beach makes; other European 'kit' manufacturers are springing up fast as interest mounts. A new British make is the C.G.V. and, in addition, there are Belgium's Apal, Austria's Austro Vee, South Africa's Peco and Australia's Elfin, as well as Autodynamics, Zink and Bobsey, three US makes. A European Formulae Vee association was formed in 1965 ('Formel Vau Europa'), when there were already more than four hundred Formula Vee cars racing in and about the Continent, and in 1967, a British association was formed (Formula Vee Association of Great Britain), which staged its first race in Summer 1967 at Silverstone. Formula Vee races on the Continent in 1967 were held at the Grand Prix meetings in Monaco, Spa, and Nurburgring, and the Volkswagenwerk today offers prizes for the European championships. Across the Atlantic, the Grand Prix for Volkswagens at Nassau, Bahamas, is an annual event and drivers who are usually seen at the Grand Prix races in Monaco have taken part (and won). The 1966 winner was Austria's Grand Prix driver Jochen Rindt, driving a Formel Vau racer produced by Austria's VW importer, Porsche Konstruktionen. Average speed of the winner: 82·397 mph. The experience, says one driver, is a bit 'like riding a roller-skate at 70 or 80 mph and, since all cars are the same, it's the best driver who wins'.

'The car often winds up in some stickily sentimental situations,' Huston Horn wrote in *Sports Illustrated*. 'In Florida not long ago, a bride stuck a miniature VW in the confection atop their wedding cake, a Kansas couple sent out birth announcements when their VW was delivered by the dealer, a Long Island man built a house for his, complete with shutters, weathervane, eagle over the door and geraniums in the window boxes, and an Iowa man gave his wife a Mother's Day present of a VW station wagon, which she thereupon filled to capacity with their nine children.' In addition, Horn says, Texas cowboys ride fence in Volkswagens, a Nashville man delivers money in a bulletproof VW, Los Angeles bank robbers have made their getaways in a VW, and Senator Robert F. Kennedy has campaigned through the sunroof of a VW station wagon. A North Hollywood drugstore which uses a beetle for deliveries has 'Medicine Dropper' painted on its door; the same may be said of a Rexall Drug outlet in Reno, which proves that when a VW fad starts, it gets around. At Ohio University and on other American campuses, students have 'crammed' Volkswagens as they once used to jam public telephone boxes (a record of 18 university students have been squeezed into a sunroof sedan and 62 into a sunroof Microbus station wagon). University pranksters in America regularly bury VWs in autumn leaves, not to speak of 'toting' them about, a feat which spread to Australia, as has already been noted.

Not only has the compact size of the car, which allows it to be carried (and rescued from floods), become the subject of good-natured humour, but also the fact that the beetle has not changed its basic design over the years. Sargent Shriver, when he headed the US Peace Corps, compared his organisation to a Volkswagen: 'We continue to improve it all the time inside, but it remains just about the same externally.' The same theme is echoed by comedian Jerry Shane, who claimed he met his local VW dealer at the post office one morning; the dealer asked Shane whether he recognised him. 'Of course I do,' Shane claims he answered. 'You're exactly the same as last year.'

The VW also benefits from that 'reverse snobbery' which prompts the rich and glittering elements of American society to avoid flashy cars like Cadillacs. Merriman Smith reports in *The Good New Days* that it was 'important to keep down with the Joneses' in Washington during the administration of John F. Kennedy. One way to do so, he says, was to drive a Volkswagen. This is an attitude the company has encouraged; a Volkswagen advertisement has even been head-lined: 'What year car do the Joneses drive?' The 'Joneses', in VW's case, include King Badouin and Queen Fabiola of the Belgians, Britain's Princess Margaret and Lord Snowdon, as well as two cousins of the King of Siam who operate the Volkswagen agency in Bangkok. Charles Lindbergh, according to *Esquire*, drives a Volkswagen, and Dr. Benjamin Spock, America's famed baby doctor, arrived at a White House dinner in a rented VW. Society columnist Jane Gregory of the Chicago *Sun-Times* writes that 'the snappiest car we've seen of late was not a Rolls-Royce or a Mercedes-Benz or a Jaguar, but a Volkswagen convertible Mrs. Otis Hubbard drove to lunch the other day in Lake Forest'. She reports that 'the finishing touch of *eclat* is a discreet monogram lettered in gold on the door'. VWs are popular not only in chic Lake Forest, Illinois, but also in American high society's watering-hole, Newport, Rhode Island. The Boston *Globe* noted that 'Rolls-Royces, Mercedes-Benzes and the ubiquitous Volkswagens' were omnipresent at Janet Auchincloss's début there. The Washington *Post* reports much the same at embassy parties. Clearly then, the car is 'in', at least in the United States, and driving one has there become a sign of good taste. 'The latest in status symbols,' says *Road & Track*, may be the installation, summer and winter, of a pair of skis on the top of a VW, an affectation noted on the campus of the University of Colorado. In Beverly Hills, when VW drivers Princess Margaret and Lord Snowdon were being fêted on their visit to the USA, actor Paul Newman and his actress-wife Joanne Woodward emerged afterwards and asked an attendant to bring their beetle. Says Gene Youngblood of the Los Angeles *Herald-Examiner*: 'The stars drove off in the tiny car amid the cheers of the crowd who saw some 15 Rolls-Royces, three Bentleys, and scores of Jaguars and Cadillacs in the jammed parking lot.' In Rochester, New York, Del Ray told readers of the *Times Union* that 'A woman wearing a mink stole and riding in a motor-car driven by a uniformed chauffeur arrived at the Eastman Theatre the other day. That's not very unusual, even in the informal Great Society. But the car the uniformed chauffeur was driving was a Volkswagen—and you've got to admit that's different!' The ultimate accolade nowadays, however, comes not from society, but from the royalty of the Big Beat, the Beatles. As one might expect, a Beatle would have to own a beetle and, as was already noted, John Lennon does, although he also stocks a Rolls-Royce and a Ferrari, as well as a chauffeur.

The kind of Americans who drive Volkswagens strike syndicated columnist Sydney J. Harris of the Chicago *Daily News* 'as having what traffic officers call "the right attitude" on the road. . . . They seem sensible people, with decent values, and I would wager a sizable amount that the accident rate is quite low among them.' Harris is right; American insurance rates are often lower for Volkswagen owners than for owners of big cars. As for their being people with 'decent values', Harris may also be right in this, according to the 'Police Blotter' column in the Sudbury, Massachusetts, *Citizen* shows. 'On Saturday night,' it reported, 'a VW sedan struck a stone wall on the Haynes property on Morse Road. The next day a young man returned and rebuilt the wall.' Stephen Baker, writing in *Advertising Age*, believes, however, that the man who 'prefers Volkswagens to Cadillacs' is 'an intellectual snob' who 'prefers to display intellectual instead of material wealth'. Dan Greenburg, writing his 'Snobs' Guide to Status Cars' in the July 1964 *Playboy*, set down ground rules for 'how to own a Volkswagen' and, in doing so, somewhat supports the 'intellectual snob' theory advanced in the advertising trade press.

'. . . If you're not married,' Greenburg tells American VW owners, 'take women who are college graduates to little theatres or terribly smart cocktail parties or to a picnic in the country, but don't do anything with them until you're married and then, when you're married, make a slat bench and have at least three children and name them after characters from *Winnie-the-Pooh*. Take out your contact lenses before making love. Use a lot of Freudian terminology in your speech unless you have been through psychoanalysis. Go through psychoanalysis. Own the complete works of Copeland or Vivaldi. Read the *New Yorker* and check off all the movies in the front of the magazine after you have seen them. Read *Time* but hate it. Spend a lot of time on your modest hi-fi and leave the components exposed. Enjoy Joan Baez. Tell people you voted for Stevenson the first time he ran but not the second. If you are Jewish and somebody should ask you what kind of car you drive, say: "A VW, and I know, but it's a helluva solid little piece of machinery." Go to any Ingmar Bergman movie and correctly identify Max von Sydow and at least three other actors, telling what roles they played in *Wild Strawberries* and *Smiles of a Summer Night*. (If your Volkswagen is a Karmann-Ghia, you should have been able to interpret *The Seventh Seal* on at least three levels.) It is all right to take a Volkswagen to a concert, to an indoor art exhibit, or to a university extension class. It is not all right to take a Volkswagen to a Great Book discussion or to a meeting of the Birch Society . . .'

To be sure, typical VW owners in the USA are unlike *Playboy*'s ideal. As a matter of fact, VW owners on the whole 'defy classification by any conventional criteria', according to R. L. Polk and

Company, statisticians to the US car industry. They seem to have
all kinds of jobs, 'from lawyers to prison guard lieutenants, to bar-
tenders, to advertising executives', Horn writes, and they enjoy the
most diverse sports and hobbies. 'They like to do everything from
skeet shooting to skiing, to gem cutting. They read the *Wall Street
Journal* and *Mad* magazine. [They] range from introverts to phony
gladhanders.'

On the whole, they tend to be more sophisticated than those
who buy Detroit cars and live in urban West and East Coast areas.
Arthur Stanton of World-Wide, Orangeburg, NY, is, as stated, the
largest-volume VW distributor anywhere in the world; the 75,000-
plus VWs he sells annually through his dealers in New York, New
Jersey, and Connecticut, represent a fifth of *all* VWs sold in the fifty
states. Asked whether a large number of American VW customers
are of German extraction, VWoA market analysts reply that the
company sells more cars in Atlanta, Georgia, where there are few
German-Americans, than in Milwaukee, Wisconsin, where there are
many. Pro- or anti-German sentiment seems to have little influence
on VW sales in the United States. To some extent, the economic
level of prospects does. 'The poor shun Volkswagen,' Horn says,
'. . . probably because it costs too little to represent status. Owners
also tend to have two or more cars, to live in the suburbs, to have
college education, to be younger than the average car buyer and to
be slightly more inclined to outdoor sports than to bowling or going
to the movies.'

A survey of Volkswagen buyers, conducted a few years ago by a
firm in Princeton, New Jersey, revealed that 40 per cent of VW buyers
are graduates and 60 per cent attended university. The proportion
of VW families in the professions or in management was 51 per
cent, about twice the ratio of these groups versus semiskilled, unskilled and service groups throughout the USA. More recent surveys
report that less educated, lower-income Americans have got the
bug, a development VWoA has devoutly hoped for and encourages
mightily.

The attitudes American owners entertain about their cars emerged
from another VWoA survey, conducted by *Small World* magazine
among five thousand of its readers to determine both likes and dis-
likes. Complaints were minor and few in number. 'The beep horn
has no authority in freeway driving,' a Californian wrote. Another
correspondent from that state complained of the 's-q-u-e-a-k-y
brakes'. The biggest gripe at the time (12·8 per cent) concerned

ventilation and heating.[1] Less than 10 per cent complained of passenger room, but some pleaded for more storage space—a problem many VW owners have solved imaginatively for themselves. A Navy man in San Francisco urged the company to redesign the engine lid to increase clearance with the rear bumper. *Small World* commented 'Maybe you're right' and referred the suggestion to Volkswagenwerk designers in Wolfsburg, who have done just that since then. Others complained about the lack of a cigarette lighter and about the location of the battery beneath the rear seat.

Most owners were less captious. A Wisconsin woman said, 'This car belongs to me—I don't belong to it!' and another owner wrote: 'It has to take one hell of a motor-car when my mother reminds me to change oil!' A New Hampshire man reported that his current VW was his fourth. Significantly, a large proportion praised the company for its service facilities and seem to agree with Hahn and Perkins that Hermann Bruns has established the 'best motor vehicle service network in the USA'. Those who reported that they were switching to a Detroit car usually gave their growing families as the reason (VWoA hopes to sell such persons its station wagon, which will hold a family of nine). An Illinois owner warned, 'If you ever change the styling of the beetle, I will change to a different type of car.' A Kentucky VW owner advised, 'Let the others load on the gadgets.' Finally, a Columbia, California, man proposed, 'Every VW owner should be forced to drive a loosely sprung, monstrous, four-eyed car over a narrow gravel road once a year. Call it Appreciation Day.'

One untypical American Volkswagen owner in whom the company takes considerable delight is a seventy-eight-year-old justice of the peace in Ocento Falls, Wisconsin, named Albert Gillis. Judge Gillis bought a bright-red 1962 VW sedan after what appears to be three decades of resistance to car salesmen. His first and only other car was a Model A Ford, vintage 1929, which was still in his garage when he bought his beetle. He had kept the Ford 'like a barber keeps his scissors', VWoA reports. 'When a part looked like it was wearing out, he replaced it.' He even jacked the car up every night to save the tyres. When Judge Gillis bought his Volkswagen, VWoA's *Weathervane* picked up the story and passed it on to VWoA's ad agency; '33 years later, he got the bug', Doyle Dane Bernbach later headlined

1. In reply, *Small World* suggested that opening a vent window improves the heat flow, that respondents' heater flaps might need adjustment, and that keeping the car in low gear for short runs provides more heat. 'This means you'll hear air rushing, but it's a cozy, warm sound.' Since then, VW heaters have been improved considerably.

an ad. Judge Gillis, it reported, bought a Volkswagen because he 'heard they hold up'. Otherwise, Gillis was cautious. 'Your inspectors sure do a good job of inspecting,' he allowed. Then he mentioned that he and Mrs. Gillis took a trip of 6750 miles in the VW for their fifty-fourth anniversary. The judge spent only sixty-two dollars (or £22) on petrol and fifty-five cents (four shillings) on oil throughout the trip. Then he murmured, 'I didn't think they were supposed to burn any oil.'

Another VW owner in whom Volkswagen of America, Inc., takes pride is the man who owned the oldest Volkswagen in the United States. In 1959, the company started hunting for him, intending to present him with the 500,000th VW then being imported to the USA. In April 1960 the man was found. He was Harold Kuhn, an Emerson, Nebraska, farmer, who had bought his VW from a US Air Force sergeant named Duane R. Margeson, of Dalbo, Minnesota, who, in turn, had picked it up in Germany. The factory records showed the car had been built on December 30, 1945. Just as the company prepared to celebrate the event, it learned that the farmer had never obtained clear title to the car and that both the veteran and the farmer now claimed the reward. Rather than sour the occasion, VWoA presented each man with a brand-new beetle.

As has been noted, it took some courage for men like the Air Force sergeant to drive a Volkswagen in the USA before the car became popular there. Owners then often banded together for self-protection, to bolster each other's resolve, and for good fellowship besides. They had, after all, something concrete in common. It became logical for a handful of them to establish the Volkswagen Club of America in 1954, 'back in those days when there was something terribly lonely about being the first in your block to own the beetle', as Huston Horn has put it. Members kept their eyes peeled for other Volkswagens and, encountering them, they honked and waved joyously and, perhaps, with relief. Those days have gone. Ten years later, driving in a VW with my wife and children, I tested out the responsiveness of US Volkswagen drivers in 1964. Despite the fact that we honked and waved at well over one hundred VWs, we got just one return salute. It struck me that the other drivers whom I greeted thought I might be somewhat mad. Certainly they did not seem to know the password, or perhaps they considered the gesture antediluvian. In 1954, matters were more fraternal. Alvin Outcalt, a founder of the Club, says, 'Of course a lot of foreign-car owners were waving and tooting in those days, but with us it went deeper

somehow. You didn't just wave; you stopped and crossed over and
shook hands with the guy and asked him how many miles he was
getting and did his heater keep him warm like yours didn't. You felt
a kinship, you know?'

Although it wasn't hard for the Club's founders to enrol members,
it was difficult at first to convince Volkswagen of America of the
Club's merits. 'Anyone coming from the outside world today,' Heinz
Nordhoff had said once, 'either wants to harm us or sponge on our
work.' His cautious spirit then infected VWoA as well. The company
at first forbade the Club to use the name of the car in its title, but the
Club chose to ignore the order, and ultimately VWoA surrendered
completely to the enthusiasts. Today, it supports the Club in sundry
ways and staff members rarely miss its conventions. Upwards of
4000 VW owners currently belong to the Club and many of them
sport Club insignia on their shirts and car bumpers. They even travel
together to Wolfsburg where, they say, 'we stand around in that
factory like pilgrims in a cathedral and think reverent thoughts'.
They also meet frequently at events sponsored by local branches
throughout the United States. Rallies and VW caravans to races and
motor shows bring them together. It is, for example, possible today
for a VW owner to attend the national convention of the Club, a May
Frolic in the New Jersey area, an *Oktoberfest* in Illinois, and a *Herbst
Festtag* in the Philadelphia area. In Britain, South Africa, and Australia, Volkswagen owners have similarly formed VW clubs; the
enthusiasm of some of these seems even greater.

One of the ties that bind is the Club's official publication, the
VW Autoist, put out in Delanco, New Jersey. 'Dedicated to helping
the Volkswagen owner enjoy his car to the fullest,' as its mast-head
proclaims, it furnishes members with regional news, technical information, and such services as the Emergency Listing Service
('Stuck somewhere? Check the list and call the names [of Club
members] nearest to where you've broken down.') The magazine
also sponsors a Club Host Plan, whereby VW travellers can spend
the night en route at the homes of other Volkswagen buffs. A typical
issue of the publication described the meetings of the Philadelphia
club (members had a lively evening discussing cornering, shifting,
and driving for economy), reported that cash on hand for the
National Volkswagen Club of America totalled about £640, offered
details on the national convention in Cleveland, Ohio, and announced that a second pilgrimage to Wolfsburg was planned, the first
having proved a sell-out. Oddly, their enthusiasm seems enduring.

VWoA vice-president Arthur Railton addressed them in 1964 and told them of his interview at VW before he was hired to head public relations. He was told that VW wanted a 'nuts and bolts approach' to its publicity. Railton told the assembled Club members his response: 'I said I wasn't sure I knew where all the bolts were in a VW, but I'd been to a few VW Club conventions and I certainly knew where the nuts were.'

A car that provides legends becomes, inevitably, the subject of many jokes and stories in America, all of which popularise the car even as they *seem* to mock it. One of the earliest and best known Volkswagen jokes—created before its rear engine became familiar to Americans—tells of a stalled American owner peering sadly inside the car's front luggage compartment. 'My engine's missing,' he says to another Volkswagen owner who happens along. 'Are you in luck!' the other one answers. 'They gave me a spare in the back.' As Huston Horn says, the car 'is the butt of some of the sorriest jokes since they told your grandfather he auto get a horse'. Typical of the kind of humour Horn says 'convulses Volkswagen owners' is the story of the drunk who was knocked down by a Saint Bernard dog, then was hit by a VW as he struggled to his feet. 'The dog didn't hurt so much,' the drunk told bystanders, 'but that tin can tied to his tail mighty near killed me.'

Texans, he reports, claim local VW ads say, 'Take home a six-pack today', and a newspaper dispatch from that state claims an eagle attacked a Volkswagen, smashed the windshield and clawed two rabbit-hunters inside, apparently under the impression the bug was edible. The story is told of the Texas millionaire who bought himself a big air-conditioned Cadillac—and took his change in Volkswagens. Yet another has a Texas oilman showing his beetle to two friends, who sneer that it isn't air-conditioned. 'No,' he admits, 'but I always keep a couple of cold ones in the refrigerator.' Columnist Dick Hitt of the Dallas *Times-Herald* tells of a local VW owner whose beetle *is* air-conditioned and 'who gets 40 miles to the ice cube'. Finally, the Phoenix, Arizona, *Weekly Gazette* talks of the Texan who bought a VW to drive from his home to his garage. (Air-conditioned beetles are becoming increasingly popular in sections of the USA, as well as, of course, in South Africa.)

Americans have called the beetle a 'humpbacked roller skate' and a 'pregnant roller skate', and, more recently, a 'pregnant skateboard'. Columnist Jack Guinn of the Denver *Post* recently amused his readers by asking them to suggest words defining a group of

Volkswagens. A 'vainglory of Volkswagens' was submitted, along with a scurry, an insolence, a peasantry, a churl, and a batch of beetles. A reader named Burton Beebe told Guinn he liked the sound of 'a chuffle of Volkswagens', and wrote that a subspecies known as 'the double-throated chortler' gets excited in the presence of 'the high-crested overbore'.

Volkswagen owners occasionally still festoon their bugs with special signs such as 'Half Car, Will Travel', 'Student Porsche Driver', and 'Transistorised Rolls-Royce', and at least one VW sports a licence plate which spells out MYBUG. In Los Angeles, according to Bennett Cerf, there is even a parking lot with a special section for Volkswagens, bearing a sign which reads 'The Nursery'. And the Indianapolis *Times*'s Irving Leibowitz writes in his column that he saw a car parked in town with a sign reading 'Conservatism is Americanism'. The vehicle, of course, was 'a true-blue Volkswagen'.

Much of this humour is whimsy. Thus, *Time* magazine, referring to Pasadena, California, said that 'for 364 days a year [it is] a gentle cultivated city populated by little old ladies who sit behind lace curtains and, according to legend, knit Volkswagens'.

Some of the humour purports to be based on fact. Henry Mullen of Cleveland, Ohio, reported in *Gasoline Retailer*, a trade magazine, that an elderly gentleman drove a Cadillac into his petrol station, followed by a Volkswagen. 'Jumping out and dashing back to the Volks,' Mullen writes, 'he began hurling invectives at the small car for "tailing him". Then he abruptly fell silent. Surmising that something was amiss, the attendant rushed to the scene—only to find that there was no driver in the Volks. At that moment, the police pulled alongside the Caddy in search of the Volks, whose owner had reported it stolen. . . .' What had happened, says Mullen, was that 'the Caddy had backed into the Volks, locked bumpers and had been towing it around'. Columnist Herb Caen of the San Francisco *Chronicle* says he saw a municipal bus and a Volkswagen come 'nose-to-nose at an intersection and the VW refused to blink'. Caen writes that the bus driver reached under his seat, produced a can of insect powder, opened the door and sprinkled some on the VW's bonnet. The expression on the VW's driver as he backed off, the columnist claims, was memorable.

Jerome Beatty, writing in *The Saturday Review*, commented that next to a couple of Volkswaven owners trading motor stories, 'the funniest conversation to listen to is two people talking about their electric blankets' (or, as a subsequent issue of the magazine had it, about their contact lenses). VW owners like to trade statistics such as the one supplied by the Waterloo, Iowa, *Courier*, which reports that the fuel used to power a Boeing 707 for one hour would drive a beetle two and a half times around the world. They enjoy stories about how easily the car handles, such as one which appeared in the Portland *Oregonian*, telling of a VW whose battery went dead in the wilds of the American Northwest. The owner 'was in a place where he couldn't coast or be pushed', writes columnist Francis Murphy. Appealing to a neighbouring camper for help, he was told to jack up the car and turn on the ignition. 'Then the neighbour spun the rear wheel by hand and the car started up with the greatest of ease.'

Volkswagen of America does more than smile at all such stories; it collects them in the archives of its public relations department and periodically circulates them to newspapers in mimeographed form. VWoA's *Small World* magazine is probably the only customer publication issued by a major car manufacturer anywhere in the world which lists customer complaints; it is hard to imagine one of Detroit's Big Three circulating gripes to 500,000 owners. The Volkswagen company, however, recognises that its honesty is appreciated. It also knows that the VW is not just a mode of transportation (which was, ironically, the only purpose for which Porsche designed it); it knows that the car amuses and delights, as well as transports, its owners.

Volkswagen humour (like decals which read 'Made in the Black Forest by Gnomes') appeals perhaps only to the less sophisticated of the usually sophisticated Volkswagen owners and was more prevalent in America in the 1950's than it is now. The bumper-strips have also changed with the times. Bill Fiset of the Oakland, California, *Tribune* says he saw one VW recently which bore two bumber strips: 'Support Planned Parenthood' and 'Make Love, Not War'. More complex is the clowning around of a Broadwater, Nebraska, TV repairman named Bud Hathaway, who installed an electronic system in his VW bonnet which allows him to trigger engine and accessory controls from a portable transmitter. Hathaway parks his VW in a crowded place, crosses the street, and watches passers-by stop in amazement as the car's engine starts, wipers move, headlights and tail-lights blink on and off, and turn signals flash, apparently of their own free will. After the inevitable crowd gathers, he broadcasts his voice through the car's bonnet.

Not only TV repairmen but also most other Americans with an engineering bent seem fascinated with the car. This fact has resulted in the space age adoption of a good deal of VW references. When astronauts James McDivitt and Edward White spent four days in orbit, the Associated Press quoted Norman Shyken, McDonnell Aircraft Corporation Gemini spacecraft crew engineer, as explaining: 'Ed and Jim's living space has about as much room as the front of a Volkswagen.' Another Cape Kennedy report, originating with Larry Van Gelder of the New York *World-Telegram and Sun*, said: 'The first stage of the Titan engine generates 430,000 pounds of thrust at maximum, or the equivalent of the thrust that could be generated by 219,000 Volkswagens . . .' Astronaut Frank Borman, an Air Force colonel, gets around at home in a four-year-old Volkswagen, reflecting the viewpoint which Ed Ramsey offered in the Trenton, New Jersey, *Trentonian*: 'Volkswagen is the most modern of cars, as any observer would agree. It features a fast-back design, bucket seats, and four-on-the-floor manual transmission. Its basic design was formulated 30 years ago . . .'

Does that design prove adequate for today? Roy Newquist wrote in the Chicago Heights, Illinois, *Star* that other cars 'have lost ground as status symbols'. He says 'the Ford which looks like the Plymouth is only a bit different from the Cadillac which resembles the Lincoln. Only the Volkswagen, which resembles a pregnant beetle, and the Rolls-Royce, which suggests a large bank account, seem to have any individuality whatsoever.'

Is the beetle really as cramped as the front end of a space capsule? One car expert says flatly, 'It offers surprising spaciousness', and claims: 'The front seat legroom is greater than many big cars, as is the headroom.' This editor, Mel Martin, a member of the Society of Automotive Engineers, says: 'There's also space for a surprising amount of luggage. Two good-sized bags go under the bonnet (so does the spare and you don't have to move anything to get at it). Other luggage may be carried in the carpeted, three-foot compartment behind the rear seat.' Martin also refers to the back seat as 'the best riding section of the car (the cradle between the four wheels)'. He concludes his report by calling the car 'one of the world's best motoring buys'.

David Felts of the Decatur, Illinois, *Herald* reports a news story which appeared on the front page of a Chicago newspaper. The news was that a young mother, en route to the hospital, had given birth to a baby in the back seat of a Volkswagen. 'Now who can possibly doubt that there's all the room anyone can need in the back of that popular car?' he asked. The total number of babies born in beetles throughout the world may never be known, but VWoA has handed out more than forty-five 'awards' for such performance since 1964. The company, which apparently regards itself as a sort of godfather, presents each family with a US Government savings bond and a letter of congratulations (for 'helping to prove there's always room for one more in a VW'). Parents have responded just as graciously. One mother wrote VWoA, 'I never knew having a baby could prove so exciting.' Volkswagen in America, in turn, announced its offer of Bonds for Babies Born in Beetles in *Small World* magazine, saying, 'Act now! This offer may be withdrawn at any time.'

While the beetle may have room for obstetrics, it is nevertheless no car for the five or six adults who can comfortably get into a full-sized American motor-car or into the newer VW Fastback, Square-back (Variant) or Microbus models. The beetle was designed for four and it was, furthermore, not designed for grouches. Driving a beetle is somewhat like driving a VW 'bus' or station wagon. As one US owner says: 'You just have to be young—at heart anyway—to drive a bus.' It seems encouraging that so many Americans still fit that description.

Craftsmanship and the New Cars

Growth throughout the world for Volkswagen has inevitably meant changes back home as well. New Volkswagen models have been introduced (just as years ago, VW introduced its 'bus' and truck, together with its Karmann-Ghias, to supplement the beetle); corporate changes have taken place; prosperity brought on a contest with those who had saved for KdF-Wagens before 1945, and the little town of Wolfsburg itself has undergone changes of its own. These stories help round out the picture of the car, the corporation, and the city it brought to life.

Wolfsburg, in which the story unfolded, is today a pretty, modern town, and about as dull as most factory towns anywhere, though it is unlike any others in most other respects. Its 85,000 inhabitants live by the factory whistle; they either leave the plant at 2 pm and go to bed early in the evening or they start working then and quit at 10.30. There isn't even any crime to speak of in Wolfsburg and its policemen, motorised in beetles, lead a life as routine as its postmen and other civil servants, all of whom drive Volkswagens as well. The town has no tradition and no history. What social life exists, goes on at home and on week-ends.

Wolfsburg, however, was far duller under the Nazis. As they originally planned the city, it was to be a mere fungus attached to the factory and work at the plant was to provide the only meaning of life for its workers. Peter Koller sketched a city lying in a semi-circle facing the factory, its homes oriented towards a city core consisting of Nazi Party office buildings and assembly halls. Only fragments of this original plan were used in building postwar Wolfsburg, and Peter Koller, who returned after being released from Russian captivity, finally was able to plan a city along human lines. A devout Roman Catholic, Koller also began building churches, which were not included in the Nazi plan. The presence of these churches after the war, and their absence under Hitler, symbolise the changed atmosphere, as do the experiences of Monsignor Antonius Holling.

Pastor Holling of Wolfsburg's St. Christopher Church is today the spiritual head of the town's Roman Catholics (who include Heinz Nordhoff). The day Holling arrived in Wolfsburg, March 1, 1940, was the start of a five-year battle concerning freedom of conscience which he waged with the Gestapo. Ultimately, he outfoxed them and outlived them all.

'You won't last one month here, priest!' the Nazi Ortsgruppen-leiter shouted at Holling when he first arrived, carrying all his worldly possessions in a cardboard Persil Soap box along the road from the Fallersleben railway station. He refused Holling a room in which to sleep and a place in which to say mass. The 'City of the KdF-Wagen', he told him, was a model National Socialist community and the only shrines permitted bore a *Führerbild*, a picture of Adolf Hitler. He notified the Gestapo of Holling's arrival, a fact which Holling says ultimately was reported to Heinrich Himmler himself.

Holling was twenty-seven years old at the time, son of a West-phalian innkeeper. He looks less heroic than stubborn and, one imagines, he survived by eroding, rather than vanquishing, the Nazis. He himself does not know how he managed it, unless he had divine protection. 'But then,' he says with a smile, 'I am a believer, pro-fessionally you might say.' His bishop, Joseph Godehard Machens, had sent him to Wolfsburg from Hildesheim, telling him he would not be able to help him once he got there. 'Watch your step—and be clever!' the bishop had told him. Holling proceeded to do precisely that. Without telling his bishop what he was about, he packed up for Berlin after being rebuffed in Wolfsburg. Brashly, he decided to visit the papal nuncio to Germany, Archbishop Caesar Orsenigo.

His request was equally brash. He told the apostolic delegate that there was an Italian labour battalion in Wolfsburg and that these workers were permitted to attend mass, said by an Italian priest. He had gone to see the priest, to ask him whether he could use his facilities (a dance hall) to say mass for the German Catholics in town. While the priest hesitated, the Fascist commander of the Italian workers had attacked Holling, almost throwing him out of the hall bodily. Holling now wanted the nuncio to have both the priest and his commandant recalled to Italy and replaced by two Italians who might be more charitable. What he was requesting, in effect, was that the nuncio embroil the Roman Catholic Church in the municipal affairs of a Nazi German city, as well as involve itself in the relations between Rome and Berlin. Surprisingly, the nuncio agreed to help.

After leaving Berlin, Pastor Holling visited a shrine, where he stayed for a few days, and from where he wrote a bold letter to the Gestapo in the 'Auto-City'.

'I have been to Berlin, where I visited the highest authorities,' he wrote. 'As a result of these conversations, I shall say mass upon my return.' He ended the letter with a 'Heil Hitler!'—which was meant to confuse the Gestapo even more. He did not tell them, of course, that the authority he visited was in fact the nuncio ('They would have told me to go to hell,' he says) but he let them infer that he had seen governmental or Nazi Party leaders. When he returned to Wolfsburg, he started saying mass in the dance hall. The members of his congregation, all workers at the VW factory, were photographed by the Gestapo.

Soon Holling was reported to the Gestapo for not having a *Führerbild* in his room, a sign of disaffection apparently tantamount to harbouring treasonous sentiments. 'So I got myself a picture of Hitler, put it on the wall, and notified the Gestapo,' Holling says. 'The photograph even showed both Hitler and Mussolini. They were walking down a flight of stairs, heads bowed. It seemed appropriate to me, because I saw clearly that they were both going downhill and I knew instinctively that Mussolini would be first to be punished, as it showed in the photograph.'

The harassment continued throughout the months and years of the war. On one occasion, Robert Ley shouted at Ferdinand Porsche: 'Burn the priest's home down and throw him out!' but Porsche, a devout Catholic, ignored the command and actually helped Holling find himself a permanent room. Shortly thereafter, Holling was saved from further Nazi badgering by a German Army officer, Major Bruehl, who commanded the 2000-man Army punishment battalion working in the factory, and who appointed Holling battalion chaplain. Holling bought himself black breeches and boots, and wore these under his clerical collar, black shirt and jacket. 'I looked like a warlord [*Feldherr*],' Holling chuckles. He recalls that the Gestapo glowered helplessly, not wishing yet to quarrel with the Army in the midst of the war.

In April 1945, the Nazis moved out and the United States Army moved in. Now services could be held with impunity and Holling started building churches for his flock. Many of these are today strikingly modern and controversial, as though architects who endured the culturally stifling atmosphere under the Nazis sought relief after the war in designing an eruption of bizarre architectural shapes. Not only German architects were used, but Finland's famed Alvaar Alto was brought in to design Wolfsburg's Church of the Holy Ghost, while Peter Koller designed Holling's own St. Christopher's Church, and Koller's son built the jagged, crown-shaped Church of St. Henry.

In 1946, while Peter Koller was still in Russia, urban development became the province of Baurat (town planner) Dr. Heinz Reichow, a man of considerable talent and reputation who, however, found himself without funds with which to do anything. Before he quit in 1948, he developed a new plan for the city, along the modest lines befitting those years. Wolfsburg was to lie like a long rectangle on the bank of the Mittelland Canal, opposite the factory. Even these plans were visionary, for the fate of the factory had not yet been decided.

At the end of the war when Dr. Reichow took over, the city consisted of barracks accommodating 10,600; as well as 2358 flats, quarters for 550 in the factory's home for unmarried men, and about 50 half-completed blocks of flats. When Heinz Nordhoff arrived in 1948, he saw the urgent need for more and better housing. 'I called the city authorities to get them to finish those fifty houses, but they said they had no funds,' Nordhoff recalls. 'When I told them the factory would come up with the money, it took them three months even to reply to the offer. They were doctrinaire socialists who hated to take money from a capitalist.' As one citizen remembers it, the town authorities spent those early post-war years wallowing in self-pity and writing lengthy memoranda to higher functionaries, detailing the miseries of the population. Finally, however, they agreed to accept 15 million marks over the next three years. More than one thousand homes were built by 1951. In November 1951 the plant's new bachelor quarters were put up at a cost of three million marks.

On the twenty-fifth anniversary of the founding of the city, July 1, 1963, Heinz Nordhoff reminisced about these events. After the city fathers accepted the company's money, Nordhoff says, 'we threw overboard all the old plans and began to build a modern workers' city, first modestly and later in broader perspective and dimensions.' He said he was 'bitterly criticised' when he suggested the town double the width of Porschestrasse (Wolfsburg's main street). 'But now we have easily the only European town with no traffic problems, no shortage of parking space, open, light, airy, centrally heated by the Volkswagenwerk, without smoke or soot, a town which offers more than many which call themselves a resort. This city of Wolfsburg was planned intelligently, so as to grow not through the mere addition of more streets and blocks of flats, but in almost completely self-sufficient groupings, all closely related to nature, to trees, woods, and meadows.'

When Peter Koller returned from Russia, he did indeed scrap Dr. Reichow's plans calling for a rectangular-shaped city facing the factory. Instead, he started building the suburban community which Wolfsburg is today.

The city is laid out in seven distinct areas, each containing its own bank, post office, shopping centre, market place, and church, and separated from each other by woodland or parks. Two major construction companies in which Volkswagen has a financial interest do most of the building; one of these, VW Wohnungsbau GmbH, is a wholly-owned subsidiary of the factory. They build mainly three- or four-storey blocks of flats, many with balconies, and all supplied with full central heating and electricity from the VW factory's power plant, which produces all power for the entire city. Interspersed with these smaller buildings are a few as tall as nineteen storeys, many prefabricated. Private homes are available also, although no one may own land in Wolfsburg. All land is owned by the city itself.

Peter Koller finally left Wolfsburg on October 1, 1960, to become professor of urban planning at West Berlin's Technical University, but he stayed long enough to see the town evolve the way he had wanted it to for over twenty years. It remains his personal monument and is still growing fast. New areas are being developed on the factory side of the canal, which originally was not planned for housing. My family and I spent several weeks living there and all of us felt as though we were living in a garden community. There is no question but that it is a lovely, sparkling, modern city spotted with ample parkland, pools and recreation facilities, as unlike any 'factory town' as one can imagine.

Eventually, the town will hold 130,000. Eventually, it may even develop a town spirit; its failure to do so for many years troubled its thoughtful citizens, including Heinz Nordhoff. From the start, he has tried to divorce town from factory. The Volkswagenwerk has no factory-run hospital, nursery, or other similar facilities, as the Nazis had planned. Nordhoff believes firmly that the company should be a place in which to work, not a centre of life. Despite his wishes, the factory inevitably dominates the life of the town. Wolfsburg is populated entirely by its workers, executives, their families and those who provide services to them. More than 70 per cent of its citizens are refugees from East Germany or from those portions of Germany which are under Polish administration. Their average age is thirty-three, about ten years younger than the national average. The population of the town increases by about five thousand a year, as new homes are made available in the never-ending Wolfsburg building boom, but these newcomers may also find it difficult to find roots there. The ties they have in common all originate at the factory in which they work.

About half the Volkswagen's employees commute to the factory from towns surrounding Wolfsburg, simply because the city cannot yet accommodate them. Some 75 per cent drive to work, mostly in Volkswagens, and about 33 per cent of the workers own their own cars, the rest riding in car pools. They are prosperous and live the lives of *petit bourgeois*. The factory parking lot is a brightly coloured sea of Volkswagens. All of them belong to the workers who buy them for 950 DM (about £85) off the local list price, irrespective of the model they purchase. Nordhoff showed me more than a dozen empty sheds, east of the lot. 'Those sheds symbolise the changing times,' he said with pleasure. 'When I arrived here, they held the workers' bicycles. Now everybody drives and the sheds are almost completely empty.' Porsche's dream of motorising the factory worker on a bicycle has come true, particularly in Wolfsburg. The town has more cars per capita than any other German city.

Salvatore Salis, a twenty-two-year-old native of Sardinia, arrived in Wolfsburg on January 15, 1962, the first Italian worker to arrive at the Volkswagenwerk since Mussolini sent Hitler three thousand unemployed construction workers. Only three two-storey wooden buildings had been erected for the Italians when he arrived, but new ones were being built at the rate of two a week. Ultimately, forty-six were completed, plus two large community halls. Together with trees, lawns, and gardens, the area in which Salis and his compatriots live today is called the 'Italian Village'. It has its own homes, canteens, administration, post office, hospital, athletic field, chapel, and priest. It is no Italian ghetto, but rather a place in which, the company hopes, these Italian workers can feel at home in the strange, cold and alien North German landscape.

More than four thousand Italian workers have come to Wolfsburg since Salis arrived. They are a symptom of and a palliative for the principal ailment which plagued the Volkswagenwerk for years, a shortage of workers. The company is not unique; West Germany as a whole employs more than one million foreign workers in its prospering industries. While the vast majority have in the past come from Italy, that country's growing prosperity has begun to absorb many of its unemployed. The composition of foreign workers in West Germany is now shifting to include more Spaniards, Greeks and Turks. West Germany today plays host to more than 300,000 Italians, 120,000 Spaniards, 110,000 Greeks and 200,000 Dutch, Austrians, Yugoslavs, and Turks.

The Volkswagenwerk tries hard to make them happy, hoping they will stay on beyond the end of their contracts. It organises a special train to take the Italians home in July, vacation month at the factory, and also at Christmastime. Homesickness, more than anything else, is the Italian disease here. Father Enzo Parenti, chaplain to the Italian workers, says: 'There is no cure for that, neither a full pay-envelope nor medicine from the drugstore.' About three hundred Italians—mostly young men from South Italy who felt miserable in the North—were freed from their work contracts and sent home. Still, as Father Parenti notes, most workers return after vacationing at home. Nordhoff is grateful. 'We are very satisfied,' he told the press recently. 'And I think they are satisfied with us too, because only a few have left us. They are capable, flexible and as good as German workers. We will soon have four thousand of them here.'

The acute need for skilled and semi-skilled workers prompted the company to establish four schools for apprentices in its Wolfsburg, Hanover, Brunswick, and Kassel factories. More than 1600 boys and girls (nearly one out of every eight employees is a woman) between the ages of fifteen and nineteen received training here under government supervision. They receive forty hours of instruction a week in the humanities as well as in one of fifteen specialised trades, and are paid a stipend while attending. At Wolfsburg alone, about 870 youths finish their training each year. Although they are not required to do so, most of them take jobs with Volkswagen.

The company employs a total of 100,000 workers in its four West German plants, 49,000 of them in Wolfsburg. The German steel-workers' union represents about half of them, its members electing a committee which meets with company management. Labour troubles are virtually unknown. Nordhoff, *Der Spiegel* claims, won his workers to his side not by offering to meet every demand for a wage increase, but precisely because he rejected such demands when he first arrived. 'The decision which the workers made at that time, to go along with Nordhoff, marked the turning point,' says the news magazine. 'The workers made up their minds to accept a joint responsibility. The new, hopeful *esprit de corps*, the "VW Spirit", was born then.' For the first years, Heinz Nordhoff did not represent 'capital', stockholders, or the state. 'It is our car, our factory, and our town,' Nordhoff said when he accepted the Sperry Award. 'And everybody is proud about it. This, like Professor Porsche's design, is sound.' It is also the reason the workers felt little class-consciousness.[1]

In 1945, Nordhoff instituted profit-sharing throughout the Volkswagenwerk. This annual bonus has risen from 1954's four per cent to today's eight per cent of annual pay. Workers also receive free accident and life insurance, a VW pension in addition to old-age benefits from the government, emergency loans, emergency medical aid (and also, if necessary, several weeks at VW seaside or mountain rest homes), as well as long-term interest-free loans for construction of homes in Wolfsburg. Workers who are transferred to less strenuous (and lower-paid) jobs because of advanced age are compensated. If they are fifty and have worked fifteen years, they get 75 per cent of the difference between the two wages; if fifty-five, a hundred per cent. 'Class warfare is dead,' *Der Spiegel* quotes Nordhoff as saying, and the magazine itself adds, 'In Wolfsburg, class warfare is as dead as Lenin's mummy.'

Just who owns the company was finally settled, fifteen years after the war ended, on May 9, 1960. The company had been state property under the Nazis and the organisation controlling it, the German Labour Front, had been declared criminal. Allied Military Government requisitioned the factory and placed it under the administration of trustees. In 1949, in accordance with Ordinance No. 202, it relinquished control of the property and empowered the Federal Government of Germany to dispose of it in accordance with Articles 89, 90, and 134 of the Bonn Constitution. The Federal Government took over the trusteeship and then delegated control of the factory to the state (*Land*) of Lower Saxony, in which Wolfsburg is located. For the next several years, Lower Saxony and Bonn argued endlessly over who owned the company. At the same time, a settlement of some sort had to be made with those who had paid for Volkswagens under the Nazis.

---

1. In those days, it was said that in France the government owned Renault; in Italy, Fiat owned the government; and in Germany, nobody knew who owned Volkswagen.

An organisation to press the claims of the 'KdF-Savers' was formed on October 7, 1948, by one Karl Stolz. Registered in Niedermarsberg as the *Hilfsverein ehemaliger Volkswagensparer* (Association of Former VW-Savers), it quickly gathered a few thousand members at dues of 50 pfennigs (about a shilling) a month, and on May 5, 1949, began pressing its case in court. The test case demanded the delivery of a factory-new Volkswagen, upon producing proof that the claimant had actually paid 990 marks into the savings programme of the German Labour Front. Since the West German government had assumed the obligations of the Nazi Reich, the claimants had a point. From that date on, the case bounced around West Germany's courts. In 1950 a Hildesheim court decided that the Volkswagenwerk were indeed the contractual partner of the 'Savers' but could not be held responsible today for the fulfilment of the contract. A year later, another court agreed that the contract was valid, but again refused to charge the company with its fulfilment. In 1954 the Supreme Court (Oberster Bundesgerichtshof) decided that the Nazi Labour Front was the true partner of the Savers, absolved the Volkswagenwerk of all responsibility, and referred the case back to a lower court. Both sides continued to argue. In 1956 and 1958 the company met with the Savers to try to come to an agreement with them, but Stolz rejected the company's offer. Finally, on October 10, 1961, the Supreme Court got them together once more. An agreement was hammered out and approved by both sides, as well as by the court referees. Savers who had completed their payments could receive either 600 DM (approx. £52) credit towards a new Volkswagen or 100 marks (approx. £8 8s.) in cash. By mid-1964, 93,000 Savers had submitted their claims and 87,000 were upheld. About half had decided to purchase cars.

It was, under the circumstances, a generous settlement. Six hundred deutsche marks are worth 6000 Reichsmarks, for the Reichsmark was exchanged at the rate of ten to one in 1948. In actuality, a person who saved the full 990 Reichsmarks should have received only 99 of the new, post-1948 deutsche marks. Nordhoff, however, was anxious to settle the long-drawn-out court battle so that he could concentrate on a final disposition of the company itself.

Now the company was transformed legally from Volkswagenwerk GmbH into a shareholder-owned corporation, Volkswagenwerk Aktiengesellschaft, or Volkswagenwerk AG, which is its status today. Forty per cent of the corporation is today owned by the Federal and *Land* governments, each owning 20 per cent of the shares. The remaining 60 per cent is owned by the general public. A foundation (the Stiftung Volkswagenwerk) was organised to further science and technology through education and research. It received the proceeds from the sale of the small shares and continues to receive all dividends paid out to the Federal and *Land* governments. It also received all profits earned by the Federal government prior to the sale of the shares, but is obliged to lend these sums back to the Federal government at low interest for the next twenty years.

The sale of VW shares to the general public created a great deal of excitement in stock exchange and other financial circles. In 1959 the capital of the company was increased to 300 million marks and in 1960 to 600 million. Then, on June 30, 1960, the upper house of the West German Parliament placed the Volkswagenwerk's shares on the open market. More than 1,500,000 persons applied for the 3,600,000 shares available. The issue was more than 84 per cent oversubscribed and two-thirds of the subscribers received two shares each, while one-third received three shares. VW employees (who totalled 65,000 in spring 1961) shared this enthusiasm; the company has the highest percentage of employee stockholders of any major corporation in the world. Only one thousand eligible VW workers failed to buy shares and these one thousand, Nordhoff among them, failed to qualify because of their high income brackets. Under the terms of the stock sale, only persons in the low and middle income groups were eligible to purchase shares. The law also restricted initial purchases to ten shares and demanded that West Germans and company employees throughout the world hold their shares at least two years before reselling. Each worker bought an average of 4·29 shares. Today, the shares are traded on the open market but the restrictions placed on the initial offering prevented large blocks from falling into the hands of major investors. Only American Telephone and Telegraph Company has more shareholders than Volkswagenwerk AG.

As the 1960's dawned, it became ever more clear to Heinz Nordhoff, his market analysts, sales executives, distributors and dealers that Volkswagen needed more than just the beetle, the bus, and the Ghia if it were to grow into the future. Volkswagenwerk AG is, after all, a motor vehicle manufacturing company and not what everyone had always thought of it as being: a 'beetle-producer' only. Nordhoff's early desire was to make his factory the largest automobile company in Europe; he had accomplished that and needed to look ahead. The great impact made on the German market by US-owned Ford and General Motors made this increasingly important.

In 1961, Heinz Nordhoff hit back at the competition with a new model, the VW 1500 saloon and estate wagon; by 1965, Volkswagenwerk had vastly improved this range of cars, made their engines more powerful, and had also enlarged the beetle's engine to 1300 cc (and, still later, to 1500 cc). The VW-1600-TL 'Fastback' was introduced and, since then, the company has gone on to two entirely new lines, the VW 411 (saloon and estate versions) and the front-engined, water-cooled VW K70, on which production began in Autumn 1970. Electronic fuel injection systems and automatic transmissions have gone far towards bringing the Volkswagen image into the 1970's.

Many crucial changes have taken place within Volkswagenwerk and its organisation throughout the world; they are still taking place. A successful producer of a single model of motor vehicles has been transformed into a multi-line corporation with models in virtually every price class. How this came about is the story of the last years of Heinz Nordhoff, and of the changes instituted by his successor, Dr. Kurt Lotz.

As 1966 dawned, the company whose fortunes had been so intimately tied to the West German economy and had contributed in large part to the 'economic miracle', found itself facing new problems as, the 'miracle' acquired some tarnish. At the beginning of that year, Volkswagenwerk completed wage negotiations, signing its biggest wage contracts yet; these compelled it to raise the prices of its vehicles in April—just as economic thunderclouds were gathering in the distance. The 12,000,000th Volkswagen (there are now more than 15,000,000) was produced that year and rolled off the assembly line as West Germany headed with increasing speed into a recession; as this recession mounted, so did the unsold inventories of VWs in West German dealers' showrooms.

The curtailment of production, which began to seem necessary, was delayed for various reasons: Nordhoff was reluctant to inflict the resulting hardships on his workers; the company was hesitant about jeopardising an increase in its capitalisation; finally, Nordhoff knew a cut in production at VW would make for big headlines and be interpreted as clear evidence that the recession was serious. It might frighten many people and create added difficulties for the West German government, already shaken by the economic distress. Action, therefore, was delayed well past mid-1966, when signs of the coming crisis were already apparent. Despite the unsold inventories, the company continued at record production for months. In August, it introduced the 1500-cc beetle; its Auto-Union subsidiary introduced the Audi 80 squareback ('Variant') and, later, the Audi Super 90.

In early 1967, the company was forced to retrench and, in so doing, was not alone. Ford and Opel, the two US-owned auto giants in Germany, dismissed masses of workers to meet the market slump; Nordhoff characteristically refused to take that step. Instead, he instituted 'short weeks'; no worker was dismissed; each, instead, got half a loaf, but it was better than none.

The recession hit hard during the first half of 1967, and until late May that year, the factory chimneys seemed to spew out more gloom than smoke: thirty production days were lost and sales of VWs dropped below the average auto industry decline.

Heinz Nordhoff hoped for energetic governmental action to spur his key industry; instead, he was dismayed when Bonn made it even more difficult for West Germans to buy cars. Petrol taxes were raised, as were auto insurance rates; worse yet, the government cut in half the tax deduction Germans enjoy if they drive their cars to and from work. Disappointed at the course taken, Nordhoff began to speak out openly in criticism of what he regarded as a shortsighted economic policy. He urged the government to eliminate all vehicle ownership taxes (which cost the average German beetle-owner 188 marks a year, or about £19 10s. at the rate of exchange then prevailing); such a move would make the purchase of automobiles more attractive and give a boost not only to the auto industry but to all who supply it with raw materials and parts, as well as all who depend on it. Hundreds of thousands of workers would have benefited. Meanwhile, in order to maintain VW's position in the domestic (i.e., West German) market, he produced a recession-oriented beetle at the beginning of 1967: a basic version of the 1200-cc VW which sold for about £458. Quickly dubbed the *Sparkäfer* (budget-beetle) —both affectionately and derisively—this car raised sales as knowledgeable, bargainwise Germans hurried to buy it. It did not, however, do much for profits. Yet it served a public relations function; it kept the beetle's virtues alive in the public consciousness, emphasised VW's good value, and helped the company ride out the recession.

The fact that Nordhoff criticised the government's policies provoked a counter-blast from that ebullient Bavarian, Franz-Josef Strauss, who had become Finance Minister in the Great

Coalition government which entered office in late 1966. Strauss icily rejected Nordhoff's call for tax concessions—and then proceeded to attack VW (and by implication, Nordhoff himself) for having produced 'too many cars and too few ideas' as well as 'the wrong models'. He criticised the fact that only 30 per cent of VW's production was sold to Germans and asked, 'What happens when the Americans stop being amused by the beetle?'

Of course he neglected to point out that less than half (32 per cent) of VW's total exports go to the USA; in reality, 70 per cent of VW production is not dependent at all on whether Americans continue to be 'amused' by the bug. Finally, every Volkswagen owner knows something which then seemed to have eluded Strauss: that the beetle's success in the USA is *not* based on its 'entertainment value', Walt Disney's *The Love Bug* notwithstanding.

It seemed less of a coincidence than part of a calculated plan that a small army of minor Bonn officials soon began bursting into print with the same 'Strauss line'. In retrospect, it seems clear that governmental policies had helped accelerate the economic slump in the key auto industry and elsewhere—and that government apologists were understandably happy to find a scapegoat and a public whipping boy: Nordhoff.

That this hurt Heinz Nordhoff deeply is a fact of which his friends and associates were all painfully aware. With considerable justification, Nordhoff saw himself as having to a large extent contributed to the nation's economic miracle. Furthermore, the Volkswagenwerk had been almost unique in West Germany in that it succeeded without ever having asked for or having received any governmental aid. Now that Nordhoff for the first time asked for tax concessions to help his industry (not just VW), he was being slapped down for it. These attacks hit Nordhoff at a time when he was no longer vigorous enough to engage in a slugging match with the redoubtable Strauss: at a time when his health was very much in question. He had been ill since the previous December. Although he continued to work every day, his colleagues noticed a growing irritability and impatience as well as a marked loss of appetite. Even his much-loved wines seemed to have less appeal.

It was at this time that, against his doctor's advice, he went to England at the invitation of the Institute of the Motor Industry, who wished to humour him with their highest award. On April 18, 1967, at Church House, Westminster, London, he was presented the Lord Wakefield Gold Medal for outstanding contributions to the motor industry—the first non-Britisher so honoured. At the ceremony he spoke on 'Management Revolution: A Broader View'. Perhaps as an answer to his government critics, Nordhoff said, 'Management today must spend less of its time looking down into the factory, and more time looking out at the world and ahead into the future.'

In a wide-ranging speech, he foresaw the need for increased industry concern about the pollution of our environment: 'There is a critical need for management to widen its view from the private interest to the public interest. . . . Companies must become more than private enterprises devoted to making profits for the stock-holders. Today's corporation must accept responsibilities beyond this. It makes little sense to return a profit to the stockholder at the same time we take away from him, as a citizen, some of his rights to clean air or clear water.'

At an intimate formal dinner that evening, the top men of the British motor industry heaped praise upon the man who had created the miracle of Wolfsburg. It was an evening that Nordhoff often recalled during his remaining time.

He returned to Wolfsburg renewed and refreshed, invigorated by the recognition showered upon him in London. Mrs. Nordhoff commented to a friend that the British trip was 'the best medicine he had ever taken'.

But the effects were short-lived. He suffered a sharp decline in May 1967.

Plans for the eventual retirement of Heinz Nordhoff had been underway since June 1966, when Dr. Josef Rust, an industrialist and one-time aide to Franz-Josef Strauss (when the latter was Defence Minister), moved from deputy chairman to chairman of Volkswagenwerk's Aufsichtsrat, or board of directors. The press came alive with speculation that Rust's main job was to find a successor to Nordhoff (then sixty-seven years old) and comments abounded about the need for new management at VW.

There was certainly a pressing need for a succession—simply because Nordhoff, already well past the customary retirement age of sixty-five, had spent his energies, was ageing, tired and ill. He himself planned to retire at the beginning of 1969, just short of his seventieth birthday. The search for a successor was, accordingly, pressed. The board of directors and Nordhoff's colleagues on the Vorstand all realised it would take an extraordinarily big man to fill the biggest industrial job in the biggest industrial nation in Western Europe.

Just such a man fortuitously became available: one not only big in size (6 feet 5 inches), but big in accomplishments. This was Professor Dr. Kurt Lotz, then fifty-four and a head of the West German branch of Brown, Boveri & Cie., a vast Swiss-owned engineering firm and the third largest electrical corporation in Germany.

Rust knew Kurt Lotz, as did Dr. Hermann Richter, another member of the VW Aufsichtsrat, for both Rust and Richter were also members of the Brown, Boveri board of directors. Nordhoff also knew him, for he and Lotz were both members of yet another board of directors. As Kurt Lotz recounted it to me, he and Nordhoff got to know each other particularly well during these meetings —simply because their initials (L and N) were so close alphabetically that they were often seated beside each other. Lotz's company had also been among several which wanted to sell the Volkswagenwerk turbines for a power plant opened in 1962; Nordhoff gave the contract to Lotz partly because he was very much impressed that Lotz had been the only top industrialist among the bidders who had made a personal effort to make that sale.

In 1966, just prior to VW's search for a successor, Kurt Lotz had resigned as head of the Swiss parent company of Brown, Boveri. He continued to be head of the German branch of that corporation in Mannheim, and he seemed to many West German firms to be a man who might now respond to an outstanding offer. A good many such offers had already come to Lotz and more were coming now; it was at this juncture that the Volkswagenwerk entered the picture.

Kurt Lotz describes these events in the following words:

'One doesn't exchange letters about such matters. What happened is this: I got a telephone call from Professor Nordhoff, in which he asked me to meet him at the Frankfurter Hof [a hotel in Frankfurt am Main]. When we met, he told me that he needed to find a man who could succeed him as chairman of the Vorstand. He offered me the job.'

Lotz said he'd think it over; when he did, he realised this was the challenge of a lifetime. In mid-April 1967, the announcement was made that as of June 1, Lotz would become deputy chairman of the Volkswagenwerk management board.

As it turned out, Lotz arrived in Wolfsburg not a moment too soon. Nordhoff, as previously noted, had become seriously ill at the end of May and his physicians declined to be responsible for him if he addressed the June 28 shareholders' meeting. That information was communicated to the Aufsichtsrat on June 27; Lotz was advised at 5.30 p.m. that he would have to fill in for Nordhoff literally overnight: he would have to represent the company at the meeting at 10 a.m. the following morning.

Lotz found Nordhoff's prepared speech 'too typically Nordhoff', 'too personal' and, moreover, too peppered with criticisms of the government. In order that he might have his own speech to deliver, Lotz assembled a staff in temporary offices in the basement of the company's Rotehof Guest House in Wolfsburg, and he himself checked into a room in the same building. Work on that speech went on throughout the entire night; Lotz snatched a couple of hours' sleep before being awakened at 4 a.m. to be shown a draft. After going over it, he awakened Dr. Rust at 5.30 to show the draft to him; the re-write then went back to the basement for a final typescript—which was thrust into Lotz's hands as he hurried into his car for the meeting in Wolfsburg's Town Hall. 'I made my last corrections onstage seconds before I spoke,' Lotz remembers.

That weekend, Heinz Nordhoff entered a sanatorium in Zürich, Switzerland; his heart was giving way.

Because Nordhoff would remain in the hospital until late October, Kurt Lotz was again called upon to speak for the company at the Frankfurt Automobile Show in mid-September 1967. There the company introduced quite a line: Volkswagens with automatic transmissions and advanced electronic fuel injection systems; a fundamentally redesigned Type II Transporter (the VW 'station wagon' and/or truck in the USA; elsewhere the 'Microbus'); the new Audi 60; the Audi 72 and Audi 80, both with technical improvements.

Critics did a *volte face*; suddenly, Strauss's blast of four months ago seemed totally irrelevant. Sales of Volkswagens began to pick up sharply during the second half of 1967: first outside West Germany but, shortly thereafter, within the Federal Republic as well. The automobile industry—and its leader, Volkswagenwerk AG—was pulling out of the recession. Recognising this, the company decided to enlarge its capacity, at first cautiously by introducing extra shifts and hiring more workers, then more aggressively, by building yet another Volkswagenwerk factory in 1968 at Salzgitter, not far from Wolfsburg.

It had been the custom to stage a New Year's reception for key

VW importers and distributors. Despite its title, this affair was not held on January 1 but on January 6, Nordhoff's birthday. Thus the reception actually became an opportunity for hundreds to honour the man who had made their own success possible—and became an expression of Heinz Nordhoff's deeply personal involvement with the company. The last of these receptions (which Lotz has since discontinued) took place in 1968 and Heinz Nordhoff was there for it, having returned to Wolfsburg late the previous October. Those who attended the January event were dismayed to see that he seemed years older: they feared they might be saying goodbye to the man who had led them so brilliantly for two decades. Then, to everyone's amazement, Nordhoff seemed to improve sharply in the weeks following the reception, almost as though the sight of old friends and associates and the reliving of old triumphs had buoyed him up. Sensing himself stronger, he even insisted on working a more or less normal week.

That improvement proved, tragically, to be an illusion, for a decline soon set in again. At the beginning of March 1968, the board of directors pushed forward the date of Heinz Nordhoff's retirement from January 1969 to May 21, 1968. With appropriate ceremonies, Nordhoff was to be named 'Honorary President' of the company.

So very much had Nordhoff identified himself with his company for twenty years that he was understandably reluctant to lay down his responsibilities and retire from active leadership. It was not a fear of boredom that caused him to dislike retirement; as previously noted, Nordhoff was not a man whose world began and ended at the office door. He fully recognised and accepted that it was necessary for him to step down but what the mind accepts is not always reconciled with old habits. Thus his friends became aware of a painful contradiction: during those months in 1968 when his health seemed to be improving, he repeatedly introduced Kurt Lotz to others as the man he had personally chosen as his successor, but the very presence of *any* successor at all merely underlined for him the emotionally unpalatable fact that he needed to step down. It was a difficult time for 'the old man'—and for everyone.

It was in deteriorating health that Heinz Nordhoff exerted himself once too often in mid-March 1968, shortly after the board of directors had communicated to him the painful news that he must step down seven months ahead of his own schedule. He raced south to deliver a speech in Baden-Baden almost as though he wished to prove to himself and others that he remained as vigorous as he had always been throughout more than forty years in the auto industry. That speech and that trip proved too much. During the flight back from Baden-Baden on March 15, the day he gave his speech, Nordhoff collapsed in the company turboprop and needed to be given oxygen, a supply of which was now never far from his side. On landing at Brunswick, Nordhoff was raced home—and from there to Wolfsburg city hospital.

It was almost as though fate were setting appropriately solemn dates for these last events: Nordhoff was stricken on the Ides of March and died on Good Friday, April 12. Early that morning Mrs. Nordhoff and her eldest daughter, Barbara, were summoned to the hospital. Nordhoff had suddenly begun to weaken. He was surrounded by doctors and assistants. His old friend Monsignor Holling arrived shortly afterward to administer the last rites.

In a few hours, however, he rallied and asked his wife and daughter to have a glass of champagne with him. The champagne available at the hospital was not chilled, so Barbara quickly drove home and returned with several bottles of his favourite brand. The three members of the family sipped the champagne and Nordhoff appeared to be gaining strength. He felt well enough to spend some time writing Easter greetings on his calling cards and he asked that they be sent with flowers to certain of his friends (who received them after he had died). Later that afternoon he weakened suddenly and died quietly. With him at his death were Mrs. Nordhoff, his wife of thirty-eight years, and Barbara.[1]

As telegrams from the President and the Chancellor of West Germany, as well as from countless others, poured in, all work ceased for a minute's silent tribute in all VW factories the world over. In Wolfsburg, where forty-five thousand workers silently filed past Nordhoff's coffin in a factory hall, the town fathers declared official mourning—as was done also in São Bernardo do Campo, Brazil, where Nordhoff's initiative had built South America's largest automobile factory. On April 18, his coffin was driven to church on a specially modified VW pickup truck. Its cab roof had been cut away and the flower-bedecked flatbed served as a bier for the coffin as it was driven slowly through the streets of Wolfsburg. Hubert Rommel, his driver for many years, was at the wheel, and

1. Nordhoff's widow continues today to live in the Wolfsburg home she shared with her husband; Barbara, who had left Volkswagen of America, Inc., for a job in Germany, later returned to the USA and in 1969 married a New York physician (and former Rumanian prince), Dr. Dan Cantacuzino.

seated beside him was Mike Hocke, who had served as Nordhoff's chauffeur years before. A Pontifical High Mass in Monsignor Holling's St. Christopher's Church followed; when Nordhoff's body was carried there to Wolfsburg's Forest Cemetery, a guard of honour was rendered by his fellow Knights of the Holy Sepulchre.

The most meaningful honours, however, had not come from those who had delivered the official eulogies. They had come from the men and women in the Wolfsburg factory who had filed past his coffin in their everyday working clothes and from the thousands of Wolfsburg citizens who lined the sidewalks of the town to watch that black pickup truck roll solemnly through their streets. They were not dignitaries, but they all knew they had been his people.

A generation had gone; twenty years after the Wolfsburg factory was turned over to German management all its early veterans were twenty years older. The passing of Nordhoff was followed by the death of that colourful Dutchman, Ben Pon, VW's first importer, and by the death of Joe Werner, whom Ferdinand Porsche lured away from Ford in Michigan to risk his future with VW. With Werner's death, there were now only two left of that original 'German–American' contingent recruited for VW before the war: Otto Hoehne, a member of the management board, and Mike Hocke, a driver in the motor pool.

Illness had struck several. The dashing F. W. Schultz-Wenck, who had built up VW's operations in his adopted Brazil, had to step down, incapacitated by a stroke shortly after Nordhoff's death. He remained titular Director Presidente of the Brazilian subsidiary until his death on December 28, 1969. Hans Hiemenz of the Wolfsburg Vorstand, whose VW career began in 1940, also stepped down for reasons of health at the end of 1968.

Retirement further thinned the ranks of the veterans, several leaving the Vorstand because they had reached or passed sixty-five years of age. Julius Paulsen, in charge of procurement and materials, retired at the end of 1968, and was replaced by Horst Münzner, then forty-three years old. Kurt Haaf, personnel chief, also retired at the end of that year, after which the forty-eight-year-old Horst Backmann took his place on the Vorstand. Another veteran, due for retirement at the end of 1970, was Frank Novotny, who had previously withdrawn from day-to-day participation in the company's affairs, though he periodically attended Vorstand meetings. Helmut Orlich, the member of the management board in charge of Technical

Development and Inspection, left in April 1969, due to changes instituted by Lotz, who brought into the Vorstand Professor Dr. Werner Holste, forty-one, charged with Research and Development. Yet another new management board position was created by Kurt Lotz for a forty-year-old lawyer, Dr. Gerhard Prinz, to head what is called 'Participations, Planning and Organisation'. Three active members of the Nordhoff Vorstand who remained on Lotz's management team were Dr. Carl H. Hahn (still in his early forties), worldwide head of sales and service; Otto Hoehne (in his early sixties), given enlarged responsibilities encompassing both production and inspection; and Dr. Friedrich Thomée (also in his early forties), who remains the Vorstand finance chief.

When Kurt Lotz arrived in Wolfsburg, Volkswagenwerk AG was being run by a management board whose age averaged in the sixties; Lotz works today with a management team whose age averages in the forties. The way Lotz sees it, that 'rejuvenated' board is just what the company needs in order to ensure its continued success in the future.

Concern about the decades to come is not an academic exercise for Kurt Lotz; he really looks and plans ahead fifty years, a fact which became very evident during the long, free-wheeling and informal conversation I had with this extraordinary man in Wolfsburg recently. Time and again, Kurt Lotz 'returned to the future' as we spoke. Objective evidence of his concern may further be seen in the importancè attached today to Holste's 'R&D' department and to Prinz's position on the Vorstand, the latter a kind of VW 'think-tank' for the analysis of future opportunities.

This emphasis, I discovered, derives in large part from Kurt Lotz's own personal life history—and from what he has learned from it.

'My philosophy,' Lotz told me, 'is to make the best of any new situation, to invest in the future and to be willing to make sacrifices for that future. My motto throughout life—and my motto now at the Volkswagenwerk—is to pay little attention to the past if it is no longer useful for the future.'

That is the approach of a pragmatist, and apparently an approach that works, for it seems to have brought Kurt Lotz an unusual degree of success. While his rise is in some ways a peculiarly German success story (incorporating the climb up after the early postwar hardships), it is so surprisingly fast that it almost strikes one as something that ought to have happened 'only in America'. Consider these facts alone: The 'typical' German industrialist is traditionally only supposed to reach top management positions after his hair has turned a dignified grey, but Lotz made it in his forties (hence, perhaps, his readiness to staff his Vorstand with young men). Lotz attained his success without attending a university (except, briefly, night school): this in a nation in which academic doctorates are not only used in daily conversation and correspondence but where they still create social distinctions and assure many a young man a smooth entry to top jobs.[1] Furthermore, Lotz's entire business career took place after World War II; thus he had no pre-war background nor any pre-war connections on which he could rely or lean. Finally, unlike many a West German industrialist, Lotz does not come from an influential family having industrial connections, much less one having influence or wealth. He was one of nine children of a farm family; his father Konrad owned an average, medium-sized farm in Lenderscheid near Ziegenhain. When Kurt Lotz was born on September 18, 1912, he was given what by German standards was practically a 'log-cabin' start in life: he was expected to make good on his own, without family help or even a higher education.

He graduated from secondary school just as Germany wallowed in the midst of the severe 1932 depression, when six million Germans were out of work and jobs seemed impossible to obtain. One of his teachers suggested that a police job in such a time was as good as any and more secure than most. Lotz, a pragmatist even then, decided 'he had to start somewhere'; this turned out to be a police academy.

Rookie policemen were supposed to be at least twenty-five years old before becoming eligible for a commission; Lotz was commissioned a police lieutenant at the age of twenty-two. A year later, the Luftwaffe searched for young police officers, who had already proved their leadership potential, to form a cadre. Lotz was invited to join and accepted, because the prospect of flying attracted him; commissioned a lieutenant in the air force, he was sent to study air reconnaissance. Then he fell ill with the flu and, rather than miss classes by reporting himself sick, brashly attempted to cure himself with quinine—an experiment at self-medication which landed him in the hospital for eleven months, after which he was declared ineligible for flying and reassigned to anti-aircraft defence.

He got his first taste of industrial planning and his first brush with

---

1. Professor Dr. Lotz's own 'doctor' title derives (as had Nordhoff's) from an honorary doctorate given him in 1963; he had earlier (in 1962) been honoured by ancient Heidelberg University, which named him an Honorary Senator of that institution.

industry during the war when he was assigned for a time to the Luftwaffe armaments department. By then, Lotz was a captain in the general staff corps and it became his job to convey the air force's requirements to the armaments ministry and German factories.

The war's end found him (by then a major) commanding a flak unit wedged between US and Soviet lines in Czechoslovakia. The months which followed were more exciting than Lotz might then have wished; these events deserve to be recorded in detail someday, but the particulars are not relevant to the story of Lotz the industrialist. Only the fact that he escaped to find the American lines needs to be mentioned—and that only because it helps one to measure the man. His chances of escaping successfully were considerably short of fifty-fifty; he had no maps, help, or resources; even he did not entertain much hope of success. Despite these gloomy facts, he was determined to risk his life to reach his family; in doing so, he discovered resources as well as characteristics in himself which he now believes were essential for his post-war success: a willingness to dedicate himself totally to a goal, a readiness to risk everything, an ability to persevere in his aim and courage enough to act decisively when all the cards were stacked against him.

After discharge from prisoner-of-war status in November 1945, Lotz found his family on a small farm near Homberg, West Germany. By this time, he had both a wife and a daughter. (He had married Elisabeth, daughter of Professor Dr. Gustav Lony, in December 1939.) Needing to obtain food for them and himself, Lotz got a job on a farm: the one-time farm boy who had become a major in the general staff corps was back again where he had started life. But the job offered food when money was worthless; indeed, his wages for a time consisted of a sausage per day.

In the spring of 1946, Lotz was offered a small job in the cost accounting department of Brown, Boveri's Dortmund office. This paid 300 marks (approx. £30) a month—at a time when Lotz might have earned that much far more easily on the farm where one pound of butter sold on the black-market for the same amount. Taking a poorly paid job in industry at a time when no one hoped for an economic miracle would mean sacrificing the immediate well-being of his family. It was a long shot, but Lotz took the gamble.

'The decision to move from the farm to Dortmund,' Lotz told me, 'was among the most difficult decisions I ever had to take in my life. But I wanted to get into industry when it was just starting up again at the very hour of its birth, so as to get the jump on others.'

He is convinced today that he would never have reached the top so fast had he been unwilling to take the two risky decisions he took during this time: the decision to risk his life in escape; and the decision to risk his family's immediate well-being in the hope of assuring a better future.

Having been decisive then, Lotz learned the habit of acting decisively. At Brown, Boveri & Cie., he quickly came to be watched as a 'comer'. While working as a cost-control expert (having taught himself how to use adding machines), he took evening courses in industrial management to broaden himself. By 1954, his record in the company so impressed management that they promoted him to head of a corporate division.

Four years later, Kurt Lotz was chairman of the entire West German operation. Twelve years after he began work as a thirty-pounds-a-month cost accountant, the forty-five-year-old Lotz had reached the very top. He was, in fact, the youngest on the company's Vorstand (of which he was chairman), nine years younger than the next youngest man on his own management board. Then he rose even higher; he was made, in 1961, director, and in 1963 managing director, of the Swiss parent company of Brown, Boveri, while retaining his chairmanship of the German Vorstand. As we have seen, he resigned from the parent company but was still head of that German corporation when he was approached by Volkswagenwerk AG.

Volkswagen could, of course, have chosen an automobile man as Nordhoff's successor: it chose, instead, to do the unexpected. Clearly, the board of directors was convinced that the Volkswagenwerk required a top industrial manager who would feel inclined to make use of the most modern management techniques—and an outsider who could look at the company as a corporate entity rather than 'merely' as a motor vehicle factory.

It has already been noted that the VW was fortunate in that 'it was designed by a technician who proved to be a visionary, and inherited by an engineer who proved to be a master salesman'; the challenge of tomorrow seems to call for an industrialist who can operate a major industrial enterprise which today encompasses more than Volkswagen itself. Kurt Lotz is even now transforming VW into a vast, international, multi-line corporation whose story is no 'small' wonder at all.

Kurt Lotz's confidence in himself had brought success and success had increased self-confidence, yet in meeting him one quickly becomes aware of a paradox: he speaks of himself and his career without self-glorification, almost as though he were speaking about and analysing someone else. He did not refer to his managerial abilities when he assessed the reasons for his rapid rise; instead, he harked back to those two crucial decisions he had taken at the end of the war, seeing them as crossroads he had successfully traversed. He seemed less proud at having done so than thankful that he had absorbed the lessons implicit in each, and it was clear he felt that any man of similar background, who had met similar challenges successfully, might have succeeded as well—and in any field, since all careers demand resolution, intrepidity, and a willingness to take calculated risks. The thoughtful self-questioning also becomes apparent in the low-keyed manner in which he discusses his background—and in his hesitancy about conducting the conversation in English, despite the fact that he is almost fluent in that language. When he first visited Volkswagen of America, Inc., some in the American VW team were understandably concerned about the 'new boss' and what he might be like; from all accounts. Kurt Lotz disarmed everyone with his relaxed, 'American' manner, with his considerable personal charm, with his mastery of English—and with his courteous habit of listening attentively to others.

These are all characteristics I myself discovered in Lotz—and they proved a little surprising in a man who is quite overwhelming physically: 6 feet 5 inches tall and built proportionately, with big powerful hands, a generally large frame and broad shoulders, and a massive head. Twenty minutes of calisthenics each morning (before showing up at his desk at 7.45 a.m.) give him the physique of a man ten years younger; in short, this man with an extraordinarily impressive career comes across very personally impressive as well. One half expects a booming voice and a steely-eyed gaze in a man like this; instead, one finds a quiet manner and eyes which reveal a ready and often ironic sense of humour.

Kurt Lotz lives with his wife and two sons in a large modernistic house built for him close by the Rotehof Guest House.[1] While Lotz enjoys concerts and the theatre, his life centers about his work and his family. His two teenage sons, Christian and Michael, are as much affected by the times as any boy anywhere: Christian, the elder,

1. Helge, the Lotz's first child, lives in Hamburg with her husband, Edgar Hennigen, and their two children.

adamantly refuses to let a barber near him and he and his father periodically haggle about just how long he ought to wear his hair. Michael is involved in the big issues of life and occasionally chides his father for being too dispassionate. Thus the generation gap makes itself subtly felt in this Wolfsburg home, as it does in others the world over, but despite Lotz's long service as a military officer, he takes a refreshingly liberal view of it all. The fact that German youngsters today have a much freer relationship with parents and elders than they ever had in the past is something which Lotz finds 'entirely positive'. As for 'external appearances', he believes they don't matter as much as some people suppose. 'The freedom these youngsters enjoy,' he told me, 'is bound to bring in its wake some exaggerated behaviour. But, by and large, that's nothing to worry about.'

I asked Lotz whether he agreed with other top industrialists that the main job of the head of any company was to find the best men, put them in the right jobs, and give them free rein.

'That's only part of it,' he replied. 'Outstanding men are just the very ones who need to be coordinated and made into a team. Goals have to be determined and adhered to. My job as Vorstand chairman is, after all, to provide leadership.'

Setting goals is a responsibility Lotz takes very seriously; a good deal of his private reading is in books and journals which assess the world of tomorrow. For years, the Volkswagenwerk never needed to concern itself with much more than producing enough cars to meet the existing demand, but that era is over.[1] Volkswagenwerk AG, Lotz believes, does not only need plans for the immediate future or for five years hence, but also needs almost visionary thinking about the 'futuristic' future two generations ahead.

'If I had thirty free days at my disposal,' Lotz said wistfully, 'I'd spend them travelling the world and studying the automobile industry, looking for new Volkswagen markets, and particularly researching the Far East. I'd visit Japan again, spending more time there. The day may come when Japan will surpass the USA in gross national product, if not in per capita income; when that day comes, two-thirds of all the world's motor vehicles may be produced in the Far East.'

Lotz has already begun to restructure the VW corporation to

1. The fact that corporate headquarters remained for two decades (and still remains, however incongruously) *within* a factory is one demonstration of this early and long-lasting orientation of the company as a sort of production facility, rather than as hub of a worldwide enterprise.

meet the demands of the future. On April 26, 1969, the shareholders of NSU Motorenwerke AG approved a fusion of their company with the Volkswagen-owned Auto-Union GmbH; this resulted in the creation, during August 1969, of a new corporation called Audi NSU Auto-Union AG. This company, with its headquarters in Ingolstadt, is 59.5 per cent owned by Volkswagenwerk; Kurt Lotz is chairman of its Aufsichtsrat. (The awkward corporate name derives from a wish to retain all three time-honoured names.) In November 1968, Auto-Union GmbH (prior to its union with NSU) introduced its luxurious Audi 100, which proved a very big success; Audis are so popular today that they are even assembled alongside VWs at Wolfsburg, as well as at Ingolstadt, so as to meet the demand.

A joint sales corporation was established between the Porsche company and Volkswagenwerk; this came to be called VW-Porsche Vertriebsgesellschaft (sales company) and markets sports cars developed and manufactured jointly by both Porsche and VW. The newest of these is the hot Porsche 914, the first production sports cars with a midship engine, providing road-holding and handling characteristics equal to those in race cars. (The joint company also markets the various other models of the Porsche.)

Thus Volkswagenwerk AG already includes two major 'divisions': Volkswagen and Audi NSU. (Porsche remains separate from the VW giant, being still a family-owned and family-managed manufacturing company. The newly formed VW-Porsche company is a marketing company only, thus allowing the engineering-oriented Porsche works to specialise in what they do best.) The future trend is obvious and inescapable: the day will come when a complete restructuring of the Volkswagen corporation will take place; it would create a sort of German 'General Motors', perhaps with an overall corporate name as vague as GM's. Whether further divisions, to manufacture still other lines of motor vehicles, will eventually be added is of course a corporate secret. Asked if he might diversify to the extent that the company would some day produce home appliances ('Beetle-brand' washing machines and the like). Lotz replied with a smile that he intends to concentrate on the motor vehicle industry for the time being. 'The wish for such diversification,' he said, 'and the fulfilment of that wish are two separate things.'

Lotz regards all these new corporate moves as logical developments flowing out of the dynamics of the auto industry. Indeed, he denies that he 'made a lot of changes' at VW after he took over.

'There was less of a need to change things,' he said, 'than to complete. There was a need to introduce additional modern management techniques and concepts, as well as to initiate further technical planning. But this was a fulfilment rather than a change.'

Nevertheless, Kurt Lotz admitted that any new corporate chief inevitably introduces not only his own 'style' into things, but also a 'personal emphasis'. This, in Volkswagen's case, did produce some changes—fulfilments, as the case may be. The biggest may be found in the competitiveness of the new divisions. They compete actively with each other and with the VW itself, are independent of each other, and have separate marketing organisations to sell their separate product lines. This separation was not achieved without creating some anguish; Lotz insisted that free competition required German VW dealers to be divested of their Audi franchises or to set up completely independent Audi dealerships, which for a while did not please these dealers. A complex method has been worked out to facilitate this divestment without hurting the men involved financially; a good many of them are today beginning to agree with Lotz that competition *per se* is a good thing for all.

Another development initiated by Lotz enlarged Otto Hoehne's responsibilities on the Vorstand and introduced Professor Dr. Holste's R&D post as a replacement for the earlier Technical Development position.

When Lotz joined Volkswagenwerk, he discovered that there often were uncertainties about 'who was at fault' when something went wrong. He also felt that VW inspection should not be limited to the production process. A customer whose VW contains a faulty part doesn't care where the blame lies—but the company needs to know. Inspection, Lotz reasoned, ought to be enlarged to control the quality of all key processes at work on a vehicle: product planning, production, and sales-and-service. For example, did the part fail due to a fault in design, in production or in service procedures? Standards for all three, not just for production, ought to be set and maintained.

Accordingly, Lotz established a new staff position called *Qualitätsförderung* ('Quality Promotion') under a thirty-one-year-old engineer named Claus Borgward, a scion of the defunct Borgward auto company, who has worked for VW since 1963. An energetic young man who speaks intensely and volubly while puffing big cigars, Borgward emphasised to me that his department now works hand-in-glove with both the planners and designers as well as with the worldwide sales-and-service organisation, to make sure that quality control everywhere remains as high as it ever was in production. If a part turns out to be defective in Baton Rouge, Louisiana or in Sydney, Australia, chances are that this part will end up in Borgward's department at Wolfsburg, air-freighted there for detailed analysis.

As for the inspectors within the various VW factories, they remain totally independent of the production staff within those factories, and even of the plant managers themselves; they continue to be able to yank any car off the production line if they spot the slightest flaw. Today, they ultimately report to Otto Hoehne on the Vorstand, because Hoehne is no longer only 'production boss' at the Volkswagenwerk; Lotz has given him the additional task of supervising inspection standards.

'His job today,' says Lotz, 'is to act as referee between the production and inspection people under him.'

One vehicle which came in for heavy criticism when first introduced in West Germany in 1968, was the 'Type IV' Volkswagen: the VW 411 (since redesigned VW 411E, for electronic fuel injection). For a variety of reasons, that line of cars failed to 'take off' in the domestic market when first introduced; in fact, in the early months, the joke went that they were called '411' because the company only expected to sell 411 of them.

Today, the VW 411E has had the kinks knocked out of it: it has increased horsepower, improved stability and a reduced noise level. Holste even ventured the surprising opinion that the VW 411 is in many ways today as technically advanced over other contemporary cars as the beetle was in 1939. It is not yet marketed in the USA, but soon will be.

The 1975 Volkswagens are already on the drawing boards in the tall Research and Development building in Wolfsburg in which I interviewed Holste. 'Every man here,' Holste said, 'knows what jobs he has to do right through 1975.' R&D breaks down into its component parts: Research, often basic, deals with engine, transmission and other changes well into the future, some twenty years hence; Development deals with the production of VW prototypes.

'It takes about five years,' Holste told me, 'to develop a car which meets Volkeswagen quality standards. We are now designing cars in all price ranges, so as to reach every category of potential buyer; no matter what a man wants to spend on a car, he ought to find one of our cars meeting his needs.

'But our interest is not and never will be to follow Detroit's direction,' Holste continued. 'We won't bring out cars each year which have been merely restyled; we won't restyle for the sake of restyling. We are interested only in bringing out new cars which are of the highest technical quality and which are really technically new.'

Each VW 'division' (Volkswagen and Audi NSU, as well as the marketing division, VW-Porsche) is meant to have a *full range* of motor vehicles—and each range is meant to be competitive with the cars produced by the other divisions. Not even a 'luxury Volkswagen,' says Holste, 'is out of the range of possibilities'; indeed, such a car would give the 'VW division' a complete line, enabling it to compete, for example, with the Audi 100, which costs up to £1595. The luxury K70, introduced in late 1970, is already a move in that direction. As for that perennial question about the survival of the beetle, Holste gave the only logical answer: 'Who wants to get rid of the beetle when you're selling 5000 of them each day?'

The beetle and its 'big brothers' remain very popular indeed in the United States, despite Detroit's sub-compacts. VW's Emden plant today produces *exclusively* for the US market, so great is the demand for VWs in the United States. The record year for VW sales in the USA was 1968, when 569,292 Volkswagens were sold; that year, VW had a 5.5 per cent share of the entire US auto market and a 55 per cent share of the imported car market. The first half of 1969 saw a general stagnation of the US auto market—plus a three-month dock strike which kept Volkswagens out of dealer showrooms for a quarter of the year. Further, the revaluation of the German D-mark in late 1969 compelled Volkswagen of America, Inc., to raise its prices (though only 2.3 to 2.8 per cent, as against a rise of between 7 and 11 per cent elsewhere in the world).

The enforced price rise does not seem to have cut US enthusiasm for the VW, for sales in the latter months of 1969, directly following the revaluation of the mark, were so good that VWoA hoped to come close to its 1968 record—and this despite losses during the three-month strike. In late January 1970, the 4,000,000th VW was produced for America.

'The big changes at Volkswagen of America,' says J. Stuart Perkins, the company president, 'are similar to those elsewhere in VW. We now also sell the Audi, the Porsche 914 and the Porsche 911's. Thus, in addition to our VW range, we have moved into selling high-performance cars—and even racing them. Porsche 917 proto-types have raced at Daytona and the Formula Super Vee has been introduced to bring the Formula Vee concept up to date.'

Changes in Formula Vee racing have been so far-reaching that there may soon be 'World Olympics' of this kind, with national champions competing against each other for the world title. A new World Formula Vee (bringing together the old World Formula Vee and the US Formula Vee) has made this possible, thanks to the acceptance of VW-1600 engines. The new Super Vee cars, which can reach more than 130 miles per hour, incorporate Volkswagen components of more recent manufacture. The greatest testimony to the entire 'Formula Vee concept' came when the Sports Car Club of America accepted the new Super Vee class without seeing a single car of that kind—despite the fact that a new class normally is accepted only after many cars have been built and raced.

Stuart Perkins restructured his American organisation early in 1970, giving VWoA two separate 'line' divisions called Volkswagen Operations and Porsche Audi Operations. Both are headed by a vice president. The new head of Volkswagen Operations is Al Breckwoldt, formerly general manager of VWoA's Washington distributorship; John Reilley is the new vice president in charge of Porsche Audi Operations.

Other company officers took over 'staff functions' under Perkins. Michael L. Sanyour, for example, became VP in charge of Corporate Marketing, while Arthur R. Railton became VP in charge of Corporate Relations. 'These changes,' says Perkins, 'make certain that both divisions are completely competitive, while both have available to them all the staff experts they need.'

The young company president then adds: 'It all amounts to a certain coming of age for Volkswagen in America.'[1]

Perhaps the most American of all Volkswagens is the 'dune buggy'. 95 per cent of these (and there are more than 25,000 in Southern California alone) are based on the standard VW chassis, cut down about 12 inches. A fibreglass body is then put on it; VW's light weight air cooling and traction do the rest. 'Volkswagen,' says Art Railton, 'has even become American enough to get into the Sears, Roebuck mail order catalogue.' (Sears sells a dune buggy conversion kit.)

The US dune buggies are a far cry from the standard Volkswagens, but even the Volkswagenwerk and its own subsidiaries have recently introduced rather surprising, specialised cars meant for a limited

1. So much are the two divisions being kept apart and kept competitive that Doyle Dane Bernbach, advertising agency for Porsche Audi as it has been for VW, established an entirely separate 'unit' to make sure no PA copywriter would write VW ads, or vice versa. The result, says Perkins, is 'a completely different advertising image.'

market. One new model is the VW 181 which sells for about £830 in West Germany and which resembles the wartime 'Kübelwagen'. Originally meant to meet vehicle requirements of the armed forces West Germany has assigned to NATO, this Jeep-like VW is also sold to civilians who like a rugged car for rough terrain.

The Australian Volkswagen organisation has also produced a somewhat similar car (though this does not resemble the Kübelwagen), calling it the Volkswagen Country-Buggy. Volkswagen do Brasil, which also produces its 'own' VWs (not sold elsewhere), stuck to a more conventional design in introducing a four-door sedan in 1969. Called the VW 1600 'Brasilia', it is based on a Wolfsburg prototype, of which there were about thirty produced in Germany; these thirty Brasilia prototypes are today used for internal transport in the VW factory.

Not only new cars have been introduced outside West Germany, but new management as well. The Australian VW organisation, which today sells about 15,000 vehicles annually and which has to date sold about 250,000 'Down under', is now headed by Dr. A. Solzer, working alongside Peter Rupp and D. Herzmer, respectively the financial and production directors. In charge of the Brazilian subsidiary since Schultz-Wenck's illness and death is R. Leiding; in South Africa, G. E. R. Eckert has become managing director. In Great Britain, as has been detailed in Chapter 9, vast changes have taken place under managing director Alan M. Dix and sales are soaring.

This vast, international export organisation is run in Wolfsburg by Dr. Carl H. Hahn and, directly under him, by Dr. Werner P. Schmidt, thirty-seven who replaced the retired Manuel Hinke as head of exports. Formerly sales manager for German Ford within West Germany (a post from which he was lured by Carl Hahn's assistant, Dr. Gunther Flüs, also a Ford veteran), Schmidt speaks fluent English (or, more accurately, fluent American), having studied at Kalamazoo College in Michigan when he was twenty. Like Lotz, Schmidt sees a big VW opportunity in the Far East. Already Japan ranks among the twenty or so nations (out of VW's total of 130 export countries) which buy at least 5000 or more VWs a year. 'The Japanese buy six thousand a year,' says Schmidt. 'That may not seem like much, but it's a day's production—and not a bad start.'

The development of such embryo markets will, hopefully, reduce the US share of the Volkswagenwerk's export business—without reducing the upward trend of VW sales in the USA. New market developments along more coordinated lines and with more centralised information-gathering facilities is a Lotz-era innovation and accompanies a rejuvenation of the export business as a whole. The pioneers, members of the first generation of Volkswagen importers, have retired or, like Ben Pon, have died; even those who do remain active have in many cases turned over day-to-day management to younger men. The effect of this is considerable.

New talents are being discovered, modern management techniques vital to Volkswagen's success in the future are being utilised and the energy of youth is being brought to bear on an organisation which is a quarter of a century old. The Volkswagen era which began with Kurt Lotz seems everywhere to be characterised by youthful, bold ideas and by younger men impatient with past accomplishments; it is this management which will help Volkswagen in its transition towards tomorrow.

Index

Schmitz, Helmut, 230, 231, 232, 234, 235, 239
Schulenburg, Count Friedrich Dietloff von der, 56
Schulenburg, Count Friedrich Werner von der, 56
Schulenburg, Count Werner von der, 55, 56, 57, 63, 73
Schulenburg, Countess Werner von der, 56
Schultz-Wenck, Dr. F. W., 152, 278, 290
Schwimmwagen, 72, 75, 88, 89, 100
Schwimmkübel, 72
Seventh Seal, The, 250
Shaw, Gavin, 181
Sherwin, Mark, 6, 11, 48
Shirer, William, 52
Simca, 134
Singer, 25
Small World, 246, 251, 252, 257, 259
Smiles of a Summer Night, 250
Smith, Merriman, 248
Snowdon, Earl of, 248, 249
Solzer, Dr. Alfred F., 180, 290
Somali Republic, VWs in, 185
Sommer, Raymond, 97
South Africa, Republic of, VWs in, see Volkswagen of South Africa Ltd.
South African Motor Assemblers & Distributors Ltd., 186, 187, 188
South African VW Clubs, 189
South Wales Echo, 161
Speer, Albert, 58, 77, 80, 90
Spencer, Lionel R. V., 171
Sperry, Elmer, A., Medal, 222
Spiegel, Der, 66, 67, 84, 115, 267
Spock, Dr. Benjamin, 249

Sports Car Club of America, 289
Sports Illustrated, 205, 228, 245, 247
Standard-Triumph, 225
Stanton, Arthur, 198, 230, 231, 232
Steinmeier, Wilhelm, 108, 109, 124, 127
Stern, Der, 123
Stevenson, Mrs. Mabel, 245
Stewart, Scott, 232, 234
Steyr Works, 14
Stolz, Karl, 268
Strategic Bombing Survey, United States, 74, 75
Strauss, Franz-Joseph, 271-2, 273, 275
Sturt, Charles, 179
Stuck, Hans, 48
Stuttgart Motor Car, 13, 14
Stuttgart University, 72
Sunbeam, 4
Sun-Times (Chicago, Ill.), 249
Sweden, VWs, in 151
Switzerland, VWs in, 151
Sydow, Max von, 250

Targa Florio, 12
Tasmanian Motor News, 170
Taunus (German Ford), 1
Theunissen, A. B., 188, 189, 192
Thomas Tillings Ltd., 162, 163, 164, 165, 168
Thomee, Friedrich, 181, 279
Time, 70, 79, 84, 103, 104, 126, 141, 250
Times, The (Canberra), 180
Times-Herald, The (Dallas, Tex.), 255
Times Union (Rochester, N.Y.), 249

Werlin, Jakob, 24, 29, 30, 43, 44,
    62, 63, 64
Werner, Joseph, 46, 58, 65, 69, 71,
    74, 85, 108, 112, 113, 130, 278
West Australian University, 178
Wheels, 171
White, Edward, 258
White Nile, The, 141
Whitehead, Laurie, 171
Wild Strawberries, 250
Withers, Malcolm, 161
Wolfsburg, 69, 70, 71, 75, 78, 79,
    82, 83, 86, 88, 91–3, 98, 99, 101,
    108, 111, 117, 122, 123, 129,
    132, 135, 137, 143–5, 149–53,
    156, 158, 164, 171, 173–4, 175,
    181, 198, 199, 200, 201–4, 206–8,
    214, 215, 217, 236, 254, 260–7
    273, 274, 277, 278, 287, 290
Wolfsburg Castle, *see Schloss
    Wolfsburg*

Wolseley, 4
Woods, Mike, 181
World-Telegram & Sun, The (New
    York, N.Y.), 258
World War I, 2, 97, 109, 185
World War II, 11, 16, 46, 48, 72,
    76, 80, 92, 109, 110, 132, 194
Wright College, 178

Xalostoc, 152

Yeomans, Athol, 171
Youngblood, Gene, 249
Your KdF-Wagen, 67

Zahradnik, Josef, 16
Zündapp Volksauto, 19
Zündapp Works, 16